CREATIVE PAINTING

English language edition for the United States, its territories
and dependencies, and Canada published 2006 by
Barron's Educational Series, Inc.
© Copyright of the English edition 2006 by
Barron's Educational Series, Inc.
Original title of the book in Spanish: *Espacio*

© Copyright 2005 by Parramon Ediciones, S.A.—World Rights
© Copyright 2005 authorized reproductions, VEGAP,
   Barcelona, Spain
Published by Parramon Ediciones, S.A., Barcelona, Spain

All inquiries should be addressed to:
Barron's Educational Series, Inc.
250 Wireless Boulevard
Hauppauge, NY 11788
http://www.barronseduc.com

ISBN-13: 978-0-7641-5928-2
ISBN-10: 0-7641-5928-3

Library of Congress Control Number 2005929081

Editorial Director: **Maria Fernanda Canal**
Editorial Assistant/Illustration Archivist: **Maria Carmen Ramos**
Authors of the Text: **Josep Asunción, Gemma Guasch**
Exercises: **Josep Asunción, Gemma Guasch,
   Esther Pascual, and Pilar Valeriano**
Graphic Design: **Toni Inglès**
Photography: **Studio of Nos & Soto**
Layout: **Toni Inglès (Juan Carlos Bermudo)**

Printed in Spain
9 8 7 6 5 4 3 2 1

SPACE

CREATIVE PAINTING

CREATIVE PAINTING

Gemma Guasch
Josep Asunción

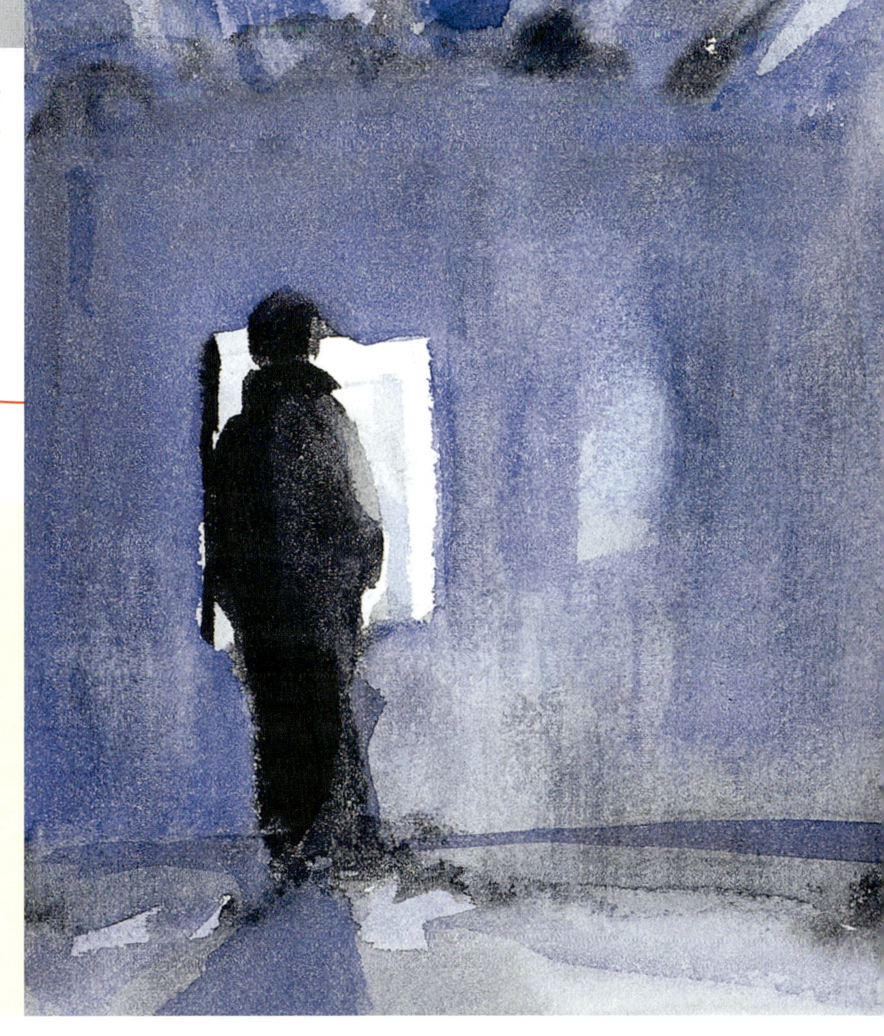

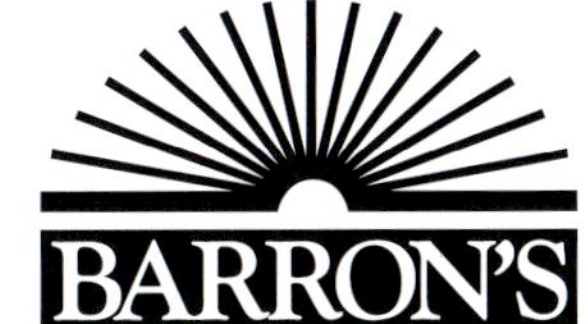
BARRON'S

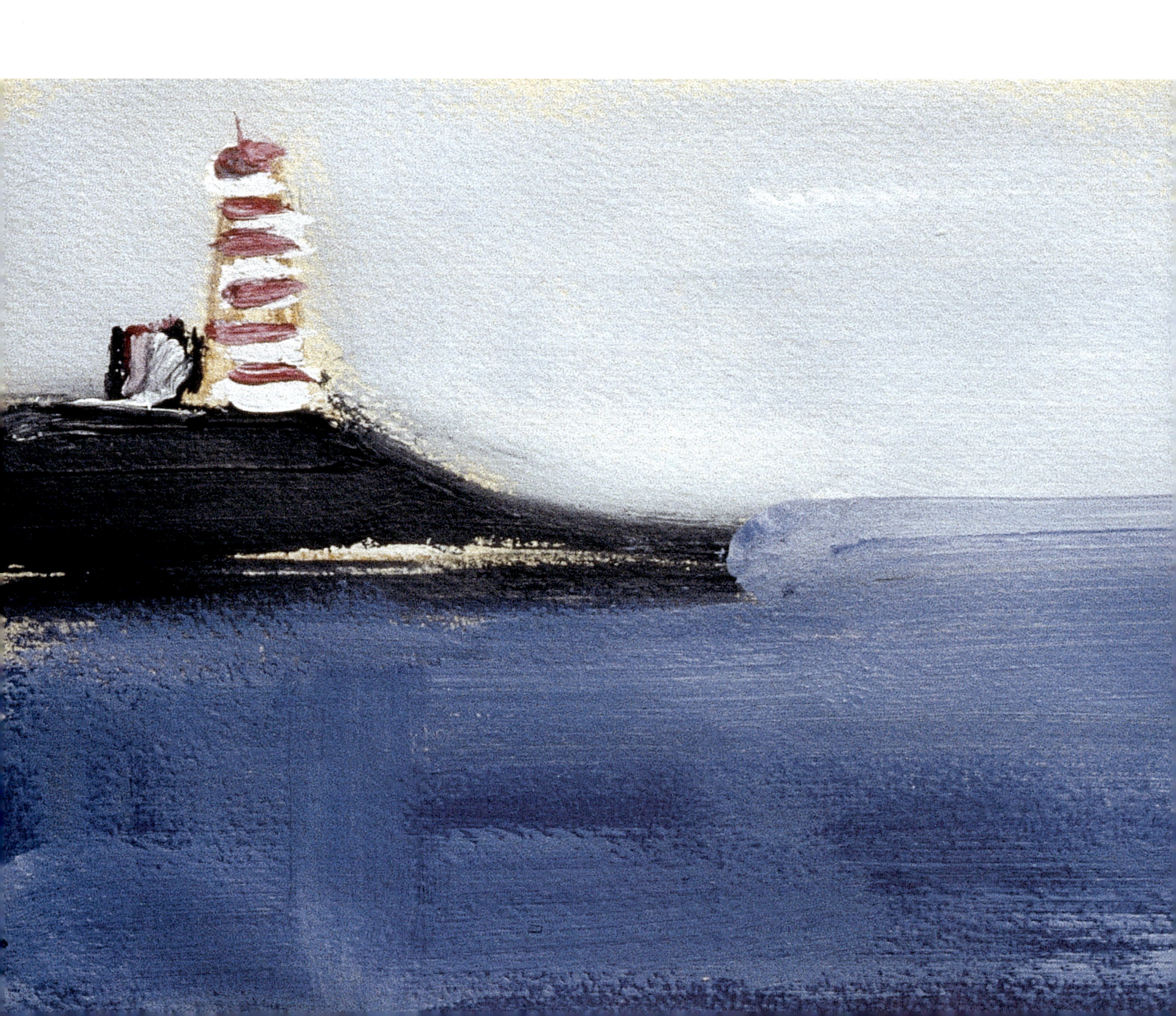

Contents

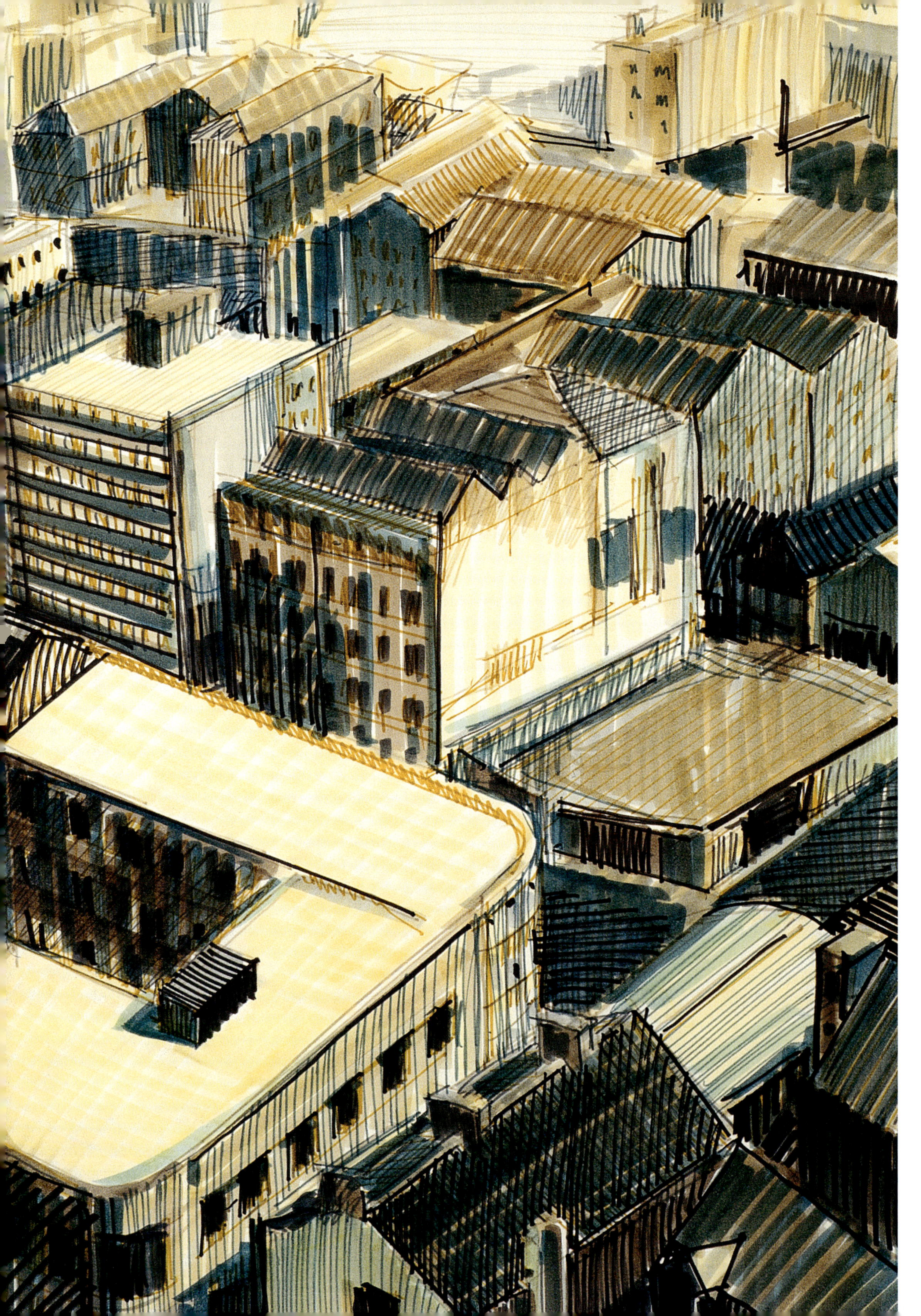

There is no art without creation. Therefore creativity is an indispensable technique that every painter must develop. Creativity involves risk and taking chances. Creativity is throwing oneself into the adventure, pursuing uniqueness and innovation, searching for the personal response. But it does no good to jump into the sea if we do not know how to swim; the experience will not last very long. Learning to paint is learning to function within the medium of painting, its visual language, just like learning to swim is learning to function in the water. This book throws us into the water while providing us with help, because it stimulates the development of creativity, and at the same time introduces us to the medium and its artistic language.

Verbal language consists of an alphabet and syntax; words and silences take on meaning in each phrase, and each phrase in the entirety of the text. It is the same in painting: artistic language is composed of elements that take on meaning in a composition, like in verbal language. The alphabet of painting is made up of color, form, space, and line. The first three elements are very much related to the image and the last to the physicality of the painting. If we compare it to verbal language again, the color, form, and space are the words, the pauses, the expressions or phrases, and the line is the tone of voice, the speed, and the emotional charge of the speaker.

It would be absurd to attempt to study each one of these four elements by isolating them completely from the others, because the four of them are interrelated in the same way that words, silences, and intonation are in speech. But it is possible to focus attention on each one of them, to really learn how visual language works and to respond creatively using this language. In this book we are going to focus our attention on one of them: space. Following an introduction explaining the theory of space in painting, there are fifteen creative approaches grouped thematically by painting genre so the reader can experiment creatively with space, in search of a personal language.

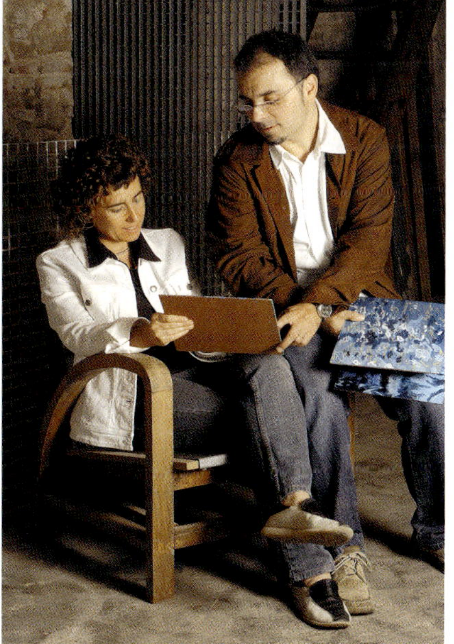

Gemma Guasch and Josep Asunción

Gemma Guasch and Josep Asunción are visual artists who combine artistic creation with the teaching of painting. Both have degrees in fine arts from the University of Barcelona, and each of them has had many exhibits in Spain, Italy, and Germany. Since 1995 they have worked together on projects under the name of Creart, a cultural association that experiments with collective artistic creation. Each one of the approaches in this book is endorsed by their extensive experience as professors in the Escuela de Artes y Oficios in Barcelona, where they direct the painting studios.

"One paints with his head and not with his hands."
Michelangelo,
Letter to Monsignor Aliotti, 1542.

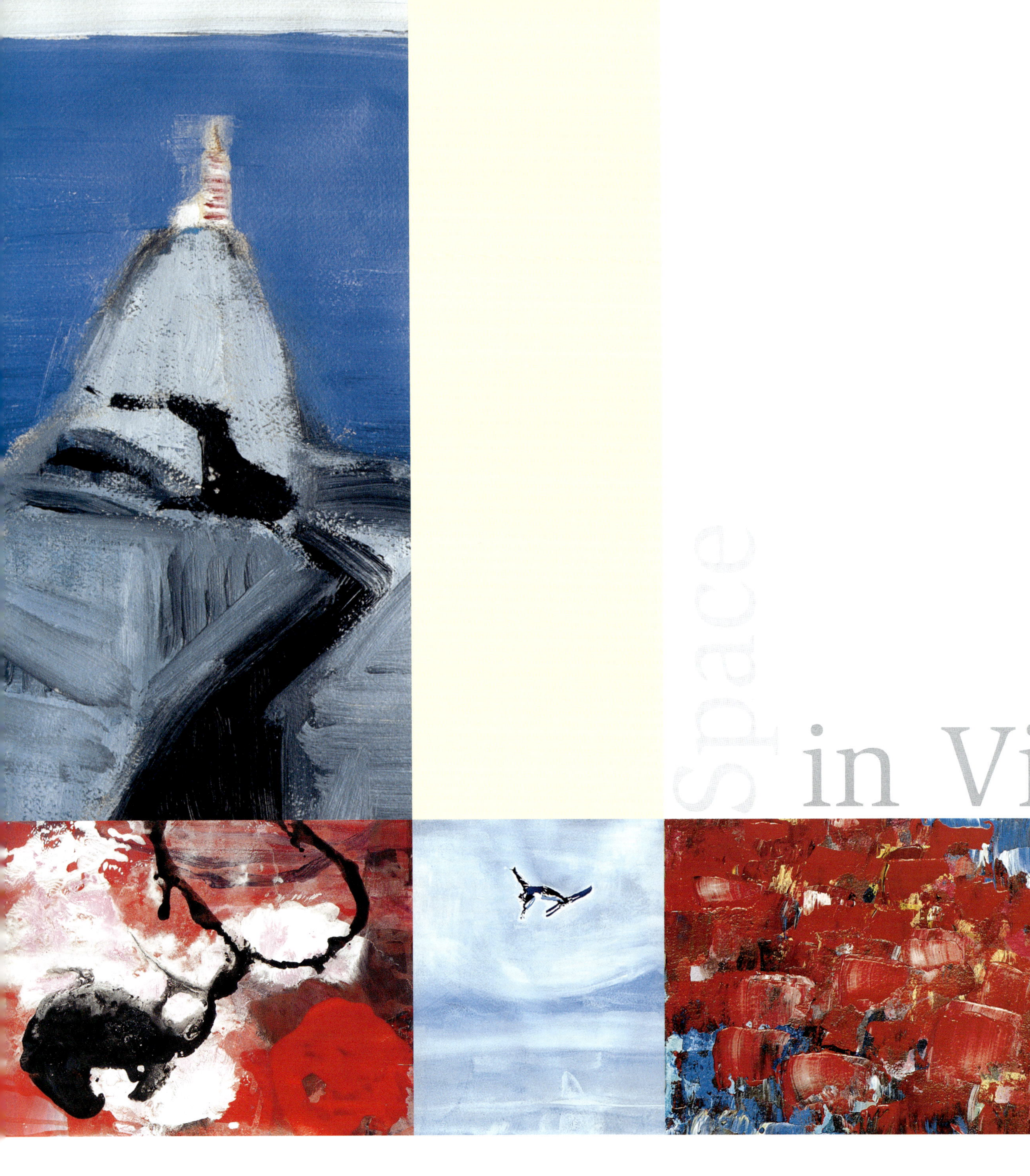

Space
in Vi

ual Language

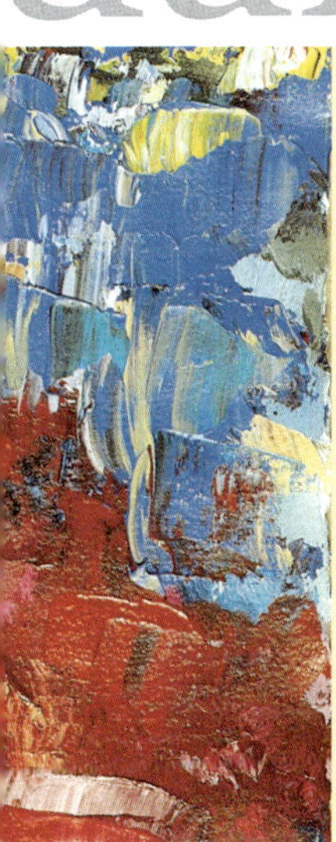

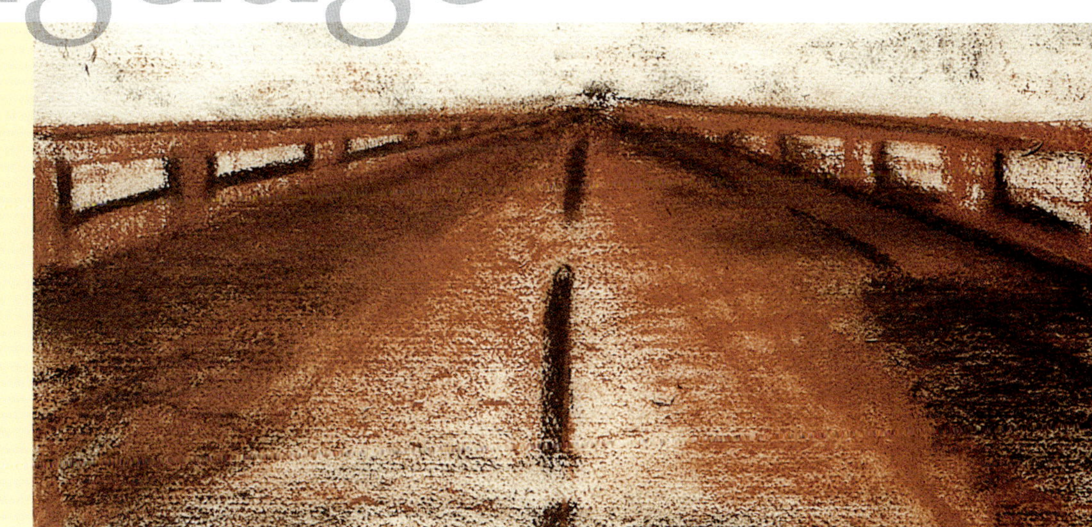

"One can only communicate an 'orientation' toward the secret, without being able to objectively express the secret."
Gaston Bachelard,
The Poetics of Space.

Space and Visual Perception

The visual perception of space is mainly the result of two factors: light and perspective. Light determines the contrast and the definition of everything in the perceived space. So, for example, a contrasting light creates great depth in the background, projected shadows separate the figure from the background, and a light modulated by fog removes all sense of depth.

Perspective establishes a sense of distance through vanishing points, scale, and definition. They are simple but important phenomena: as objects get farther away, they converge in the distance, they get smaller, and they are less distinct.

Other approaches are especially applicable at short distances to create the illusion of space: overlapping and focus. Overlapping is placing one object in front of another to cover it, and focus is controlling the clarity and definition, blurring everything that is in the distance.

A classic theme in painting is the relationship between the background and the figure, because it establishes the depth on two fundamental planes: foreground and background. Some factors that come into play in perceiving this relationship are the curve, the division, and proximity. The concave forms are perceived as background or empty (Figure **A** is interpreted as a hole) and the convex forms as a figure (Figure **B** is perceived as an object). In a horizontal division the upper area is perceived as a background and the lower as a figure **(C)**. In a sequence of lines, those that are closer together are seen as being closer, and the rest are seen as background **(D)**, naturally creating the greatest space possible between the elements.

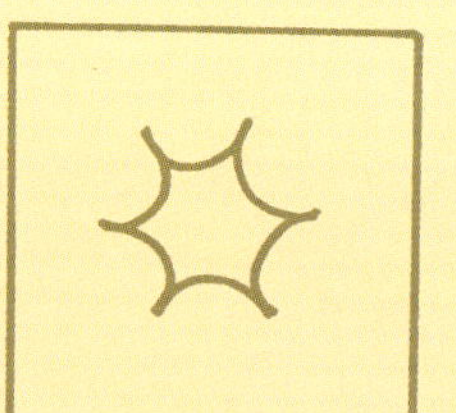
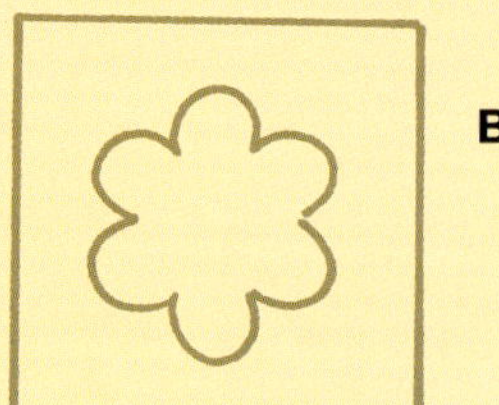
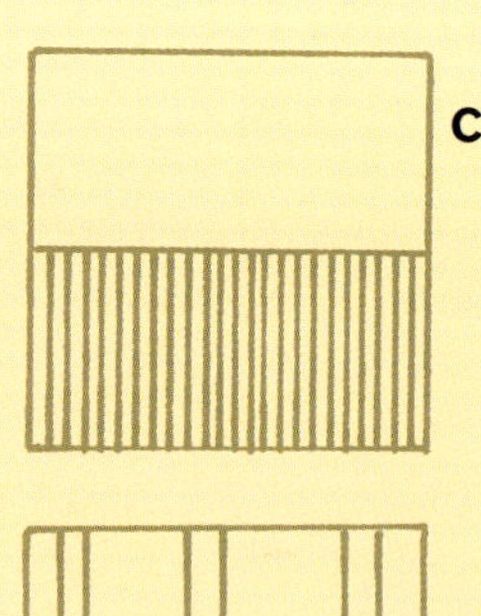

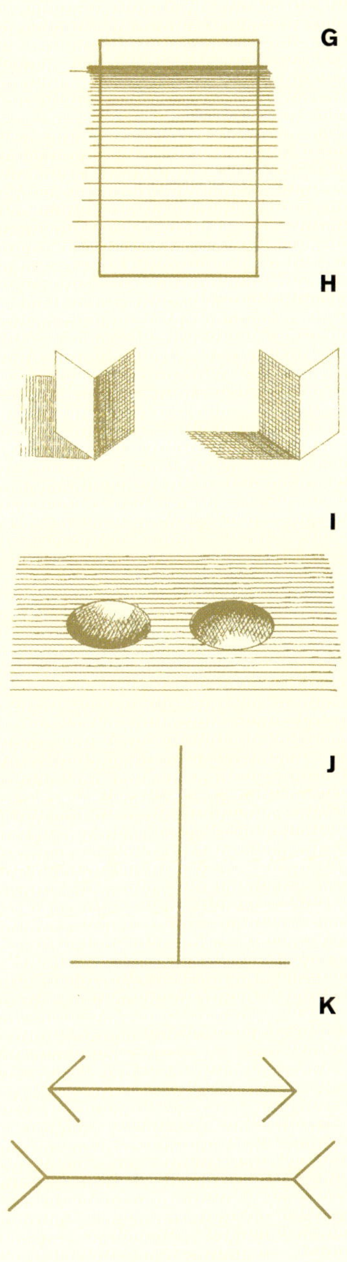

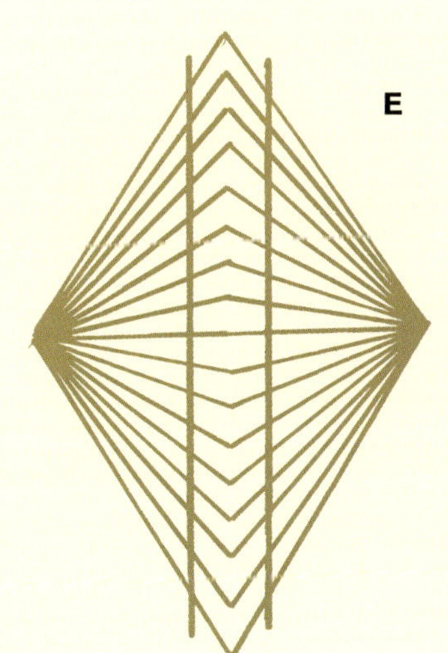

A gradation **(G)** is enough to cause a visual sense of depth. On a perceptive level darkness indicates greater distance than light.

The location of the light and shadows alters the spatial orientation of a form: the same book can be perceived as facing backward or forward **(H)**. The modeling can also alter forms that are not linear: if the light is on top, we perceive a shape, whereas if it is on the bottom, we see a hole **(I)**. Two lines of the same size will be perceived differently according to their positions **(J)**. Curiously, faced with two lines of the same length, we perceive the vertical one to be longer than the horizontal one. We also perceive them to be different according to their ends **(K)**: as we can see, the arrow shape is very powerful on a perceptive level.

When the oblique lines converge at vanishing points, a spatial structure is created that completely conditions anything found within them. The vanishing point creates an enormous spatial tension, such that the forms and lines on the structure are perceptively deformed **(E)**; furthermore, size is also perceived in the same way on this structure, causing two equal lines to seem different **(F)**.

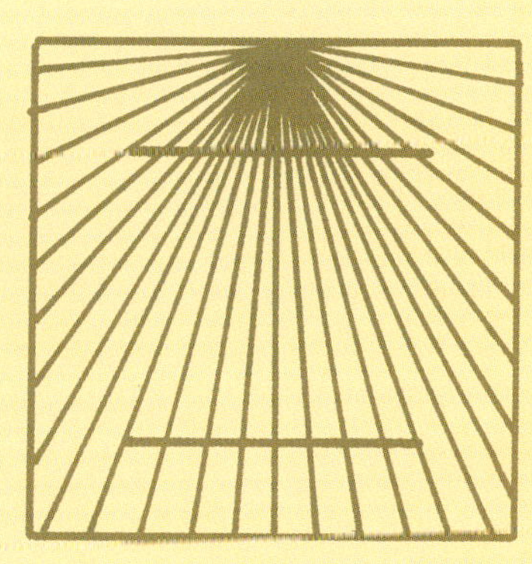

The Structure of Two-Dimensional Space: Composition

Composition is the first of the spatial aspects of painting. It refers to the distribution of forms and colors on the picture plane, independent of the illusion of spatial depth. In a composition, the arrangement of the parts obeys criteria established by the painter based on his or her expressive intention and gives meaning to the work of art. The composition controls the path that the viewer's eye follows based on a hierarchy of importance: the central nucleus of the painting, related aspects, marginal aspects, setting, atmosphere, and so on.

The Format

This is the first decision relative to the space in a painting. By format we understand two aspects: the size (large format, small format, etc.) and the shape of the painting (square, landscape, vertical, etc.). When it comes to size, certain works beg to be created and seen in very large formats and others are better suited to very small and easier-to-handle formats. Marc Rothko said, "The reason that I paint large pictures is precisely because I want to be intimate and human. Painting a small picture means placing yourself outside the experience, contemplating the experience as a stereoscopic view or through a microscope. No matter how you paint a large work, you are in it." When it comes to the shape, some formats greatly affect the composition. The feeling of a prairie, for example, is more easily produced in a horizontal than a vertical format, a centered composition is more striking in a square than a rectangle, and a very narrow vertical format completely directs the visual reading without giving the viewer many options.

Compositional Structures

All compositions have a structure, a skeleton that roughly sustains and orders all the elements of the painting. This structure is the scheme that explains the distribution of the masses and spaces in the picture plane. According to the balance or the tension the artist strives for, the distribution will be more or less complex, static, dynamic, symmetrical, etc. Despite the fact that each work has its own unique structure, there are compositional schemes that are often repeated. The most common of these are centered, diagonal, pyramidal, horizontal, slightly angled, orthogonal (in halves, L-shaped, Golden Mean . . .), symmetrical, balanced, asymmetrical, zigzag, and grid.

Rhythm

Rhythm is the unity in variety and change; it is the feeling of movement, the dynamic that is created during the visual journey across the painting. Some rhythms follow a very regular sequence; others play with variations of intensity, size, or distance between the parts to

Compositional Schemes

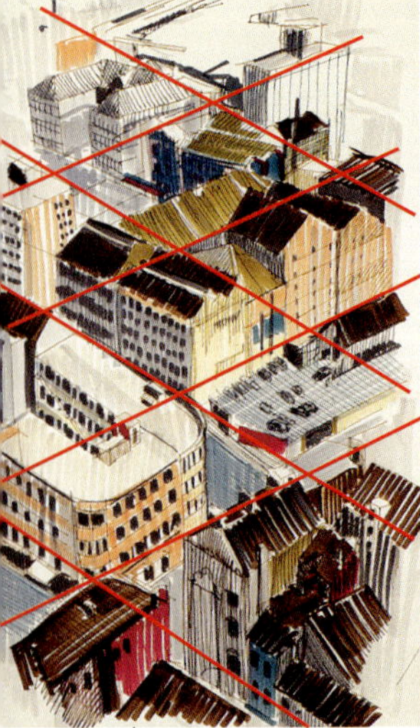

Creative Approach 8.
Diagonally gridded composition.

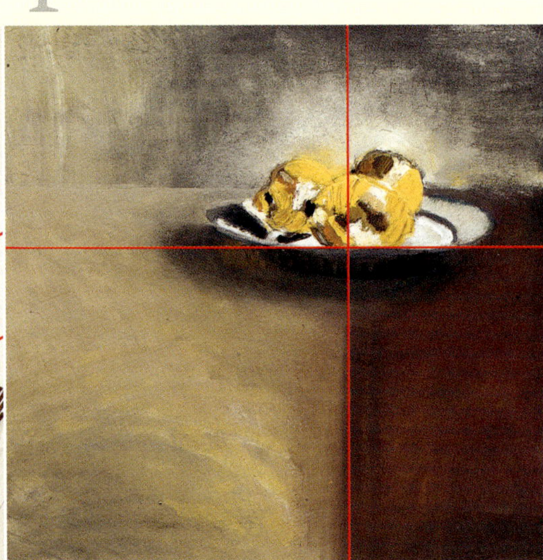

Creative Approach 3.
Orthogonal composition (Golden Mean).

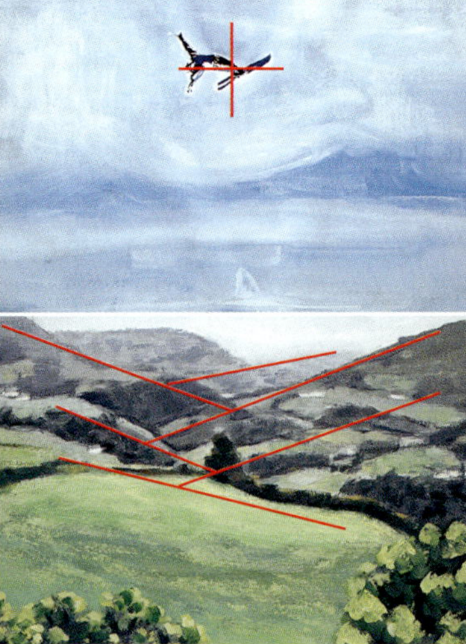

Creative Approach 12.
Centered composition.

Creative Approach 9.
Zigzag composition.

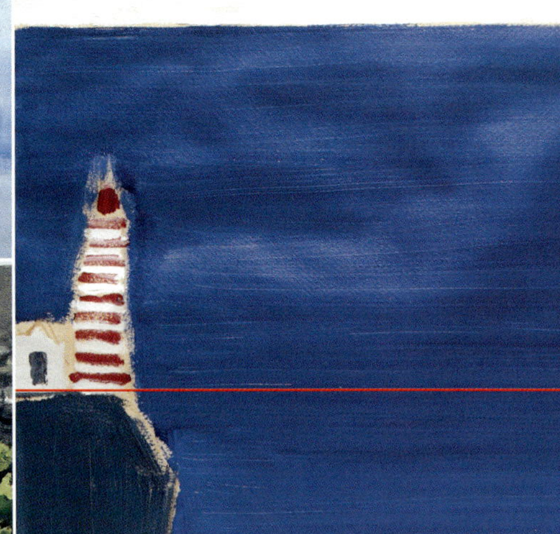

Creative Approach 6.
Horizontal composition.

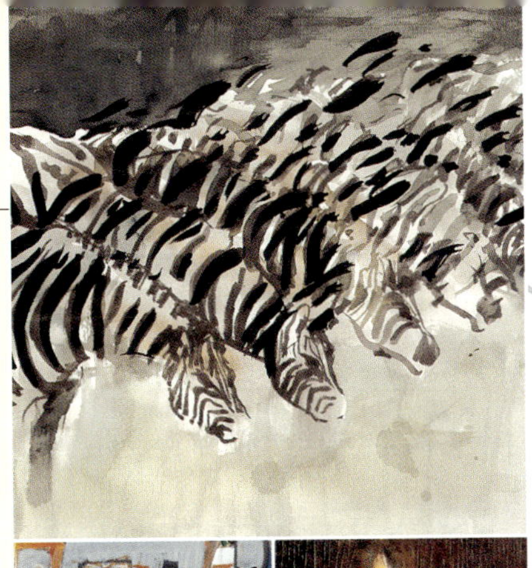

Creative Approach 1.
Rhythm in repetition and decreasing size.

create moments of shock, slow and quiet moments, monotony, chaos, etc.
The factors that create rhythm are repetition, alternating, increasing or decreasing extension, rotation, movement, and reflection.

Point of View and Framing

Point of view is the position of the painter in respect to the subject that is being depicted, and framing is his or her selection of what part to depict. These two spatial aspects are intimately related and fundamental, because the viewer will be in the same place as the painter and will focus on the same things, seeing what caused the artist to position himself or herself there and not somewhere else.

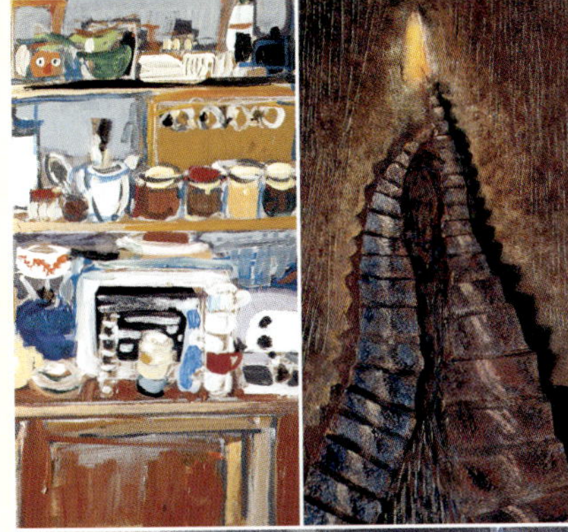

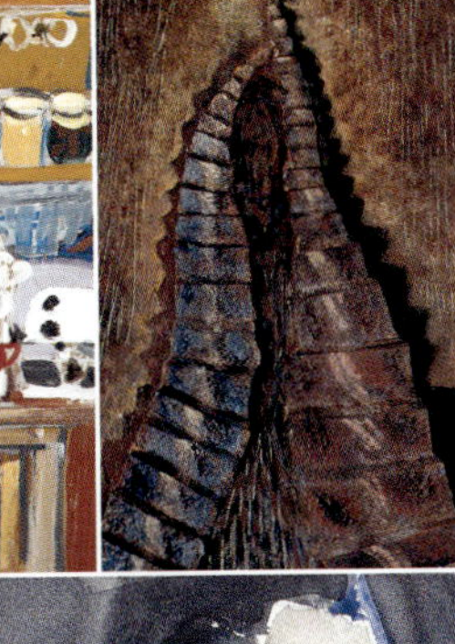

Creative Approach 4.
Frontal point of view.

Creative Approach 10.
Rhythm in symmetry.

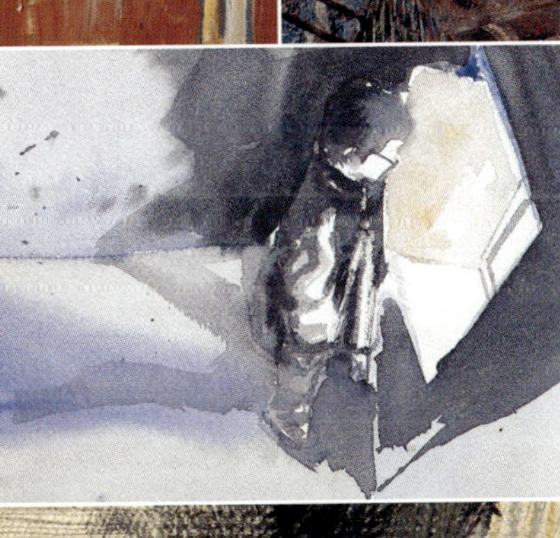

Creative Approach 13.
Elevated point of view.

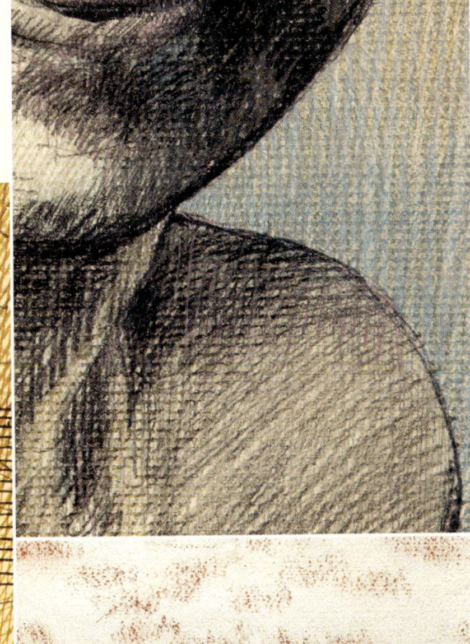

Creative Approach 11.
Very close point of view.

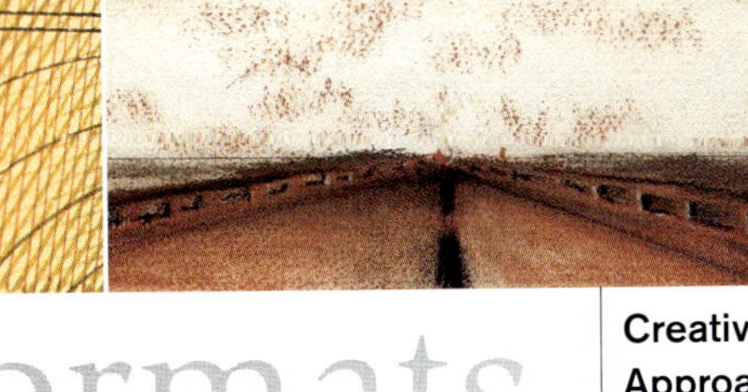

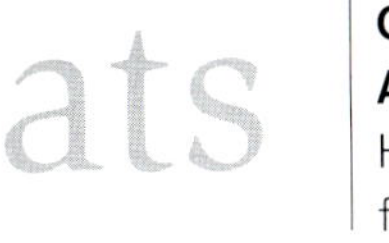

Creative Approach 15.
Square format.

Creative Approach 7.
Horizontal format.

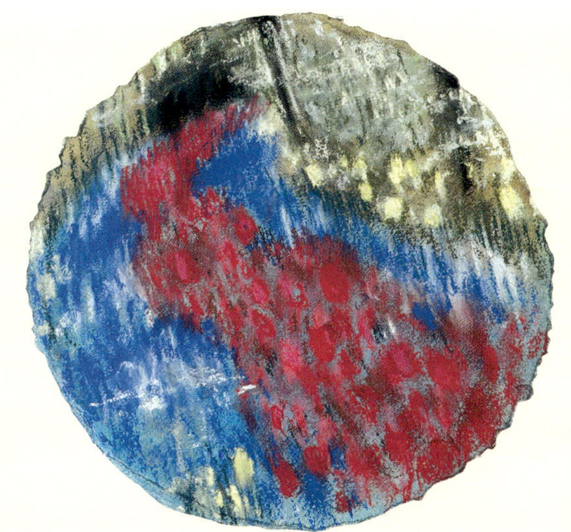

Creative Approach 2.
Round format.

The Structure of Three-Dimensional Space: Perspective

The illusion of space has been one of the goals of painting since the Renaissance, that historic moment when the foundations of perspective were laid. Cornelis Escher, the magician of the optical illusion, said, "producing a spatial reality with depth on a flat surface always fascinates the viewer because it presents him with an illusion, a mirage, turning the painting into a window through which we can observe another parallel reality."

Linear Perspective

This is used when the space is defined by lines (streets, houses, interiors, etc.). It is based on the following phenomenon: lines that in reality are parallel are perceived to vanish at a point on the horizon, which is always at the same height as the viewer's eyes. Depending on the position of the viewer in relation to the space, the perspective can be frontal, if there is only one vanishing point (a highway, for example), or oblique, if there are various vanishing points (a street corner, for example).

Aerial Perspectivea

If the space is not structured with lines, but with masses, aerial perspective can be applied. This is based on the following four points: the greater the distance the smaller the size, the less detailed, less contrast (of light and color), and more blue in the tones.

Chiaroscuro

The comprehension of space relies on understanding the light that defines it. The differences in the light are the basis of the effect of spatial depth. In general terms, darkness recedes and light advances. This principle has been followed since the baroque period, although in open spaces the sense of distance is normally produced by the opposite gradation of dark to light. The shading on the volume itself defines it, and the projected shadows define the space where the volumes are located. Other more abstract spatial effects created with light and shadow are the feeling of emptiness, leaving, depth, abyss, expansion, and atmospheric density.

Scale

The most obvious general principle for indicating nearness of distance is the change in size of all objects as they move away from us. Painting has developed some resources based on this fundamental principle; the most common are foreshortening and overlapping. Foreshortening is the deformation caused by a forced point of view that exaggerates the disproportion of the parts of a body, which change scale as they get farther away. Overlapping means placing the closest object in front of one that is farther away, partially covering it.

Creative Approach 9.
Perspective in hilly terrain.

Creative Approach 6.
Aerial gradation on flat landscapes.

Linear Pers

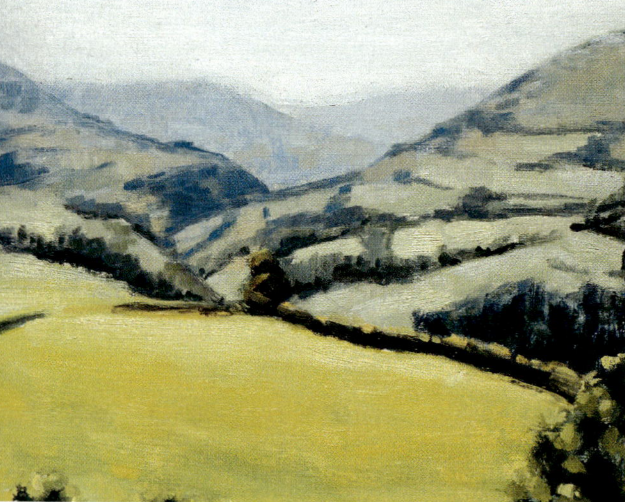

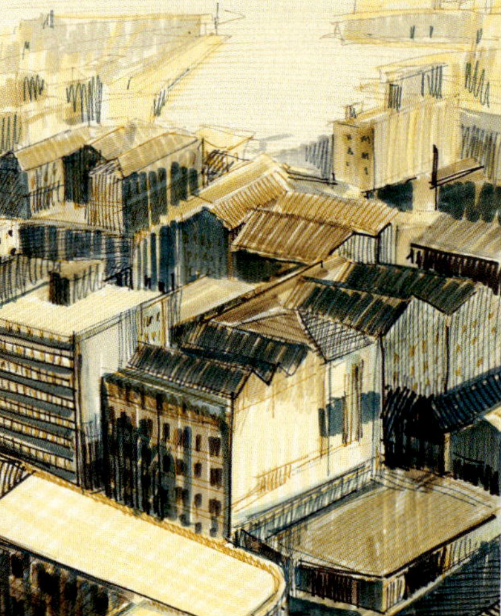

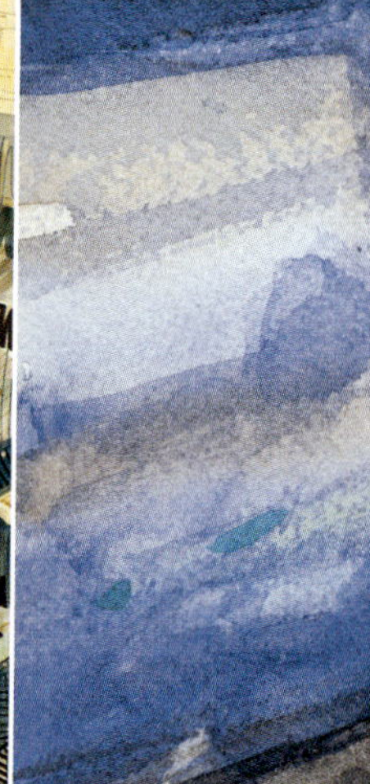

Aerial Perspective

Creative Approach 7.
Frontal perspective: one vanishing point.

Creative Approach 8.
Oblique perspective: two vanishing points.

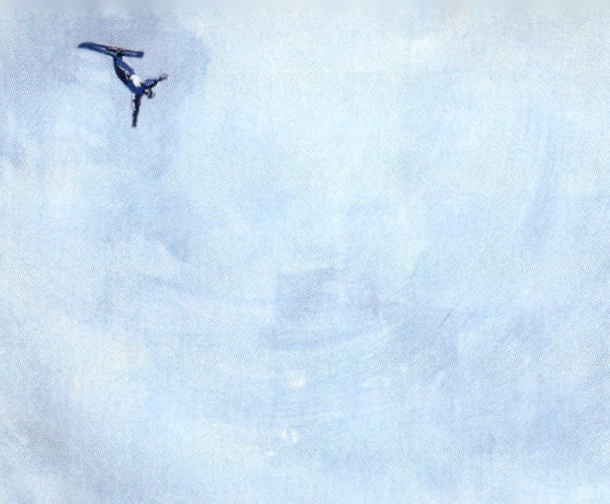

Creative Approach 12. Proportional contrast between figure and field.

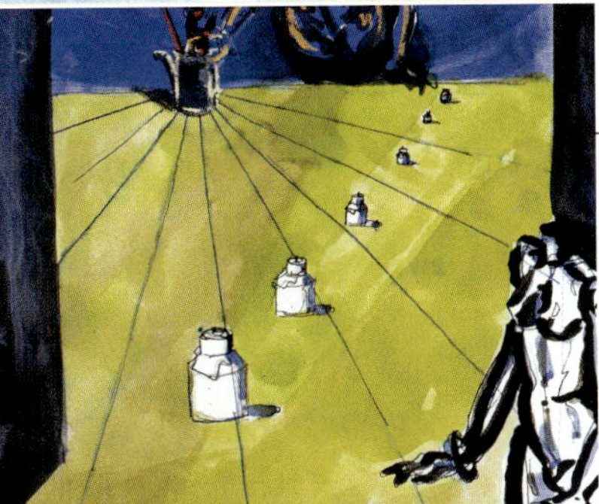

Creative Approach 5. Creating distance by reducing the size.

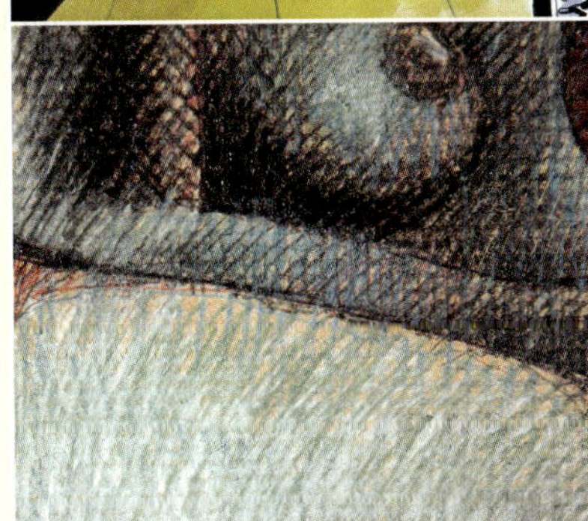

Creative Approach 11. Foreshortening.

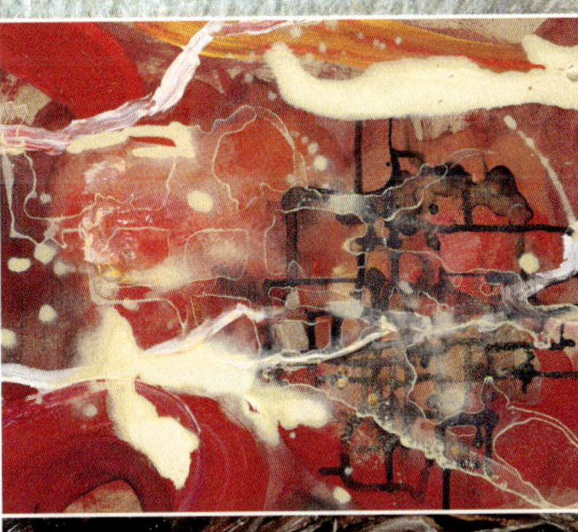

Creative Approach 14. Changes in scale and overlapping.

Scale

ective

Chiaroscuro

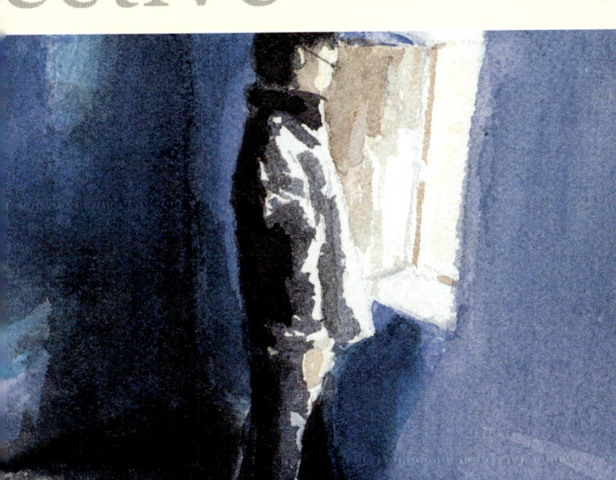

Creative Approach 13. Atmospheric chiaroscuro.

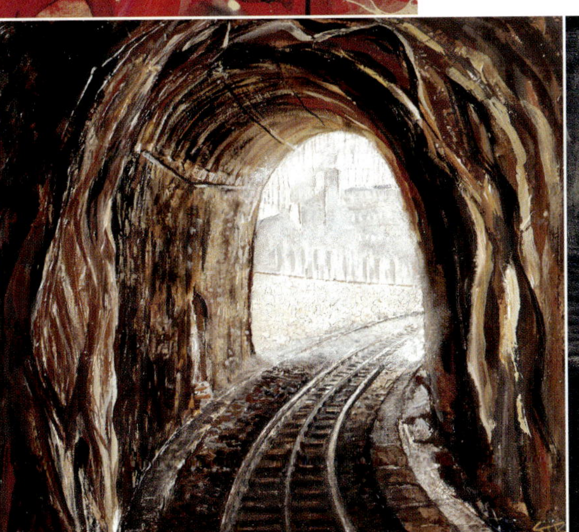

Creative Approach 10. Gradation: changes in light.

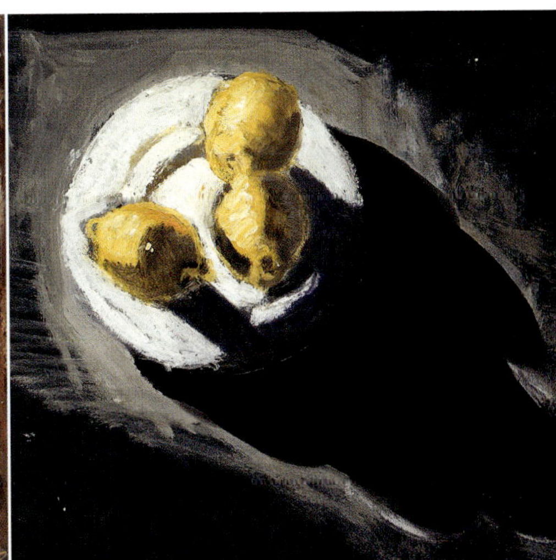

Creative Approach 3. Modeling and projected shadow.

Space in the Painting

In the painting *Las Meninas* (*The Maids of Honor*) by Diego Velázquez (1599–1660), one of the major artists of the baroque period, there is a paradigm in the treatment of space, in its studied composition and the complex structure of the background space.

The compositional structure of the work (**A**) is very rich: it is roughly divided into halves, background above, figures below, a hyperbole whose center is occupied by the princess and two concentric triangles created by the leaning figures; all this is within a rectangular grid. The positions of the heads and their expressions create the movement in the scene, along with a certain organic rhythm (**B**).

The image is like an instant photograph in which the action of a group that is visiting the painter's studio is interrupted by something that is happening outside the limits of the painting: a visit from the king and queen, who are reflected in the mirror in the background. This photographic framing cuts off figures on both sides, and the double opening in the background—the mirror and the door—expand the space in the room by opening it up in all directions (**C**). When it comes to the use of perspective, it should be pointed out that the horizon line is at the king and queen's eye level (**D**), because they are the ones viewing the scene. There is also a carefully controlled play of focused and unfocused areas (**E**) that was very advanced for the time. The great changes in scale (**F**) between the subjects give us an idea of the dimensions of the space, which is quite a large room. The light from a window that is outside the painting flows into the dark room, dividing the picture in half diagonally (**G**). A second light enters through the door at the rear, creating a strong contrast in the composition with the asymmetrical balance between the door, which is far back, and the princess, who is near (**H**); this is the focal point of the work.

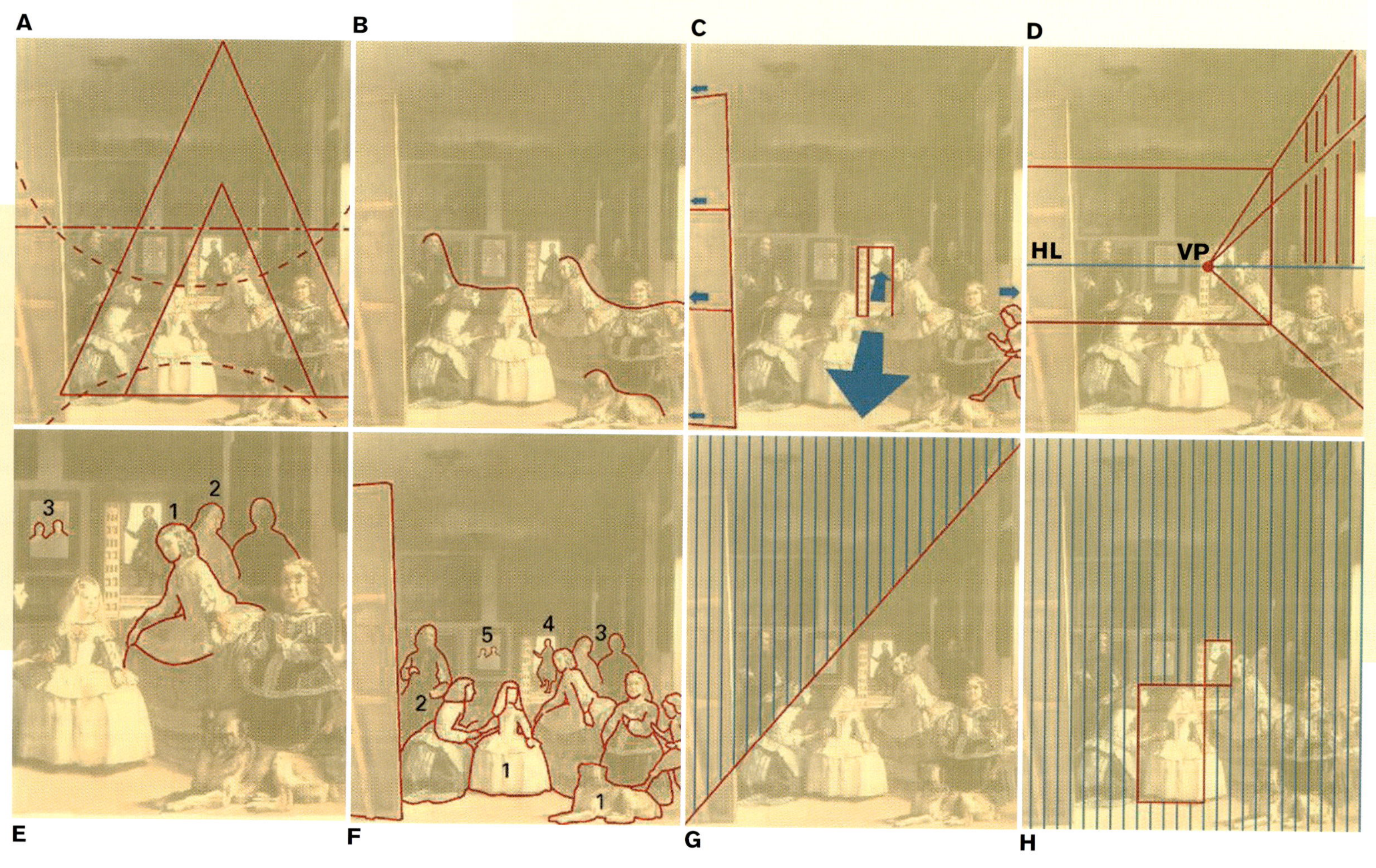

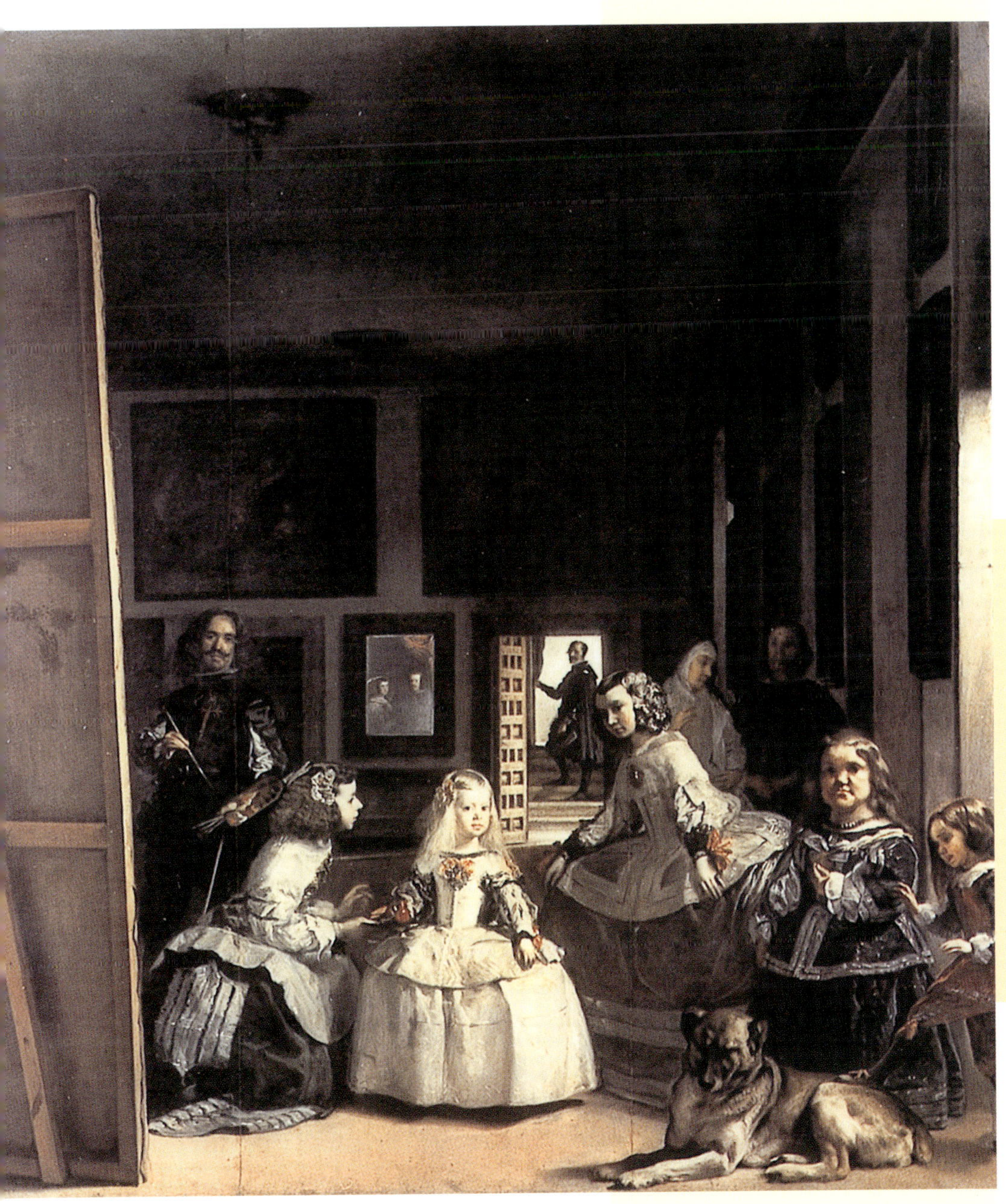

By situating ourselves as spectators in the space that would be occupied by the intended royal observers, Velázquez grants us three privileges: he allows us to visually construct the image ourselves, to be part of the canvas on which he works, and to receive homage from the characters depicted. With this painting it was not so much the artist's intention to immortalize the royal family and its entourage as to celebrate painting as an artistic achievement.

Diego Velázquez,
Las meninas, 1656.
Museo del Prado,
Madrid, Spain.

Space and Personal Expression

In the words of British artists Jane and Louise Wilson, "We deeply identify with some spaces, as much as with some people." The aesthetic experiences produced by space greatly affect the psychology of the viewer because they connect with his or her lived experiences on a very deep level. Thus, through composition and the illusion of space, the artist can awaken intense emotions and sensations with his work, like ascending, falling, abyss, claustrophobia, agoraphobia, balance, unbalance, expansion, contraction, escape, monumentality, smallness, shelter, desertion, barriers, contraction, spinning, flight, disorientation, etc. We shall see how four painters from different time periods have expressed themselves through the pictorial treatment of space.

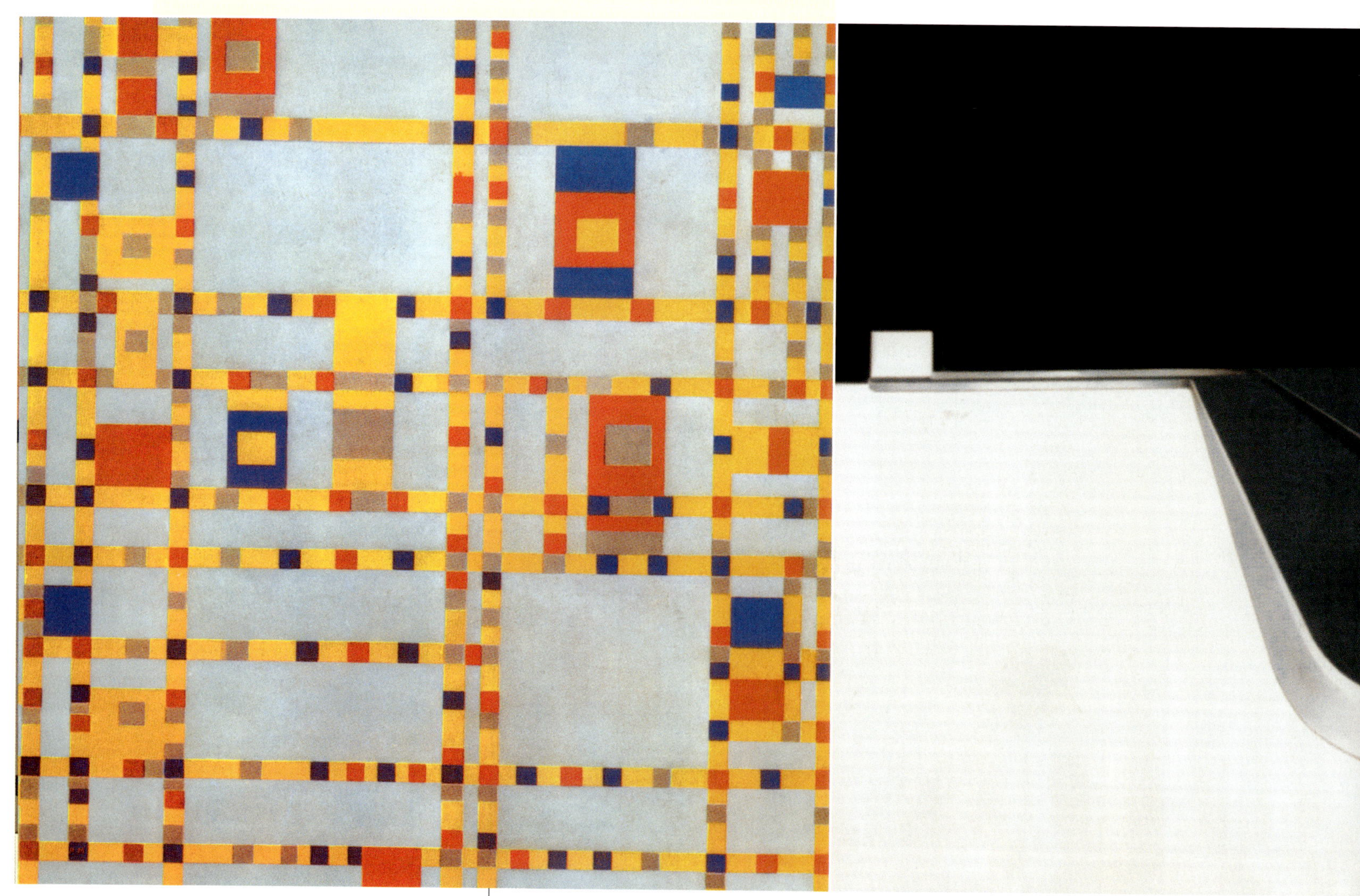

Piet Mondrian, *Broadway Boogie Woogie,* 1942–1943. Museum of Modern Art, New York, NY.

The creator of neoplasticism, Piet Mondrian (1872–1944), found a new dimension of pure and geometric space in New York that gave form to his painted works: movement. The traditional black lines of his previous paintings are replaced with color, the spaces are broken up, and the rhythm of the painting takes on a new excitement.

Caspar David Friedrich,
The White Cliffs of Rügen,
1818.
Private Collection.

This work by Friedrich (1774–1840) is full of symbols: the V-shape composition closed at the top by the trees creates the shape of a heart. This is a painting done during his honeymoon, in which the horizon line is very high so their long life as a married couple may be contemplated (the two boats sailing away). The woman in the scene is his wife, and the two men are the artist himself at two different ages and attitudes; in his youth he contemplates an idealized future, and as an older man his wife is directing his gaze.

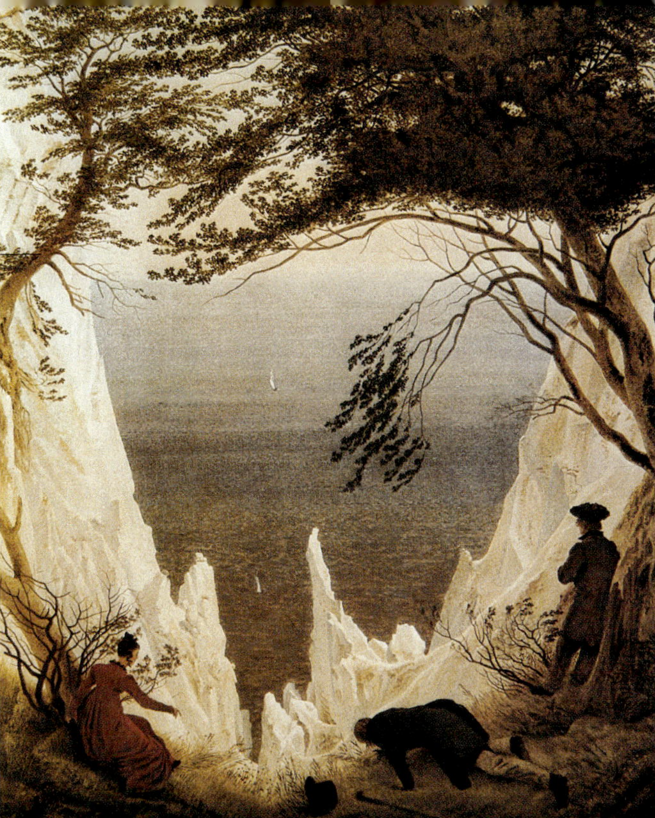

This unique fresco painted by Goya (1746–1828) during his self-seclusion in the Quinta del Sordo is a direct and moving expression of his personal situation. Three-quarters of the painting is empty, nothingness, a space that does not belong to any place and a dog looking away with nothing to support him. It has an almost human expression that speaks of solitude and insecurity.

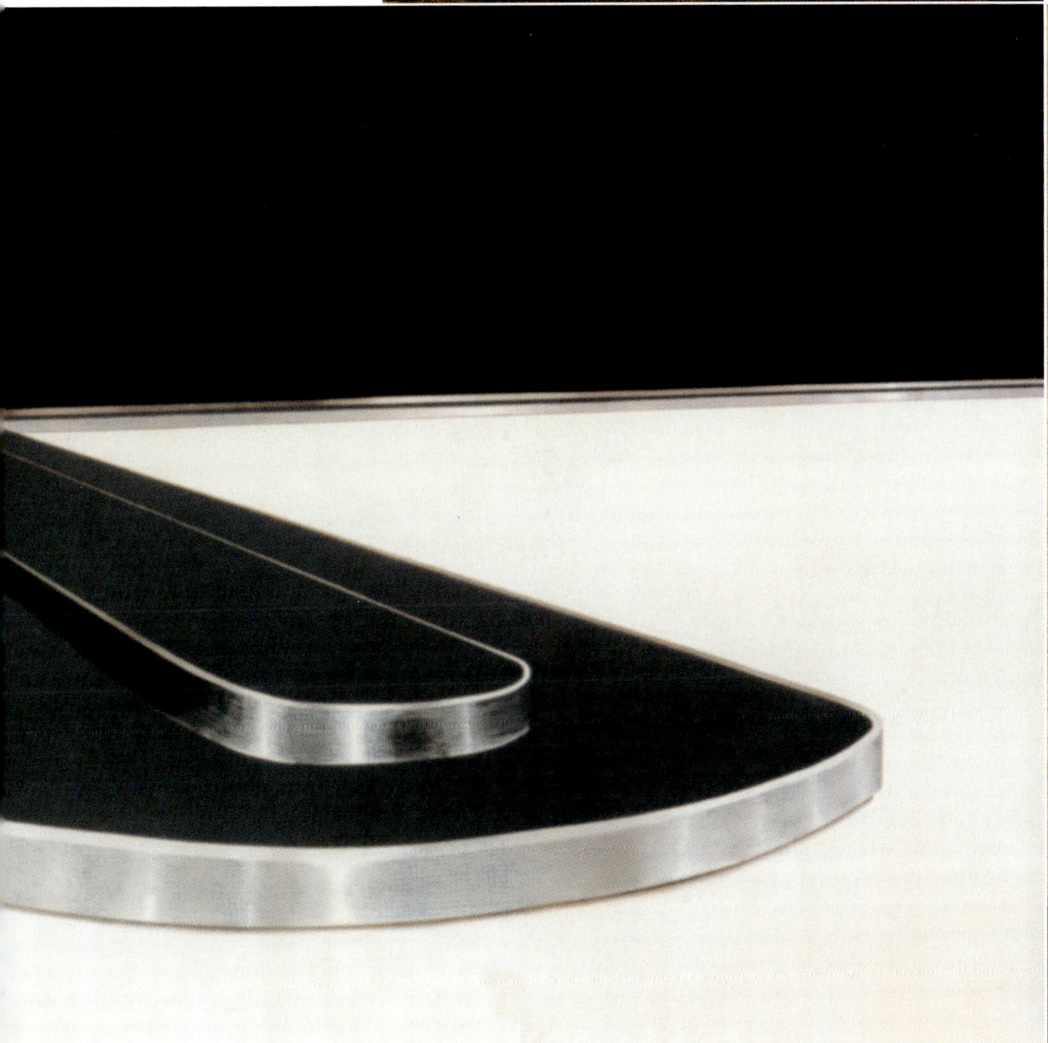

Francisco de Goya,
The Sinking Dog,
1821–1823.
Museo del Prado,
Madrid, Spain.

Guillermo Kuitca, *Terminal,* 2001.
Private Collection.

In the series of paintings by Guillermo Kuitca (born in 1961) based on airport luggage carousels we find a visual metaphor of the search for identity. The painter places the viewer before a conveyor belt that could be in any airport waiting for bags to arrive, the viewer's. Time—waiting—is here an additional conceptual value that conditions the perception of space.

Experimenting with Space

When a painter experiments with space, it is done with two realities, the formal problems on one side (composition, perspective, structure, atmosphere . . .), and conceptual problems on the other (limits, emptiness, occupation, what passes us by . . .). This double attraction has captivated numerous painters, inducing them to abandon themselves to passionate exploration; constantly searching for space in the painting, a pictorial space that is not a simple representation but a new autonomous and eloquent reality.

The source of inspiration for Sarah Morris (born 1967) is the urban landscape, although from an unusual perspective, different from that of a pedestrian at street level. The glass façades of company, bank, and hotel buildings and advertising slogans are the basis for the two-dimensional nature of her paintings, as can be seen in these large 7 x 7 foot (214 x 214 cm) canvases. Her works, made using bright enamel colors and masking tape, connect with the American pop art tradition and the works of Sol Le Witt and Peter Halley.

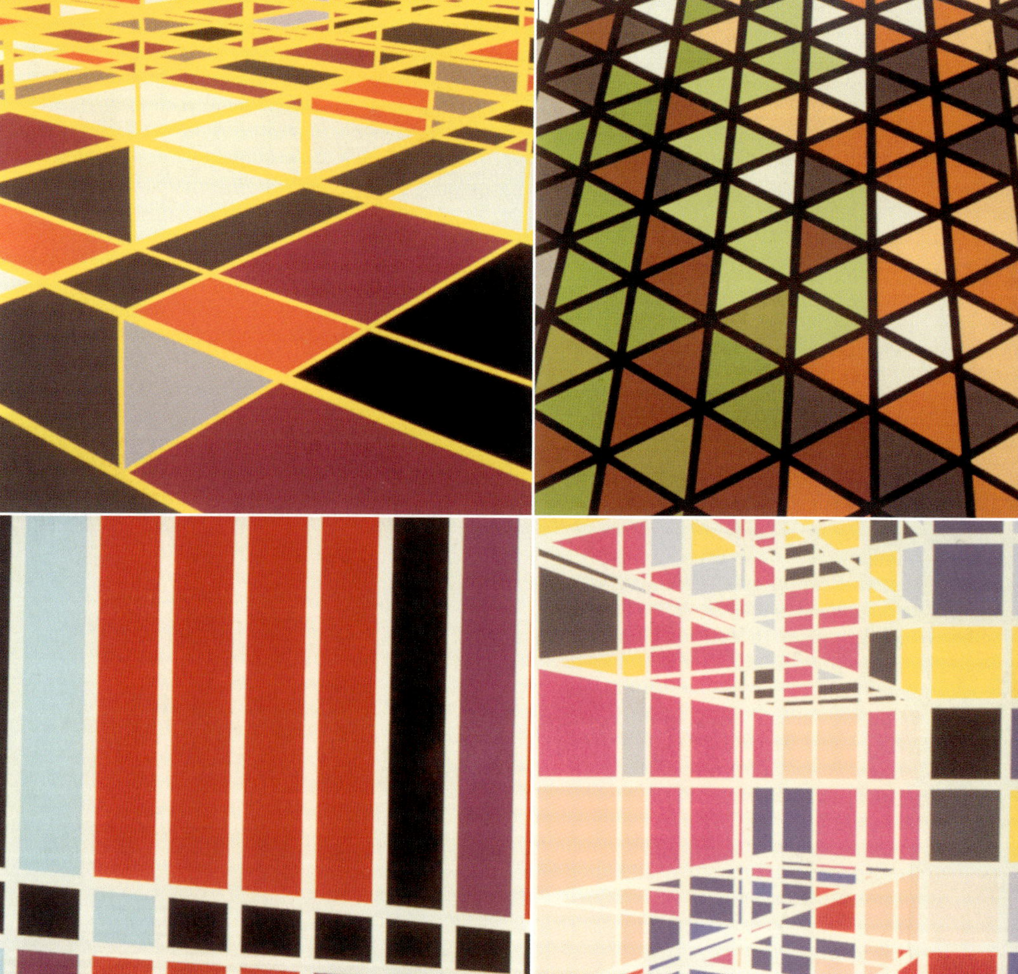

Sarah Morris,
IMF (Capital), 2001.
Private Collection.

Sarah Morris,
Neon-Rumjungle (Las Vegas),
2000. Private Collection.

Sarah Morris,
*Midtown-Chase Bank
(World Headquarters),* 1998.
Private Collection

Among the many experiments in space and perception carried out by Cornelis Escher (1898–1972), these two sketches belong to the studies that the artist made on the limited and the infinite. Two of the most emblematic works of this series are *Waterfall* and *Stairs Up and Stairs Down*, in which he created a visual *perpetuum mobile*. Both depict complex architectural spaces of absurd construction, impossible buildings with cubic structures, where by turning a corner during a stroll we find ourselves where we began.

Cornelis Escher,
Sketch for Stairs Up and Stairs Down, 1960.

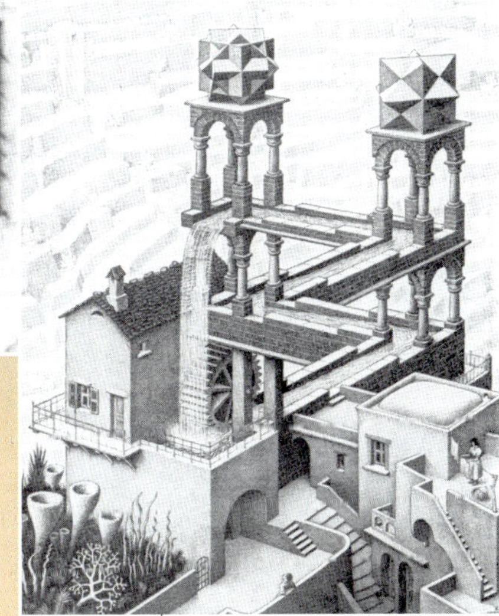

Cornelis Escher,
Pencil Drawings of the Waterfall Building, 1961.

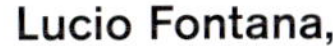

Lucio Fontana,
Concetto Spaziale 49 B2, 1949.
Lucio Fontana Foundation, Milan, Italy.

Lucio Fontana (1899–1968), the creator of spatialism, abandoned the myth of the tradition of the artistic object in his work in favor of "the act of the free spirit of all models." In his work he did not represent space as much as create it. His works are performance pieces because they contain the action over the image, perforating and cutting the canvas to create a new pictorial space born of contingency and drama. In an interview in 1968 he said, "I make a hole in the canvas with the goal of leaving behind the old pictorial formula, the traditional painting and vision of art, the flat surface. It is a prison from which I escape not only symbolically, but also materially."

Sarah Morris,
Dulles (Capital), 2001.
Private Collection.

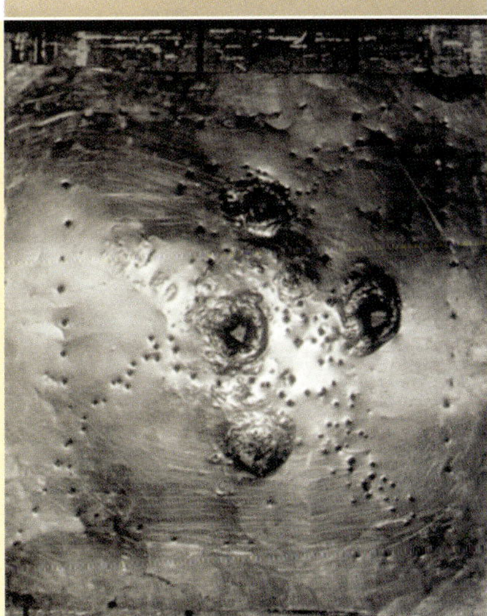

Lucio Fontana,
Concetto Spaziale 50 B9, 1950.
Lucio Fontana Foundation, Milan, Italy.

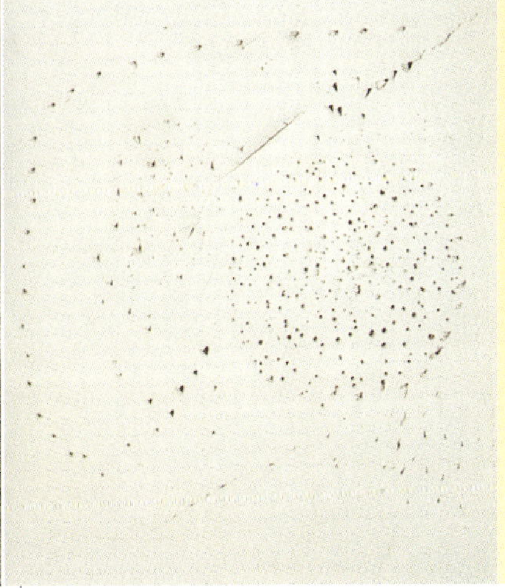

Lucio Fontana,
Concetto Spaziale 50 B4, 1950.
Lucio Fontana Foundation, Milan, Italy.

Life is lived in a habitat: the sea, the desert, the forest . . . these are living spaces. In the first chapter we are going to talk about two spatial phenomena characteristic of living beings: rhythm and grouping. Rhythm indicates movement in space; it is the order that is established through variety. There is rhythm in the stripes of a zebra, in the petals of a sunflower, and in the spirals of a snail. Grouping is common in most living organisms: forests, prairies, formations, herds, bands, hives, colonies, and so on.

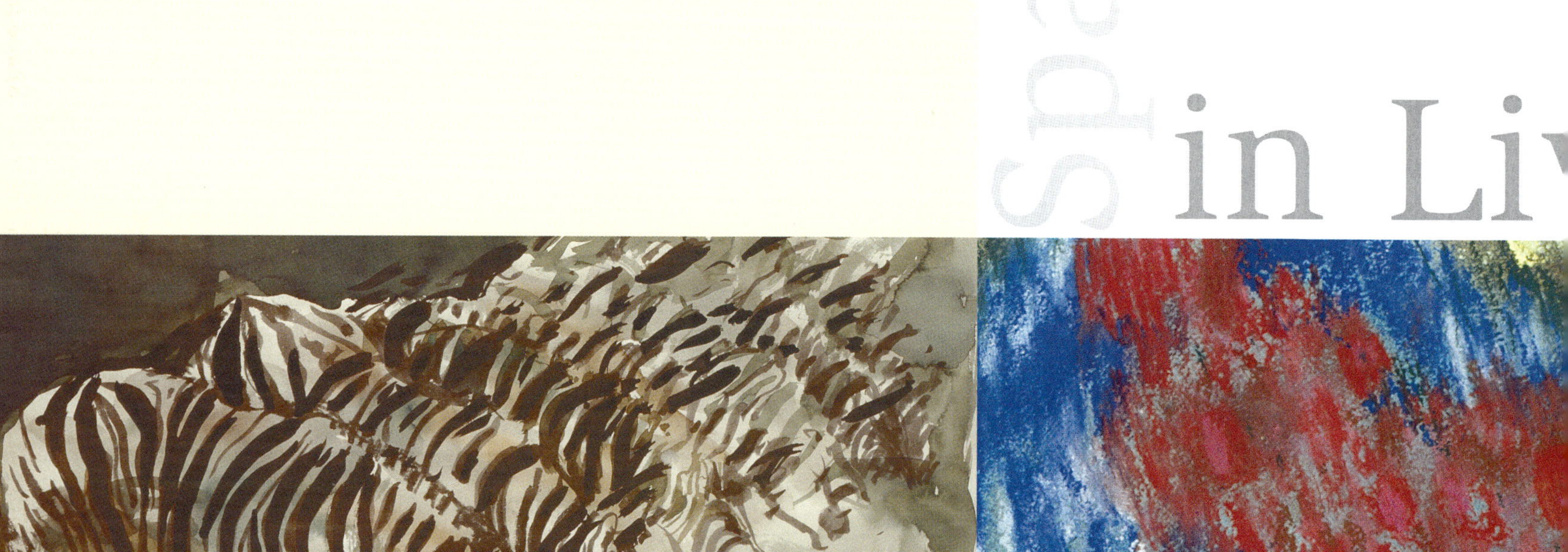

ing Nature

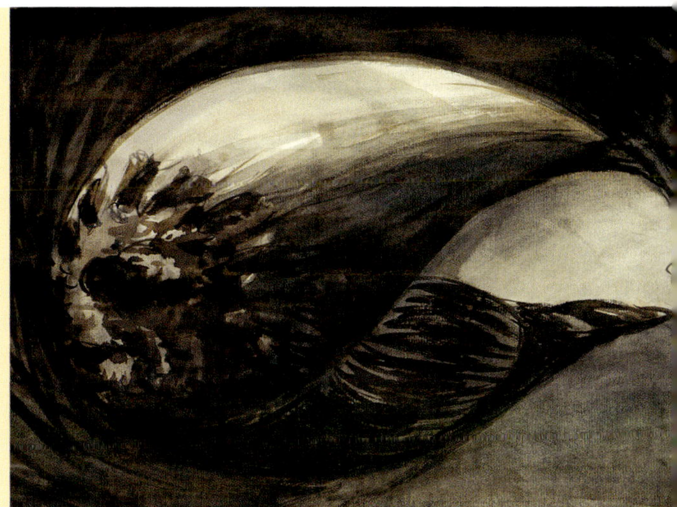

> *"The rough sea, trembling and roaring,*
> *still finds itself in its original state."*
> **Emil Nolde,**
> *Autobiography* (during his stay on the island of Alsen, Denmark),
> 1910.

Rhythmic, Ordered, and *Alternating Spaces*

24

Franz Marc (1880–1916), a German painter belonging to the group of expressionist artists known as *Der Blaue Reiter* (The Blue Rider), said, "Today we search for the things in nature that are found hidden behind the veil of appearance . . . we look for and paint that interior face, the spiritual in nature." In his paintings of animals, mainly horses and gazelles, he evoked what was later called "the interior sound," the rhythm or beat of life. The painting *Gazelles* belongs to the period in which Marc took his work, until then figurative, toward abstraction—between 1912 and 1913 he wrote his thesis on abstract art. In the works that he painted during this period the internal rhythm of living nature is emphasized, more so than descriptive forms. In this case the work is sustained by a rhythmic base with alternating interlaced arcs inspired by the horns of the gazelle. They are acute, dynamic, and graceful spaces, like the animal.

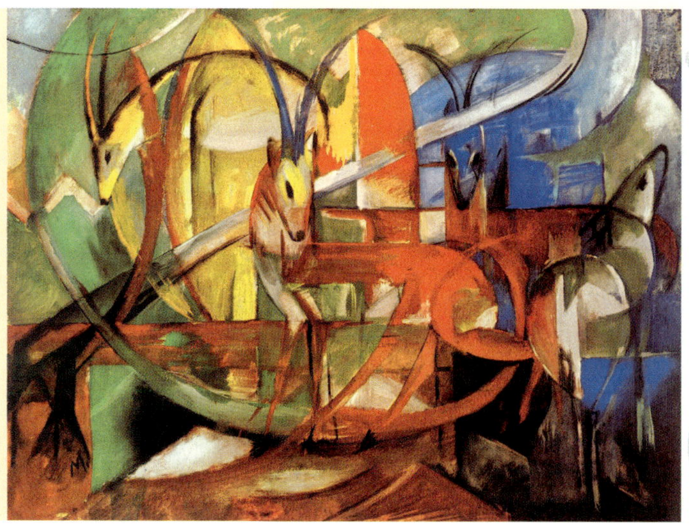

Franz Marc,
Gazelles, 1913.
Private Collection.

Rhythmic Compositions: Increasing and Decreasing Rhythms in a Herd of Zebras

Rhythm is the unit in variety, the order in change. When variety in a painting does not follow any order, there is chaos rather than the perception of unity. Since Leonardo da Vinci, many painters have observed nature to discover the rhythmic basis that orders all change: the growth of trees, the arrangement of the petals on a flower, the stripes or spots on some animals, waves, falling leaves . . . they all have some order, a logos. In this approach Josep Asunción creates a rhythmic study of the stripes on some zebras, creatively developing dynamic compositions that increase and decrease based on the animal's stripes. The medium used for this work is brush and ink on paper.

Space in Living Nature

"Order and regularity are a consequence of the complete realization of the attraction that atoms and molecules exercise upon each other."
William Bragg

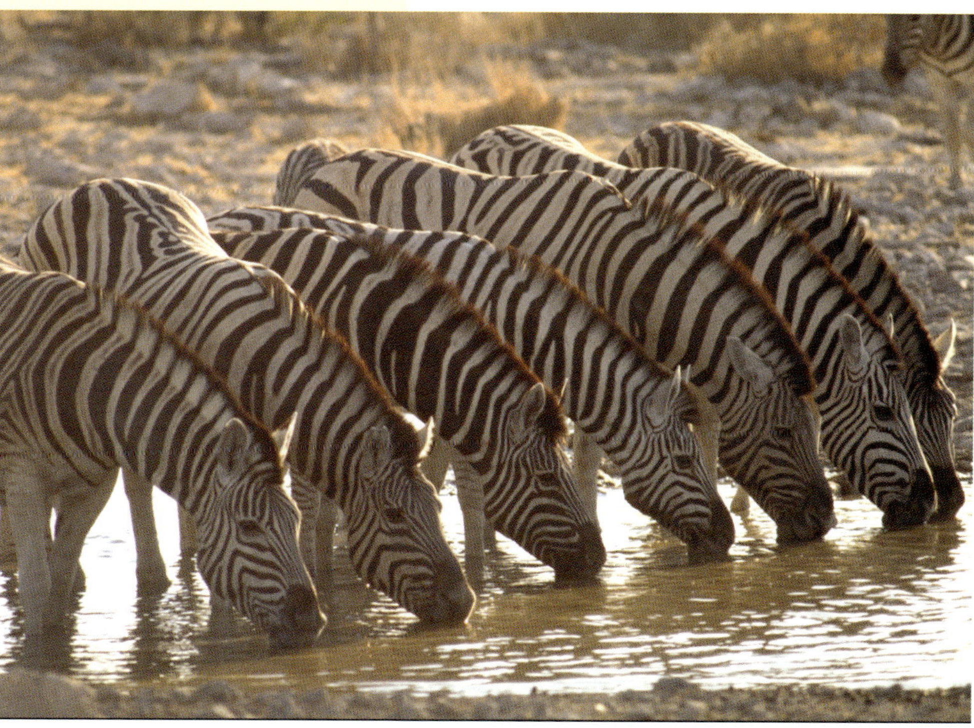

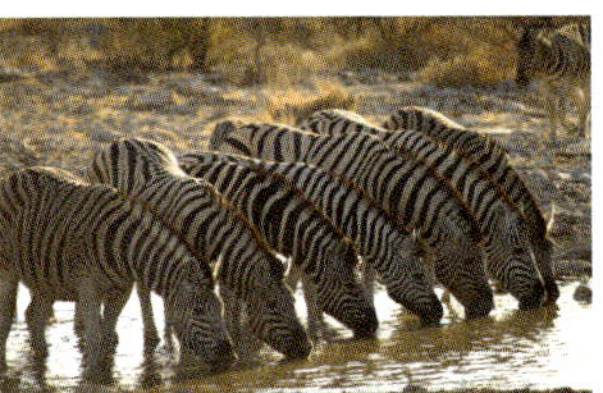

1 We apply the first brushstrokes of Prussian blue and burnt sienna colored inks to center the composition, arranging the zebras in an ascending diagonal. The colors are diluted on the paper to create gray tones that will later show through between the zebras' black stripes.

2 We indicate the stripes of the zebra in the foreground with rhythmic movements. It is very important to control the curves of the stripes to make the anatomy of the animal easy to see.

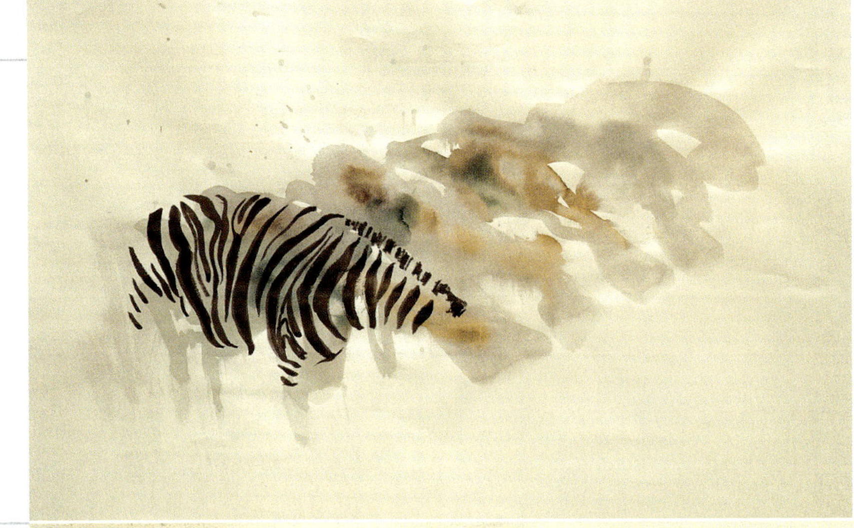

3 We continue drawing the stripes on the next zebras, controlling the form and intensity. To do this we dilute the ink more as the silhouettes move away, which helps add depth to the scene.

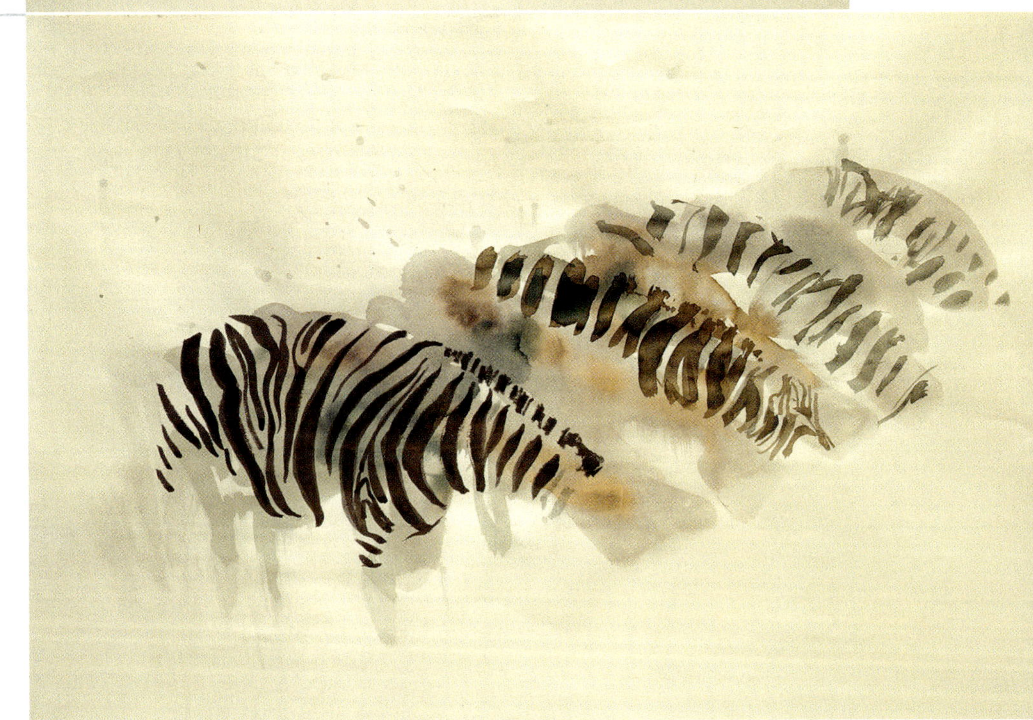

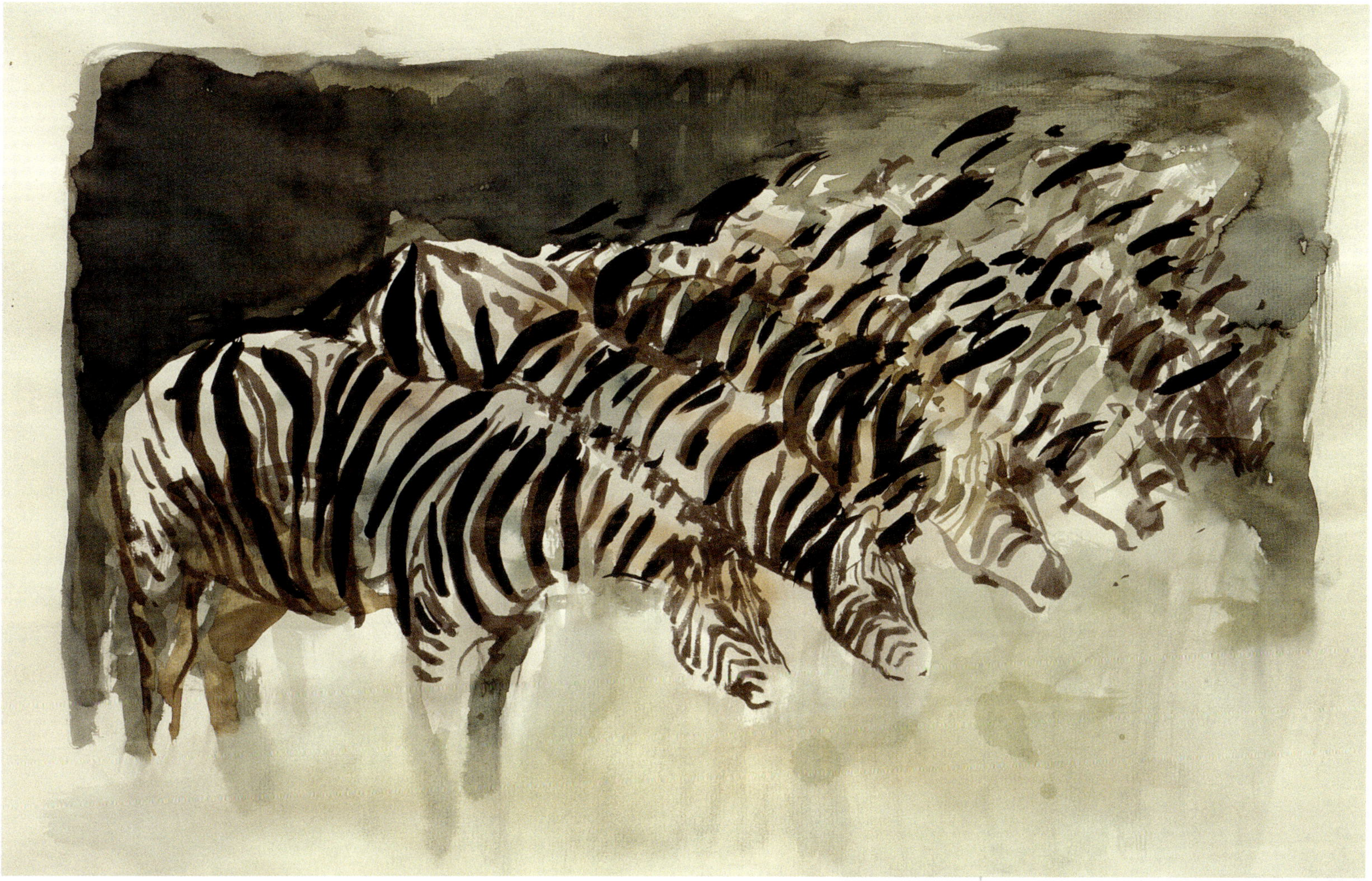

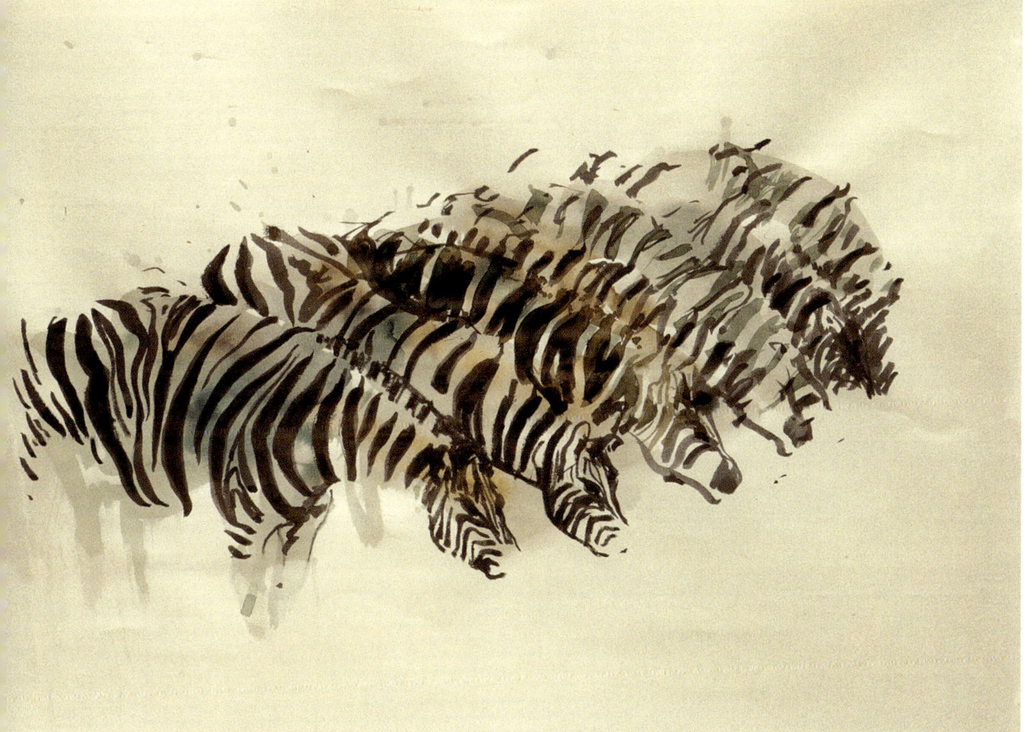

5 Finally, we create a luminous atmosphere that helps give the animals form. We darken the background and the foreground so that the light falls on the zebras and not the surroundings. We are able to use this to outline the anatomy of the animals with modeling and chiaroscuro.

4 We finish drawing the lines, varying their width and intensity so they will not become monotonous. This way we make it understood that there is unity in variety, a logical rhythm. The increasing sinuous movement that is repeated in each zebra, with slight variations, decreases as they get farther away.

The structure of this work is based on increasing and decreasing movement. The curved stripes of the zebra skins move up and to the right and decrease in size and intensity. Here we see size variations based on this rhythmic approach.

In this image the protagonist is the increasing movement and tremendously dynamic lines of the zebra's stripes. The fact that the first zebra of the group is realistically detailed and the rest are not produces a more dynamic effect. It is as if the black stripes have detached themselves and are jumping and flying into the air. It is an expansive rhythm.

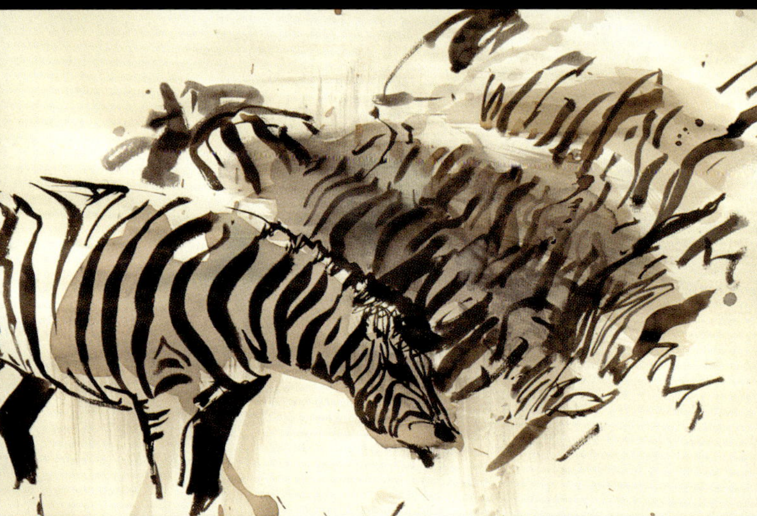

In this painting the sense of decrease has been intensified by exaggerating the change in darkness as the zebras get farther away, becoming lighter until they are lost in the background. This approach strongly accentuates the sense of grounds—foreground, middle ground, background, etc.– which adds spatial depth.

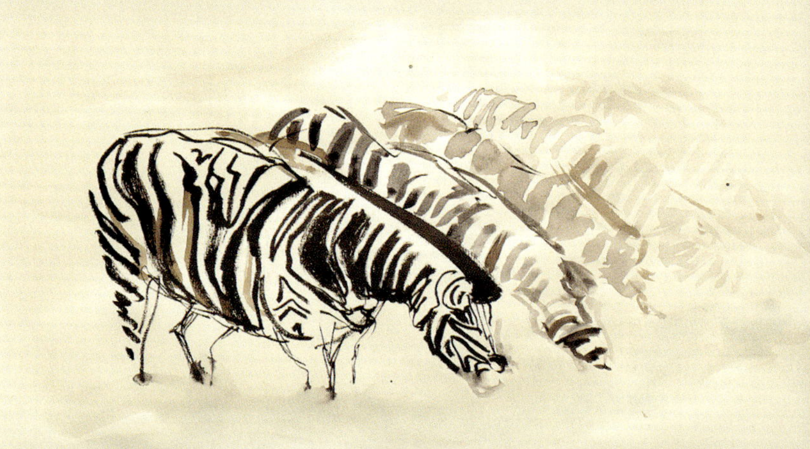

This painting makes use of the placement of the zebras to show a fan-shaped rhythm. The animal's haunches become the protagonists and the stripes take on a secondary importance. This is a radial rhythm where we can sense a center off to the left where the haunches of the zebras converge visually.

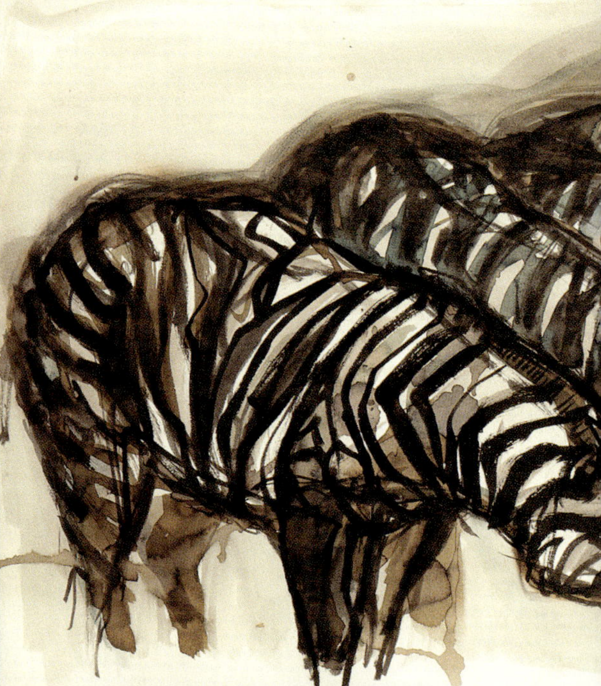

The painter created a strong chiaroscuro effect, reinforcing the directional gestures of the necks and heads of the zebras. This approach is used to emphasize whatever the artist wishes while making the rest disappear in darkness. The rhythm now points toward the bottom right, signaled by the heads of the animals.

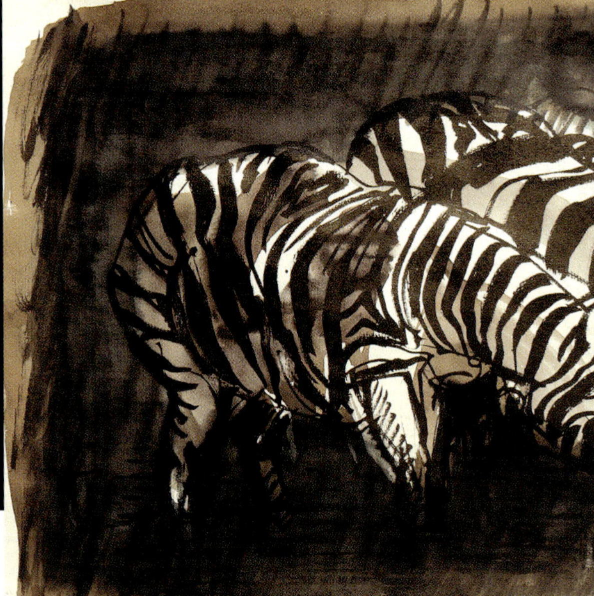

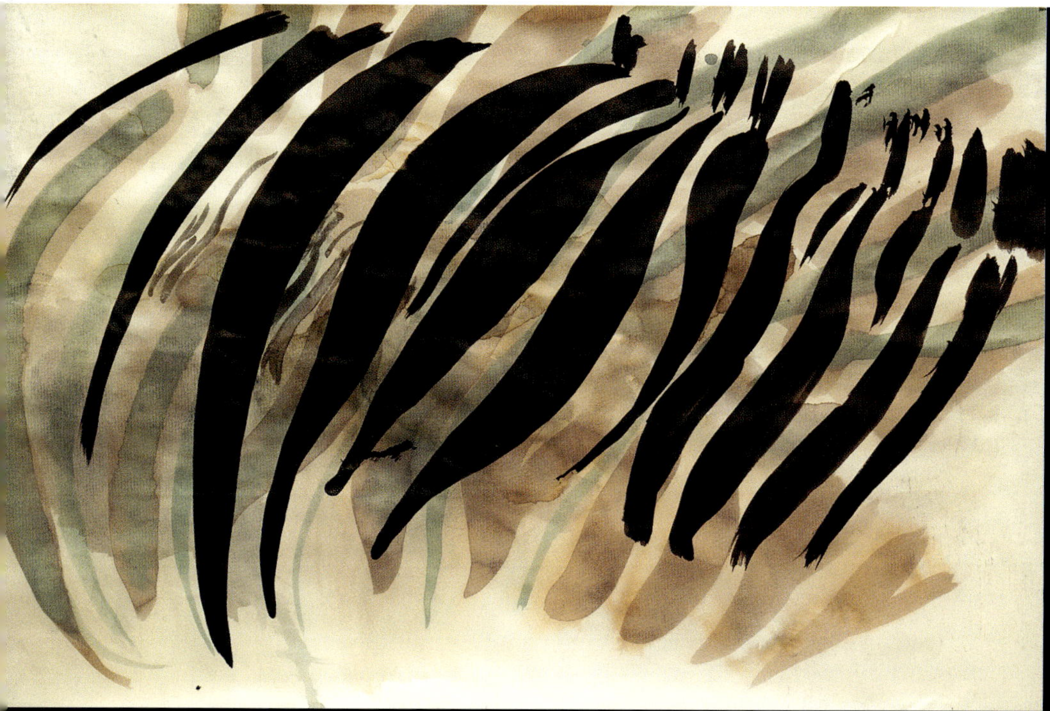

This is the most abstract composition of the gallery. The entire surface is covered by the sinuous movements of the black lines on the animal hide. The artist made the black bands vibrate against curving strips of bluish and earth tones. This is a rhythm where increase/decrease and movement come into play.

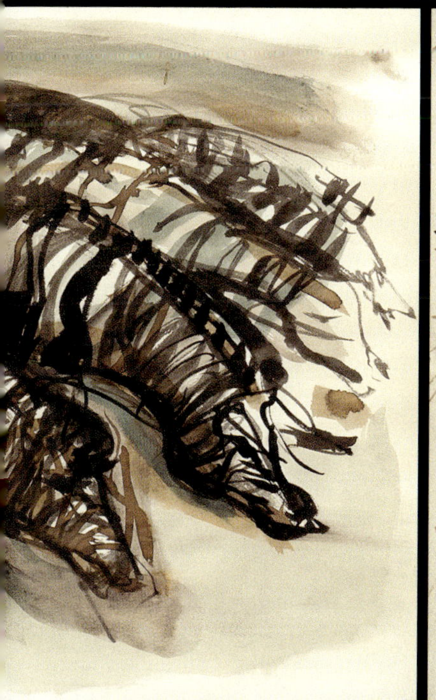

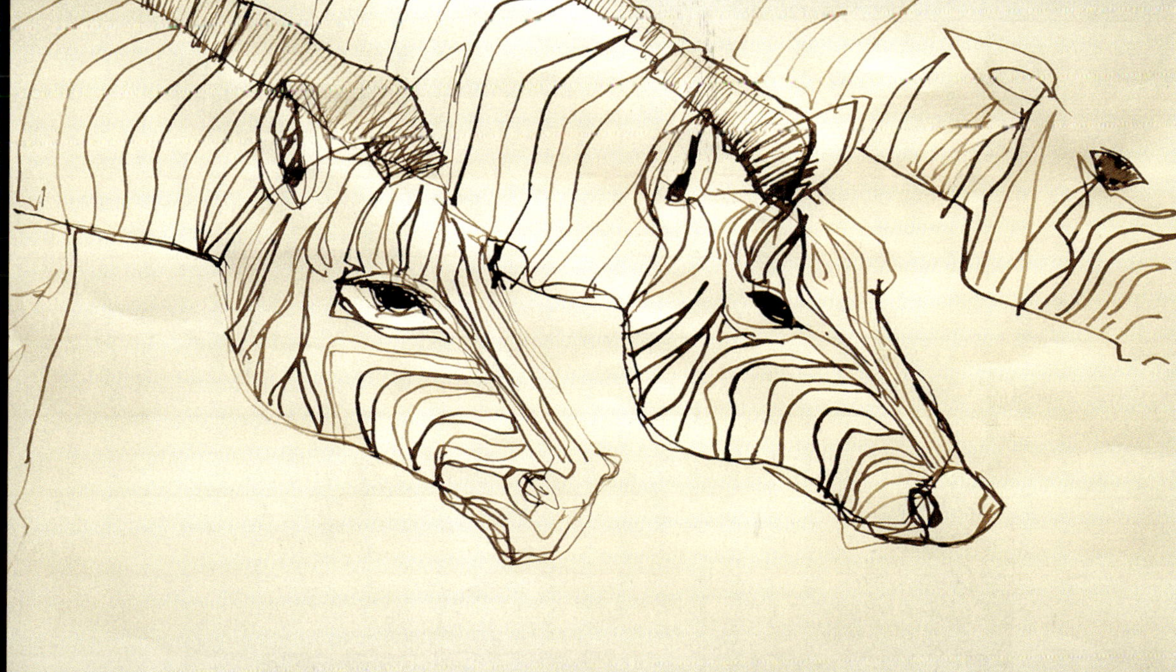

Here the lines are distributed in a very orderly manner, causing the rhythm to become regular and sequential. It has no spatial depth, like a frieze. A clean, precise line has a more descriptive and synthetic character than an area of color. The rhythm thus becomes more mental than visceral.

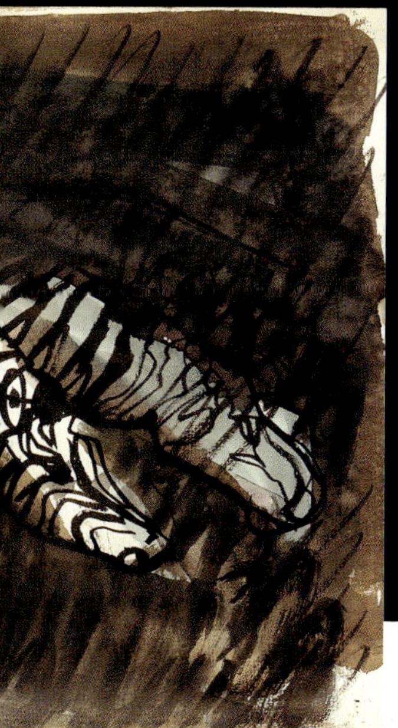

Other Models

One of the natural factors that create very attractive and beautiful rhythms is growth. The distance between the branches of a tree where they connect to the trunk obeys the tree's rhythm of growth and is always proportional. The same thing is true of snails: they have an absolutely harmonious and dynamic spiral growth, a growth that determines their form. To experiment with this rhythmic spiral space we have chosen the snail as an alternative to the zebras.

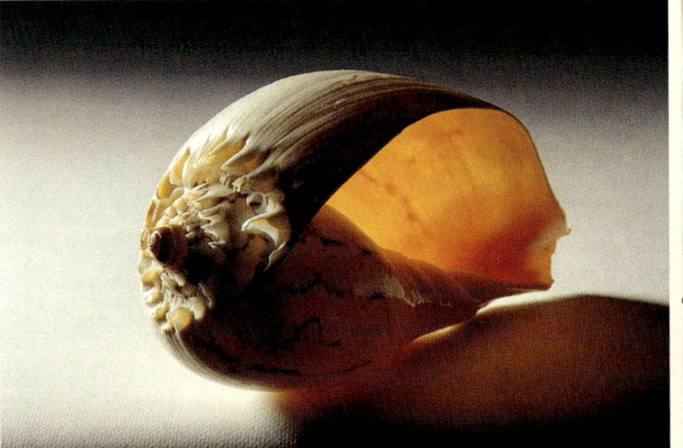

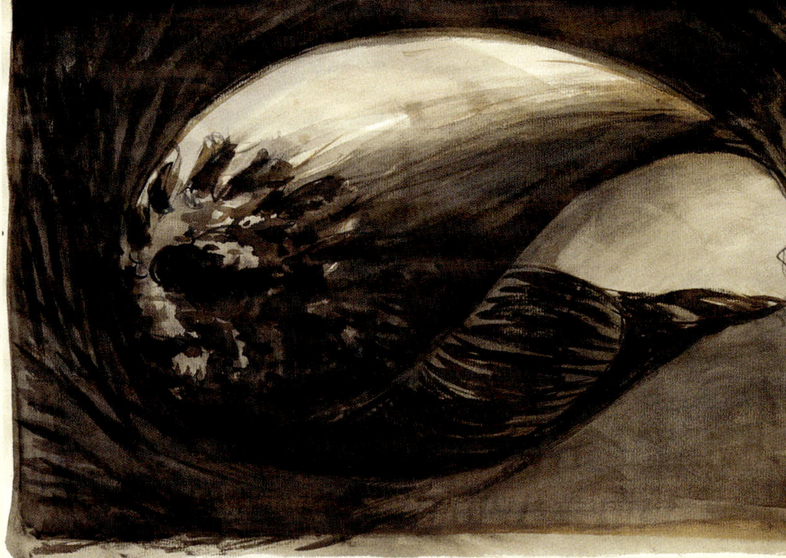

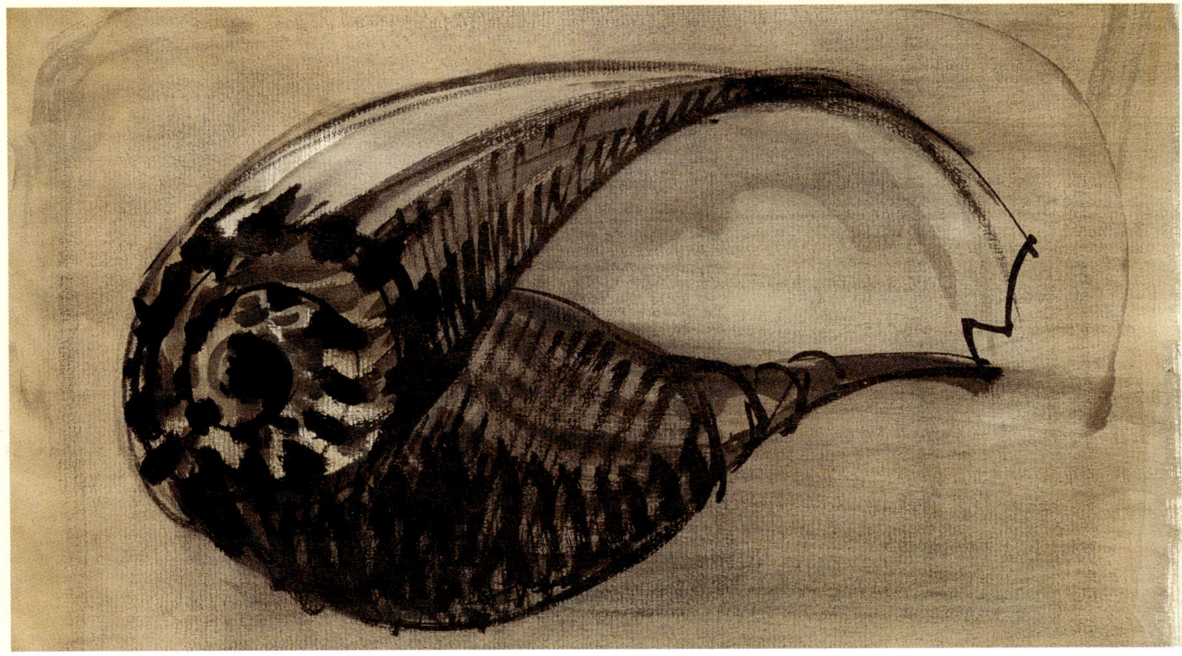

Other Media

Because ink creates a very flat and smooth result, we are going to experiment with a dry medium to add more texture to the work. In this case, we have chosen pastels for working with the intensity of the line, blending, and erasing to achieve more roughness in the final piece, more like the hide of the animal.

Other Views

Odilon Redon (1840–1916), an impressionist artist, found his source of inspiration in nature: the world of the sea, flowers, butterflies, the microscopic world, and so on. Already between 1873 and 1877 he had worked almost exclusively with snails, but in his *Underwater Vision* done thirty years later, he fulfilled the sentence written in the theoretical treatise to himself, "I have opened my eyes to the marvels of the visible world, totally concerned with obeying the laws of nature and life."

In this painting from his mature stage we find, more than fish and mollusks suspended in the water, arcs and spirals in lively movement, in a natural rhythm.

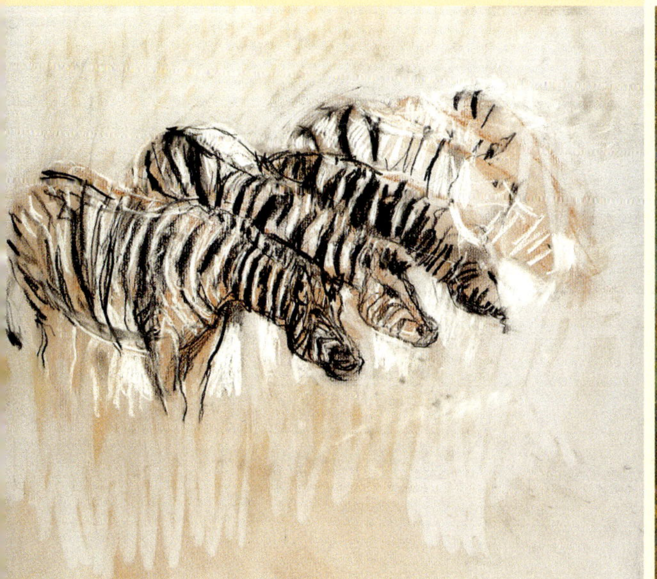

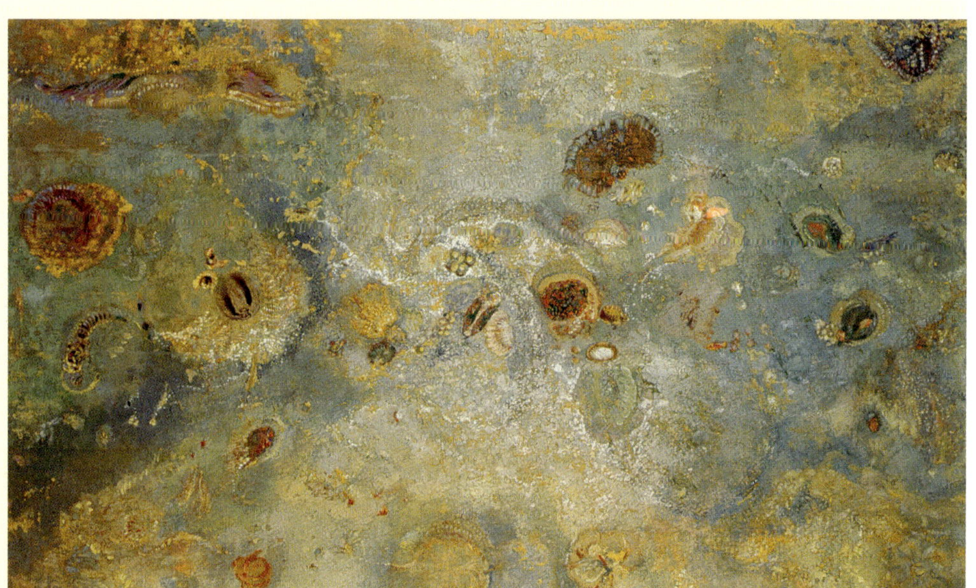

Odilon Redon,
Underwater Vision, c. 1910, detail.
Private Collection.

Grouped, Extended, and Populated Spaces

The Austrian artist Gustav Klimt (1862–1918), leading figure of the Viennese secessionist movement, approached nature from a group perspective, as extensions or agglomerated living elements with little contrast between them. In his paintings the forests, lakes, fields, and gardens look like mosaics or decorative rugs.

The presence of floral and decorative elements in his work is a result of his love of classicism and symbolism, and his background in the decorative arts. This began in his childhood through the influence of his family; gold and silver work, scene design, gilding, and mosaic work all influenced his personal style from the beginning. His work is characterized by atypical framing, decoration imposed upon the figures, textural and kaleidoscope-like spaces whose extreme profusion of decoration is woven into the structure of the painting. Influenced by Japanese prints and Van Gogh, Klimt painted the surface of nature with extreme delicacy and clear vitality, adding his personal note of luxury and sensuality.

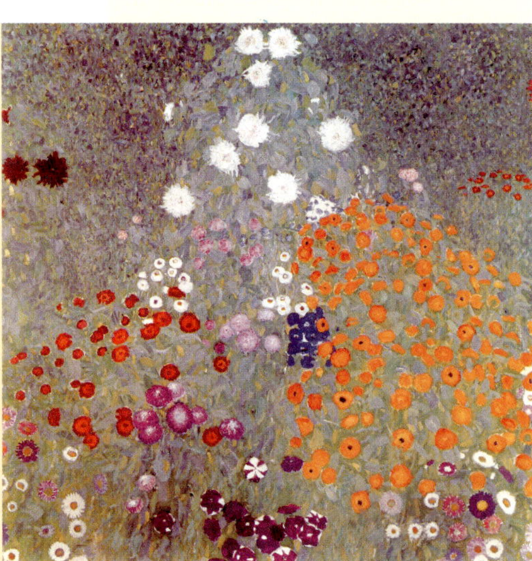

Gustav Klimt,
Flower Garden, 1906–1908.
Narodny Gallery,
Prague, Czech Republic.

Varying the Formats: Different Ways of Framing a Floral Subject

The second approach in this book deals with a fundamental theme of painting: the format. We are referring to the form adopted by the painting: square, round, landscape, vertical, diamond, oval, etc. The format is directly related to the framing and affects the composition of the image. In this approach Josep Asunción addresses a floral subject, a garden, creating a visual grouping where each flower forms part of a spatial extension, in the style of Klimt. He has used acrylic paint on paper, varying the formats (shapes of the painting) and the framing (selecting different areas of the garden).

"The garden of Utenwarf, on the side of the hill, angled toward the sun, was particularly luxuriant and covered by innumerable flowers. The roses, of a luminous red, covered the south side like waves and above, surrounding the small pond full of fish, were magnificent bushes. It had all been transformed into a magnificent spectacle. 'A small paradise,' as the people say."
Emil Nolde,
Autobiography
(visiting Utenwarf), 1916.

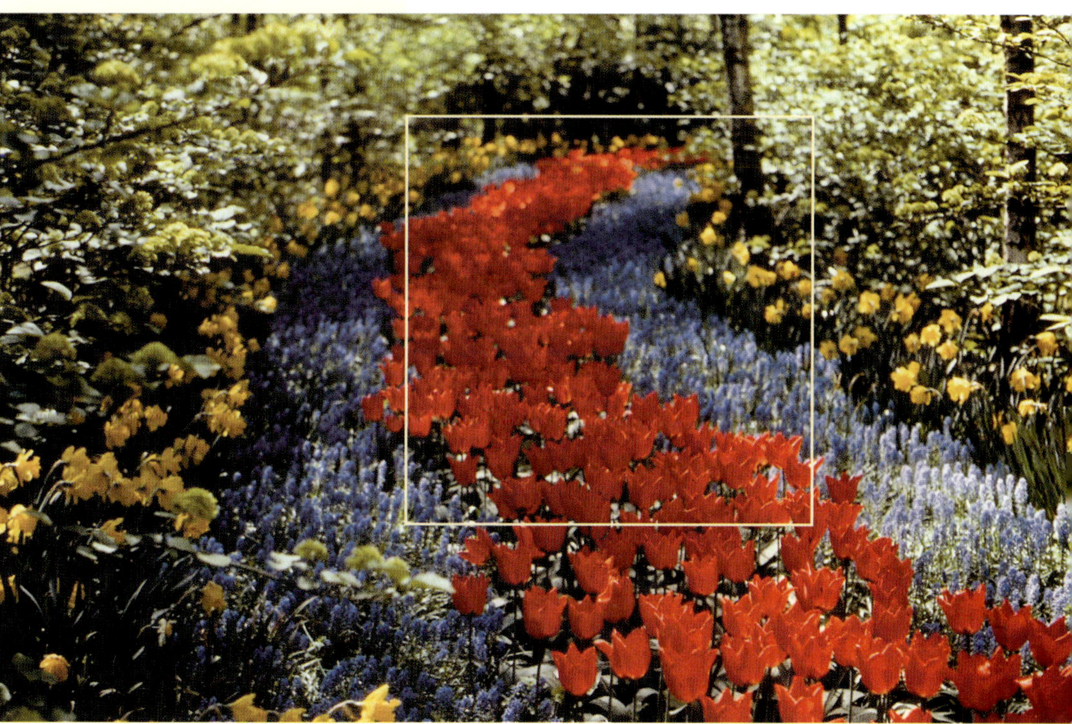

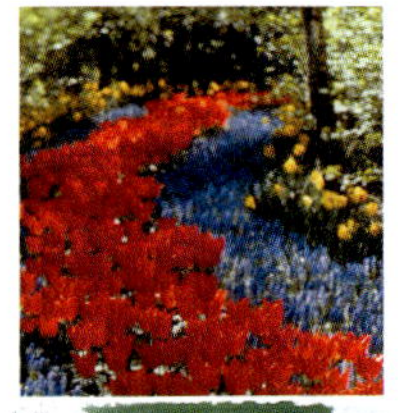

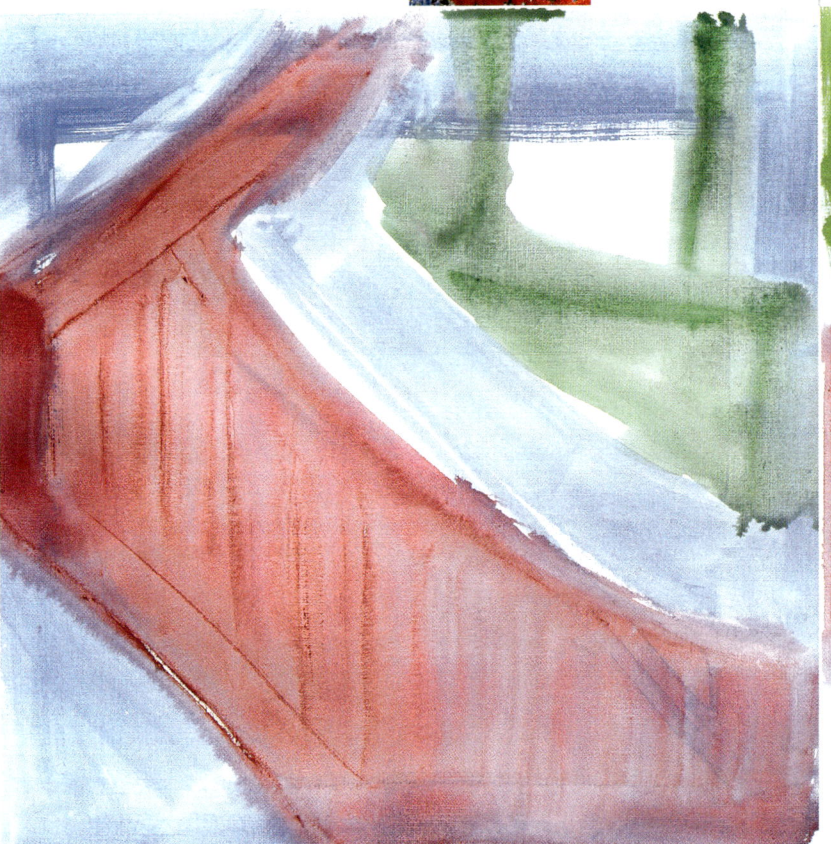

2 We locate the first dark values to begin giving the plants and flowers a sense of volume. The paint is denser and of more intense color.

1 A square format was chosen for this painting, where the framing encompasses more than half of the visual field. The artist focused on the diagonal bands descending from the upper left corner to the lower right that define the path of flowers that lead into the woods. The first diluted brushstrokes indicate each area of flowers in the composition with light tones.

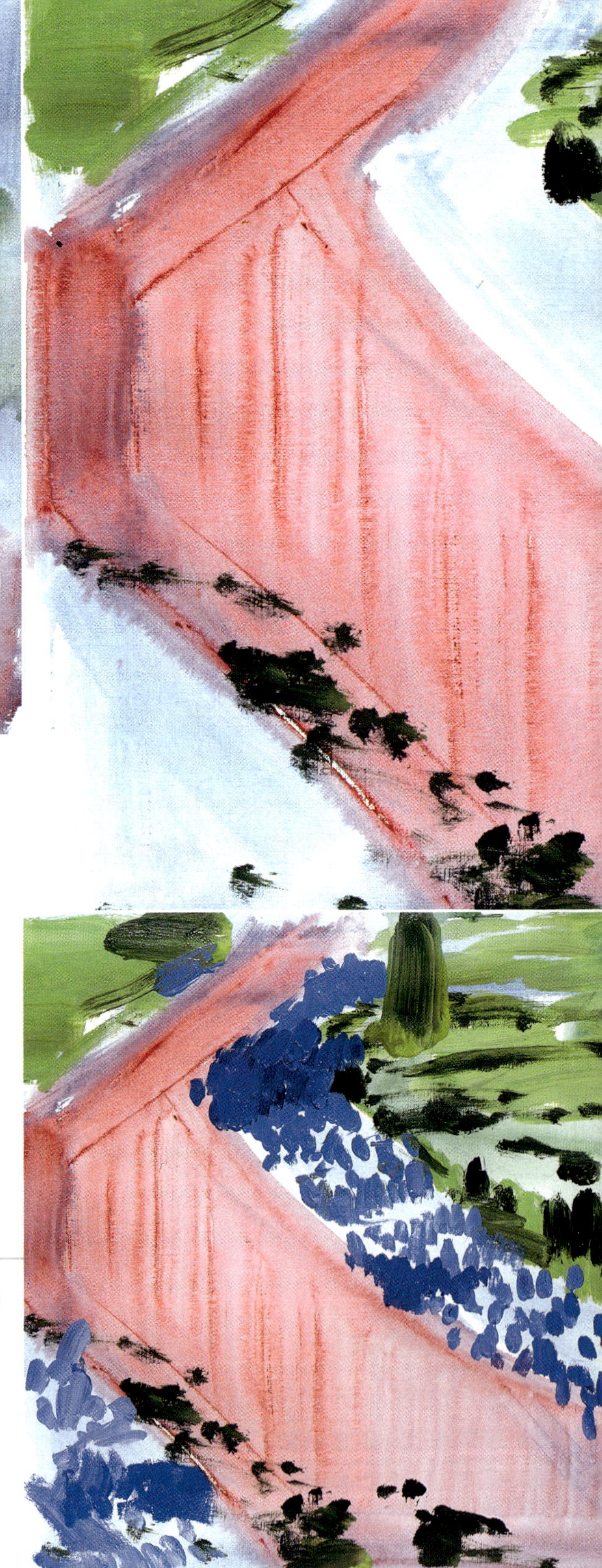

3 The first area we define is that of the blue flowers. We vary the size and number of the brushstrokes to create a feeling of deep space. The farther away the flowers, the more crowded together they are visually, until they become impossible to distinguish. We reproduce this effect with the brushstrokes.

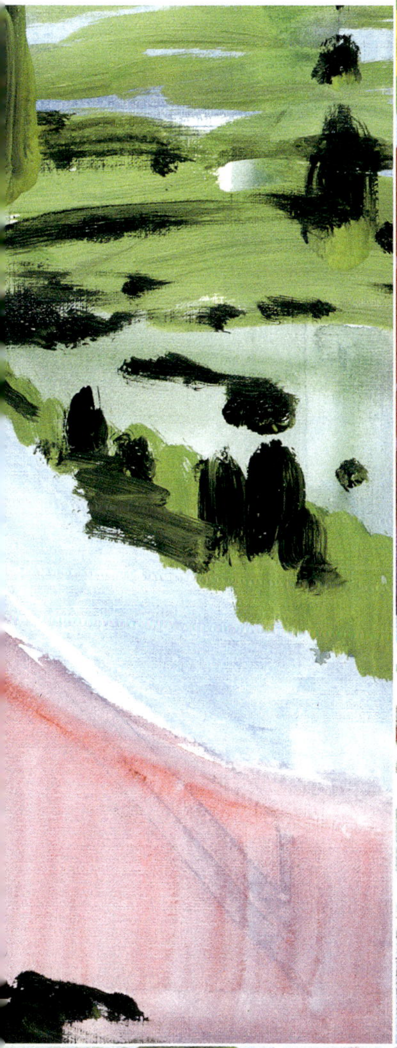

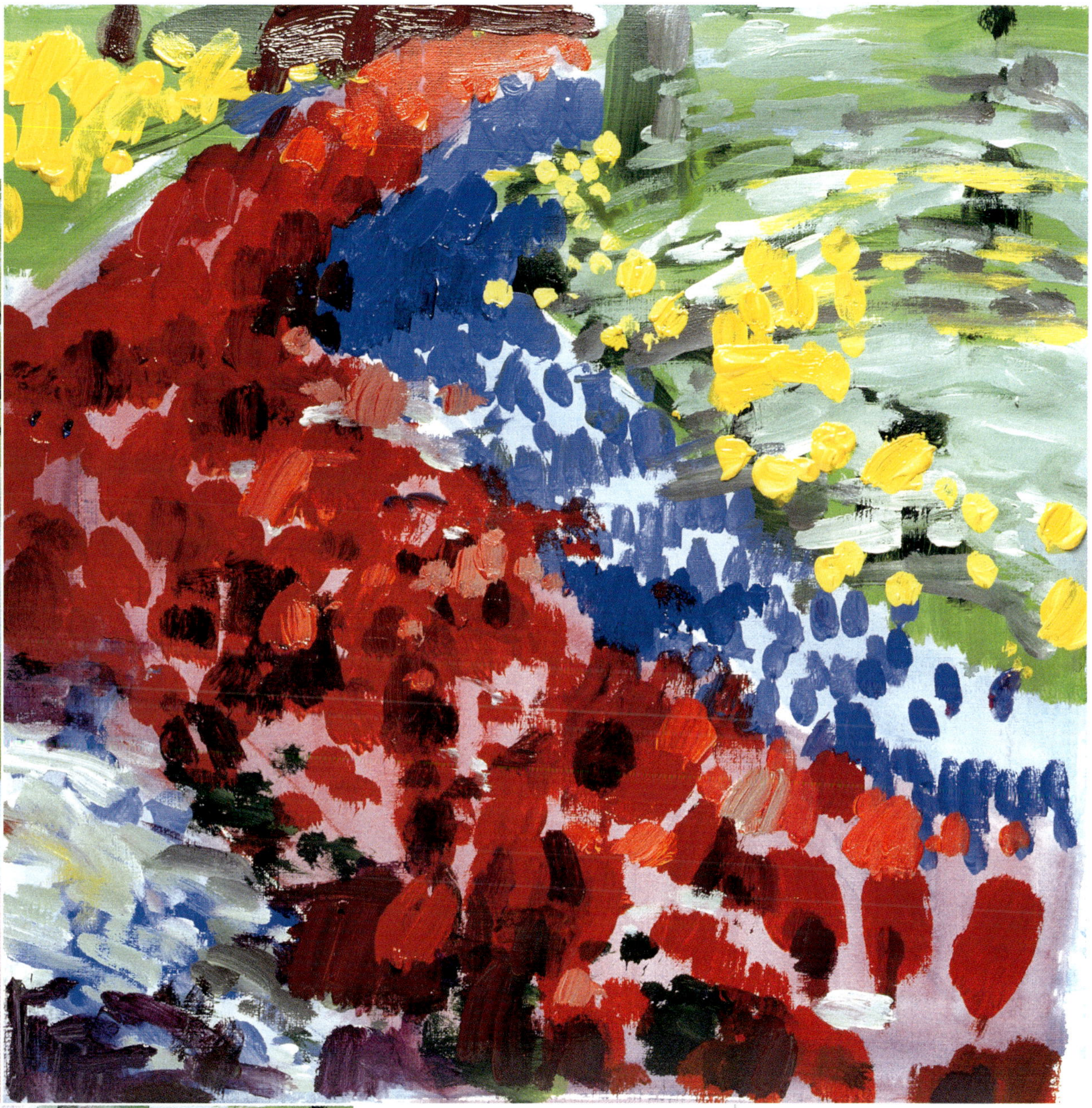

4 We apply the same principle to the red tulips. We acknowledge that there is a considerable difference in depth between the lower margins and the top of the painting, a pathway to walk.

5 Finally, we apply yellow brushstrokes to indicate the flowers that are missing from the composition and that add notes of light and vitality. Before adding these strokes of color we prepared its background by covering the ground with different areas of green light and shadow.

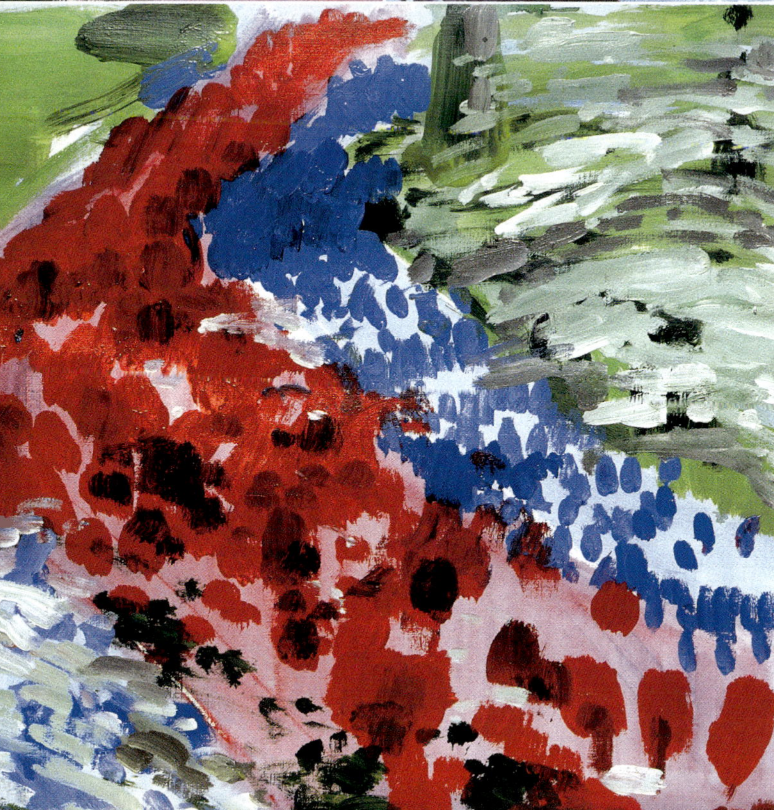

Other Versions

Here we see how the painting changes when the framing moves away from or toward a specific area of the garden, and when, in addition, we vary the format. These changes are so important that they actually cause each painting in this gallery to be completely different from one another. The artist has found a very personal view in each, just as Klimt did.

This rectangular format is not at all typical for a garden. The proportions of the sides are more appropriate for a figure study than a landscape, and furthermore, it is vertical. The focal point is very near, amplifying one of its areas: the red tulips. This allows the viewer to enter this part of the garden, bringing it much closer visually.

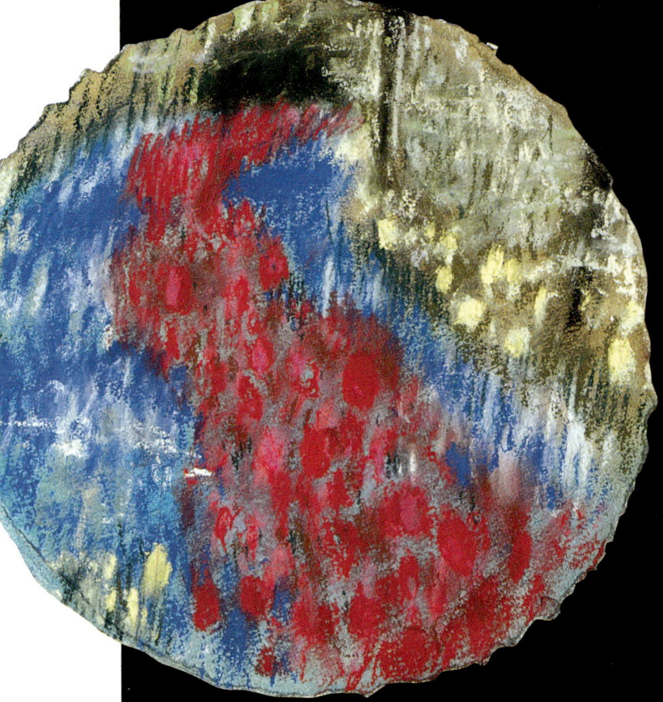

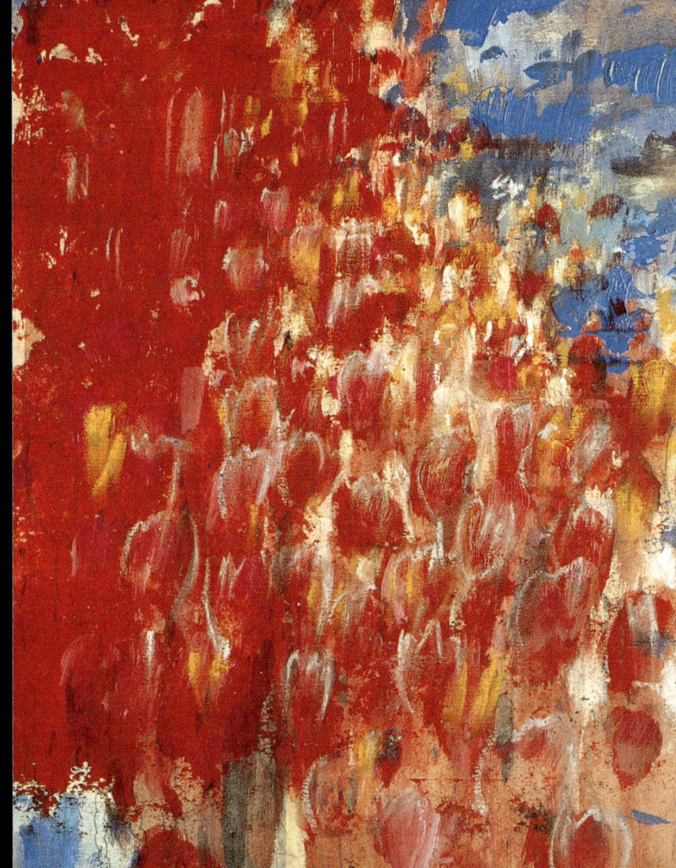

This is the circular format. It is appropriate for compositions where there is a very defined focal point, a portrait, for example, or when there is a serpentine structure like the one in this painting, because it reinforces its dynamism. The circle exercises two compositional forces, the centripetal, which focuses visual concentration toward the center, and centrifuge, which indicates that the image continues outside the edges of the painting and provokes visual expansion.

The diamond is not a typical
format. It is a geometric shape
that destabilizes the gaze and
causes restlessness. The
division of the space into
two large areas and
the zigzag edges
add dynamism
and visual tension
between the two
areas: the red and the
blue.

This is the same square format seen in
the step-by-step process, but framed to
encompass a larger visual field, causing
a different feeling. Here are two
differences: there is a horizon at the top
of the painting, and the treatment of the
paint is more tactile because it was
applied with a spatula. Each spatula
mark evokes a tulip, suggesting its
corporeality and position in the space.

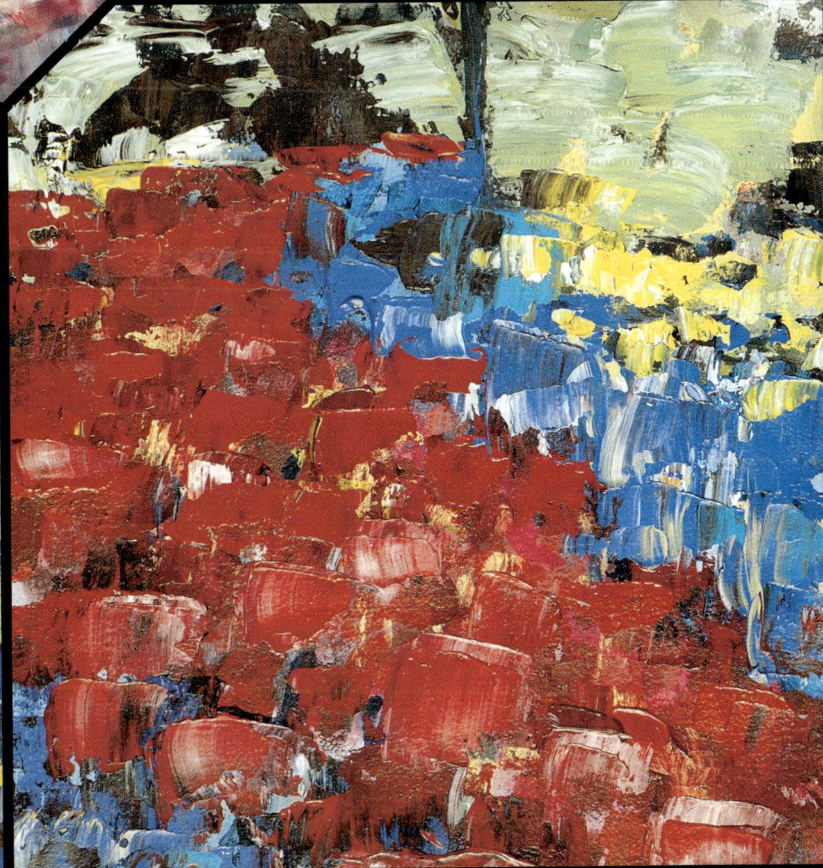

In this work the eye is drawn to the upper right part of the
visual field, the area of the trees. The flowers become the
foreground of the scene. The verticality of the format is
exaggerated by narrowing the width. This causes the tree
trunks to become stylized, and they direct the eye upward.

Other Models

The animal world contains another kind of grouping: herds, flocks, colonies, schools, etc. This time the artist has chosen a group of penguins as an amusing subject for a work that will have a painterly quality, despite the illustrative connotations of this animal, using impasto and a loose and spontaneous finish.

Other Media

The artist wished to continue experimenting with other formats and framing, but this time with other media to see how this material would work. These are two wax crayon–on–paper drawings, both in landscape format. In one of them he created a focal point with a large variety of flowers, which he made indistinct so that the fields would be perceived as areas of color. In the other he exaggerated the horizontality, varying the definition of the flowers in a rich mix of density and empty spaces.

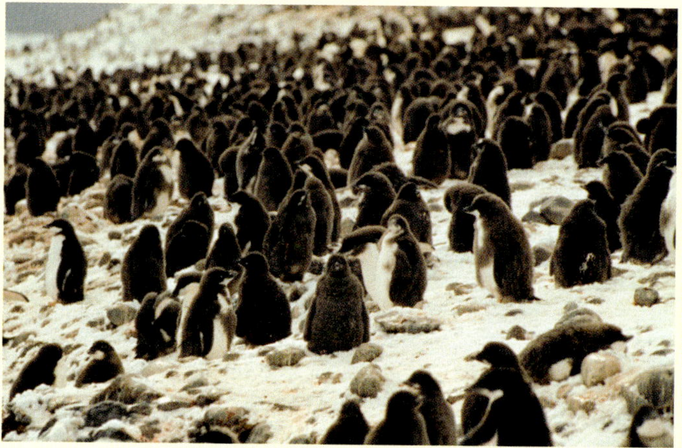

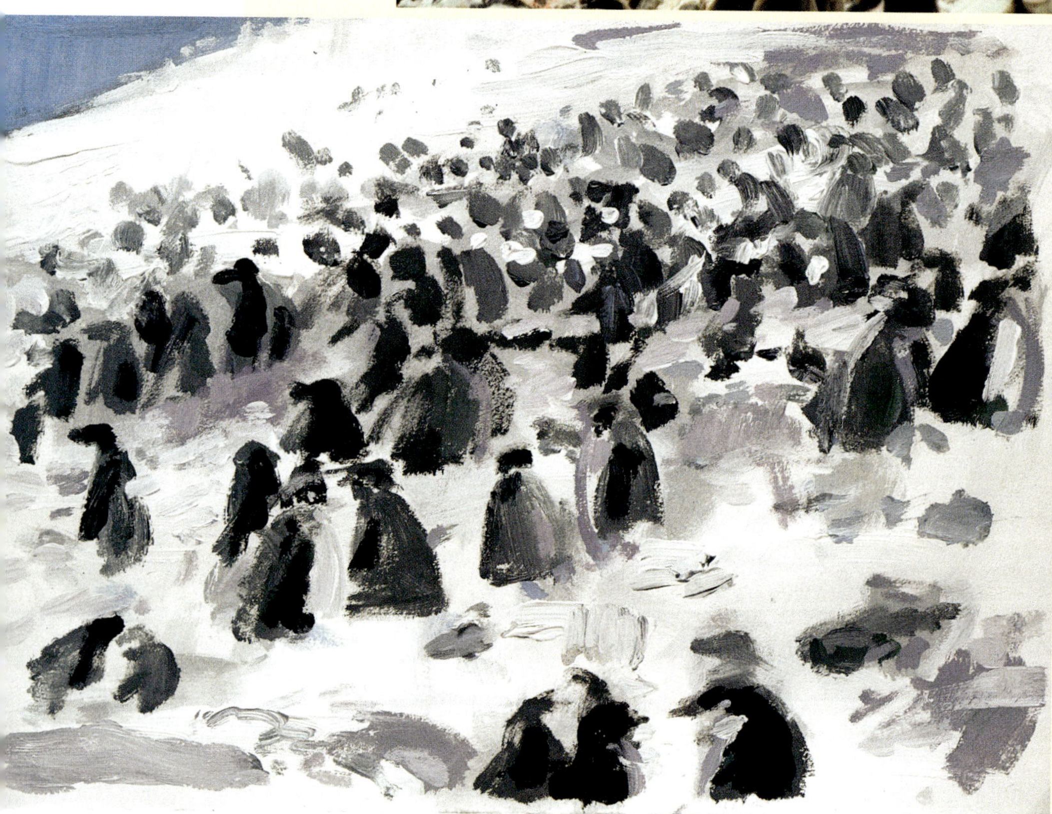

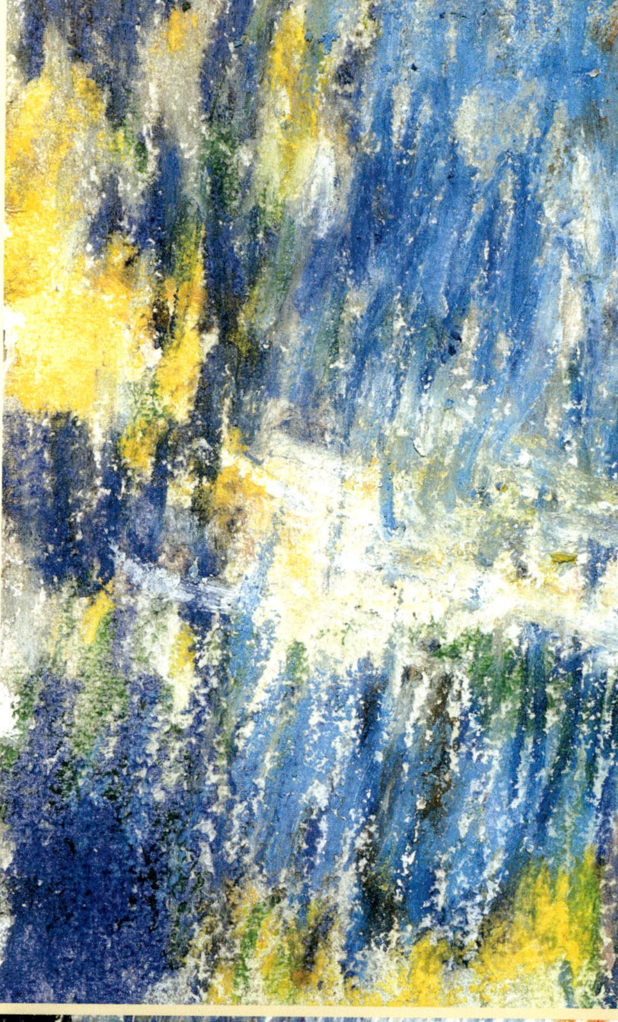

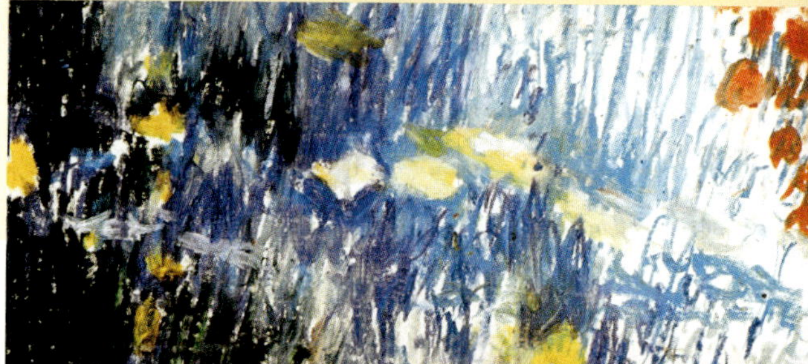

Other Views

The Catalan artist Frederic Amat (born in 1952) has always shown a great interest in the organic. In his paintings is often the presence of the animal or plant world connected with the mythical or symbolic. His painting has a very Mediterranean style that can be appreciated in the use of material (paper pulp, wax crayon . . .) and the color. In the painting *Aquari a Bibí*, Amat depicts the school of fish as a single living organism. He organized the space in a serial arrangement without perspective. The shapes are uniformly and densely spread across the picture, giving form to the subject to exaggerate the idea of collectivity, of a social body.

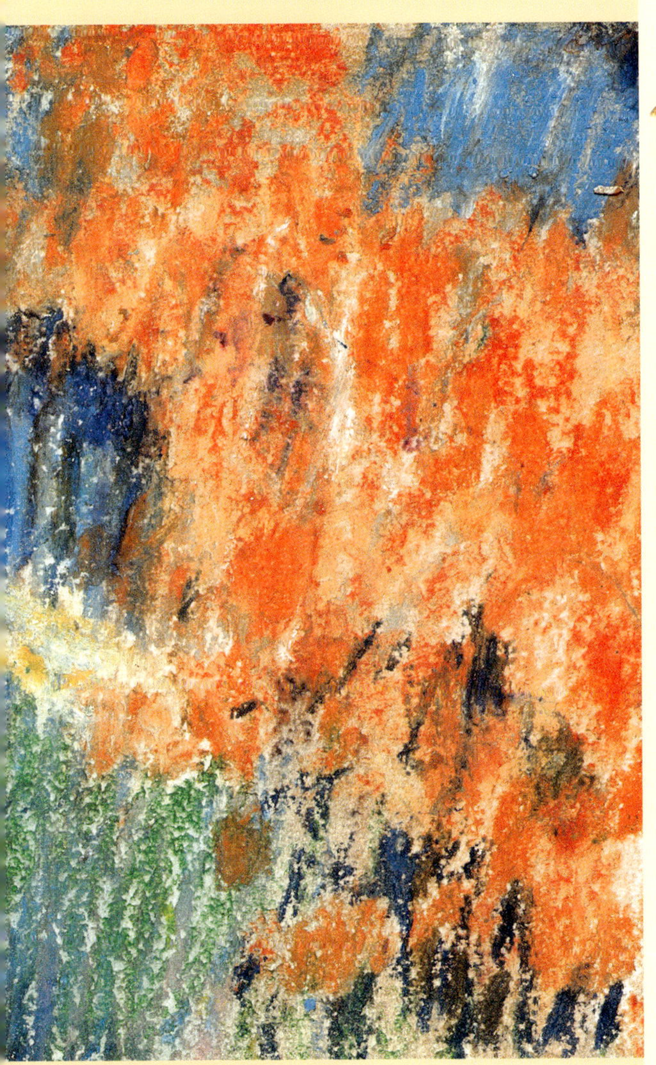

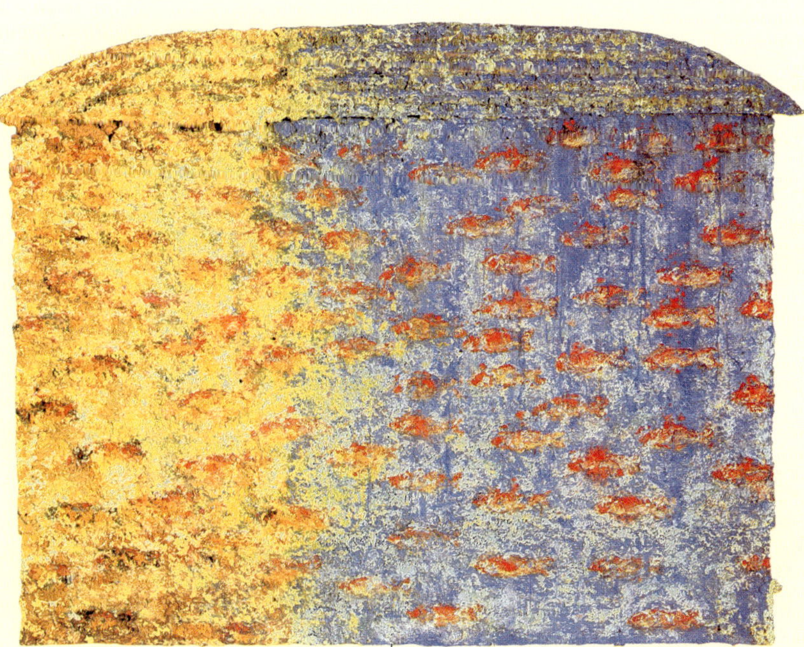

Frederic Amat, *Aquari a Bibí,* 1982. Private Collection.

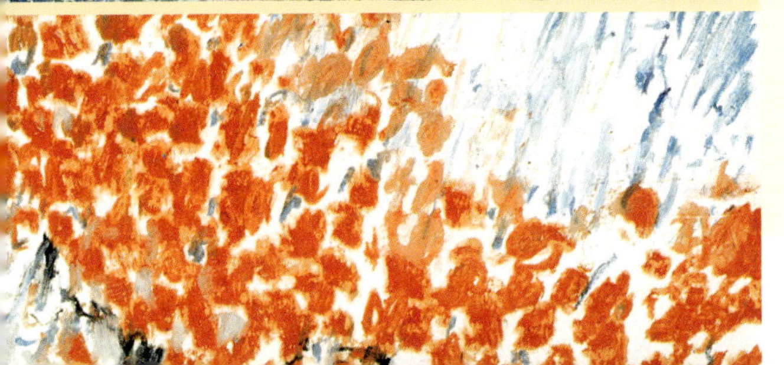

From its beginning, the still-life genre has allowed artists the necessary freedom to create their desired compositions while basing them on their feelings. In this chapter we propose three still lifes. The first is a simple still life, a plate with lemons, composed in an orderly way by following the classic laws of composition. The second is a crowded still life, where chaos reigns and empty space is denied. The third is a dreamlike still life, where an unreal space is created and the objects, through tricks of proportion, generate strange and fantastic spaces.

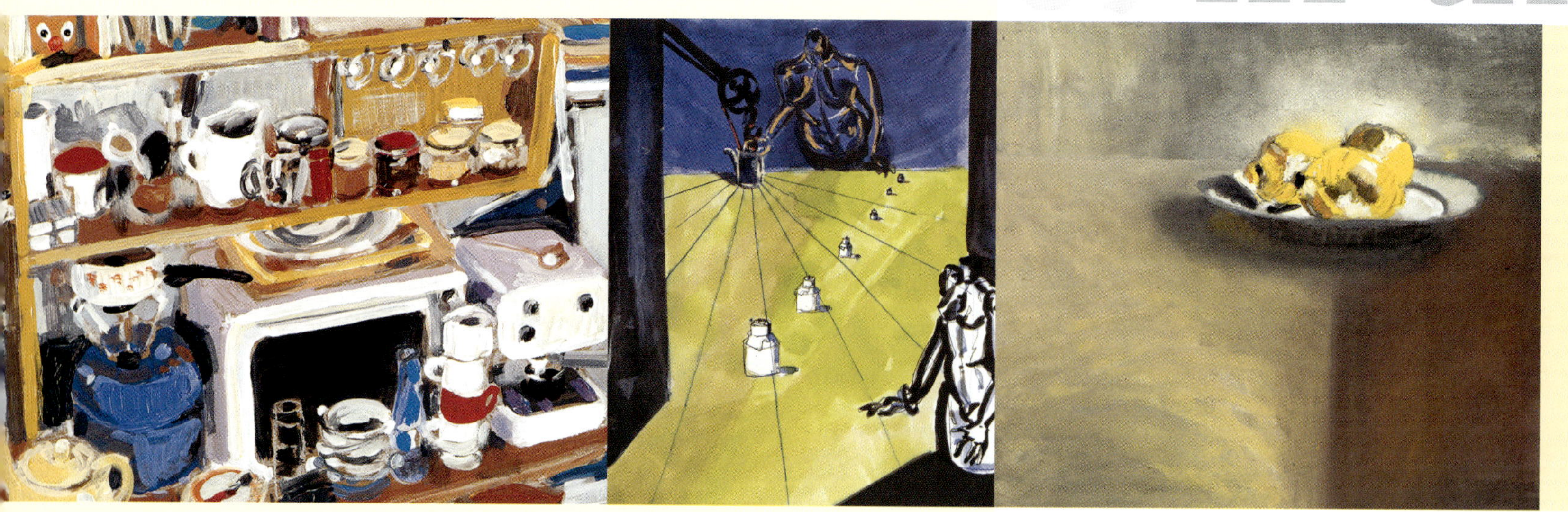

Still Life

Space in Creative Painting **41** *Space in the Still Life*

"The order in which I arrange my entire painting is expressive. The place occupied by the figures and the objects, the empty space around them, the proportions, all fulfill a mission."
Henri Matisse

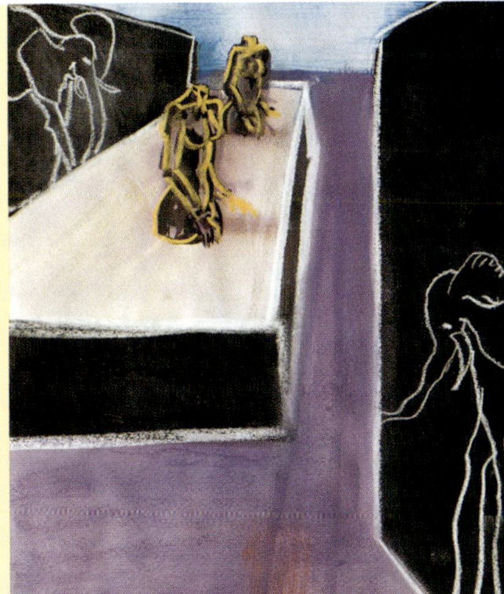

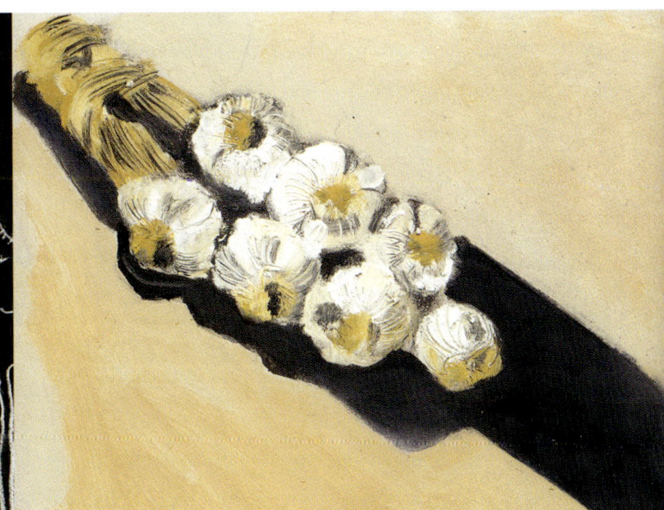

Composed and Organized Spaces

The still lifes by Juan Sánchez Cotán (1560–1627) were created in the last third of the sixteenth century, at a moment when Spanish still lifes shared a love of humble objects and sobriety in the composition, distancing themselves from the Flemish and Italian models that were more rhetorical and elaborate. Sánchez Cotán was surprising in the way he mixed the natural with the supernatural on the canvas. He presented objects straight from the pantry placed or hung in a sort of stage and surrounded by a timeless atmosphere. The backgrounds, black and tenebrous, condense the spatial depth, and the insignificant details of each fruit and vegetable are highlighted with an artificial illumination that acts as a magnifying glass and strengthens the individuality.

His compositions are careful and minutely analyzed, and most likely follow some mathematical ratio. This makes us appreciate Sánchez Cotán's scientific interest in reevaluating the genre.

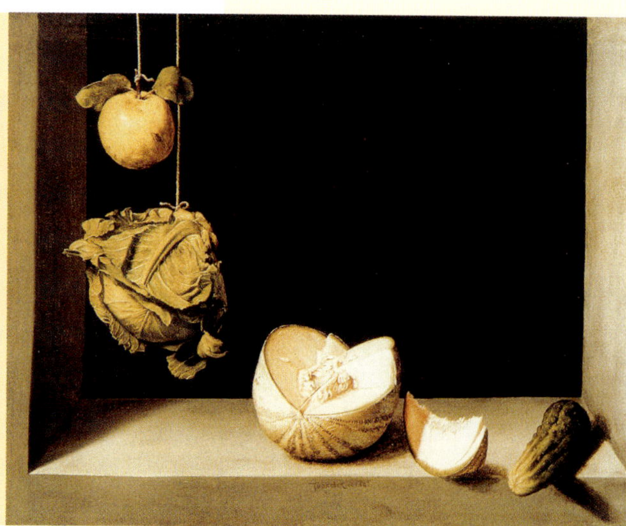

Juan Sánchez Cotán,
Still Life with Quince, Cabbage, Melon, and Cucumber, 1602.
Museum of Art,
San Diego, California.

The Composition: Applying the Golden Mean to a Simple Plate with Lemons

For the first approach in this chapter, the artist Gemma Guasch has chosen the simplicity of a plate with lemons and has applied a scientific method of composition: the Golden Mean, also known as Divine Proportion. A proportion is golden when the relation between its parts is 1:1.618. In addition, in a golden proportion the relation of the longest segment in respect to the shortest is equal to the sum of the two in respect to the longer one. To obtain the Golden Mean from any measure it must be multiplied by 0.618, and to obtain the larger proportional part it is multiplied by 1.618. The artist has chosen to work with oil on cardboard, a classic medium ideal for working with a traditional compositional application, stable and harmonious.

"Composition is the art of arranging the different elements that the painter has to express his feelings. In a painting all the parts should be visible, fulfilling the role that was given to them, whether principal or secondary."
Henri Matisse

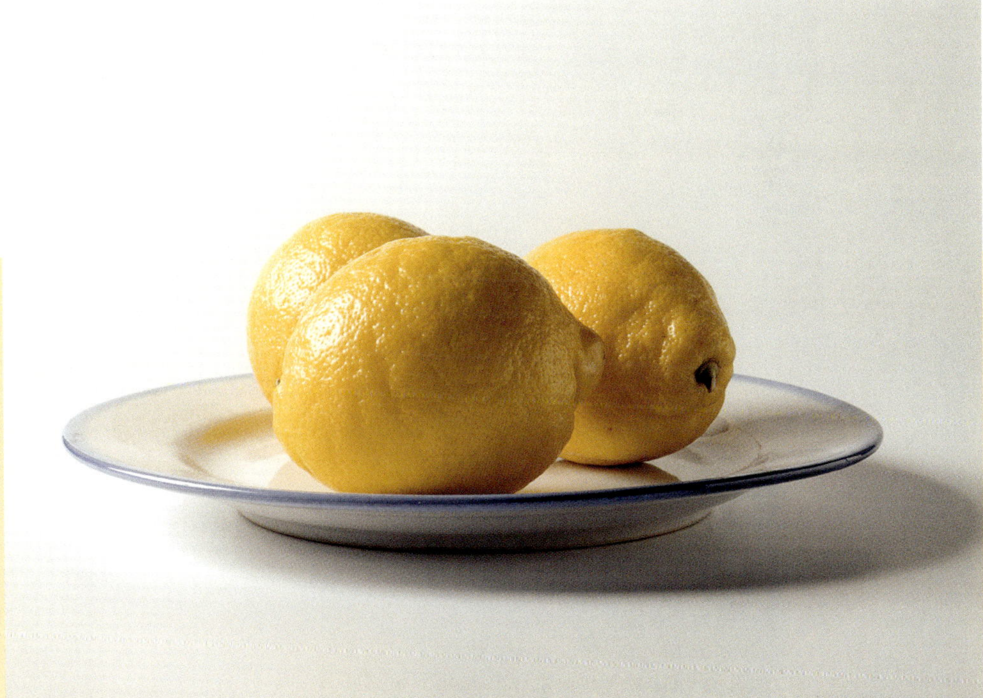

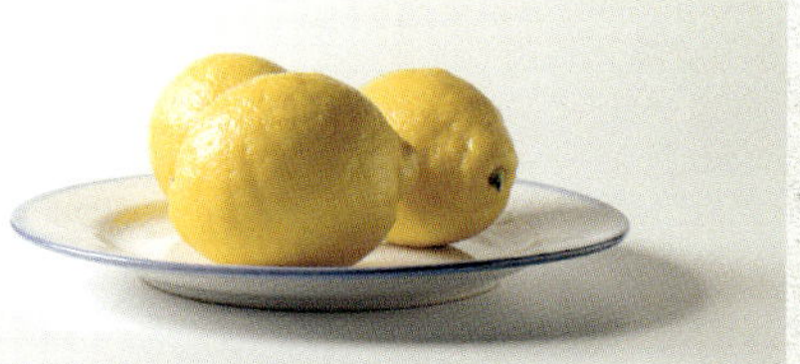

1 We find the Golden Mean point in the composition, and we place it above and to the right of the image. Using a soft graphite HB pencil we center the plate with three lemons at this point. This will give the composition proportion, stability, and solidity. Then we divide the space in two horizontally; the elements are put in the foreground and the space above is left empty, as was done with the still lifes in the seventeenth century.

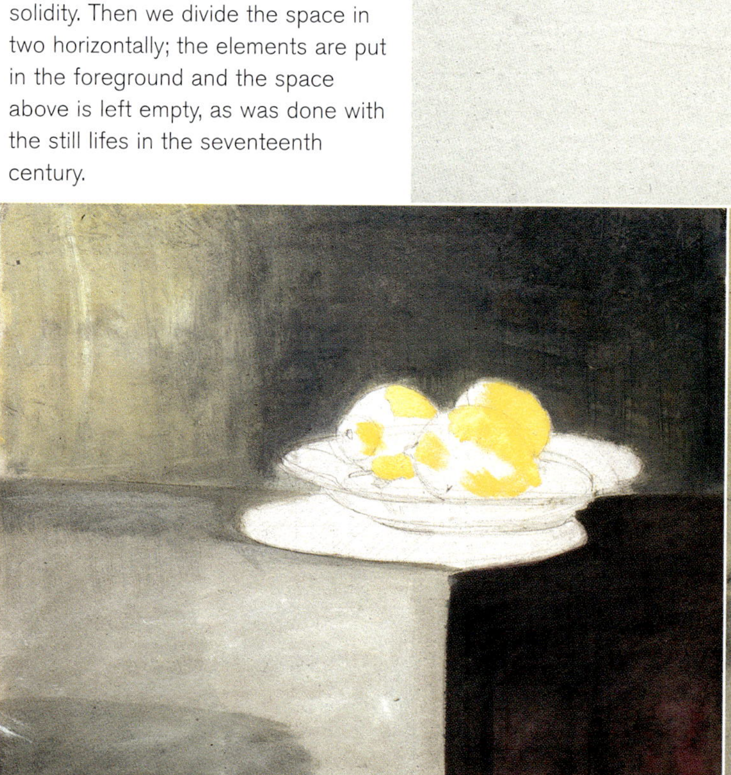

2 To reinforce the feeling of space we first work the background with a brush dampened with turpentine, applying small amounts of oil that are distributed in three tones. A gradated yellow-gray is painted in the back, carmine on the right, and pearl gray on the left. Then we apply a thick lemon yellow to the three lemons, indicating the light.

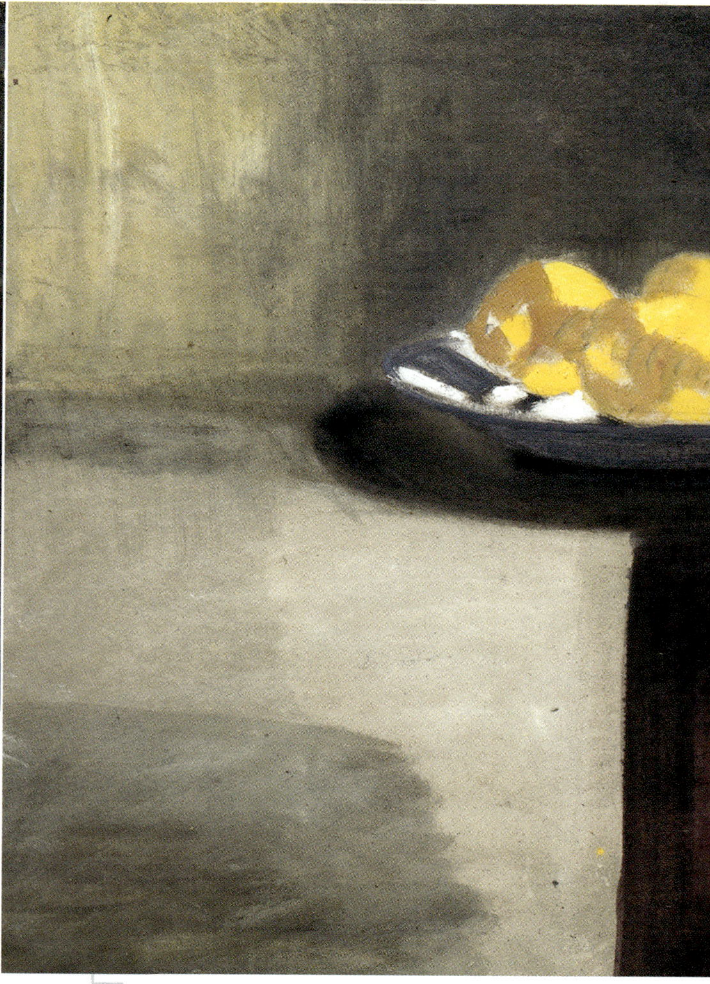

3 Now we will focus on the subject. First we paint the projected shadow with a dark tone; its placement is important for situating any object in a real and believable space. Next, we paint the plate in a contrasting manner, using black and white to accentuate the drama of the setting. Finally, we give the lemons volume, painting an earth tone on the less well-lighted parts of each of them.

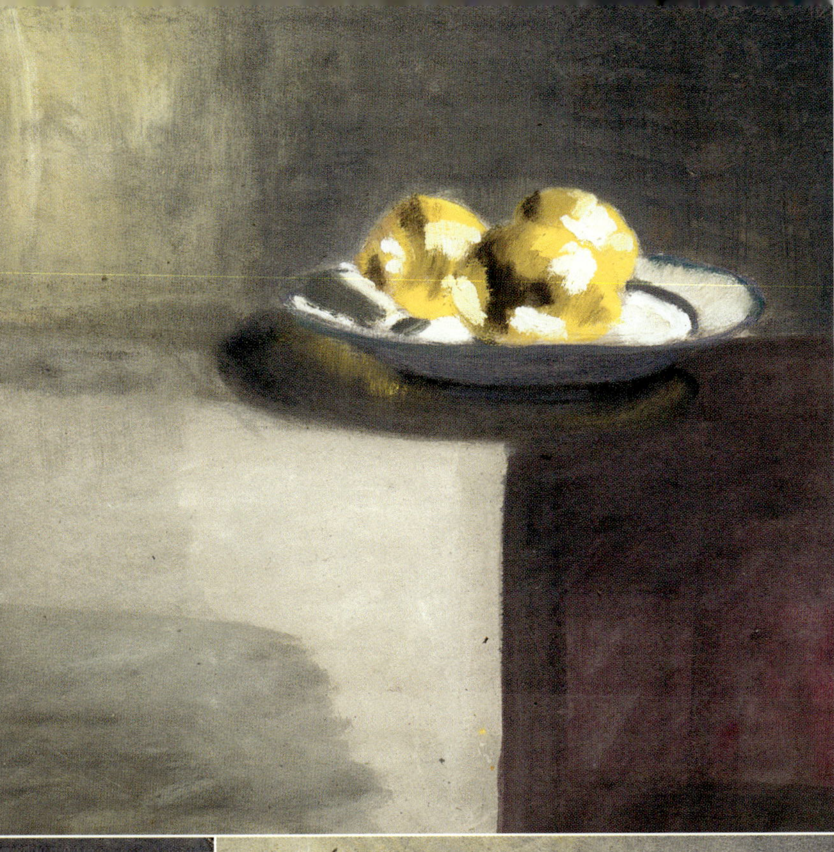

4 We give the lemons greater volume and contrast. To do this, we apply thick tones, white for the highlights and black for the darks, thus reinforcing the contrast of light and individualizing each lemon. We work on the plate the same way, giving it more light. Finally, we smooth the projected shadow, blending it where it comes into contact with the plate with light dabs of yellow-gray that spatially separate it from the plate and reinforce its planar sense.

5 Finally, we return to work on the background to create a more suggestive and encompassing atmosphere. To do this we blend the tones, especially on the back part of the lemons where we apply a tinted white to reinforce the depth and luminosity of the space to make it more atmospheric. Then we lighten the edges of the projected shadow by blending it with the background. And lastly, we make the lemons stand out through an application of oil impastos in the same tones we used before. The result has the beauty of a classic composition and the mysticism of the Spanish still lifes.

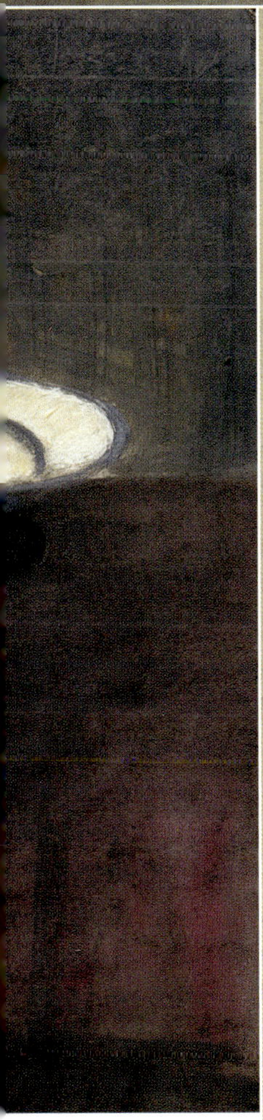

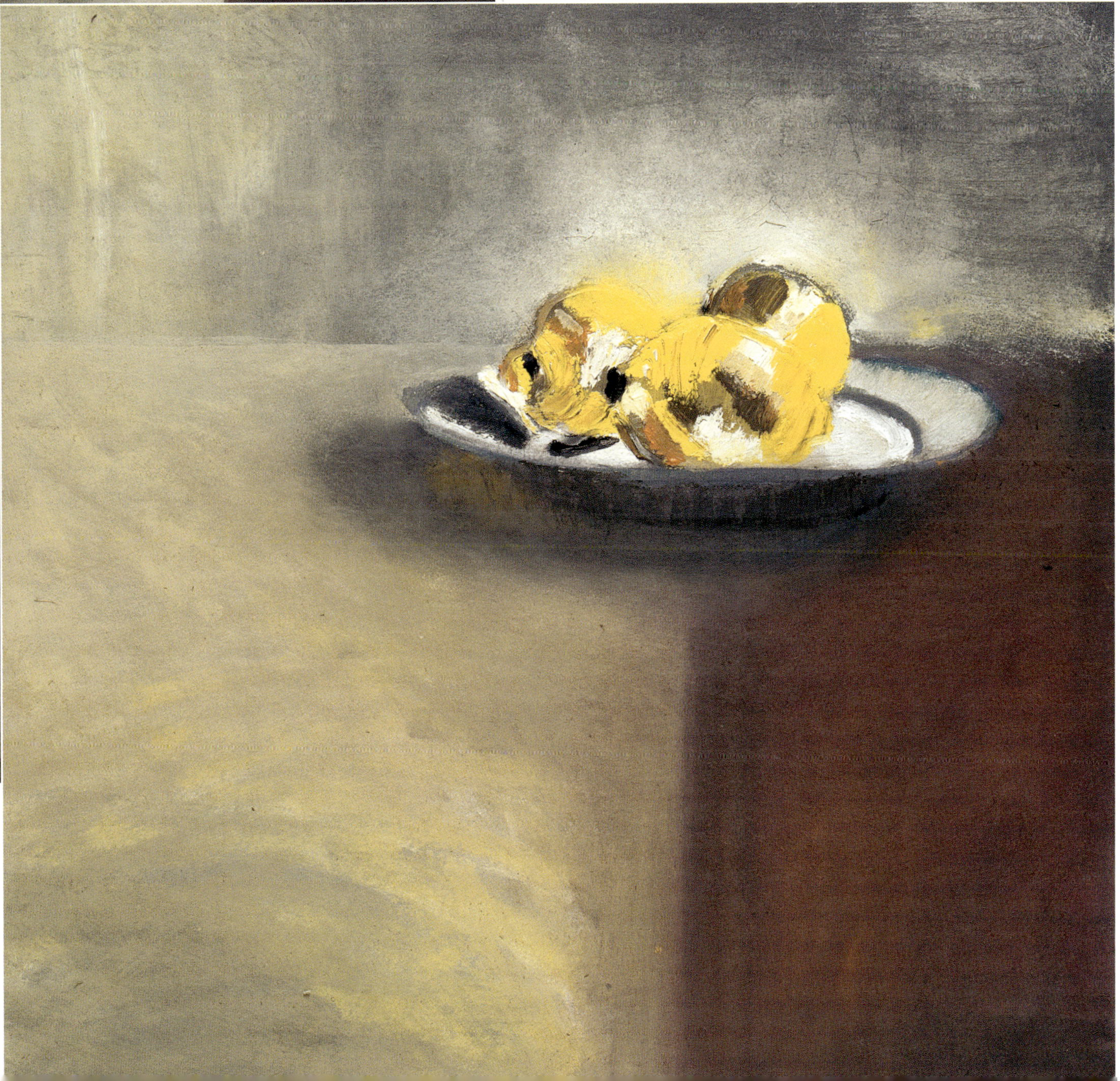

Other Versions

Different compositional spaces result from changing the distribution of the objects in the painting: dynamic or static, close up or far away, symmetrical or asymmetrical. This gallery attempts to apply in each version a different compositional scheme that helps us appreciate the message hidden in each setting.

The plate of lemons is modestly placed in the lower left corner, very much in the foreground. The rest of the space is treated as a single surface, suggesting a pleasant horizontal plane. At the slightly curved edge along the top we can see the end of the horizontal space where the objects are located. The use of creamy tones instead of dark ones strengthens the naturalness and the realism of the grouping, removing the drama and making it intimate and ordinary.

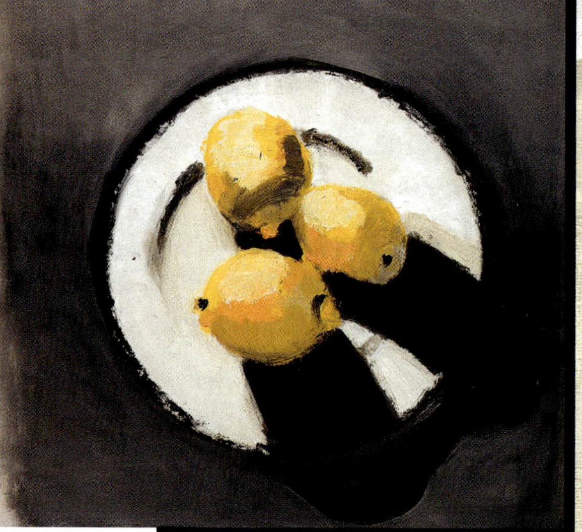

A centered composition with a very high point of view situates the plate with lemons in the center of the image. In this compositional scheme the strength lies in the elevated viewpoint that highlights the plate, a perfect circle, and the lemons. The enormous size of the objects brings them closer to the viewer. The length of the projected shadows of the lemons indicates that the grouping is illuminated from one side. The result is stable and striking.

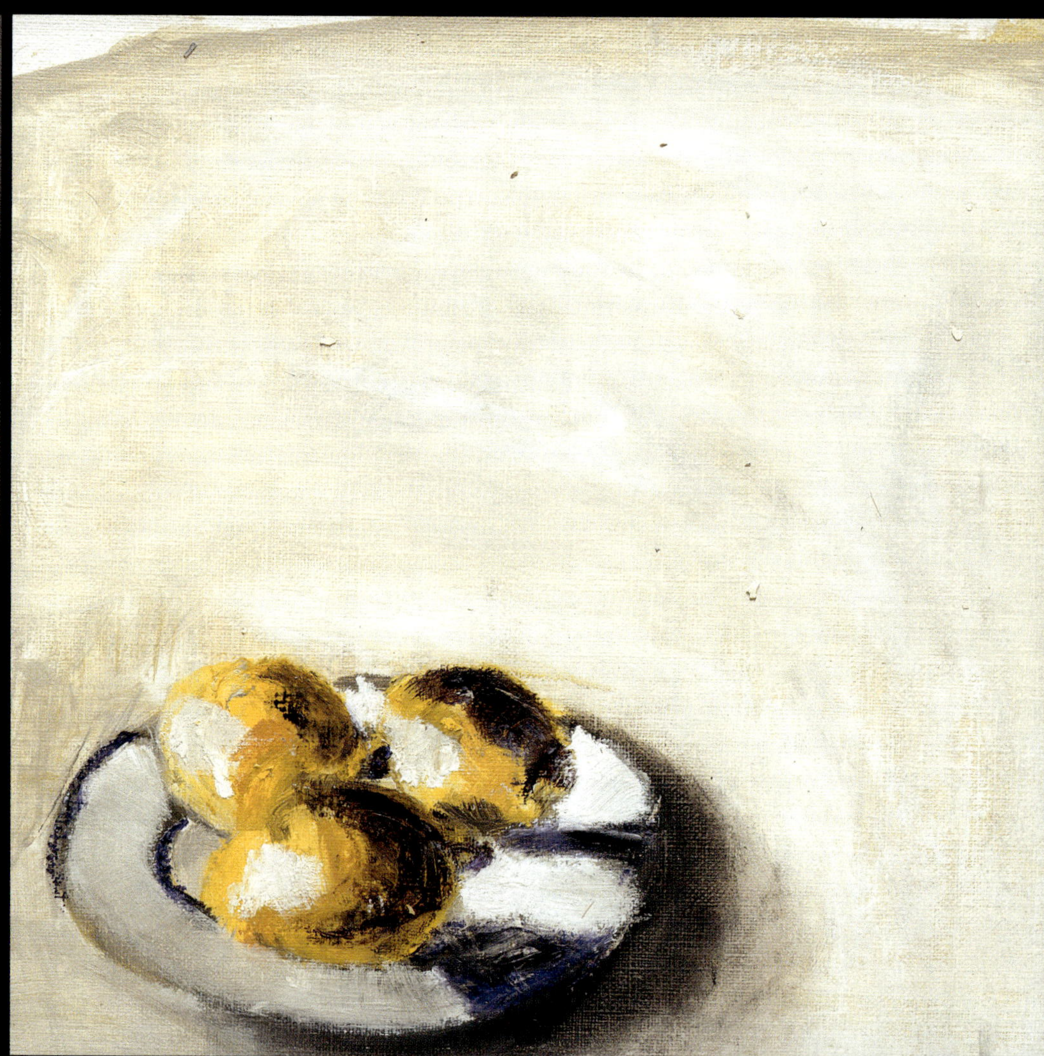

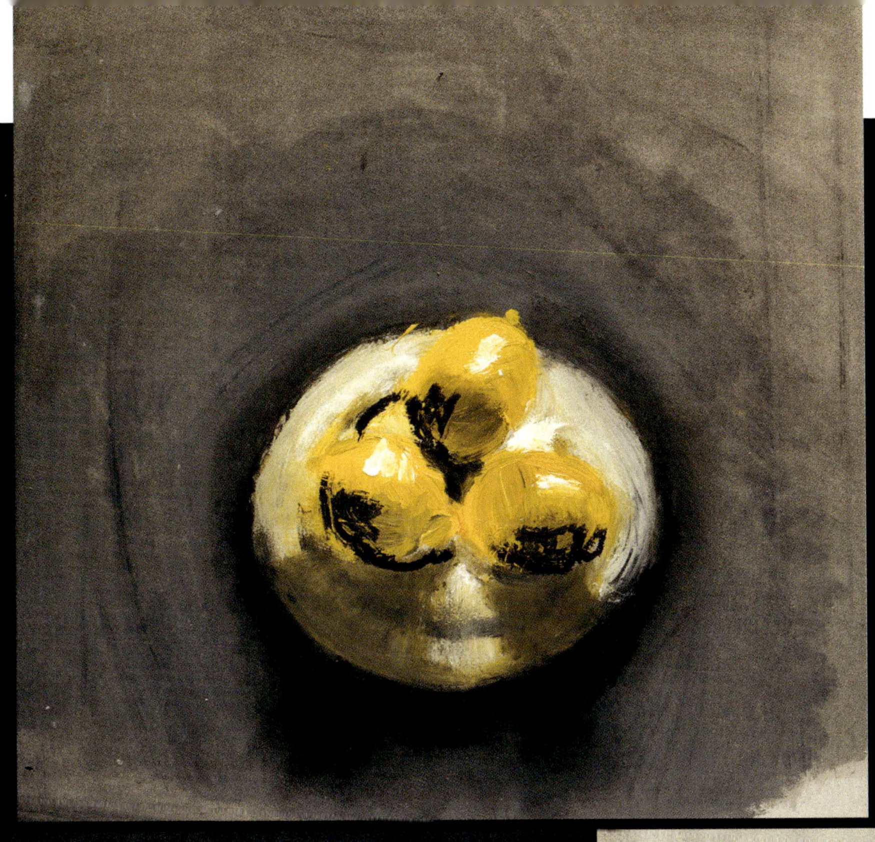

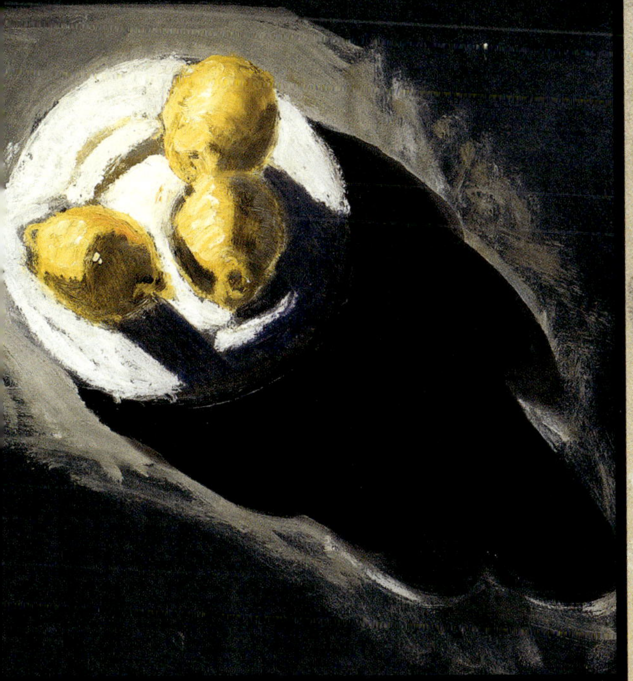

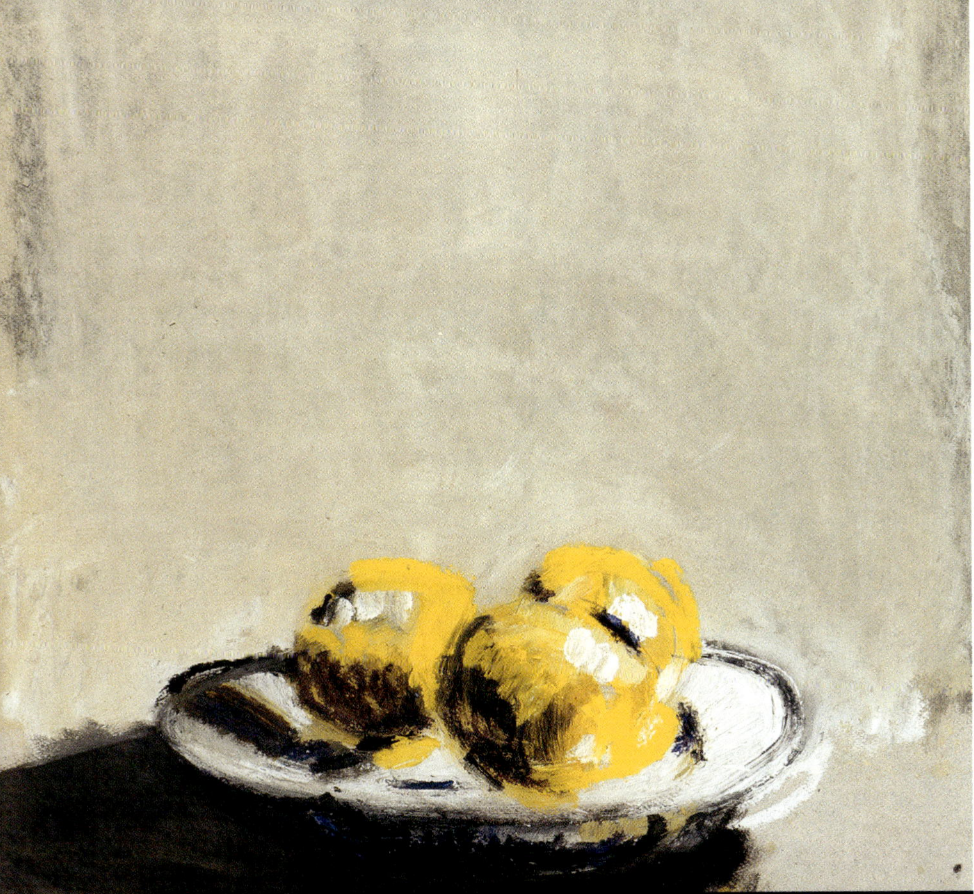

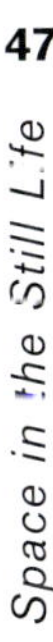

Here we have created a space in the lower center with a distant point of view that makes the plate of lemons look small. The entire scene is in a limited space with no linear perspective. The treatment of the blended background evokes a nostalgic atmosphere. The centered illumination of the elements is high and directs the gaze to the lemons. This composition has a strong compositional balance between the full (the plate of lemons) and the empty (the horizontal surface).

An enormous diagonal crosses the compositional space, giving it a dynamic and unstable scheme. The plate with the lemons is in the upper left corner and has a very high, angled point of view. The diagonal ends with a large black smudge that indicates a low source of illumination because of the long projected shadow. The edges of the shadow and the plate were loosely painted with a greenish gray tone, and the rest of the plane is in a space that has no depth.

A near but slightly low point of view of the model situates the plate with the lemons in a different position that allows us to see the depth of the background and gives the painting a large and beautiful vertical space. The lighting of the scene from the right puts the projected shadow in the lower left corner. The empty space in the background, painted a cream tone, gives us a sense of great space and light and adds a joyful feeling.

New Approaches

Other Models

Any object from the pantry is appropriate for painting a still life: nuts, vegetables, game, bread, and fish have been used by countless painters to represent and communicate that which causes them to paint. In this chapter the artist has changed the models and chosen another typical element from the Spanish pantry, a string of garlic. A diagonal composition was selected, and the garlic was placed at the top left of the image and the space left empty in the opposite corner. A long dark projected shadow indicates a low light source.

Other Media

Oil is an ideal medium for blending and painting impastos. The slow drying process allows slow and reflective work, as well as retouching. The artist chose markers and water-soluble color pencils as secondary media. These are used quickly and directly, given their fast drying time, and they have a fresh and lightly worked finish, more like a sketch, but they keep the sense of an impulsive work that is not retouched.

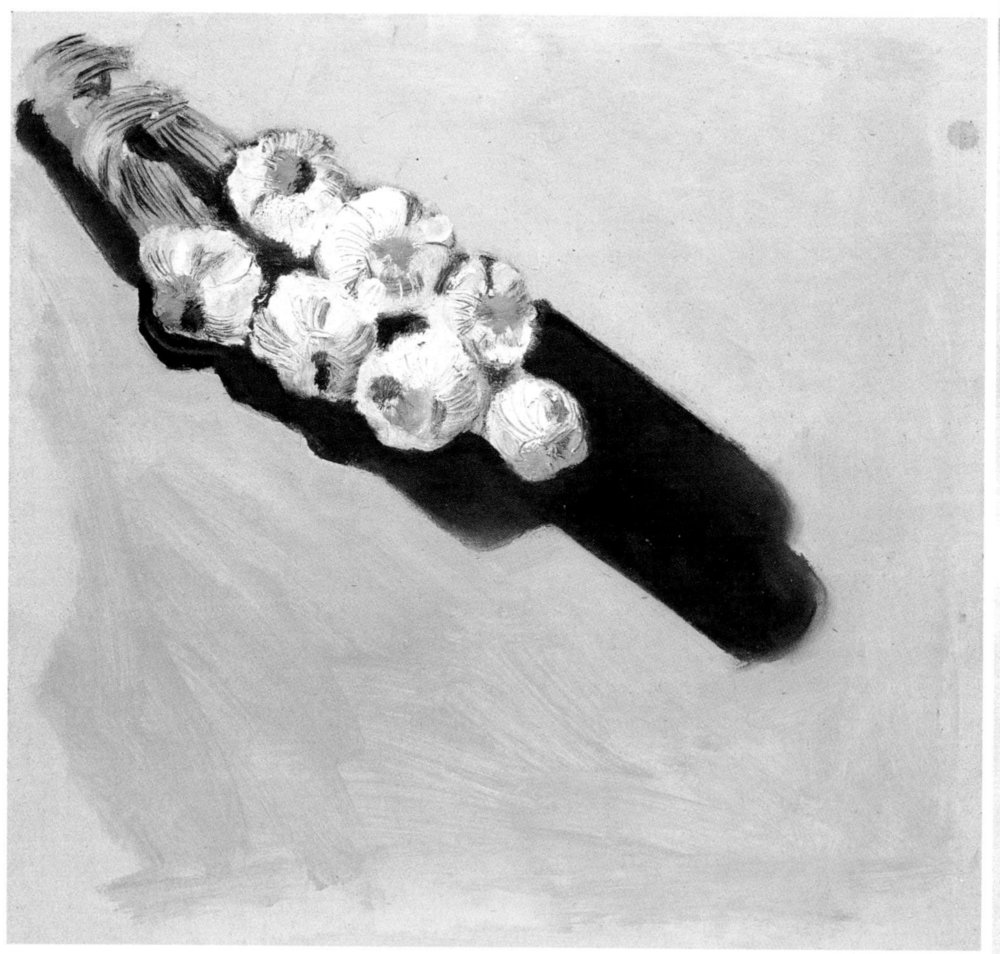

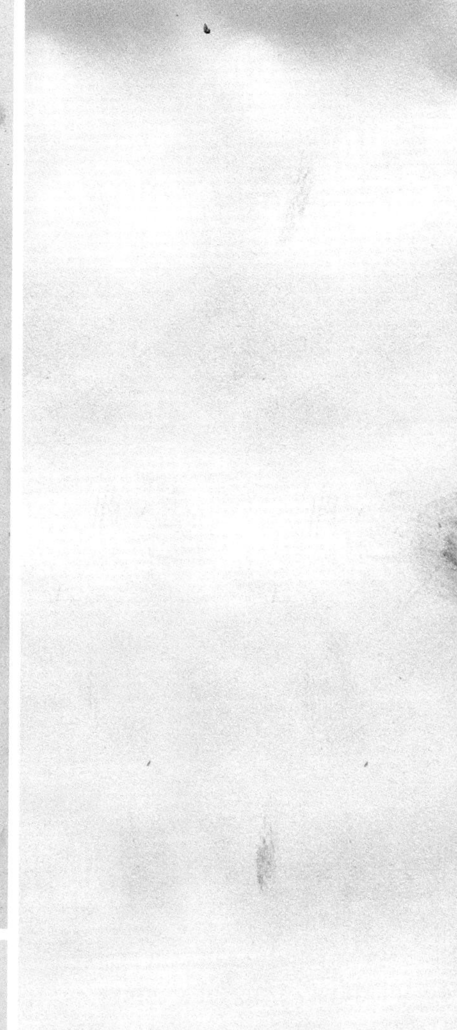

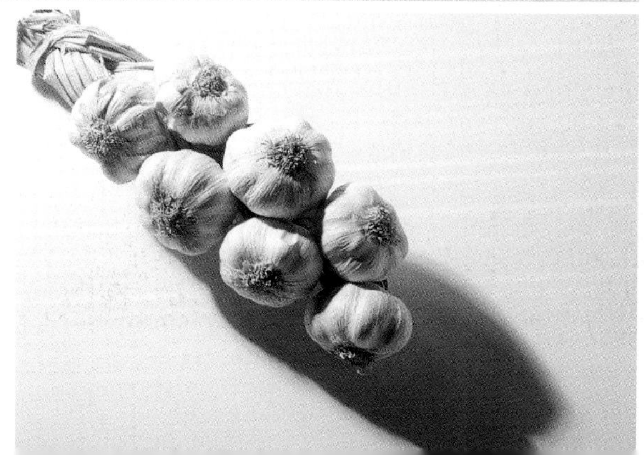

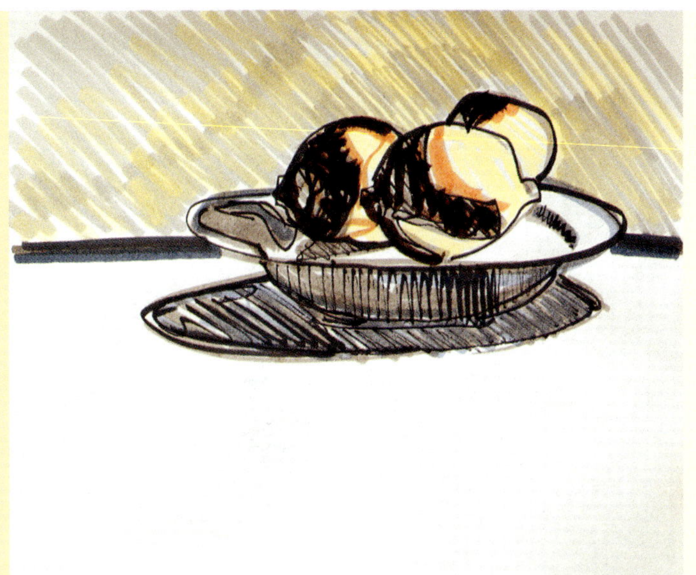

Other Views

In 1919, when Pablo Ruiz Picasso (1881–1973) painted *Still Life with Pitcher and Apples*, he was at the end of his cubist stage and wished to return to figurative work. His figurative painting is known for the monumentality of its forms, a certain neoclassical flavor, and a search for new compositional structures. The still lifes of this period show the duality between cubism and classicism. The voluptuousness of the pitcher reminds us of the female nudes that he later painted between 1920 and 1921. Thanks to a subtle and elegant treatment of light and shadow, Picasso converts everyday objects into a scene of great beauty and sensuality.

49

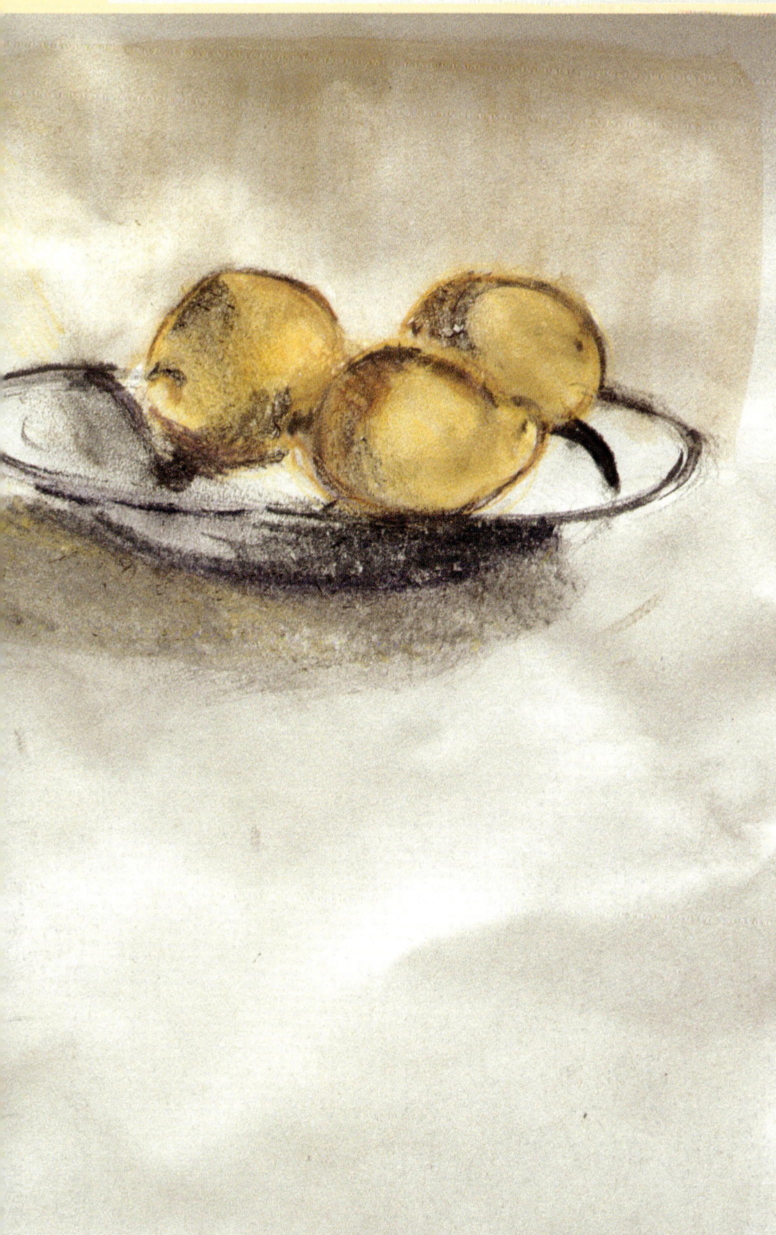

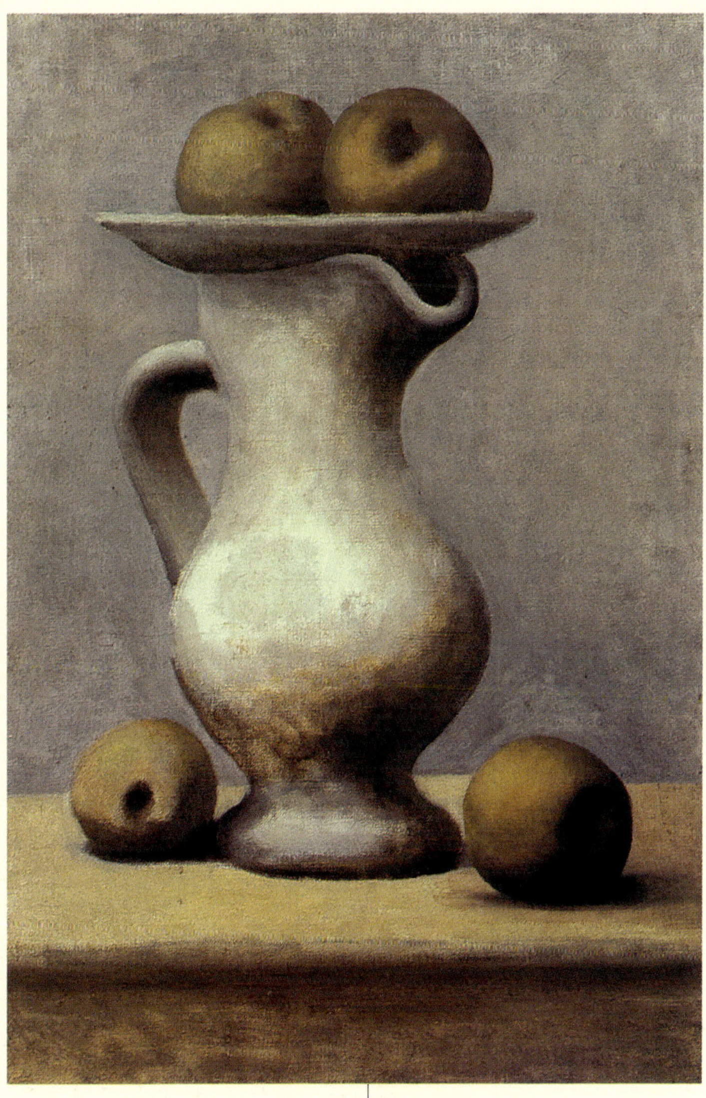

Pablo Picasso,
Still Life with Pitcher and Apples, 1919.
Musée Picasso, Paris, France.

Full, Saturated, and Crowded Spaces

Creative Approach 4

The phenomenon of superabundance originated in the baroque period (seventeenth and eighteenth centuries). Although this option seemed to obey the principle of *horror vacuii* (fear of emptiness) in the beginning, we now observe another equally important motivation, the *amor profusi* (love of fullness). Many baroque still lifes were a tribute to the lavishness of a flourishing middle class and a decadent nobility. The still lifes of the Majorcan painter Miquel Barceló fall under the second group. A taste for the material and an invitation to the sensitive in his paintings can be seen here in this series of still lifes in which animals, fruits, and vegetables flood the painting in a veritable celebration of superabundance. Still lifes such as *Soup with Red Plate*, an immense painting 93 x 112 inches (235 x 285 cm), function as icons of the decadence of developed countries swimming in abundance while the Third World dies of starvation. Other themes by this artist are paintings that are absolutely full of books, or floors covered with containers and holes, a handsome paradox: full spaces, but full of emptiness.

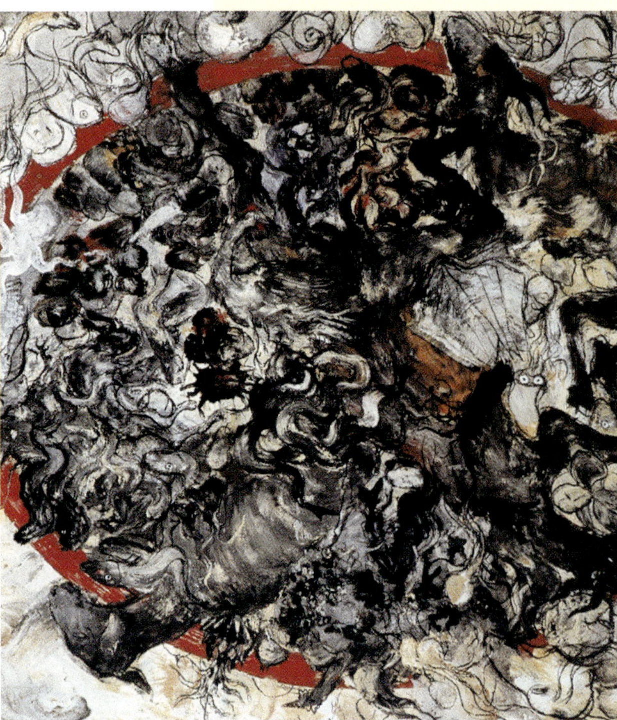

Miquel Barceló,
Soup with Red Plate,
Private Collection.

Baroque Style: A Shelf Filled with Objects as a Metaphor for Abundance

In this chapter we propose a creative project based on the superabundance of objects. For this Josep Asunción chose an everyday subject that barely requires setting up: a shelf full of objects. The chosen medium will be acrylics on a wood panel. The objective is to fill the surface of the painting to the last corner, thus perceiving a space that is totally occupied, in which the eye can follow multiple paths, pausing on each object, identifying it, and relating it with the rest.

"A total and complete impression filled my soul, which, being composed of a thousand details in harmony, I could savor and enjoy, but not understand and explain. They say the pleasures of heaven are like that."
Goethe,
On German Architecture,
1770–1773.

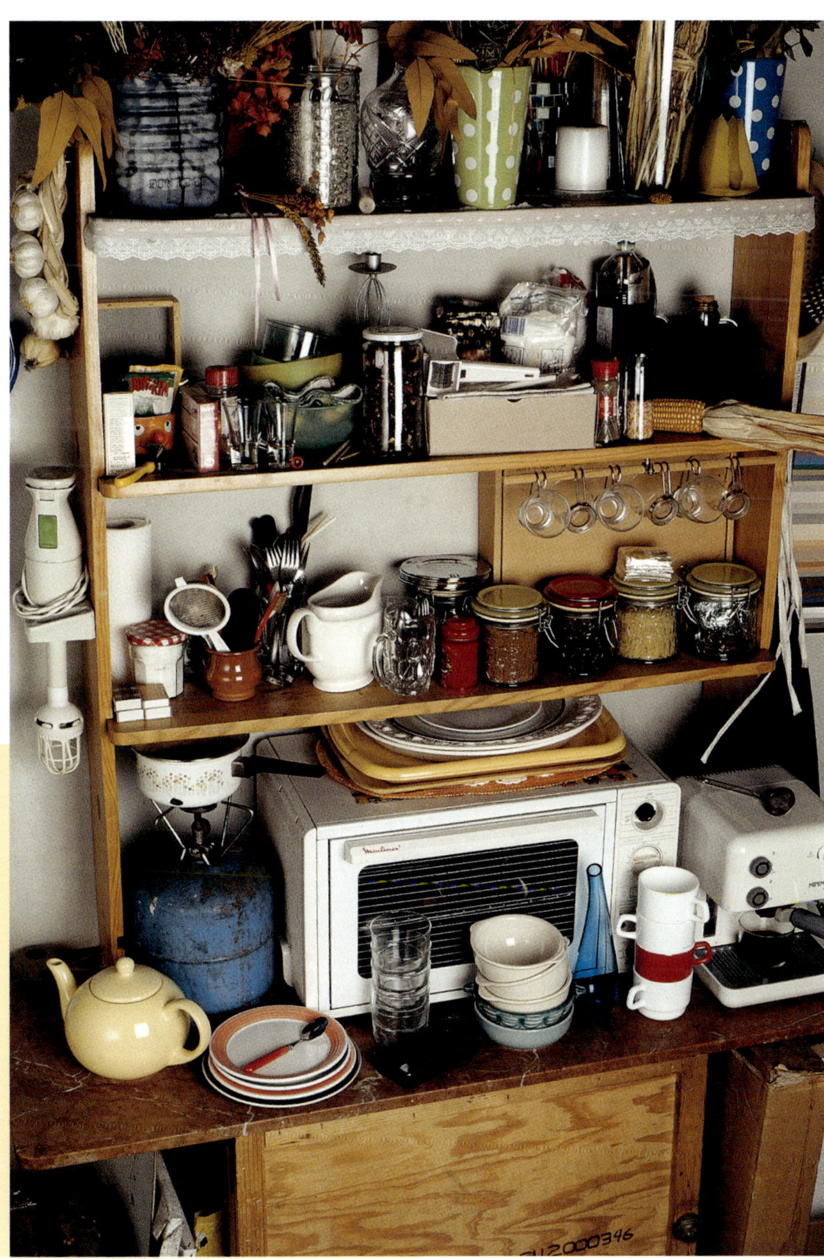

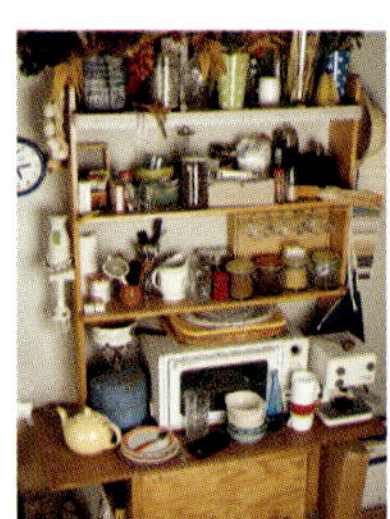

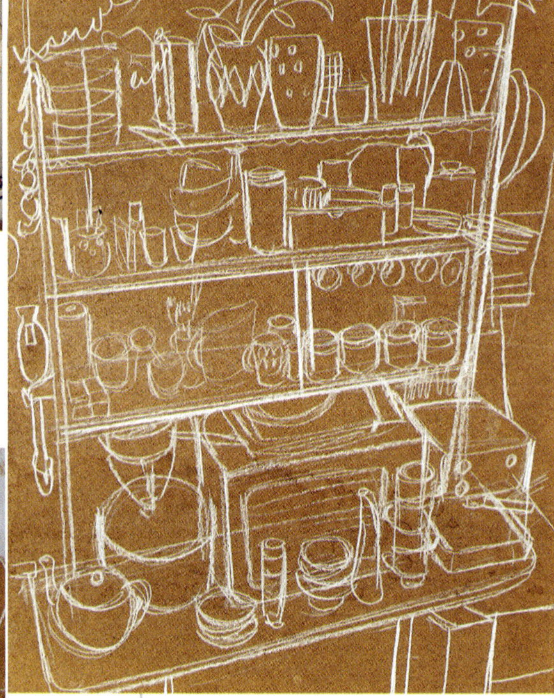

1 The preliminary line sketch is made with a white pencil so that it will stand out against the dark panel. It is important to lay out the perspective very well, and to draw each object in proportion. The drawing is the base of this work.

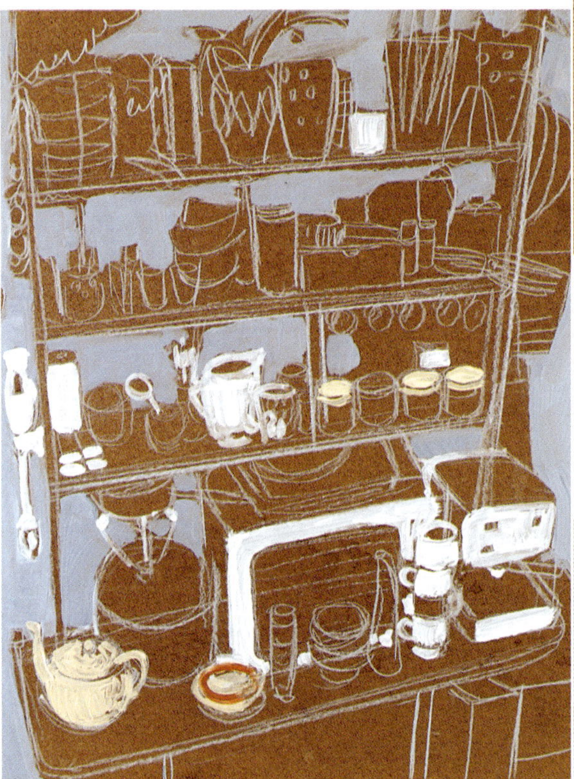

2 The first colors that we apply are the chiaroscuro values, with white and light blue-gray brushstrokes. We follow this order because the background is dark; if we were painting the still life on a white canvas, we would indicate the dark areas first.

3 Next, we work on the objects in order. Here the artist is free to begin where he wishes. We will begin with the first shelf, where the largest objects are located: the gas burner, the microwave, and the coffeemaker. We apply their dark values to create volume.

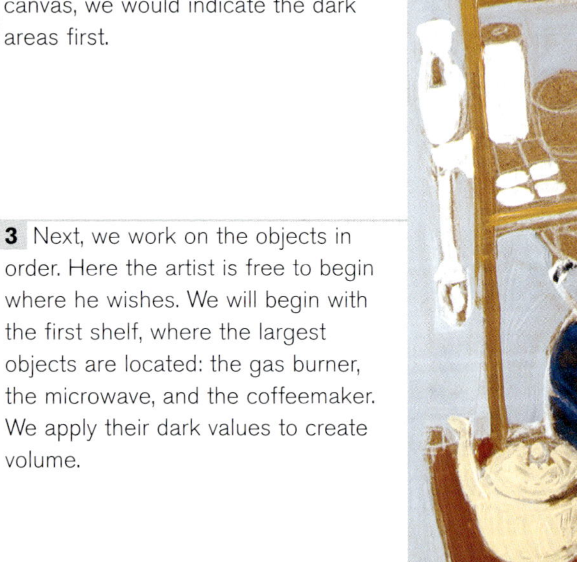

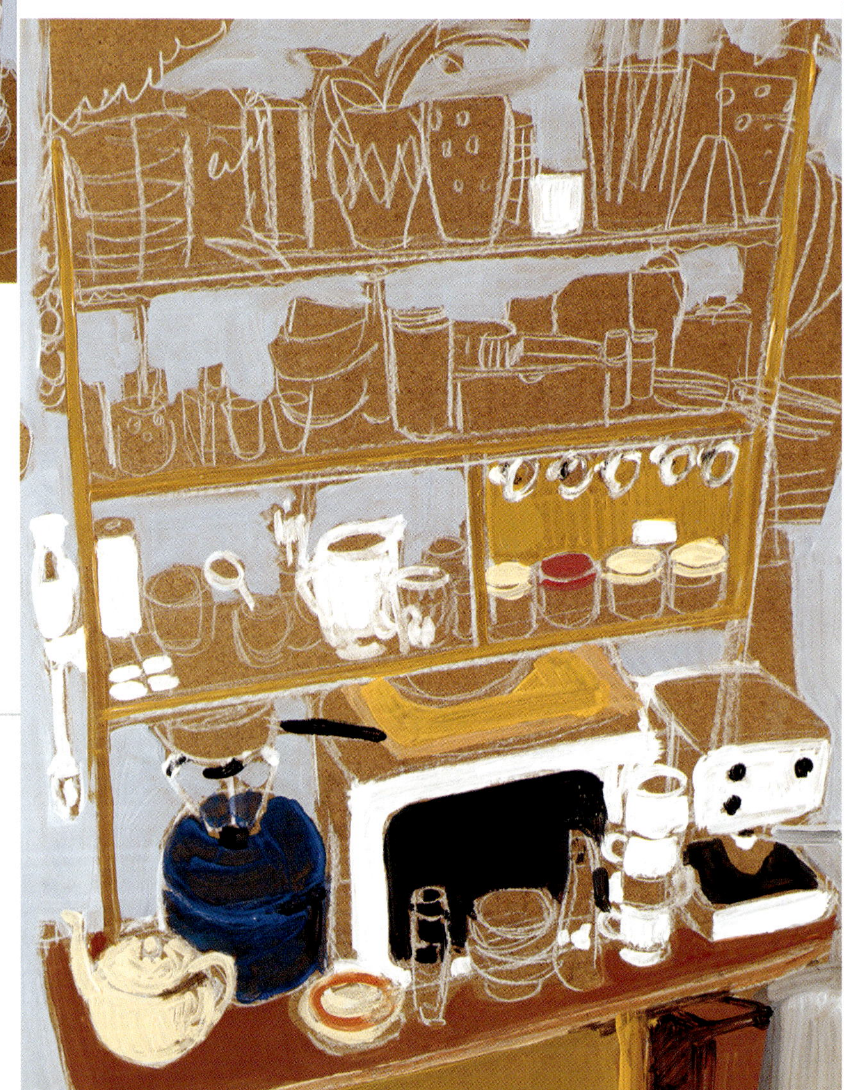

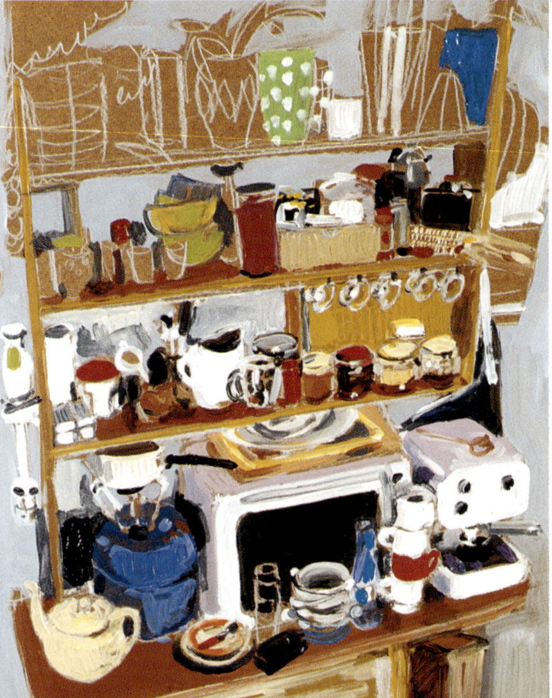

5 There are few objects left to define. This painting requires patient work, regardless of the finish. Each element should be carefully studied, although the line is loose and free.

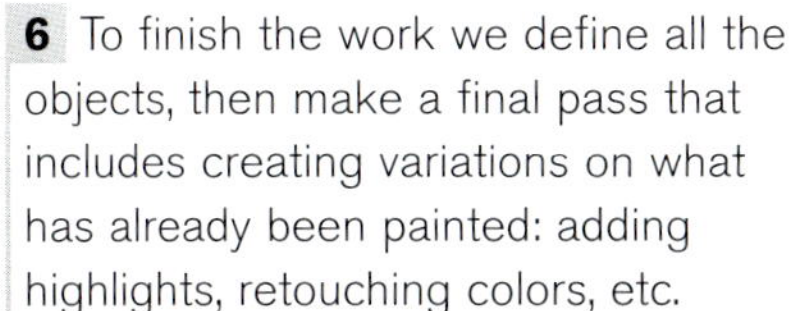

6 To finish the work we define all the objects, then make a final pass that includes creating variations on what has already been painted: adding highlights, retouching colors, etc.

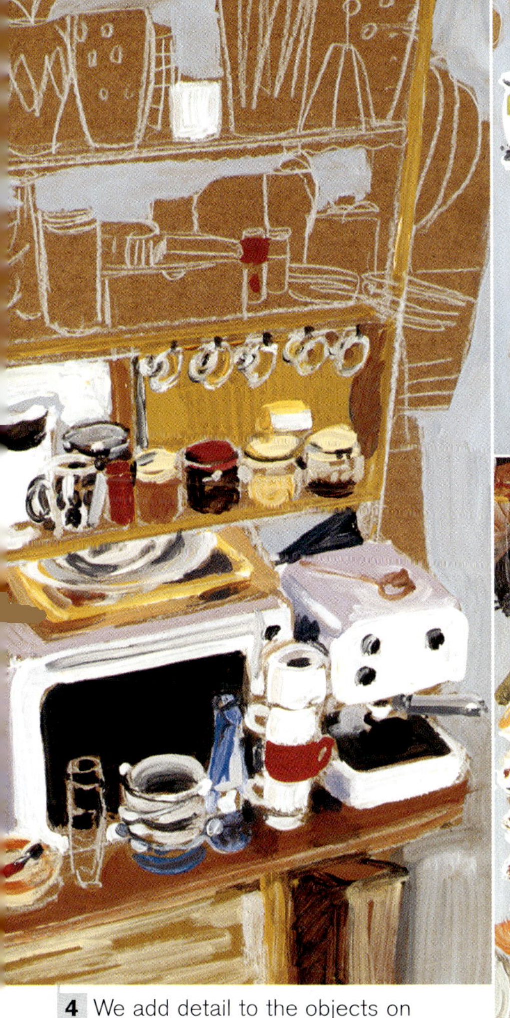

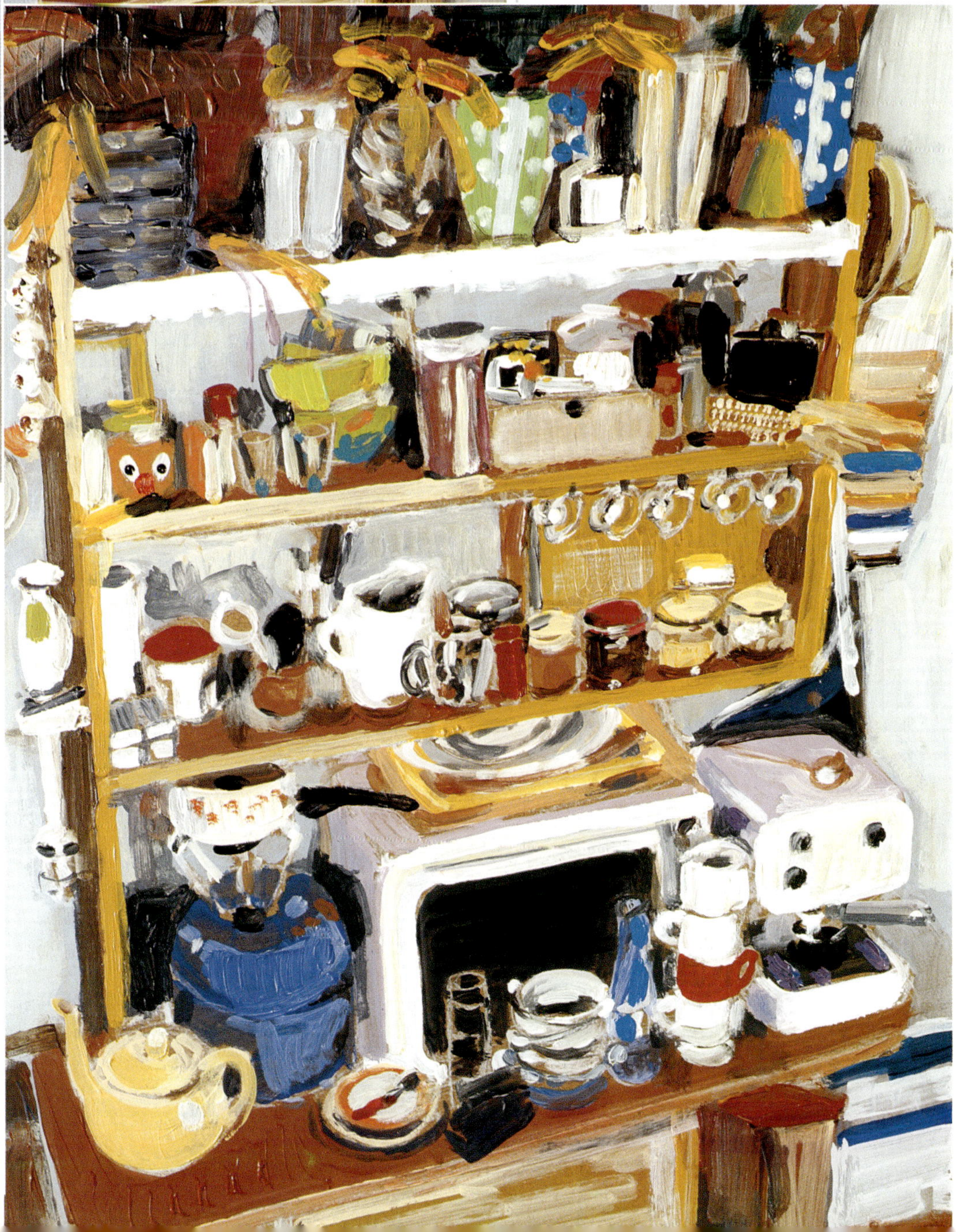

4 We add detail to the objects on the first shelf. On the shelf above we apply the same kind of lines to maintain uniformity.

Gallery

Other Versions

According to the framing, and the distance between the painter
and the model, we can create multiple full spaces. We can also
allow the painting to breathe visually in one of its corners, or blur
the objects to create a greater sense of chaos, as can be seen in
this gallery.

This is the least-defined painting in the gallery. The effect is
caused by the use of a spatula in some areas. The spatula
builds up the paint and makes it difficult to represent details.
The objects here are not outlined, but suggested, which
creates a greater feeling of chaos because of the imprecision.

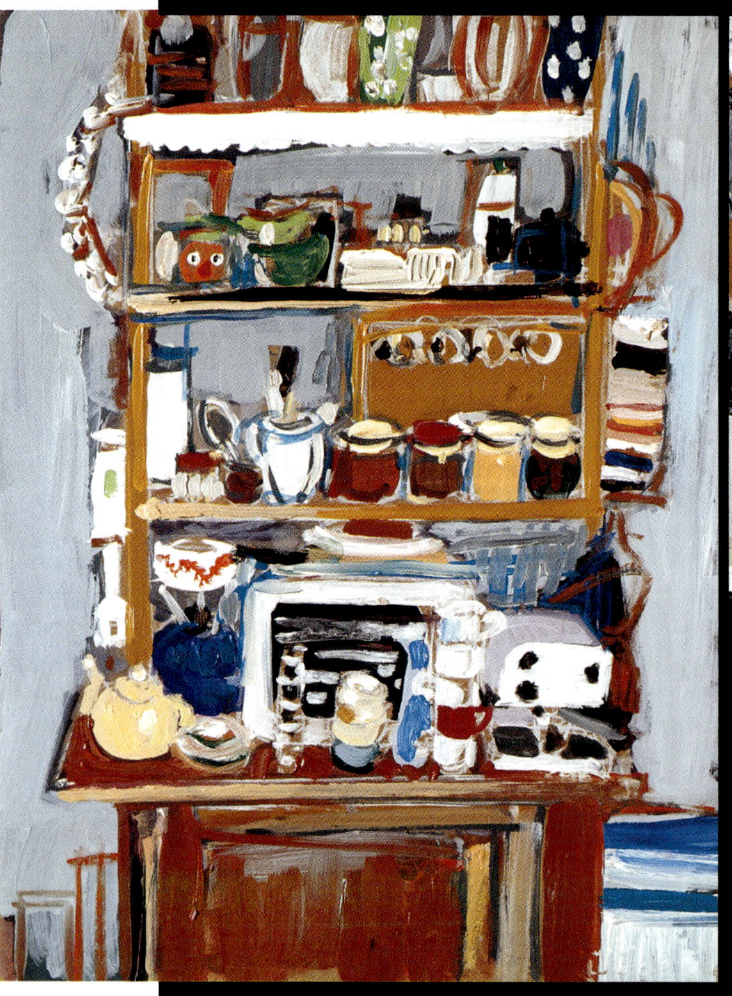

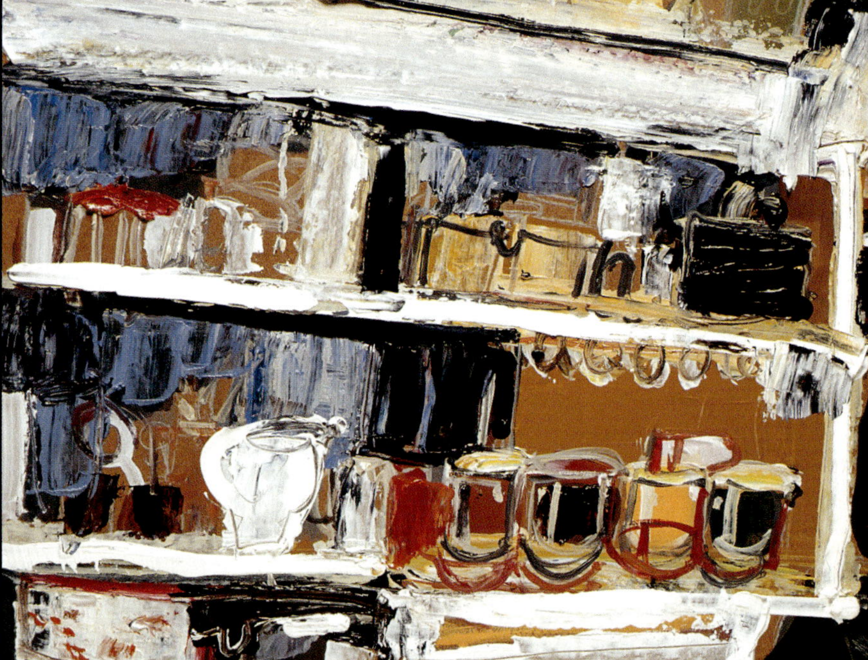

A totally frontal view and a vertical layout are the compositional
approaches that the artist used to give a sense of order in the
chaos. Despite being a full shelf it seems to be in order.

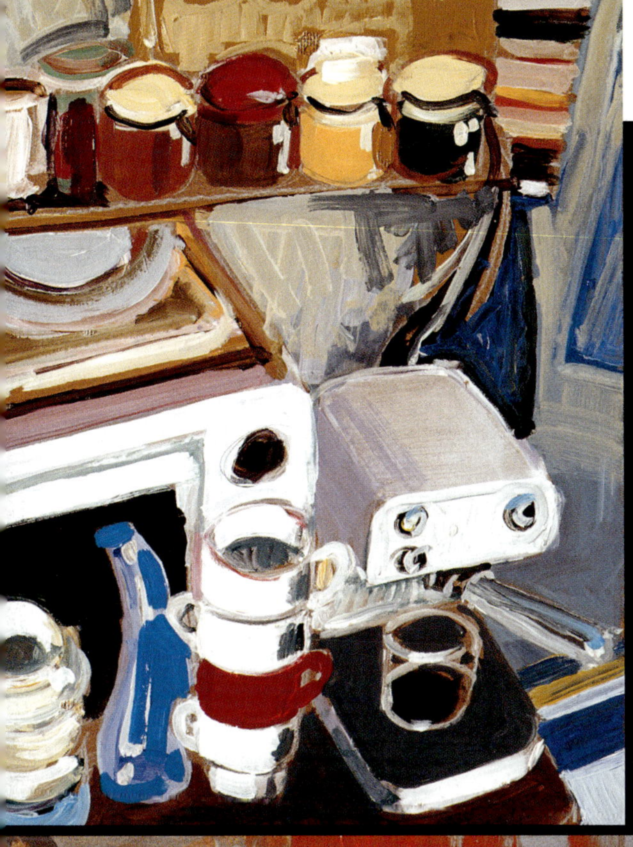

We move closer to the area of the coffeemaker and microwave. Moving close to an area is an approach that can be used to suggest that the shelf continues on both sides, and that there is so much to represent that it does not fit into the frame, reinforcing the idea of abundance. In addition, the diagonal composition adds more dynamism to the reading of the painting.

The idea of moving closer is found in this solution, although the composition follows a grid (verticals and horizontals). The image is more static and ordered.

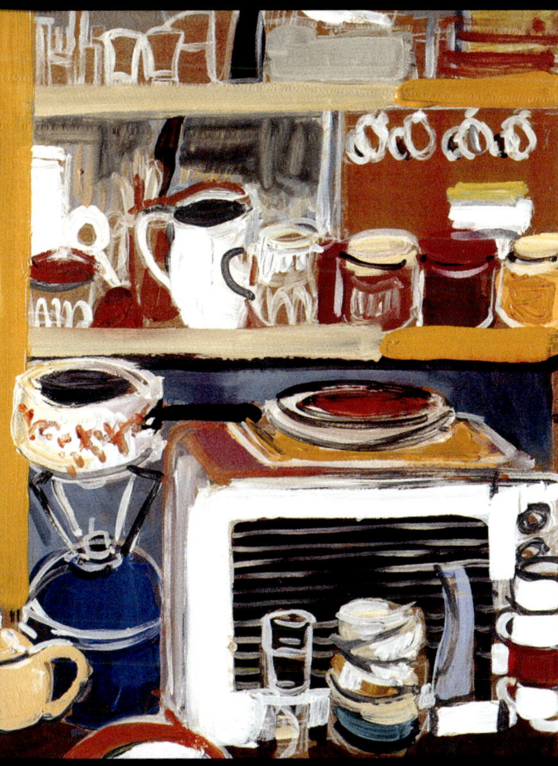

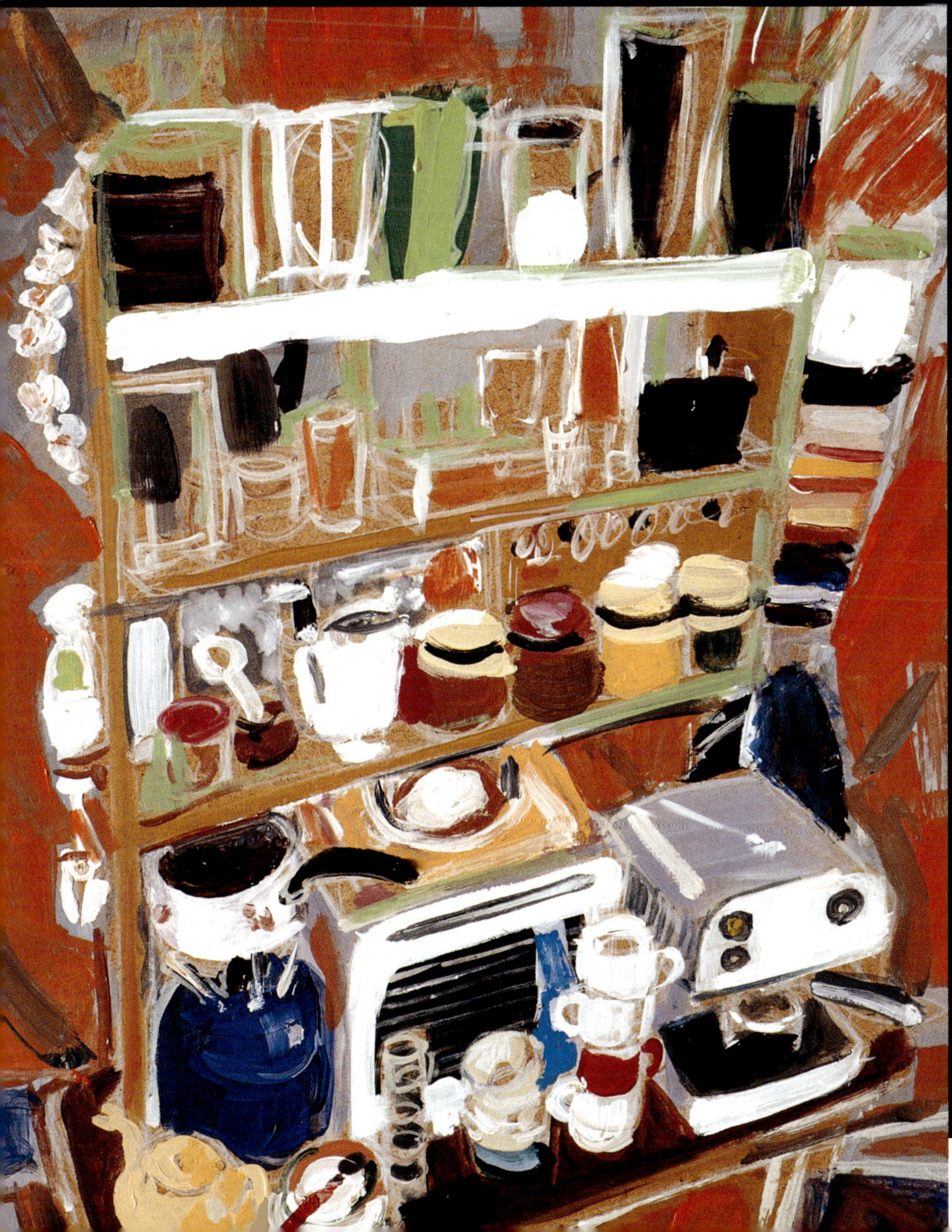

This painting represents an angled view from above, as if from the top of a stairway, to make use of a more expressionistic and striking language. Furthermore, the presence of finished objects and barely indicated objects produces a feeling of a living picture, inviting the participation of the viewer to complete it.

Other Models

To recreate the classic theme of a lavish still life, Josep Asunción found food to use as the model, but with a personal twist: bringing it up to date. Just as the Flemish, French, and Spanish baroque still-life painters represented scenes with the gastronomy of their times, this artist has created a scene that represents something of today's gastronomy. After considering packaged and canned foods, fast food, and pastries, he opted for the last subject because the image is so appetizing.

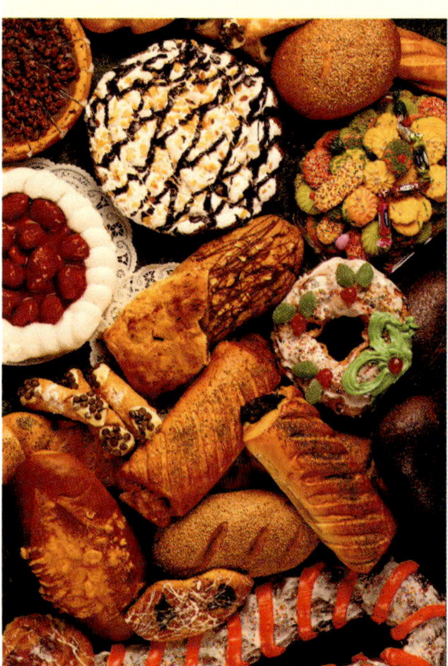

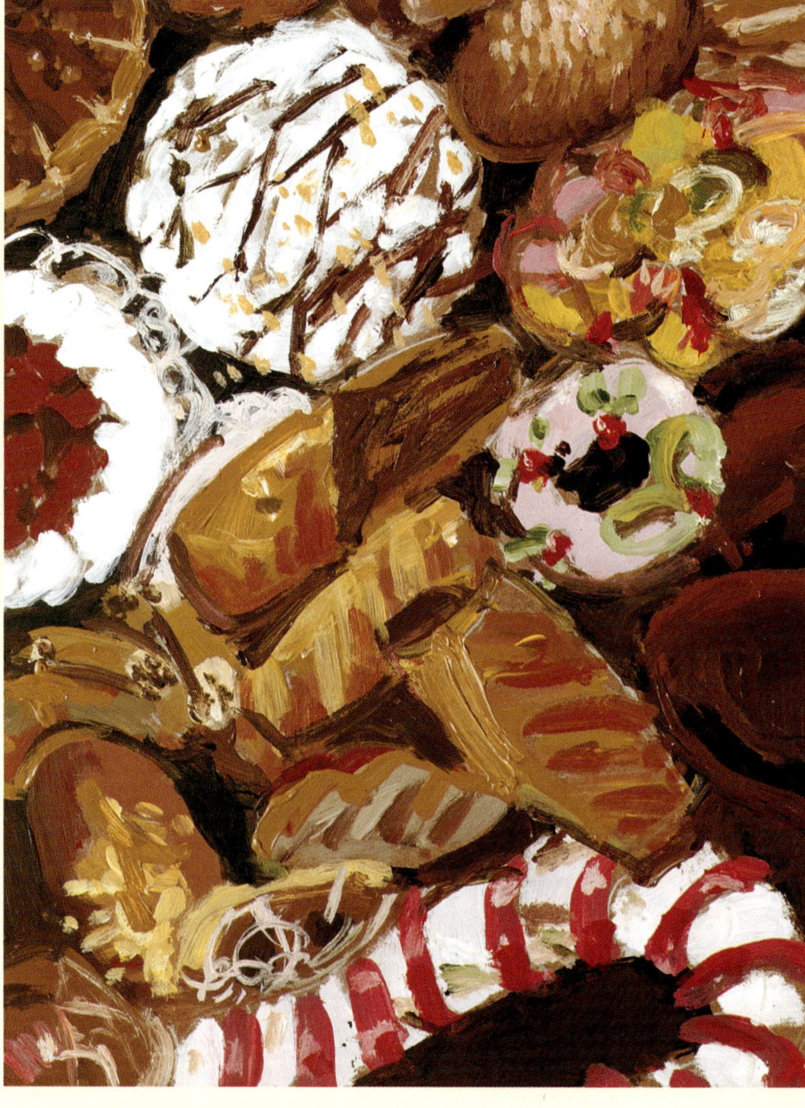

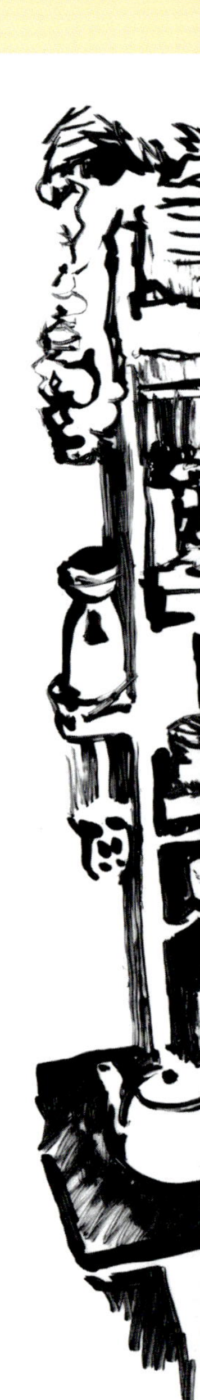

Other Media

The use of color in a painting makes the image more complex, because it contains so much information for the viewer. This time we experimented with black and white as a way toward synthesis. We used india ink applied with a reed pen and paper. It is a much more austere and direct medium that clashes with the complexity of the subject.

Other Views

Juan de Valdés Leal (1622–1690), a Spanish baroque painter, is the creator of works that stand out for their vigor and drama. With a bold yet detailed style, Valdés Leal created in his *Allegory of Vanity* a work of moralizing character. Each element in this large still life symbolizes something—the triumph of death (the skull with the laurel wreath and the snuffed candle), the impermanence of the material (the flowers that wilt), the futility of life (soap bubbles), the need to let go of fame and fortune (scattered coins and medals)—to speak of spiritual virtue as the only way to salvation in the Final Judgment that appears in the painting that is pointed out by the angel on the right.

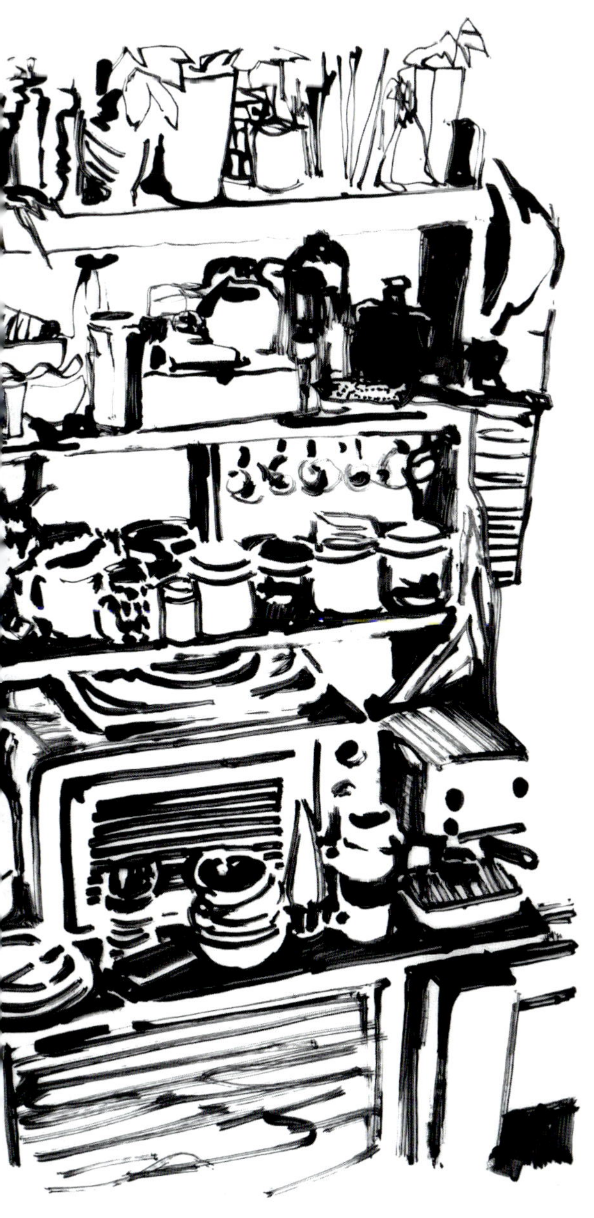

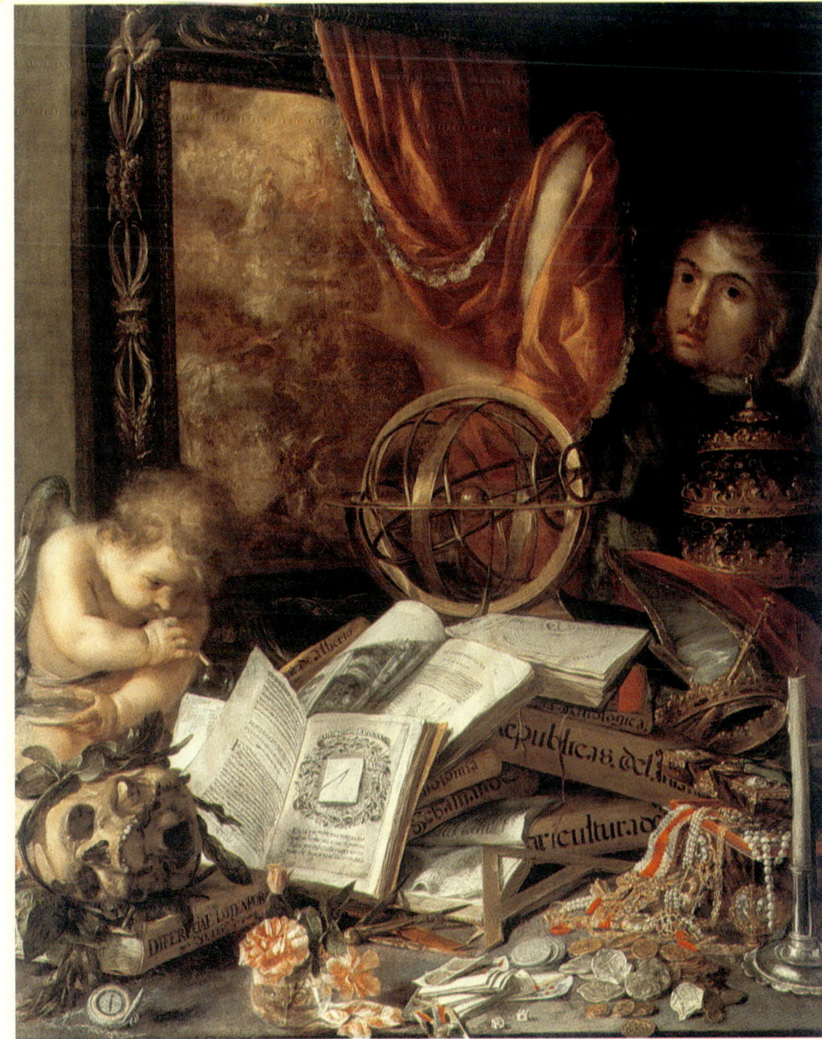

Juan de Valdés Leal,
Allegory of Vanity,
Hartford Museum, Hartford, Connecticut.

Dream, Metaphysical, *and Fantastic* Spaces

Giorgio De Chirico (1888–1978) can be defined as a painter of enigmatic spaces, chilling and solitary, urban spaces without life inhabited by disturbing figures. When exposed to this work in Paris, the poet and critic Apollinaire described these spaces with the term *metaphysical.* De Chirico's father died when he was an adolescent, and the emptiness caused by his absence is reflected symbolically in his enigmatic figures and frightening silhouettes suspended in emptiness. He showed a great interest in reading philosophy, in the Romantic painters, and in Renaissance art, which influenced the need to create silent and solemn spaces, exaggerated perspectives, illusionist fugues, and sharply defined shadows, in both his paintings and his scenery for theaters. *The Unsettling Muse* symbolizes the loneliness De Chirico experienced during his hospitalization for a nervous breakdown. The spaces in the painting are unreal and the figures are senseless. All materials in the painting are messages from the memory.

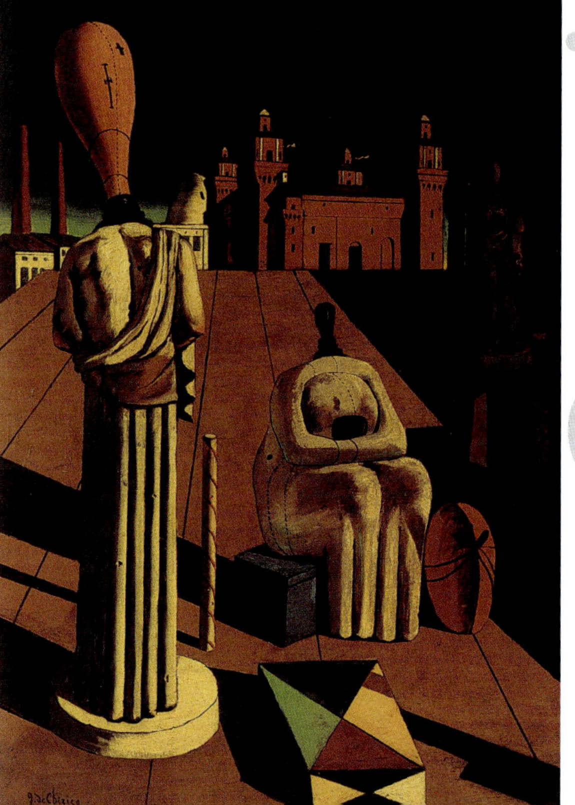

De Chirico,
The Unsettling Muse, 1917–1918.
Private Collection, Milan, Italy.

Creating Metaphysical Spaces: The Dream Applied to an Unreal Space

In dreams reality is deformed and spaces are created where the fears, worries, and hidden desires come to life, forming and defining the unconscious. In this approach Gemma Guasch decided to enter into these suggestive dream spaces to present a fantastic and enigmatic vision apart from tangible reality. The model chosen for this presents a great ambiguity. A suitcase full of unusual items with no logical connection is used for developing fantastic and unreal spaces. She used mixed media: artist's inks mixed with chalk on paper.

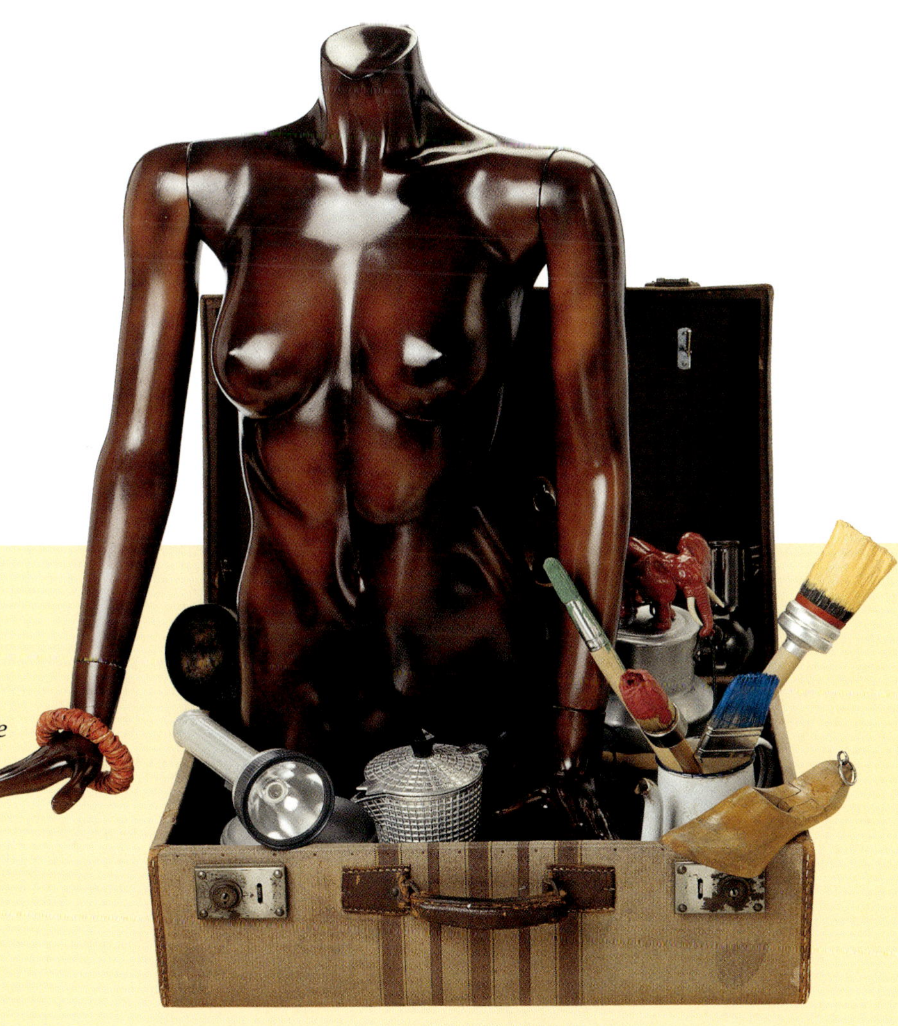

"For a work of art to be truly immortal, it is necessary that it completely leave the confines of that which is human: good sense and logic prejudice it. In this manner we can get closer to the dream and the infant mentality. A profound work will be taken by the artist to the deepest depths of his being."
Giorgio De Chirico, 1914.

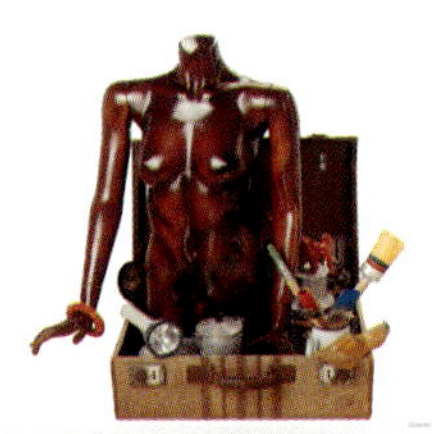

1 We create an unsettling space in which to develop the dream image. Using a pen dipped in blue ink we create a large space with a single vanishing point, and we limit it in the foreground with two enormous walls that cut the plane at angles.

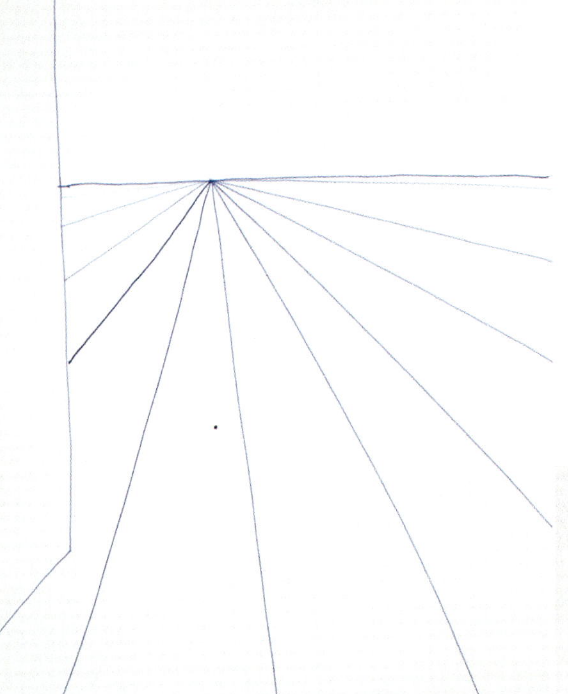

2 From among the models in the suitcase we choose the manikin figure. With a brush dipped in india ink we draw its outline in a larger than normal size, in the closest part of the foreground in the lower right corner of the picture. We generate a new space by painting a triangle in ink between the manikin and the bottom edge of the paper.

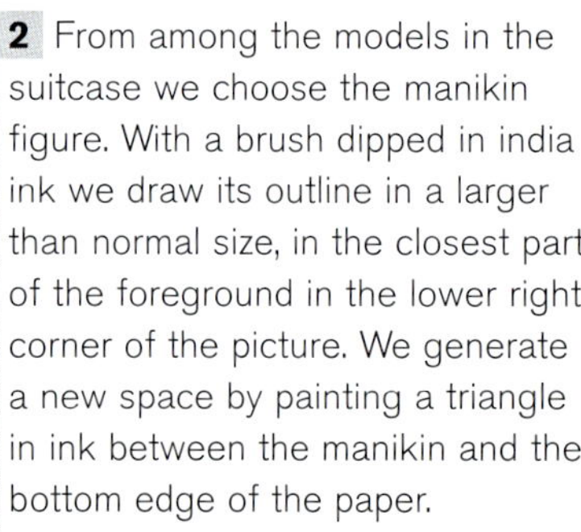

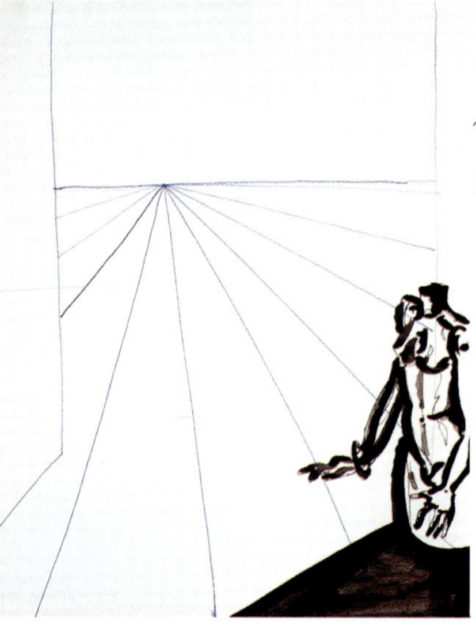

3 Using pen and ink we multiply the milk can in the space, varying its size from large to small. This accentuates the feeling of spatial immensity and creates another diagonal in the space.

4 We center and limit the viewer's gaze by painting the side walls with india ink and blue ink. A night sky is suggested in the background with blue and magenta. We place a coffeepot with brushes at the vanishing point in a larger size than would be logical for the space we have created. Finally, we paint the manikin and the right sides of the milk cans blue to give the objects volume and presence.

6 The sky is invaded by a flashlight that becomes deformed by stretching across the upper left corner of the paper, generating a play of diagonals in the background that oppress the spatial feeling of escape. Finally, we paint the ground a luminous yellow green over a large encapsulated and cold space.

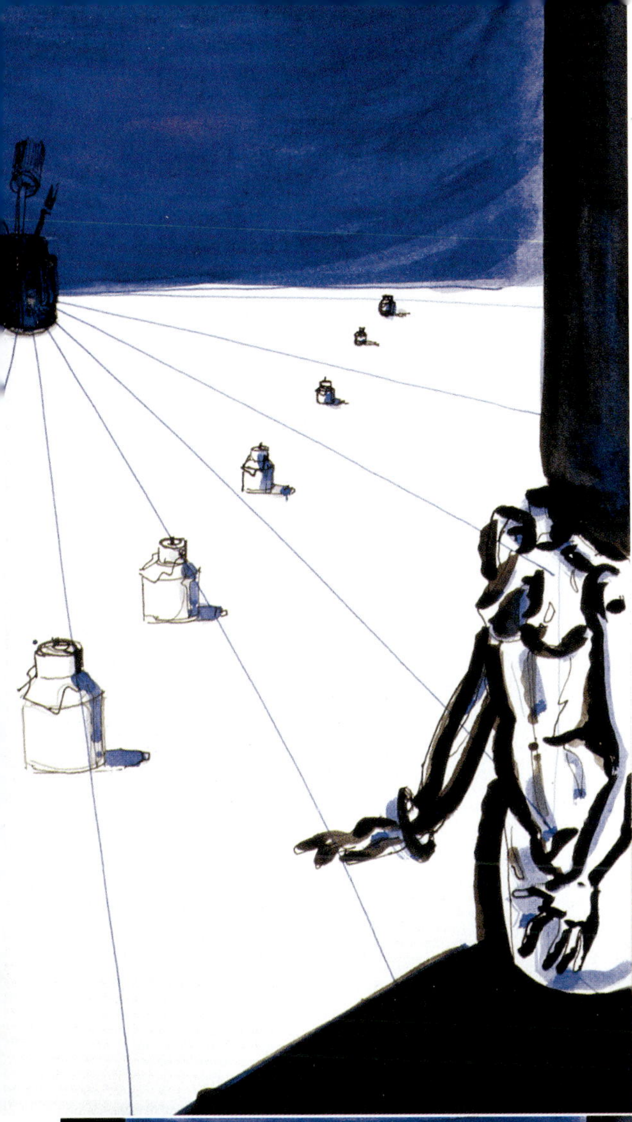

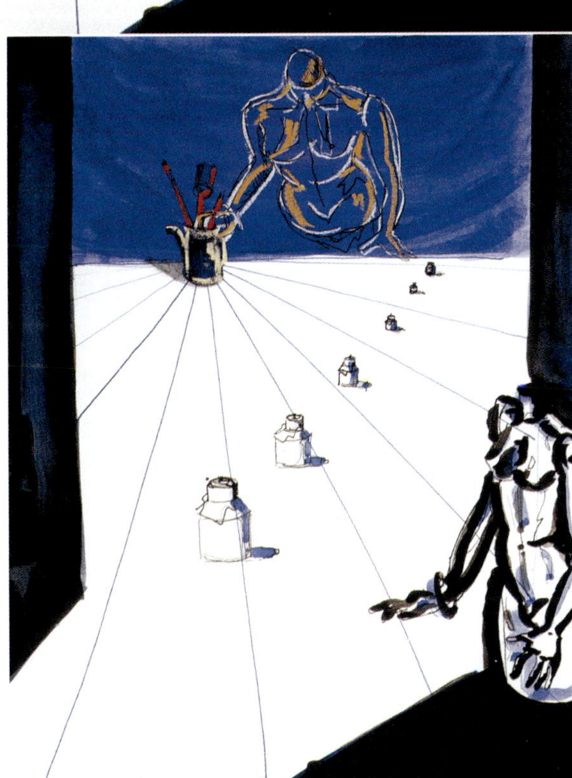

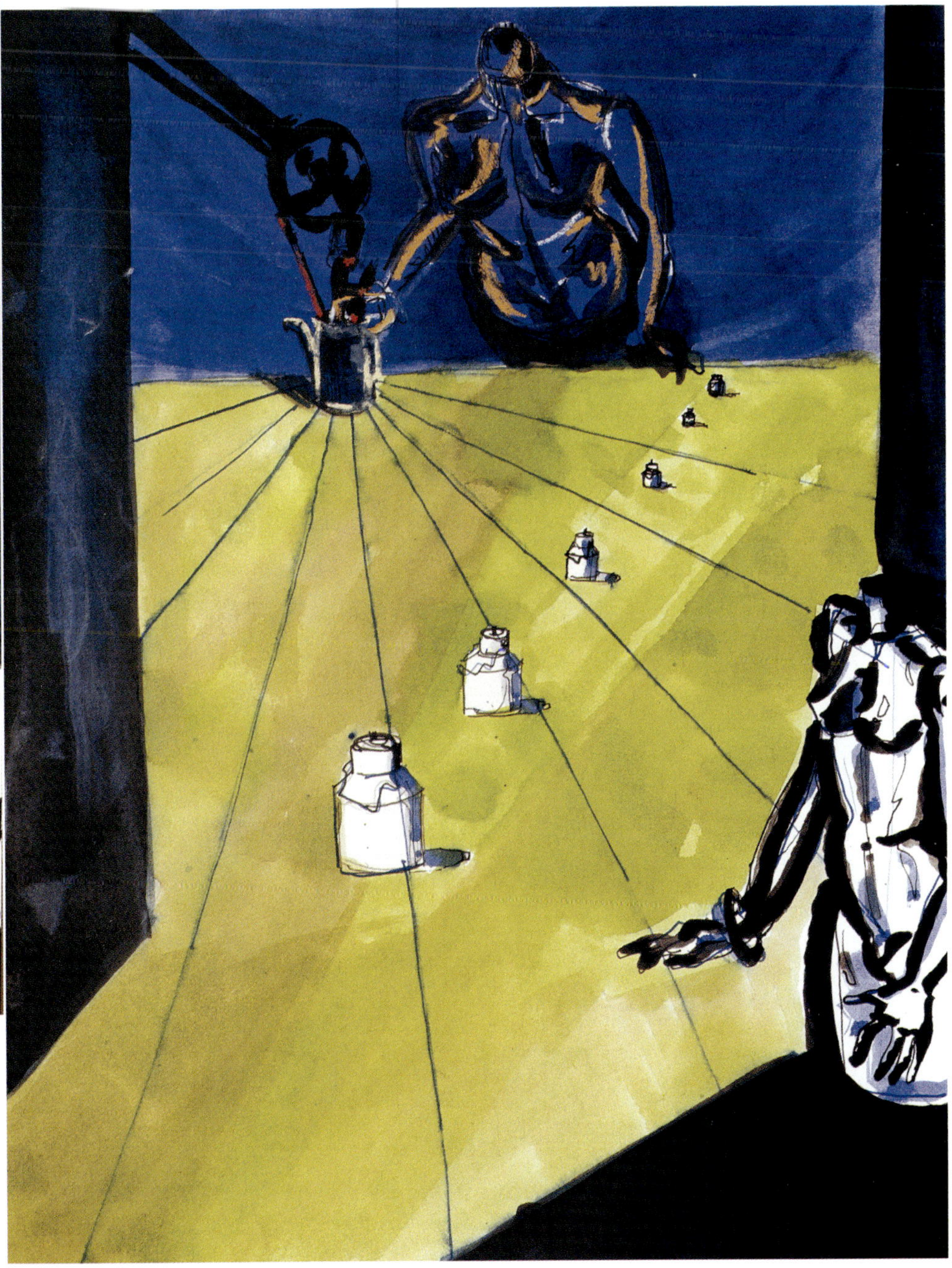

5 We draw an enormous manikin with colored chalk that invades the night sky, creating an ambiguous and unsettling presence that is intimidating in its size and position in the painting. We also apply chalk to the coffeepot and the brushes to connect them to the manikin.

Other Versions

The creation of fantastic and unreal worlds allows many, many spatial sensations: fear, attraction, weightlessness . . . Fantasy allows us to modify spatial perception. In this context the rules are not fixed and can be modified, exaggerated, and deformed according to what is being dreamed.

An unstable space in a disturbing diagonal is upsetting to the viewer who sees it from an elevated point of view. The dead ends and opposite directions disturb the general view and create ambiguity. The enormous projected shadow of a nonexistent coffeepot suggests that there are objects above the space that the viewer is not able to see.

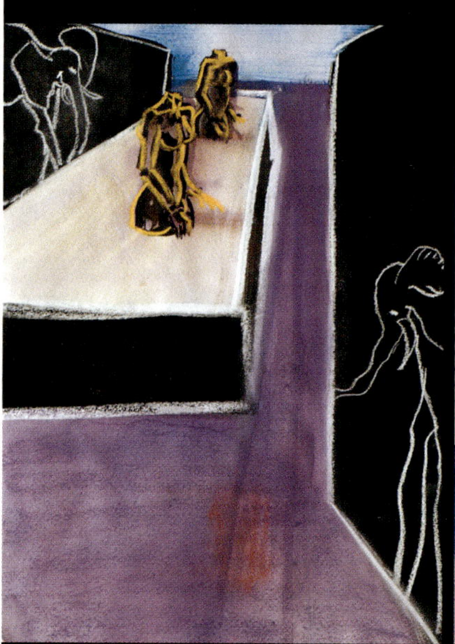

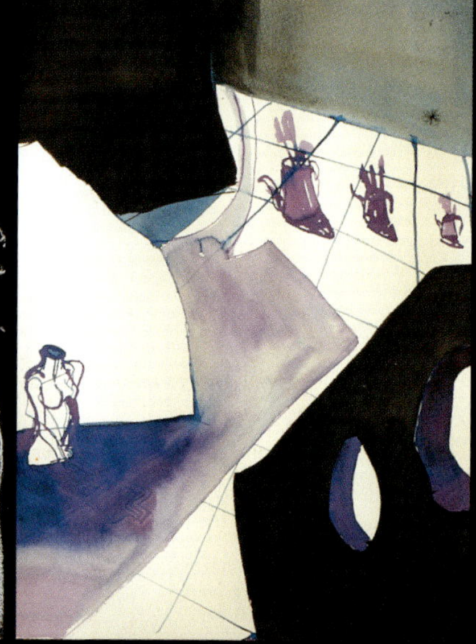

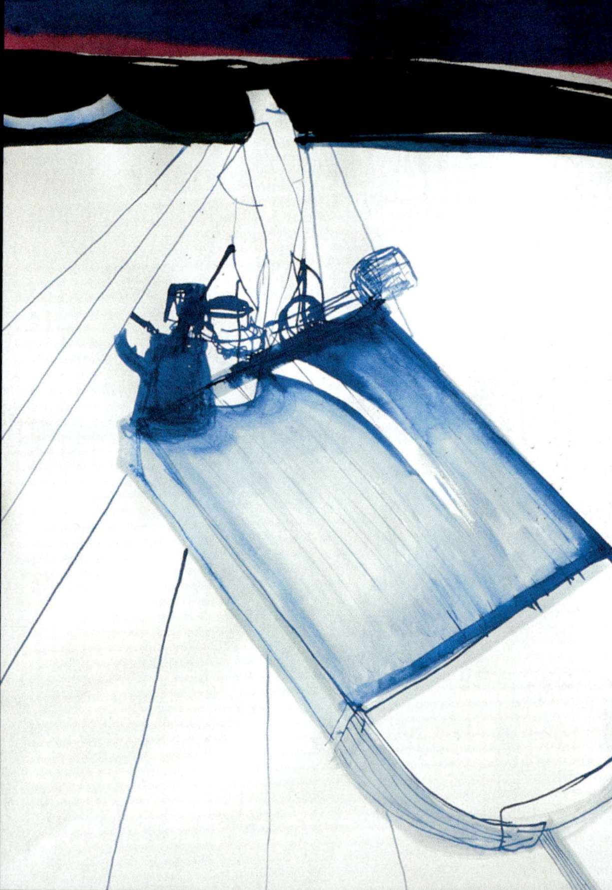

Along the sides we constructed stepped walls and platforms that protect the elements from an empty vanishing space marked by a horizon cut by a blue sky. There are few elements and there is no relationship between them. On one side are twin manikins, and on the walls are flat and enlarged outlines of an elephant. The enigmatic sensation is created by the positions of the two manikins that look toward something on one side of the scene hidden from the viewer.

The different elements find themselves in a weightless space. An enormous paintbrush juts out from the right corner of the painting into an open and endless space to serve as a platform for the rest of the elements that are grouped at one end, expectantly contemplating the infinite space.

The space created in this work shows the ambiguity of a closed space treated as if it were an airy landscape. Only an aperture on the right side shows an open landscape from which an exaggeratedly elongated flashlight invades the image and points to the fallen cup in the foreground. On the other side appears a large hand that is unable to reach anything. The disproportion between the sizes of the objects and the created space is disconcerting and intensifies the fantasy.

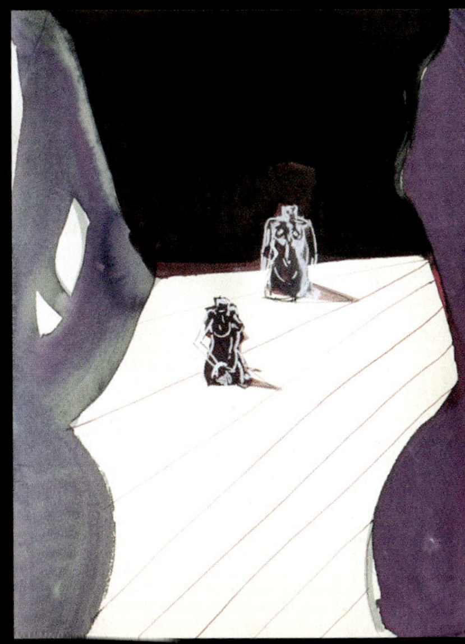

The basic theme of this work is seen in the repetition of four manikins: two giants at the sides of the paper and two in the rear, inverted in their logical perspective. The sizes were changed to reinforce the falseness of the perceived space and to situate it in dream and unreality.

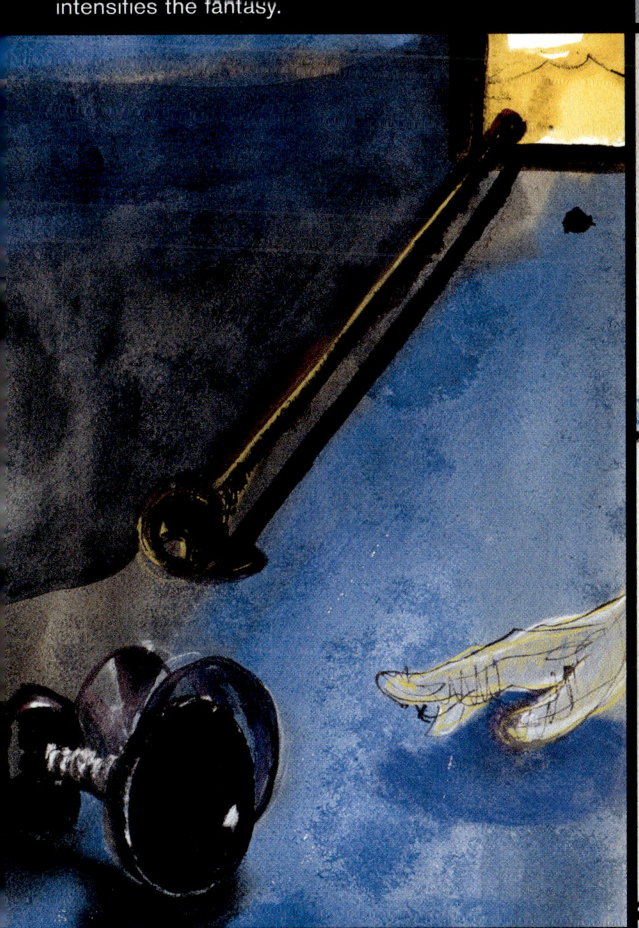

Here the objects float and meet in a pleasant sky. Below, in the distance, we can make out a familiar mountain landscape. The radial arrangement of the cup and the flashlights generate an interior movement that converges in the center of the image. It is an open and at the same time egocentric view of space.

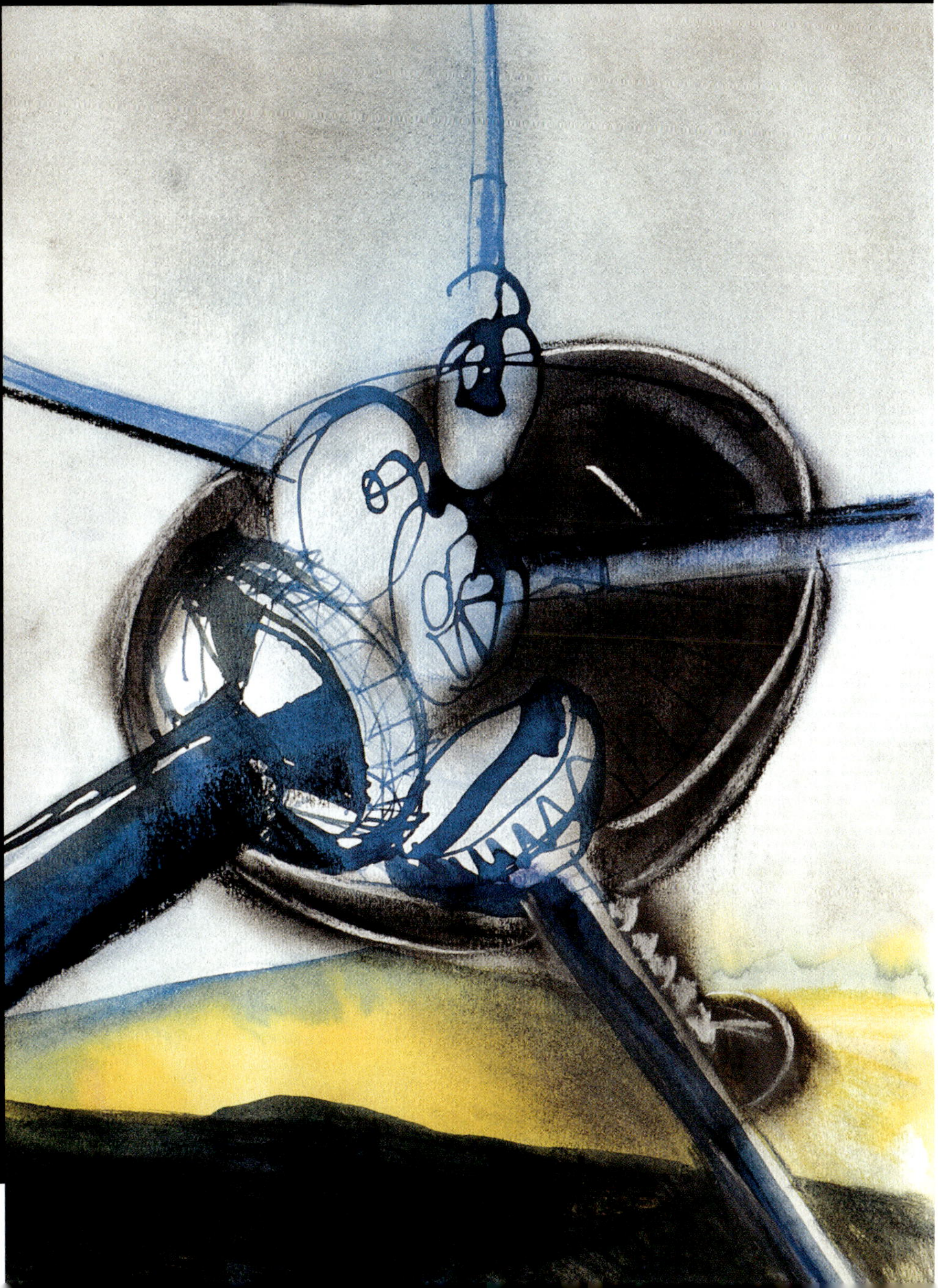

New Approaches

Other Models

To vary the dream space, the artist has chosen a quite disturbing interior setting because of the difference in scale between the miniature furniture in a real habitable space. The new subject suggests the possibility of creating spaces where the logic of gravity does not dominate the scene, by floating the furniture in the air, outside the interior space. Experimenting with reversing the contexts has generated a disconcerting and illogical space based on spatial disproportion.

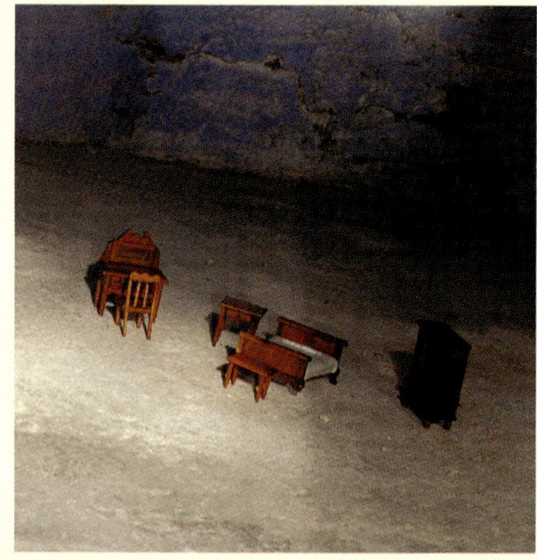

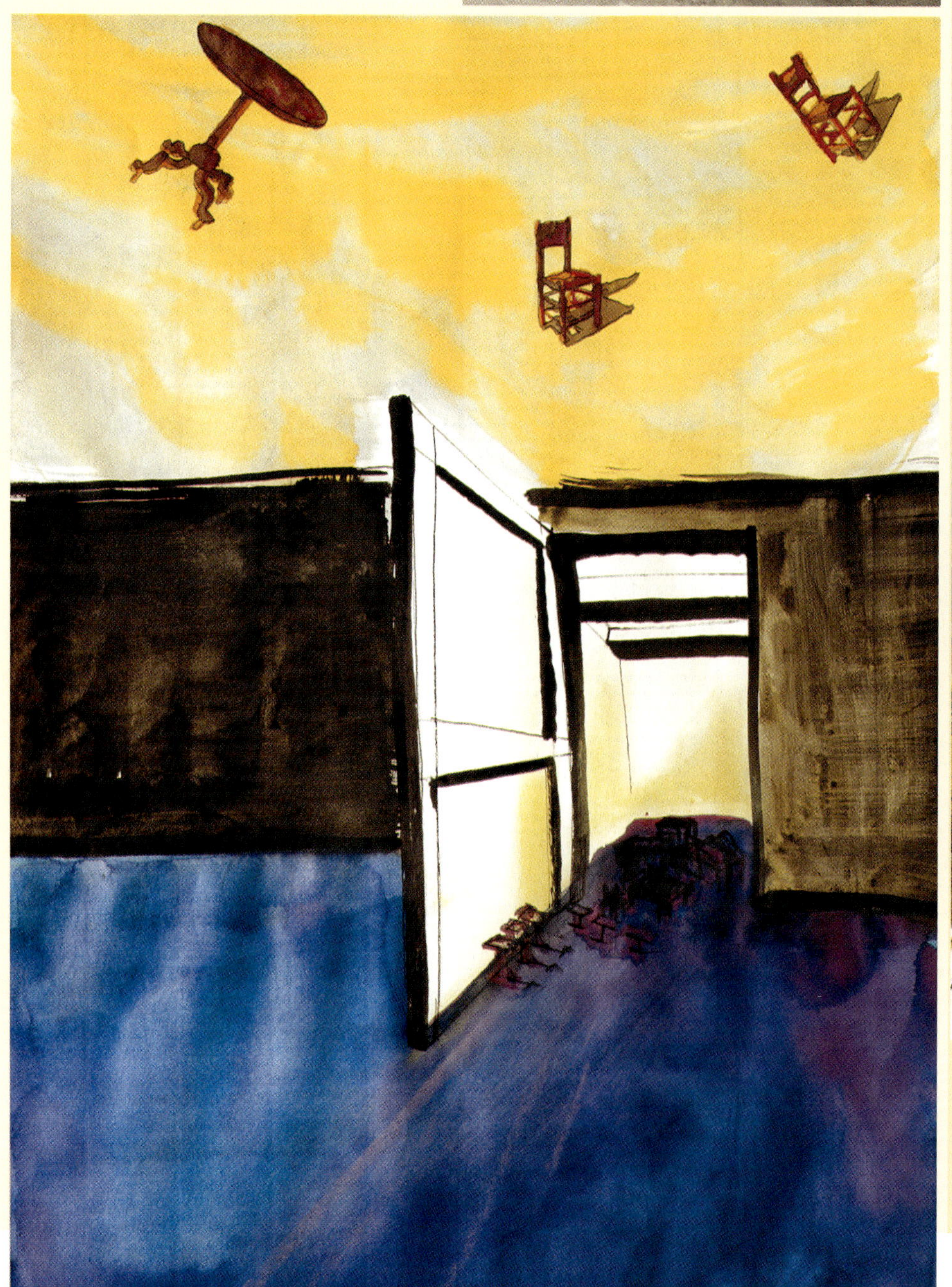

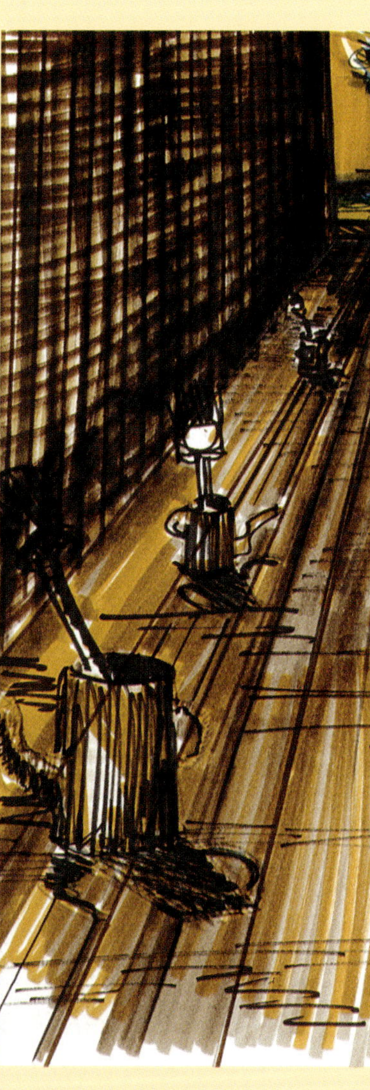

Other Media

To experiment with hatching and superimposing tones, Gemma Guasch chose markers as an alternative medium to drawing inks. They permit working with line and absorbency. Color markers are a more graphic than painterly medium, with a direct and immediate character. Drawing inks allow the intensity of the tones to be manipulated by mixing them with each other or with water. The marker, on the other hand, obliges us to work with line, creating color variations by superimposing the hatch lines.

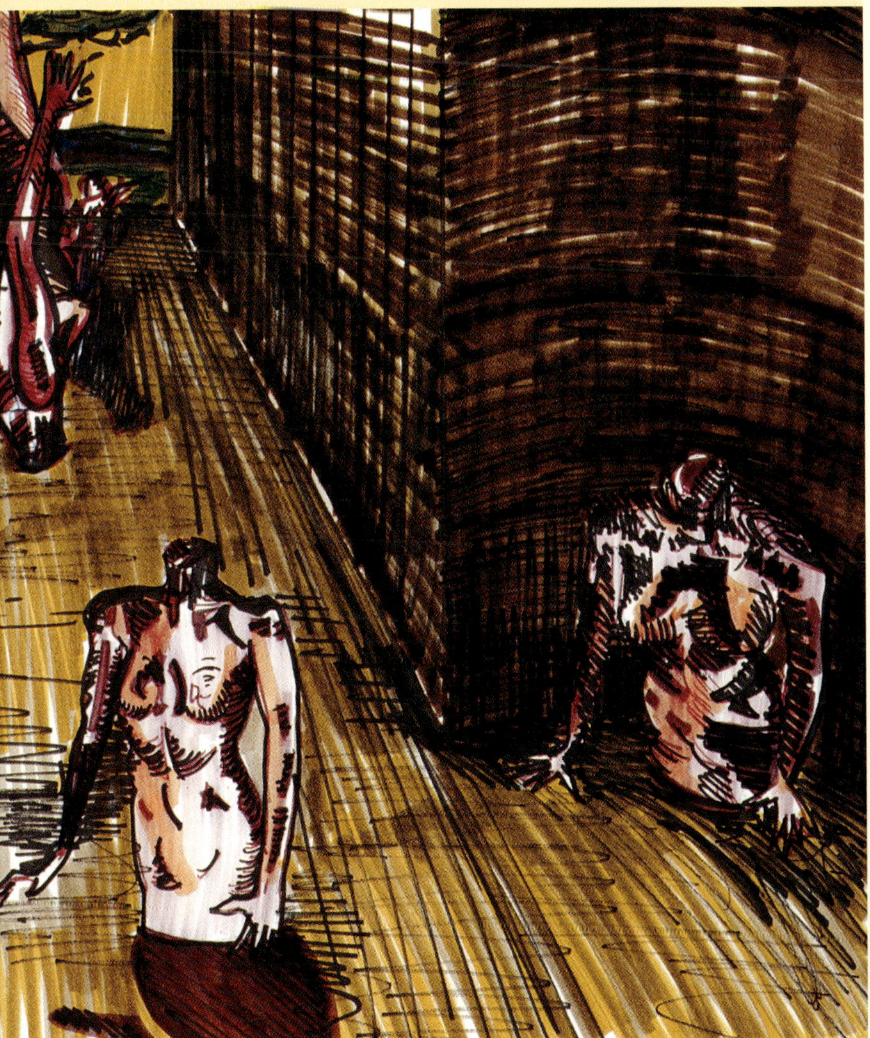

Other Views

The first *Surrealist Manifesto* was published in 1924. It paid homage to Sigmund Freud: "thanks to him the imagination is perhaps on the verge of regaining its rights." The surrealist artists defended dreams, because dreams let hidden desires and powers emerge, liberating the unconscious. Surrealist painters attempted to distance themselves from all logic, reversing established relationships to generate a crisis that would permit the creation of a free and wonderful world. In the painting *Cannibalism of October,* Salvador Dalí (1904–1989) applied the paranoid-critic method. The man in the painting is seen as a praying mantis that is about to devour the male. The cannibalism and the sublimation of the jaw cause him to define beauty: "beauty will either be edible or it will not be." The work was compared to Picasso's *Guernica* because both of them express the drama of the Spanish civil war, although Picasso considered it a political phenomenon and Dalí an anthropological one.

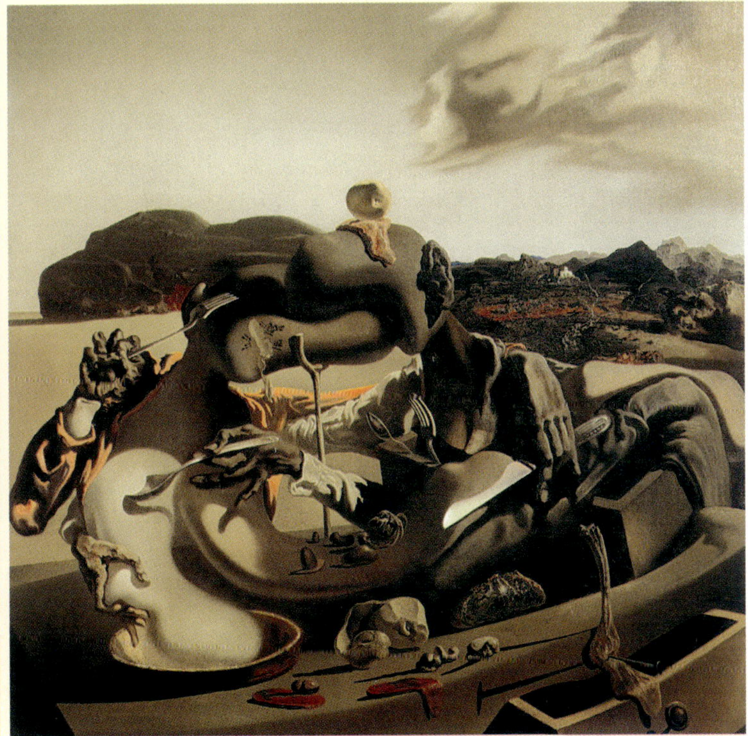

Salvador Dalí,
Cannibalism of October, 1936.
National Gallery, London,
United Kingdom.

A landscape painting is a painting of space, which is why this
chapter contains the greatest number of creative approaches in this
book. Three of them deal with traditional themes: the rural
landscape, the seascape, and the cityscape; and the other two cover
circulation spaces: a highway landscape and an interior with stairs.
This last subject is connected to the landscape and not the still life
because it is about a space without objects, in it pure structure in an
allegorical-symbolic form.

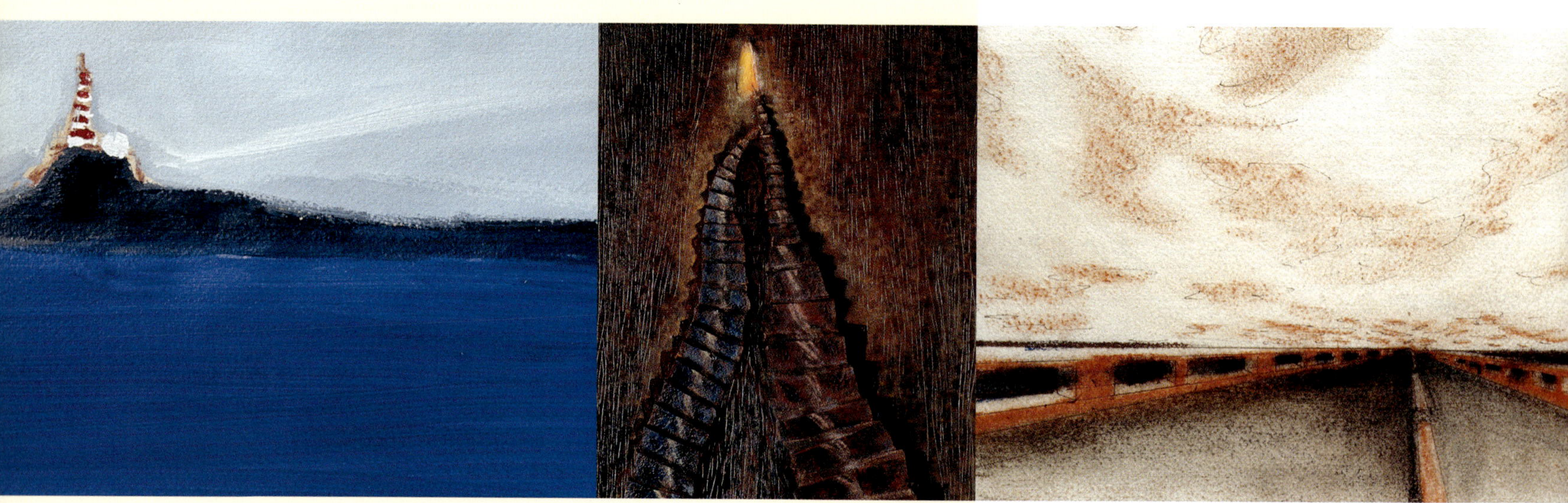

Landscape

"There is a tactile space in the landscape, a space that could almost be defined as manual . . . what attracted me most was (. . .) the materialization of this new space that I was seeing."
Georges Braque

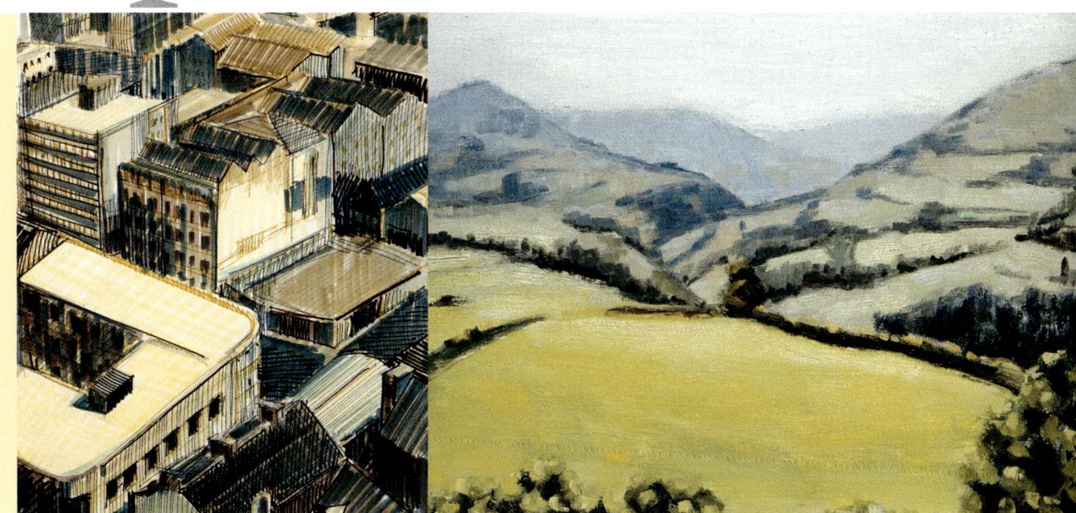

Open, Empty, and Panoramic Spaces

Caspar David Friedrich (1774–1840) painted true icons of romanticism, figures in the landscape that pay homage to nature, nostalgic ruins, and landscapes with enormous spaces that are waiting for something to happen, like the mythical painting *Monk on the Shore*. In it, on an extremely low horizon, a shoreline marks the limit between the elements and the monk, who is on the farthest point of the shoreline and is the only vertical in the painting. The sky is an infinite space achieved with misty layers of color applied one over the other. For Friedrich the figure is important because without it there is no perception of grandness. The figure determines the scale because it lets us compare the spatial proportions. The subject of the background is infinity; the viewer should place himself alongside the monk and see his extreme smallness in the immeasurable infinity of the universe. "The painting has no foreground other than the frame, as if one had removed his eyelids," said a magazine of the era.

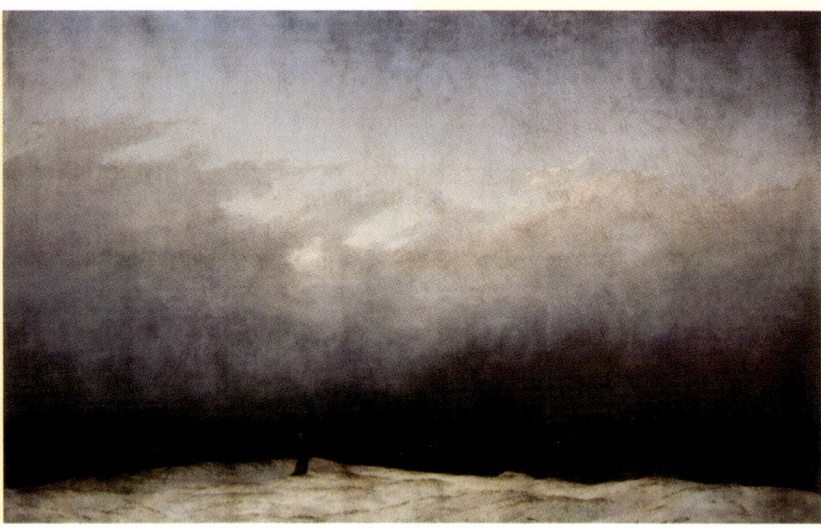

Caspar David Friedrich,
Monk on the Shore, 1808–1810.
Nationalgalerie Staatliches Museen zu
Berlin, Berlin, Germany.

Composition and the Landscape: The Perception of Emptiness in a Seascape

The most frequent spatial perception in a seascape is that of depth. This perspective must be applied, whether linear, atmospheric, or a combination of both. But what happens when no perspective can be seen in the landscape? We should make use of the arrangement of the objects on the visual plane: the composition. This is a very common case in the purest seascapes, those that depict only the sea, the sky, and perhaps some boat or a piece of land to orient us in the scale relationships, like in the creative approach that Josep Asunción develops in the following pages. He creates several compositions in acrylic on paper based on the real model of a lighthouse, combined with an imaginary sky, sea, and coast. In them he changes the arrangement of the elements, their proportions, and the format of the framing, continually searching for the emptiness, the open space, the panoramic gaze that is fixed on the horizon.

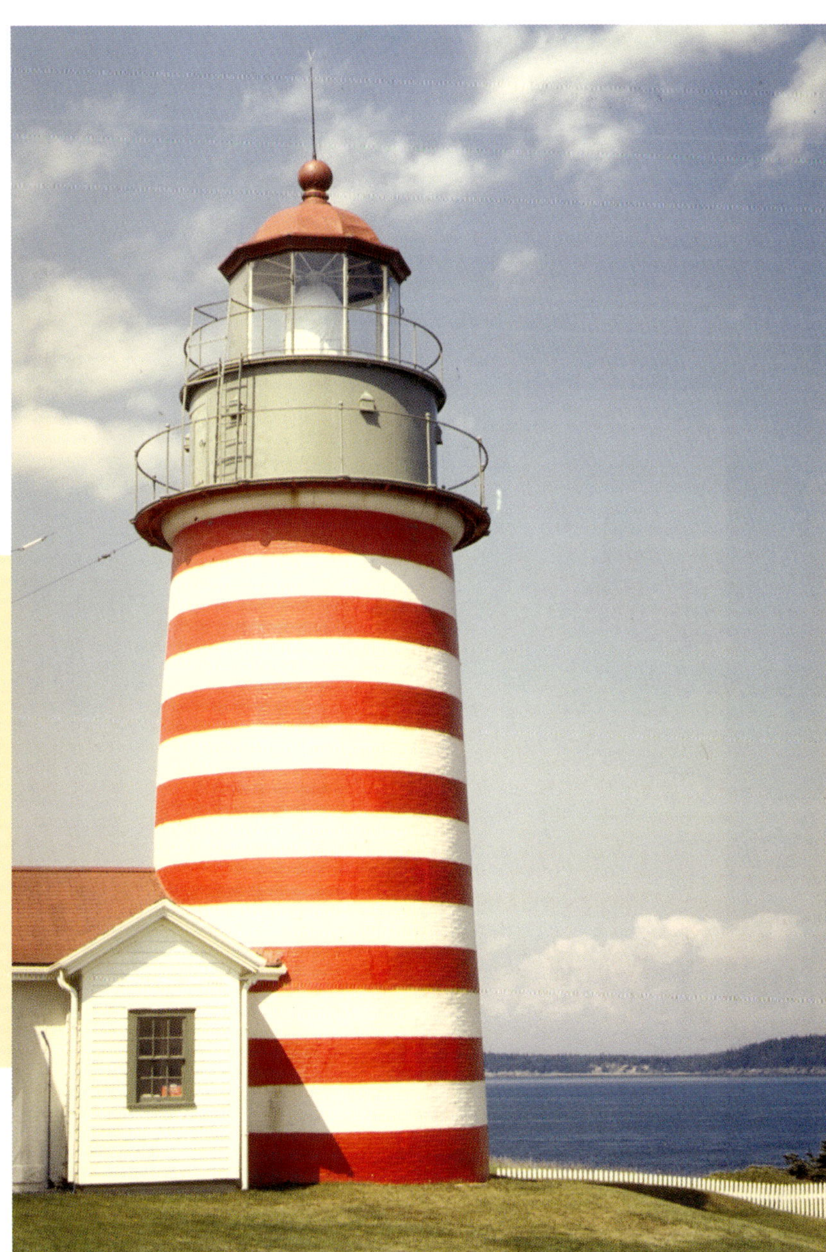

"The spectacle of the sky moves me. I feel emotional when I see, in an immense sky, a crescent moon or the sun. On the other hand, in my paintings there are very small shapes in great empty spaces. The empty spaces, the empty plains, everything in its nakedness impresses me very much."
Joan Miró,
Interview with Yvon Taillanier for
XX siècle, 1959.

70

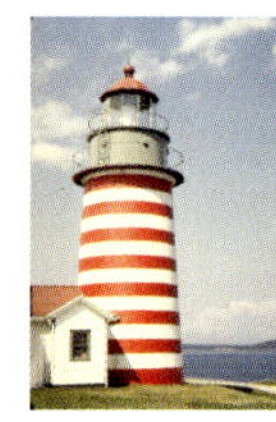

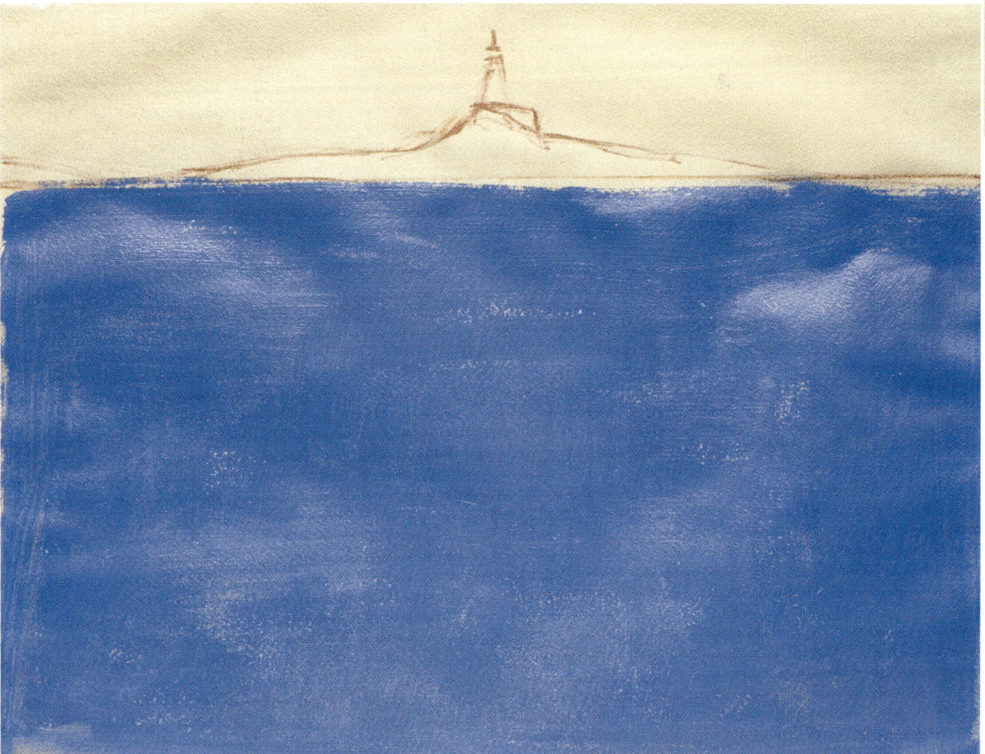

1 The first decision that must be made about this work is the choice of format. In this case it will be horizontal but nearly square to enhance the planes. The second very basic decision is to situate the horizon line; here it is high to raise the point of view and to show the immensity of the sea. The third is about the size and position of the lighthouse, which will be very far away, small, and, logically, on the coast as it would be seen by a sailor returning home. We draw this compositional structure with a fine round brush over a brushstroke of cream-color paint.

2 The sea is the true subject. We paint the entire plane blue with a wide brush. We notice how the high point of view, deduced from the location of the horizon line on the paper, indicates that this is the view a sailor would see, whether traveling in a large ship or holding the rudder of a sailboat.

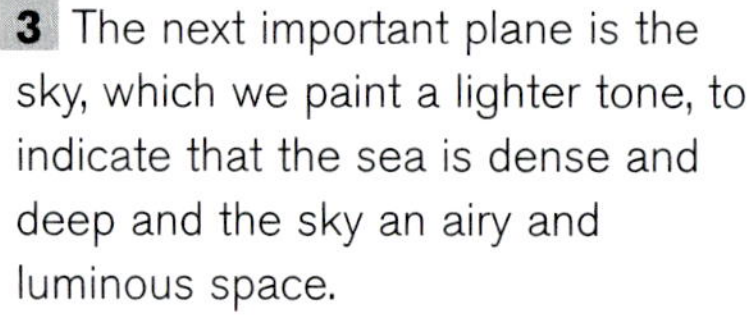

3 The next important plane is the sky, which we paint a lighter tone, to indicate that the sea is dense and deep and the sky an airy and luminous space.

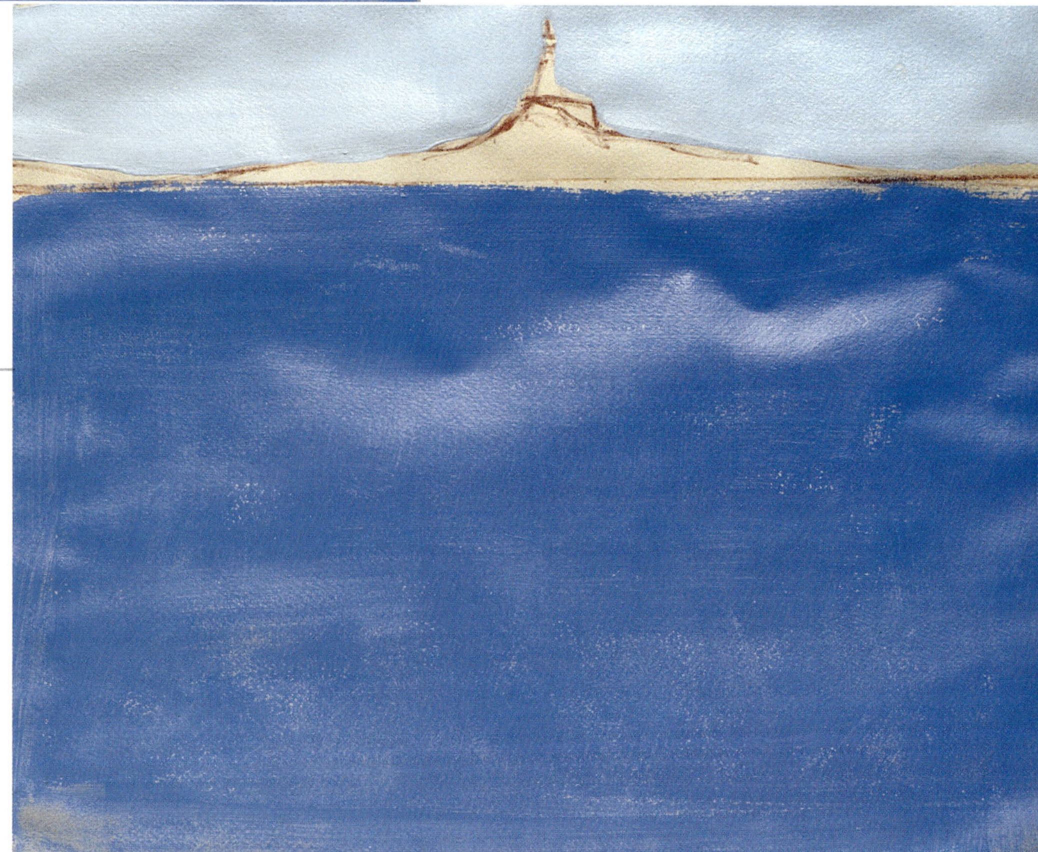

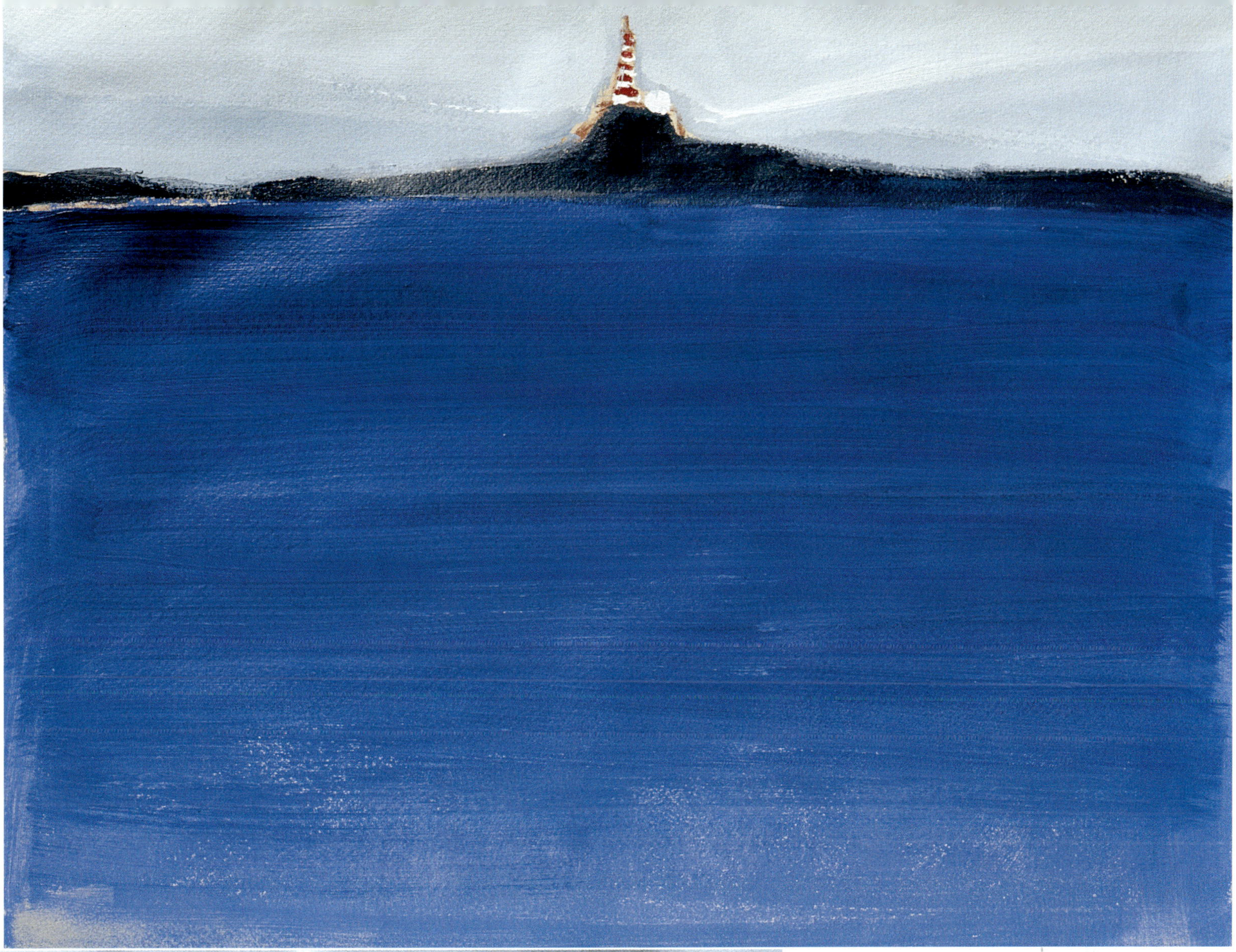

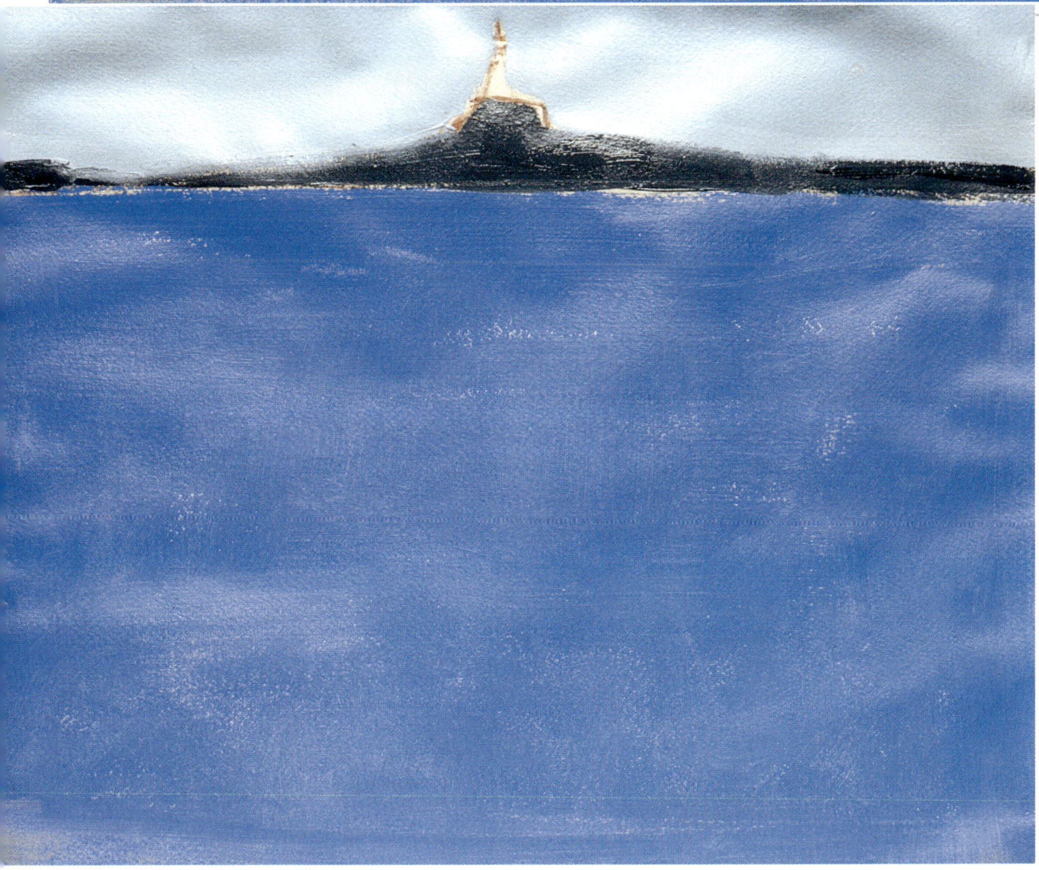

4 Next, we define the coastline, much darker with the same bluish tones to give it the same spatial effect and for the atmospheric effect of distance. The darkness is used to define the corporeal limit between the sky and the sea, and adds a solid base for the lighthouse in the center as the view of the fictional sailor, the viewer of the painting.

5 To finish the painting we lightly blend the ultramarine blue of the water with a new layer over it that becomes diluted as it moves toward the bottom of the plane. We also define the lighthouse in the distance and add some light luminous blue lines in the sky to direct the viewer's eye toward the lighthouse as the destination of this journey.

72

Gallery

Other Versions

The painting can change radically according to the compositional placement of the lighthouse and the height of the horizon, as you will see in this gallery. In addition, if we change the size of the lighthouse, we add new messages, because this will indicate how far away we are from the coast.

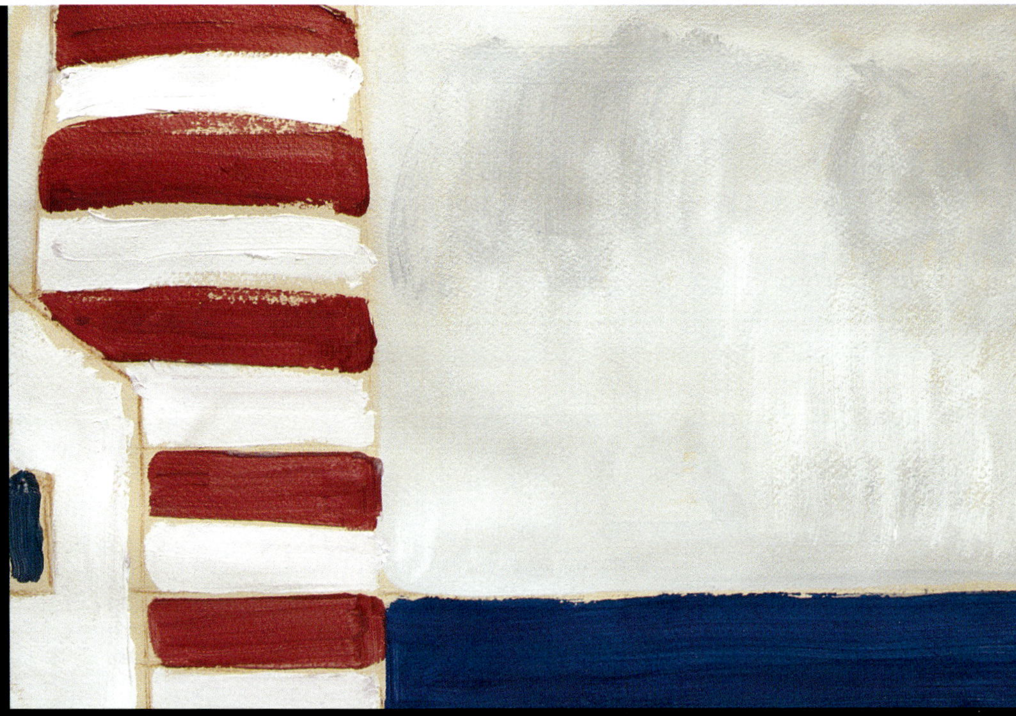

In this composition the viewer has a sense of practically standing on the coastline next to the lighthouse, which is on one side and makes us feel safe and secure before the sea spreading before us.

This work is very similar to the one we saw in the step-by-step process, but with a fundamental difference: the lighthouse is on the bottom edge of the painting. This position creates a sense of height, but it also adds distance with respect to the sea because the lighthouse is so small.

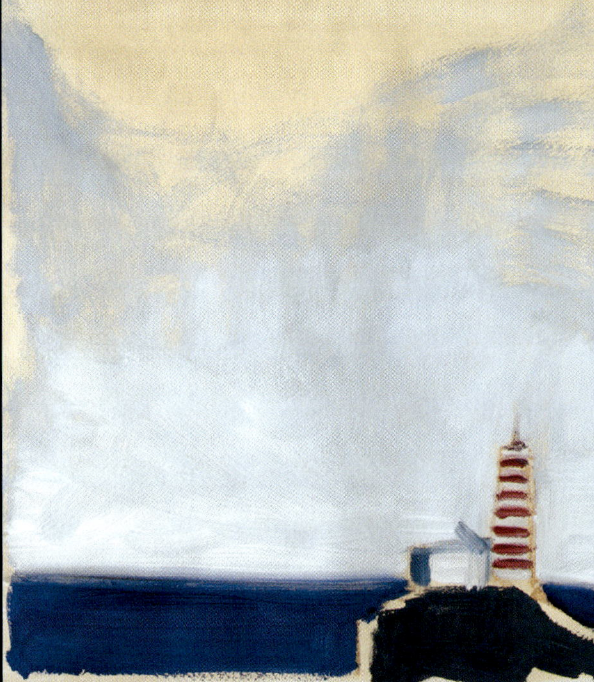

This panorama shows an open sky. The horizon line is low, placing us at the height of a passerby. There is space between us and the lighthouse, which is in the middle distance because of its size and its isolation on a hill.

This unique composition accentuates the horizontality of the horizon. Here the subject is the spatial limit that separates and at the same time connects the sky and the sea. The horizon is a visual metaphor of utopia, of something unreachable, but also of hope and that which encourages us to move forward.

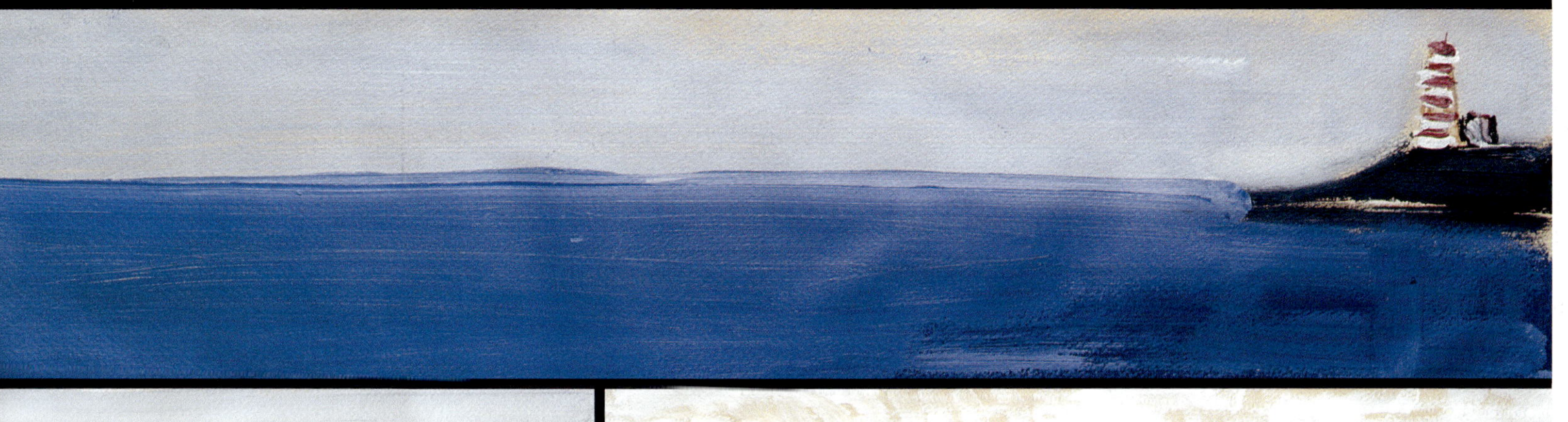

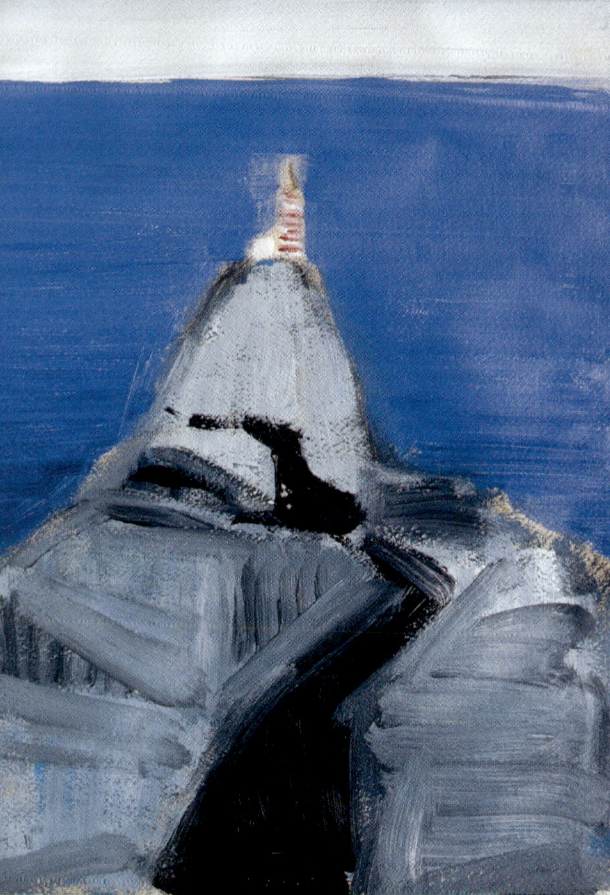

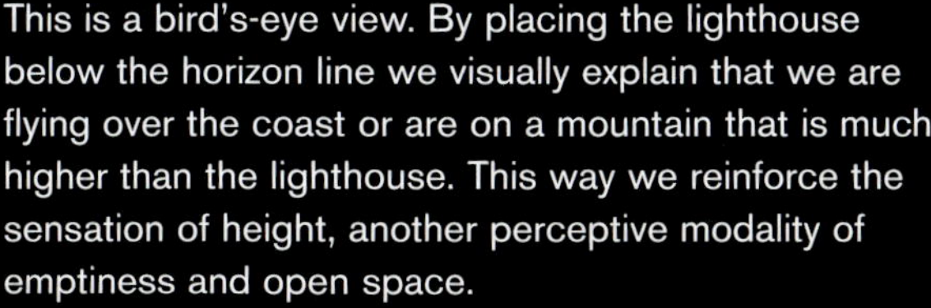

This is a bird's-eye view. By placing the lighthouse below the horizon line we visually explain that we are flying over the coast or are on a mountain that is much higher than the lighthouse. This way we reinforce the sensation of height, another perceptive modality of emptiness and open space.

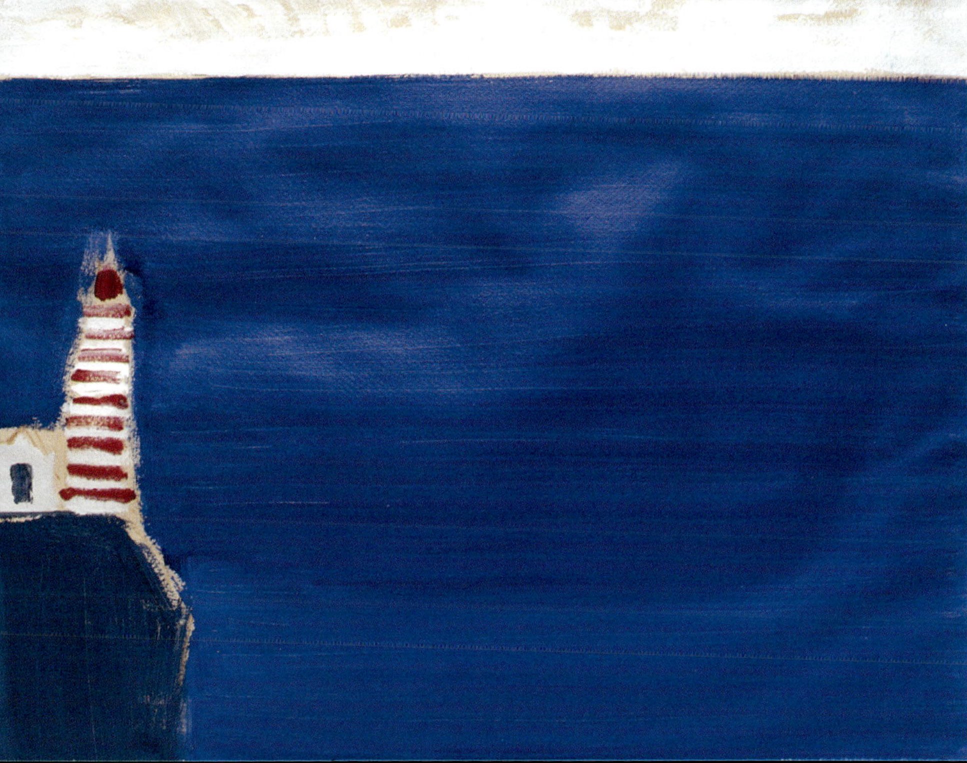

The precipice opening up below the lighthouse, on one side of the composition, is reminiscent of some paintings by Friedrich. This image associated with the abyss produces a feeling of wide-open space, but also uneasiness and danger because of the risk of a fall.

Window

New Approaches

Other Models

Following the same creative method of combining a real object with invented spaces, we have here a similar subject in the hot-air balloons. They are very expressive when it comes to open spaces, flight, horizons, bird's-eye views, etc. This time we place ourselves, as spectators, inside a third balloon from which we can see a magnificent panoramic landscape.

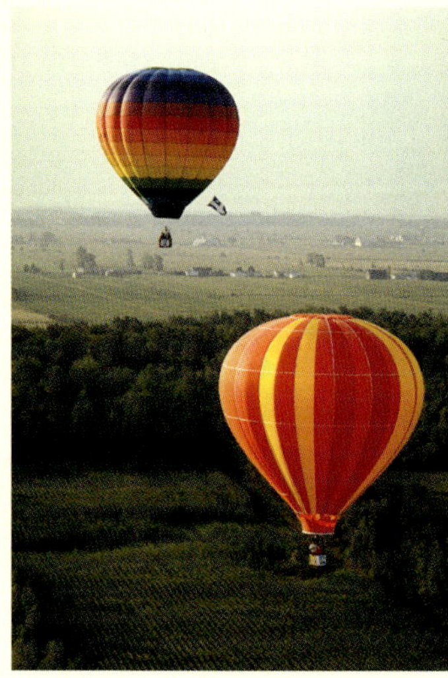

Other Media

Here we see two watercolors made as additional options for experimenting with more watery results. Both compositions have the same structure, a high horizon and a centered lighthouse in the distance. One of them brings the sea to our feet, changing the sizes of the waves, whereas the other is more uniform; but both carry us across a lively and open sea.

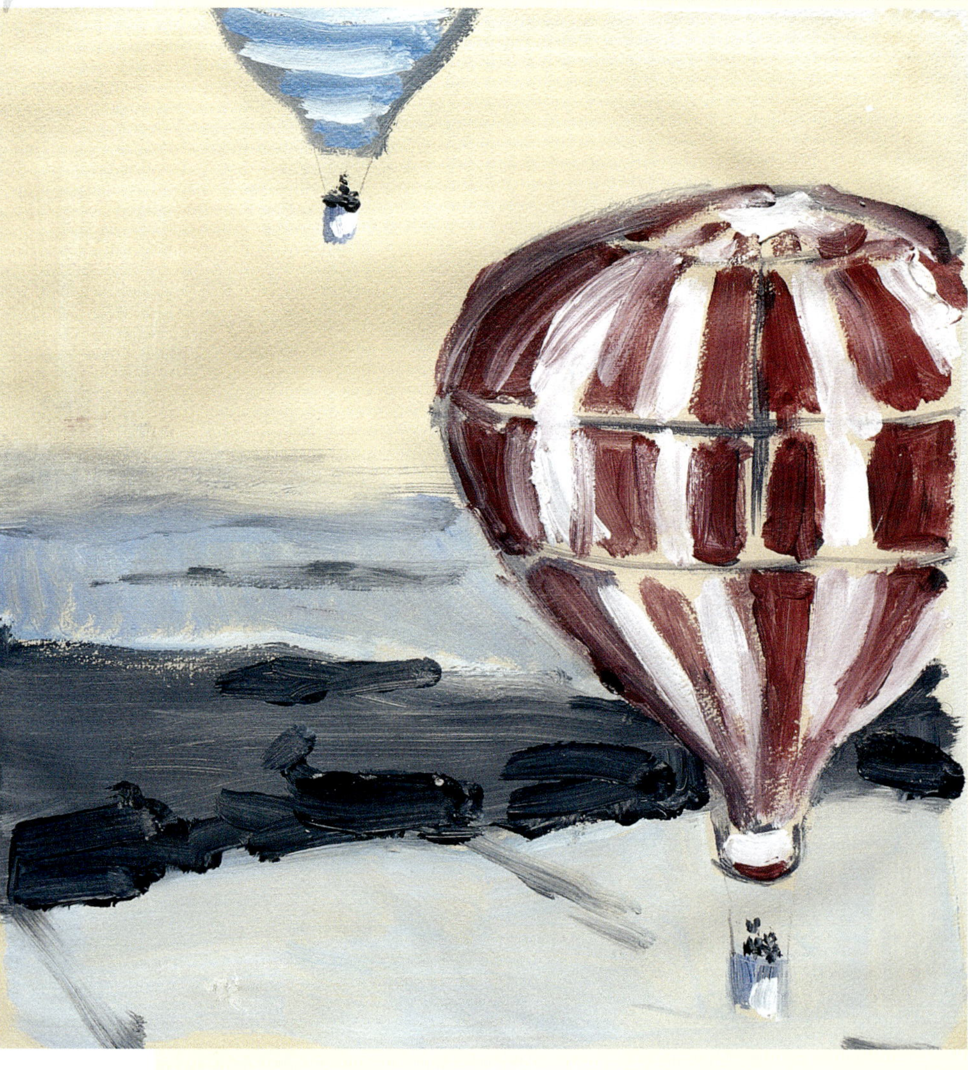

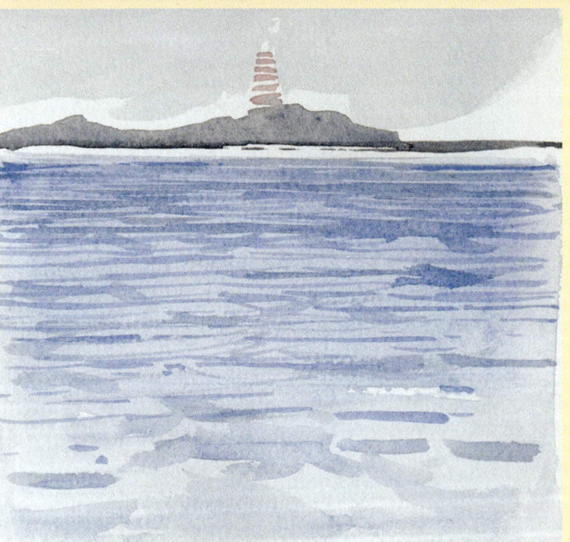

Other Views

Many artists have painted empty spaces. Giovanni Fattori (1825–1908), in the last years of his life, took on the theme of man before the vast sea that his predecessor Friedrich explored eighty years before, but this time from a perspective that was more realistic than romantic. Gerard Richter (born in 1932) is one of the principal contemporary painters. His figurative work has a very strong atmospheric feeling created through the *sfumatto* technique. In them the image is out of focus to leave room for what it conveys, for its intangible and spiritual content, not what is described but what is sensed. The landscape is perceived as a momentary perception of the self.

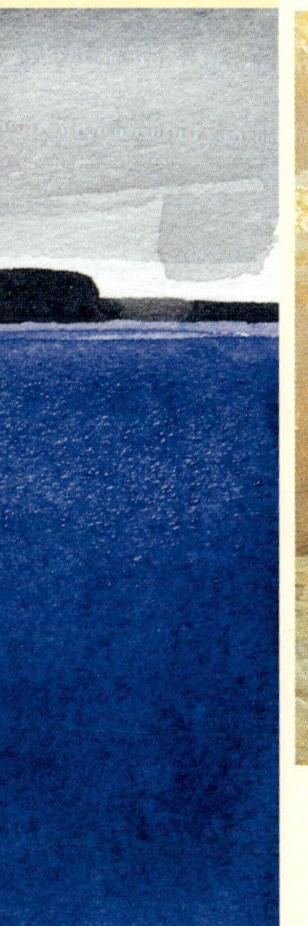

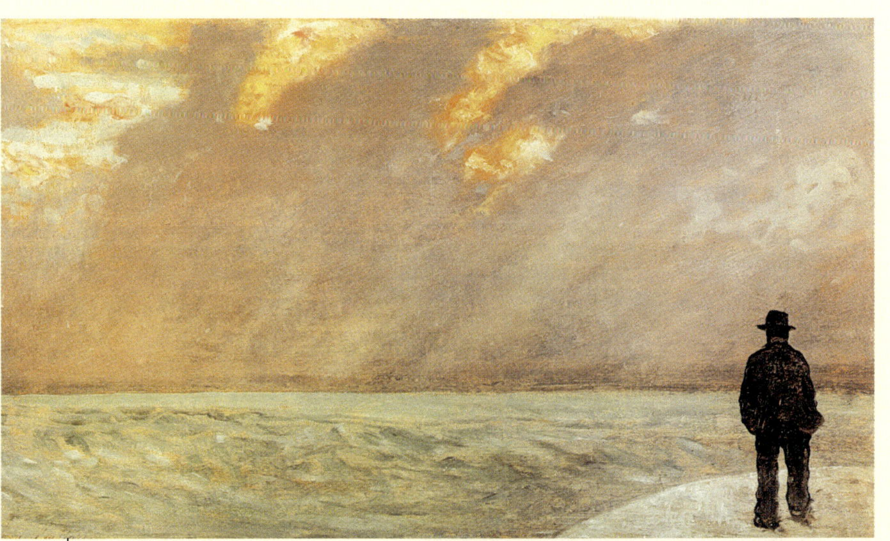

Giovanni Fattori,
Seascape at Dusk,
1890–1895. Gallery of
Modern Art, Florence, Italy.

Gerard Richter,
Bridge, 1969.
Private Collection.

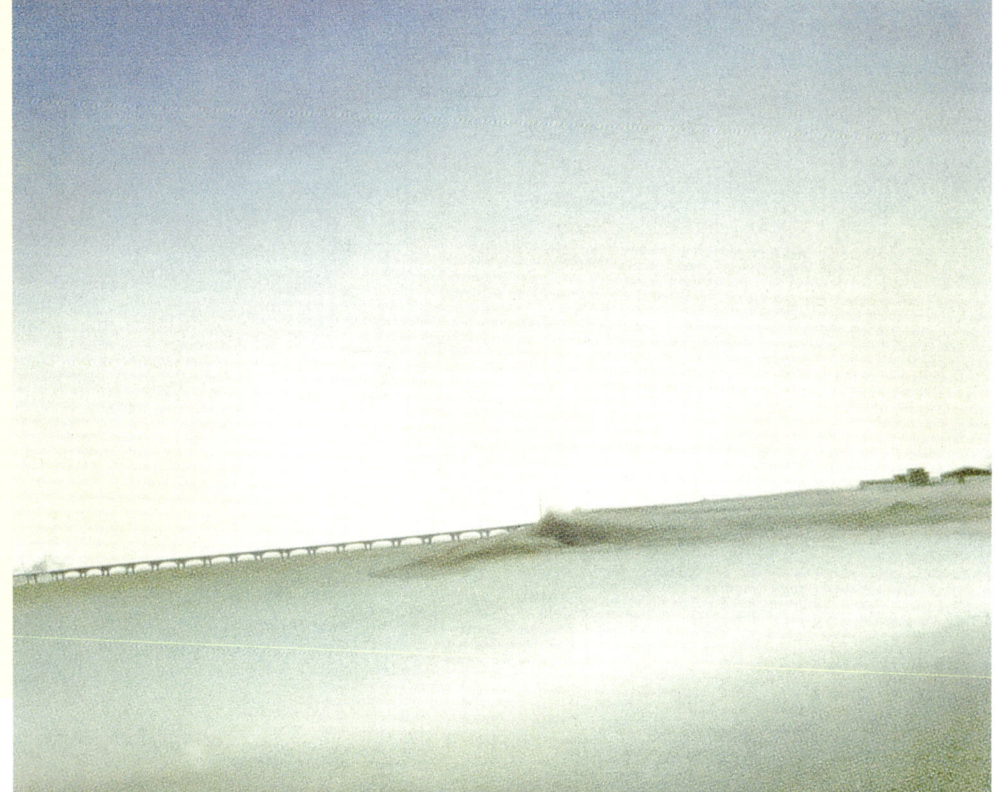

Anselm Kiefer (born in 1945) presents a body of work with a high philosophical and spiritual content. Kiefer reflects on humankind, focusing on his identity as a German and on the history of his country. To achieve that, he approaches space from two angles: on one hand, the physical or real space of the painting, always choosing formats of large dimensions, and on the other, the figurative or represented space with exaggerated vanishing points that place the viewer in front of a desolate and isolated landscape. He presents to us the history of his country, stigmatized by pain, through very large textured, rugged, and imperfect landscapes. The facts are etched in the landscape as if they were the scars on a human body, the words as tattoos, data in a memory that cannot be erased: in *The Mountain of the March*, they refer to the region of Brandenburg and to the title of a song that became a hymn in Hitler's army.

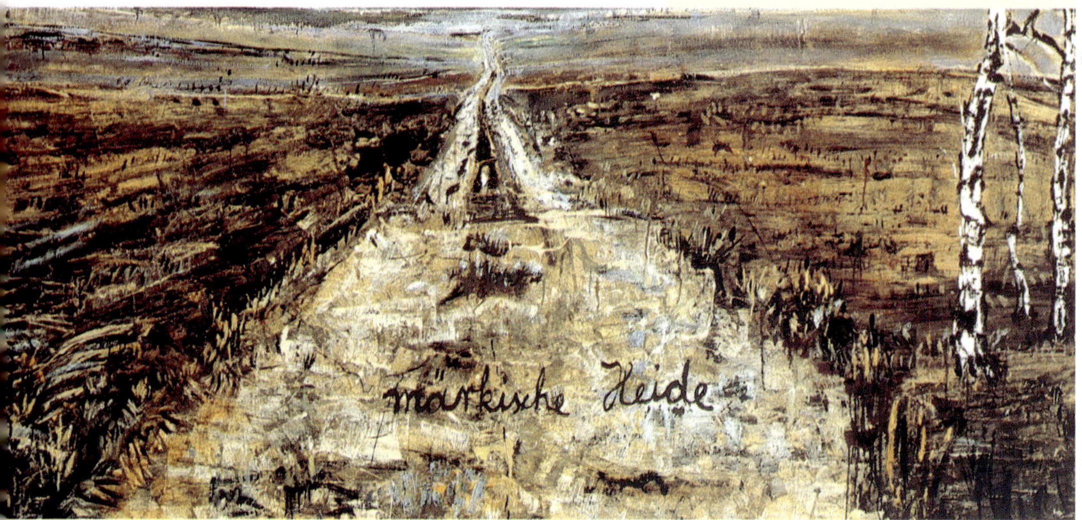

Anselm Kiefer,
The Mountain of the March, 1974.
Van Abbemuseum,
Eindhoven, The Netherlands.

One-Point Perspective: Variations in the Horizon Line and a Highway's Vanishing Point

In this approach, Gemma Guasch has chosen a road to develop a basic aspect of space: one-point (or parallel) conical perspective. It focuses on the attraction produced by the central vanishing point on the ground (road) and the sky (clouds). The two elements converge at a single vanishing point in the center, thus intensifying the feeling of spatial depth. She chose chalk, in earth and sanguine tones, contrasted with black and white. Because they have more agglutinant, they make the work easier because they do not break easily and because they provide an appealing painterly character.

"The horizontal line is the line of the home town, the line of the prairie; to contrast with that an elevation of a few inches acquires a tremendous force."
Frank Lloyd Wright

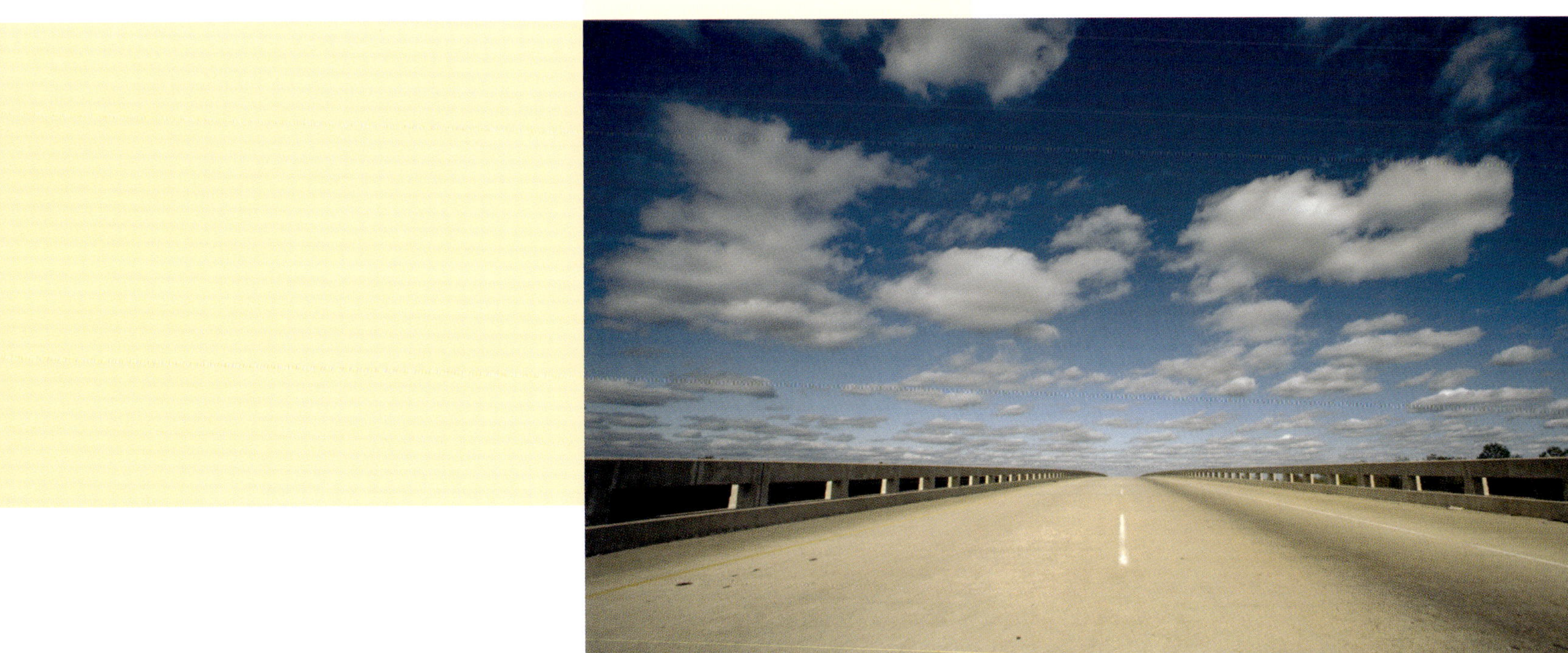

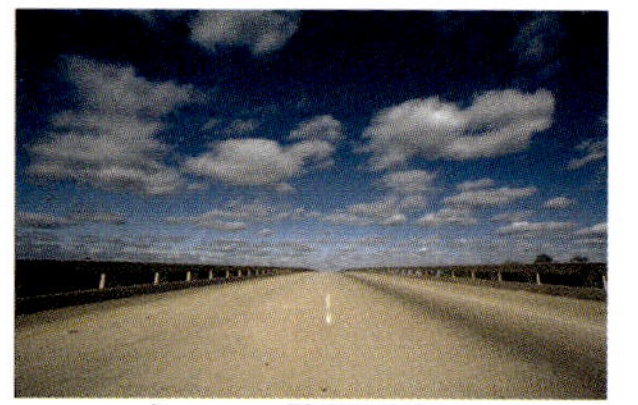

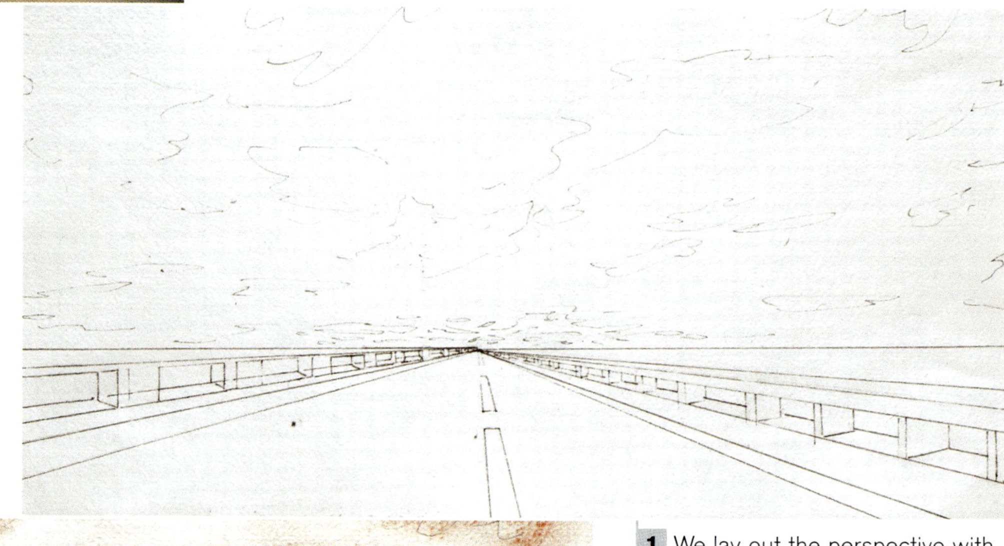

1 We lay out the perspective with a fine-tip marker: the position of the horizon line and the vanishing point, paying special attention to the line of the rail and to the position of the fan-shaped clouds. In this work, it is very important to devote time and attention to the initial development because any error in the perspective drawing will produce a series of errors that will be difficult to correct. You can also approach this work with a pencil.

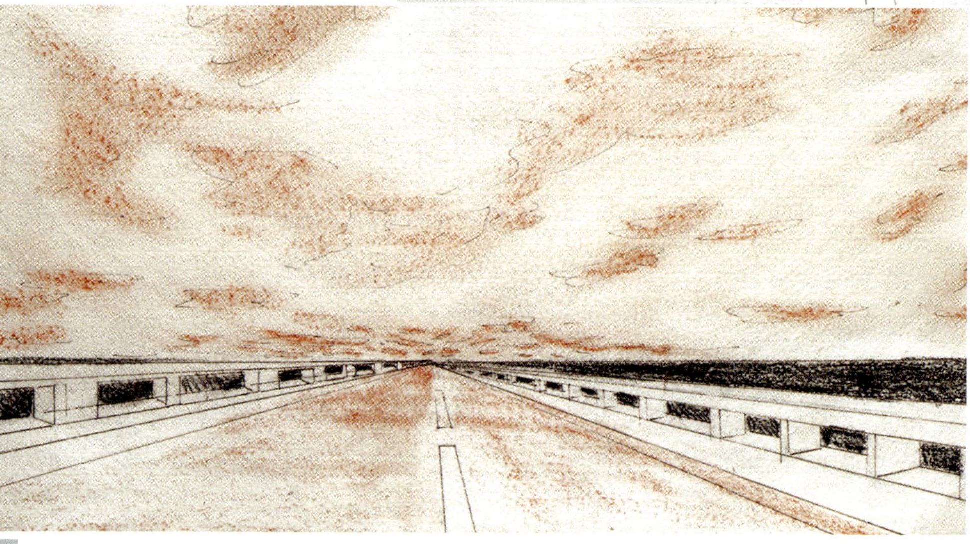

2 We direct the eye of the viewer to the center by strongly emphasizing the central vanishing point and darkening the sides of the road with black. Then we smear the sky and the road with sanguine. This airy approach contrasts with the straight and horizontal lines used to represent the asphalt.

3 We vigorously apply the sanguine to the rail alongside the road, emphasizing only the vertical lines, which stand out strongly against basically horizontal work. We also increase the feeling of spatial depth by intensifying the reddish tone of the road's central lines.

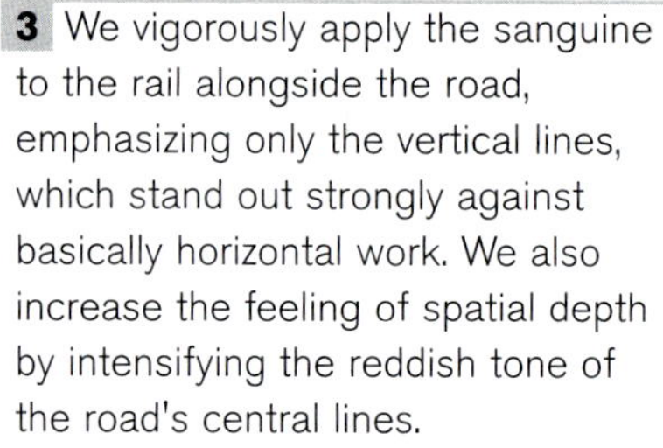

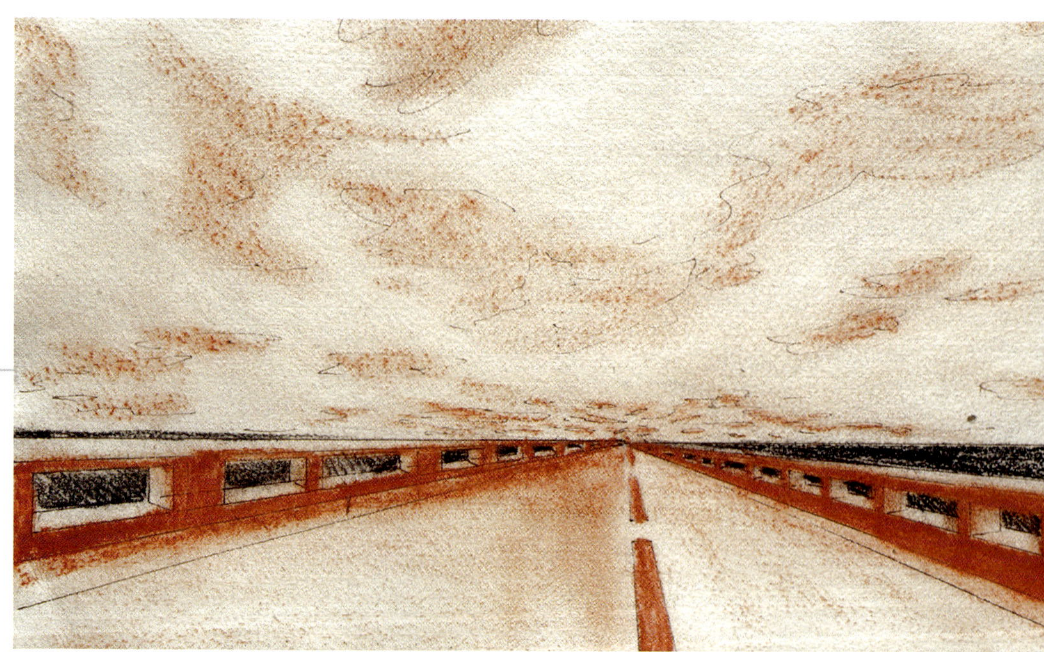

5 Finally, we add the highlights. We use the eraser to draw lines, as if it were a piece of chalk, on the horizontal areas of the rail. We also rub it gently on the asphalt of the road to diffuse and soften the contrast.

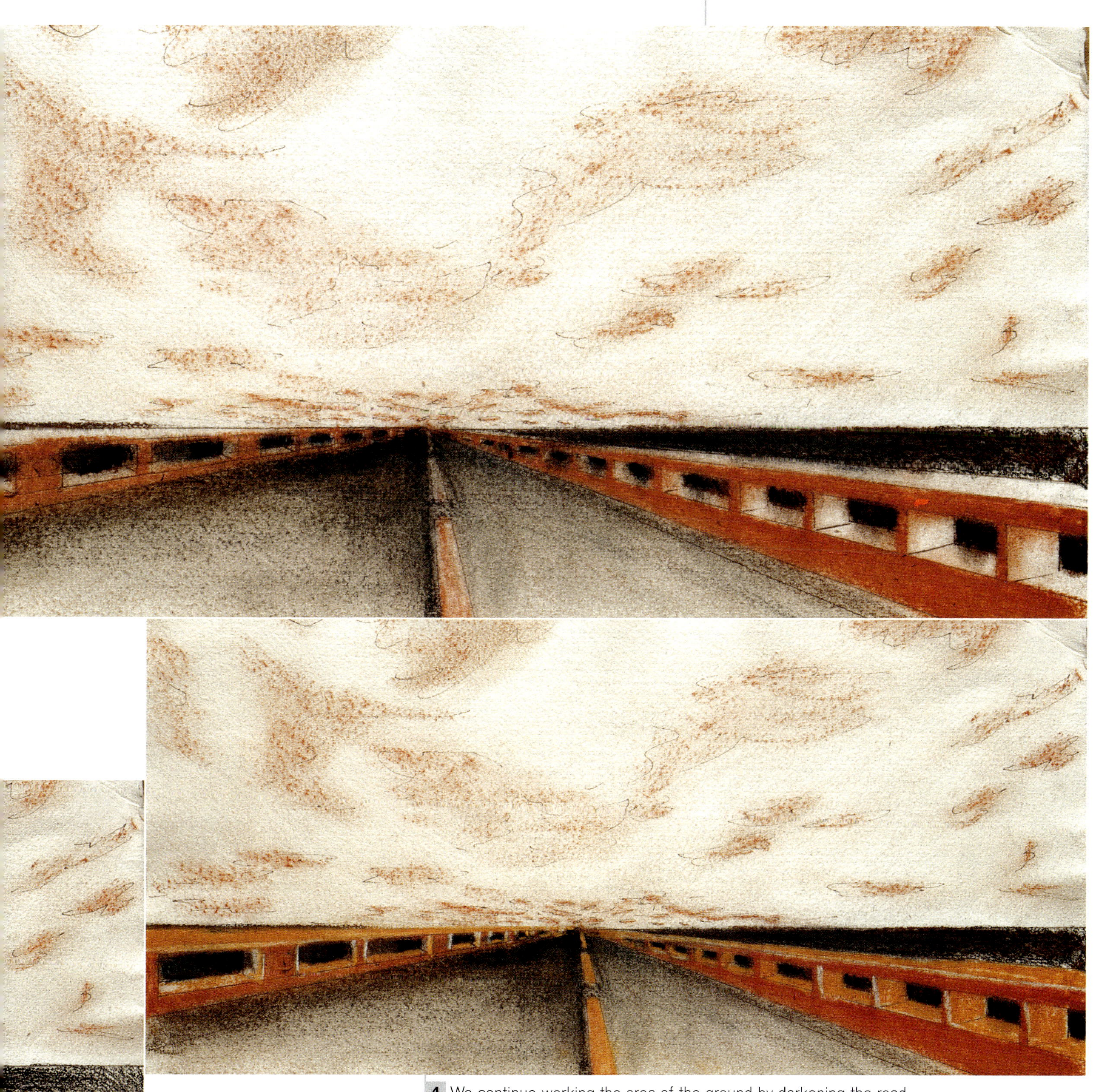

4 We continue working the area of the ground by darkening the road progressively toward the horizon and leaving the gray and white tones for the foreground. We emphasize the contrast by darkening the sides of the road with black, and we define the horizontal lines of the railing. All of this reinforces the contrast while increasing the feeling of hardness and spatial coldness, typical of the chosen subject.

The array of possibilities offered by perspective is without a doubt very interesting. In this case a one-point or parallel perspective has been used, but the same result could be achieved with two-point perspective. These are done by changing two aspects that are very characteristic of perspective: the horizon line and the position of the vanishing point.

In this work we have raised the horizon line considerably, which provides an almost bird's-eye view. The vanishing point is in the center of the image. The narrowness of the road and the tones chosen, browns and blacks, reinforce the feeling of spatial distance and intensify the steep view.

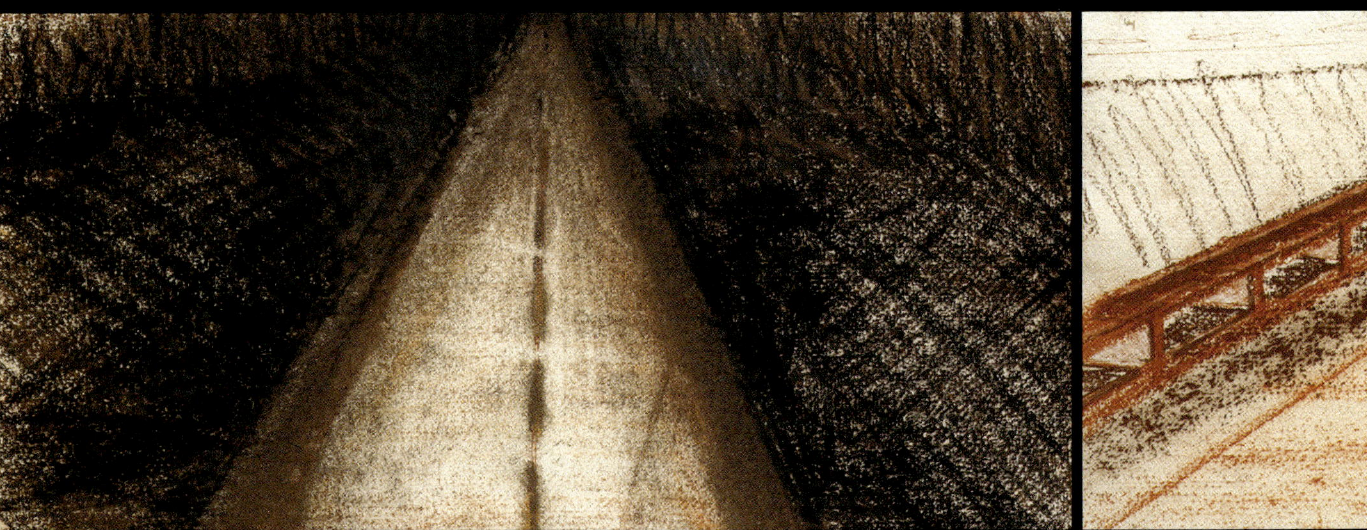

This perspective has a very low point of view, almost at the edge of the bottom of the frame; the intention is for the sky to become the center of attention. The road makes a timid appearance; it has been evenly worked with reddish tones, and the ground with brown tones. Everything reinforces the spatial idea of immensity and emptiness when we focus our gaze on the sky.

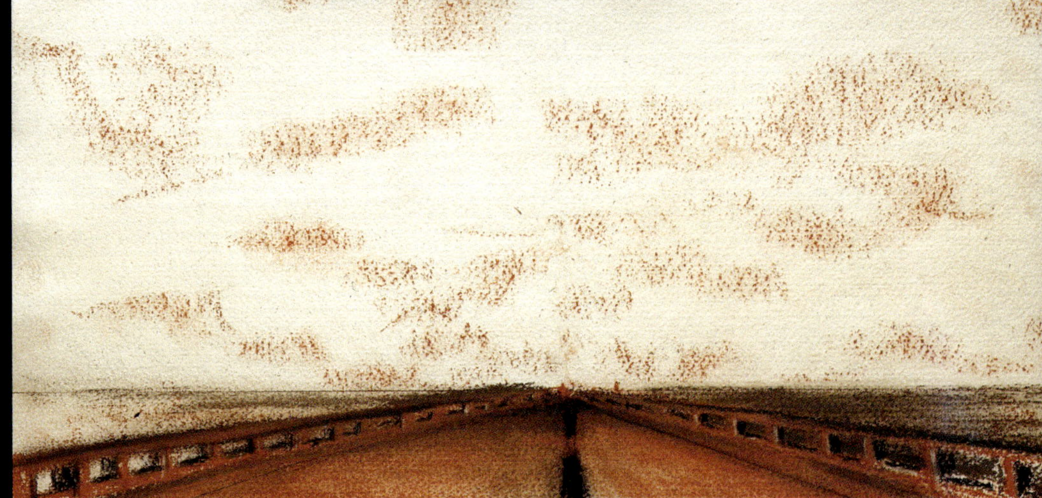

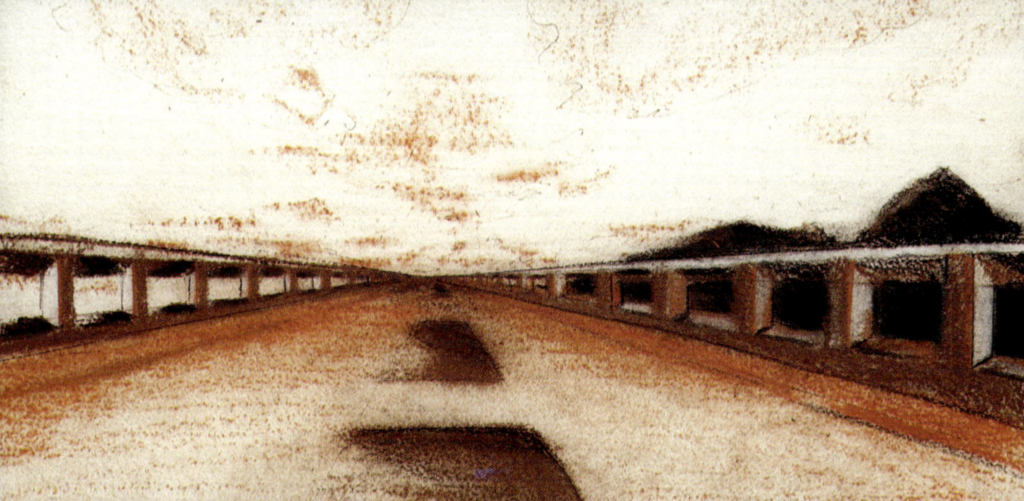

The horizon line is in the center of the paper, originating a composition of two triangles: the sky and the ground. The railing acquires more importance as a result of its drawing and its treatment. The use of dark brown, red, and white tones applied with contrasting effects helps reinforce the perspective of the railing. On the right side of the image we draw the treetops in black tones to indicate a high point of view, which lets us see the landscape above the railing.

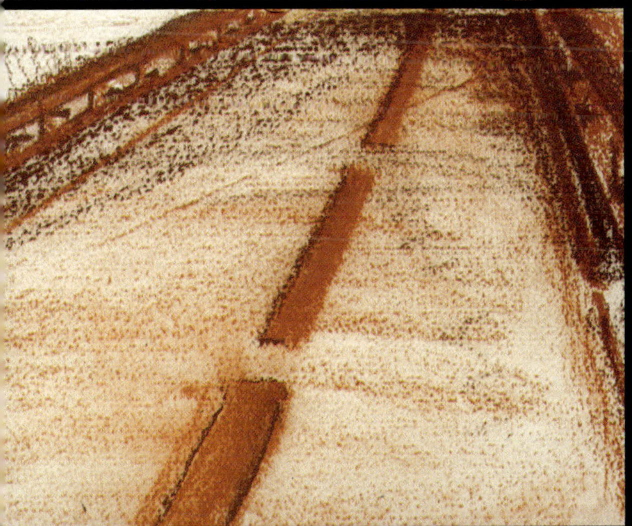

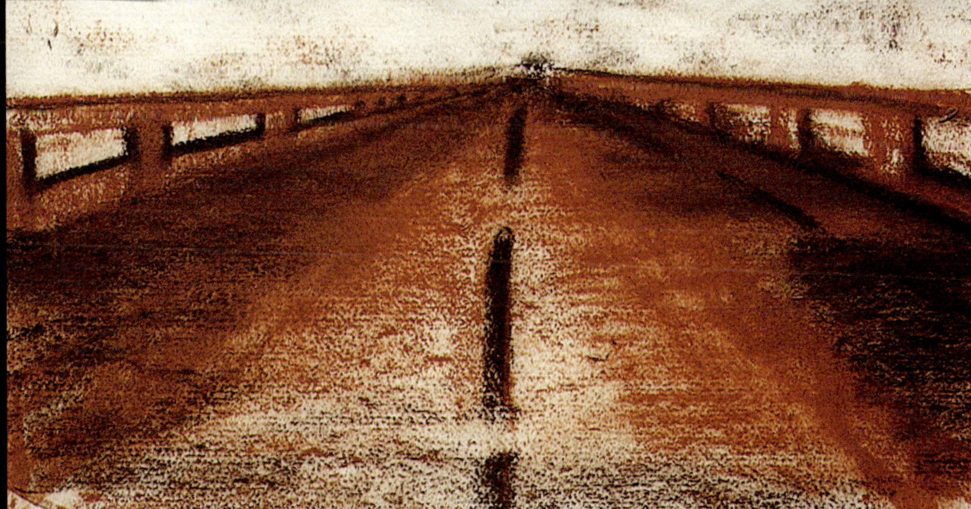

Here the vanishing point is displaced toward the right of the image, and the lines of perspective open generously on the left side, which spatially brings us to a very close and dynamic view of the road. We have sacrificed the sky completely to give maximum importance to the view of the terrain. We work loosely, only with sanguine and dark brown, in a fresh and direct manner. The result evokes speed and dynamism.

With the horizon line in the upper part of the support and the centered vanishing point, we have created a static, symmetrical, and balanced composition. The distribution of the tones reinforces the symmetry, applied very equally on both sides of the image. The view of the sky is almost an afterthought, and the spatial effect is achieved by the ground-level view.

Other Models

Many landscapes offer suggestive spaces through the use of linear perspective. As an alternative model, a field of tulips showing a high horizon line and a vanishing point toward the right of the paper has been chosen. These factors provoke, on one hand, a great aerial view of the field, and on the other, a dynamic and lively spatial feeling. The tulips break the horizontal feeling and force us to work with multiple vertical features in a more spontaneous and less rigid manner than the road.

Other Media

This time acrylics have been chosen as the medium for painting the road. They are a wet medium that provides a very different look to the same model. The dark road contrasts with the light colors of the railing and the sky. It places the horizon line in the middle of the support and transfers the vanishing point to the left of the image. With the vanishing point of the road toward the left, this acrylic provides a wide and pleasant spatial view.

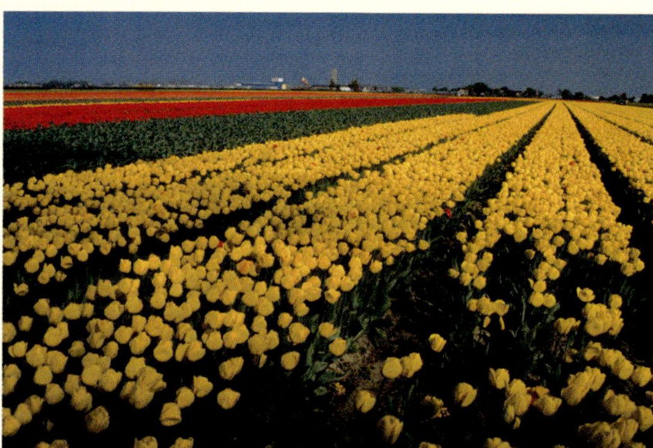

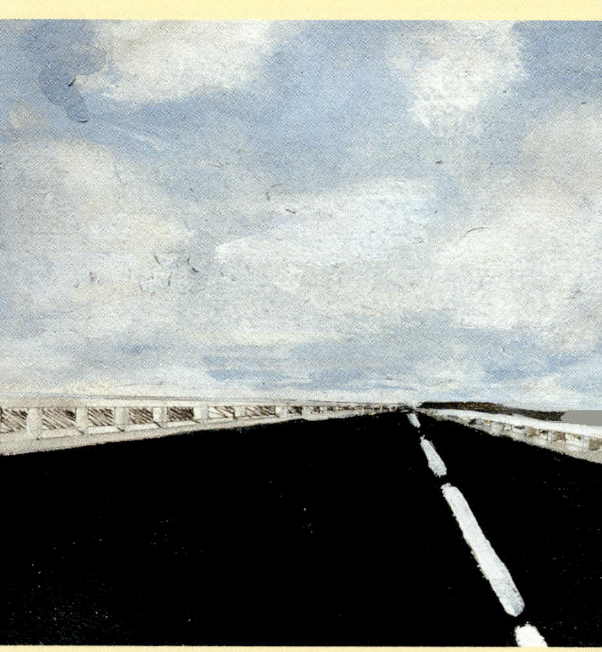

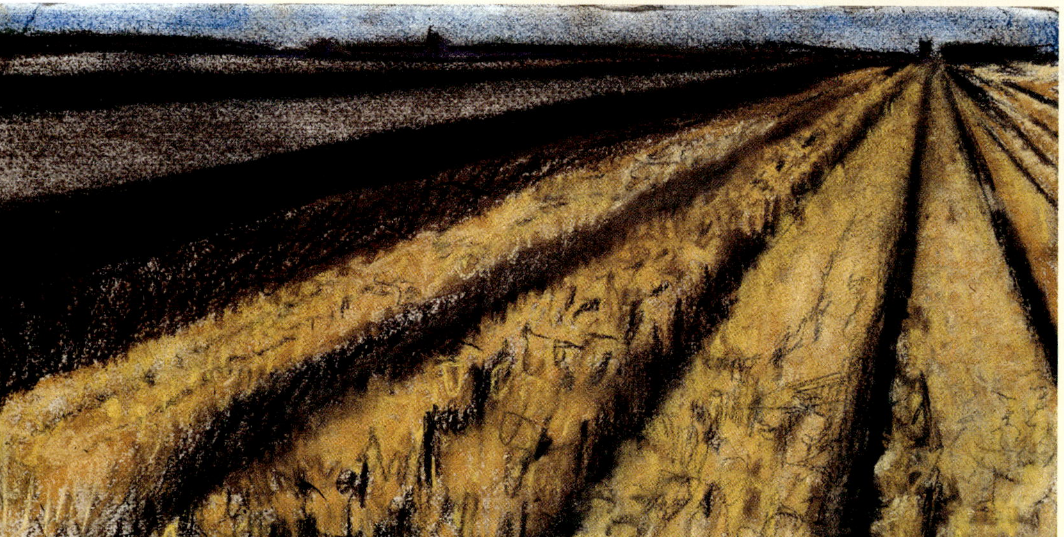

Other Views

Let's look at two very different views of a one-point perspective separated in time. Canaletto (1697–1768) very quickly acquired fame as a perspective painter. He used an optical camera to create his paintings. With it he marked, in the initial phase of his work, the horizon line and the different vanishing points of the perspective. This method allowed him to modify the perspective by intensifying the spatial effects according to the effects he wanted to achieve. In a second phase he studied the behavior of light, applying a liquid and transparent paint on the canvas to produce clear tones in open spaces. Nicolás de Stael (1914–1955) is known as the painter of absence. In landscapes such as the one shown here, the blocks of color indicate the distance between things. Those blocks acquire an abrupt sweetness and convey an impression of great uncertainty, the impression that everything will change suddenly and that it will be imbued with pain.

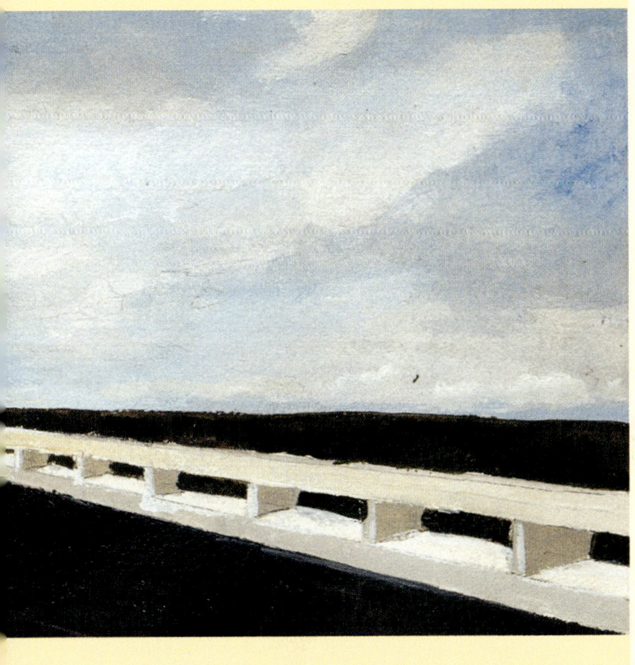

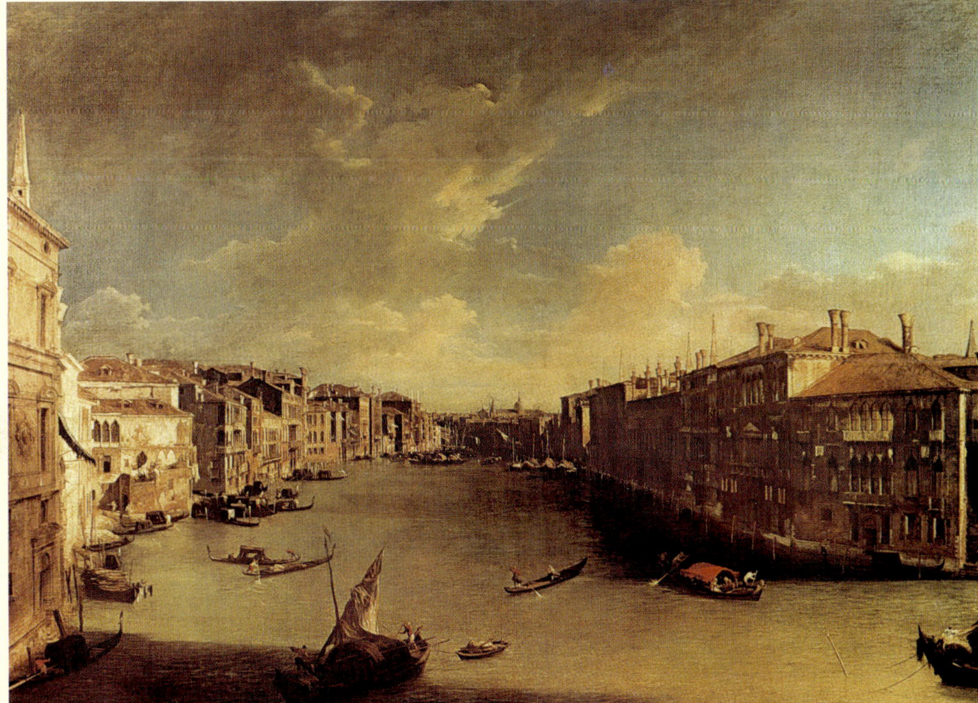

Canaletto,
The Great Canal Near the Rialto Bridge,
c. 1723.
Private Collection.

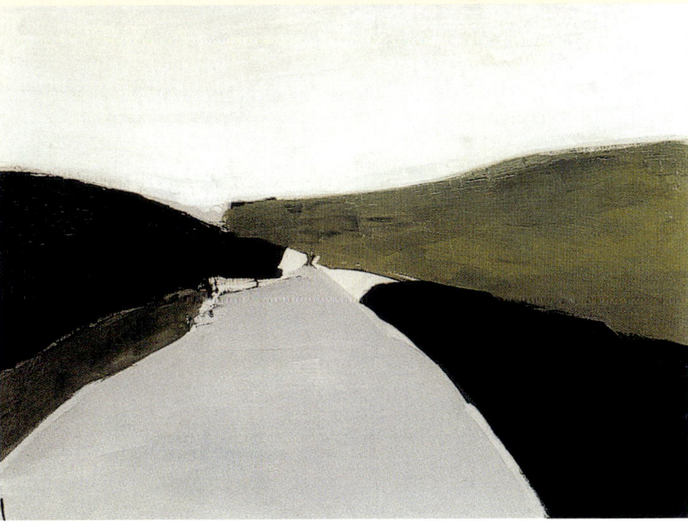

Nicolás de Stael,
The Road of Uzès, 1954.
Private Collection.

Urban, Industrial, and Metropolitan Spaces

When Canaletto liberated the urban space from the role of stage set that it had been assigned since the Renaissance, a new landscape genre emerged that had total autonomy: the urban landscape. Edward Hopper (1882–1967), one of the greatest exponents of American realism, which dealt with the subject of civilization, developed his body of work along this line. For more than fifty years, until his death, he led a quiet life in his Manhattan studio or in his summer house, representing in his paintings the daily life of the average citizen. The house is the main theme in most of his work—views of the interior through a window or of the outside from a window. His urban landscapes, painted around 1920, such as *The City*, are cold spaces, sometimes even without people, that speak of loneliness and melancholy. In them is reflected the way of life of the people of his time, forced to abandon the fields as a result of the economic depression to begin life in the city.

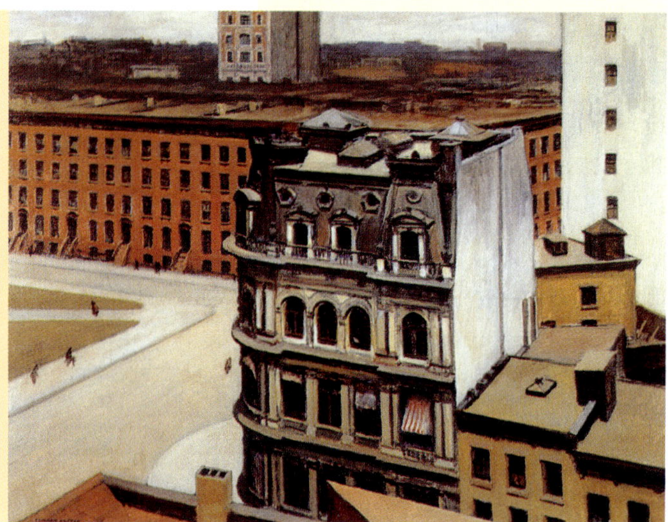

Edward Hopper,
The City, 1927.
University of Arizona Museum of Art,
Tucson, Arizona.

Oblique Perspective: The City from an Elevated Point of View

The approach that we offer in these pages is a study of the inherent spaces of our civilization: the city with its buildings, shops, parking lots, warehouses, and offices. For this, Josep Asunción placed himself in an elevated point of view that allows him to capture the maximum number of buildings organized along the city's grid of streets. The medium he chose was markers on paper. This is a very graphic medium that allows a variety of combinations of lines and areas of color of different thicknesses and widths. He places himself in a corner, resulting in an oblique perspective that promotes the use of diagonals, similar to Hopper's painting *The City*.

Space in the Landscape

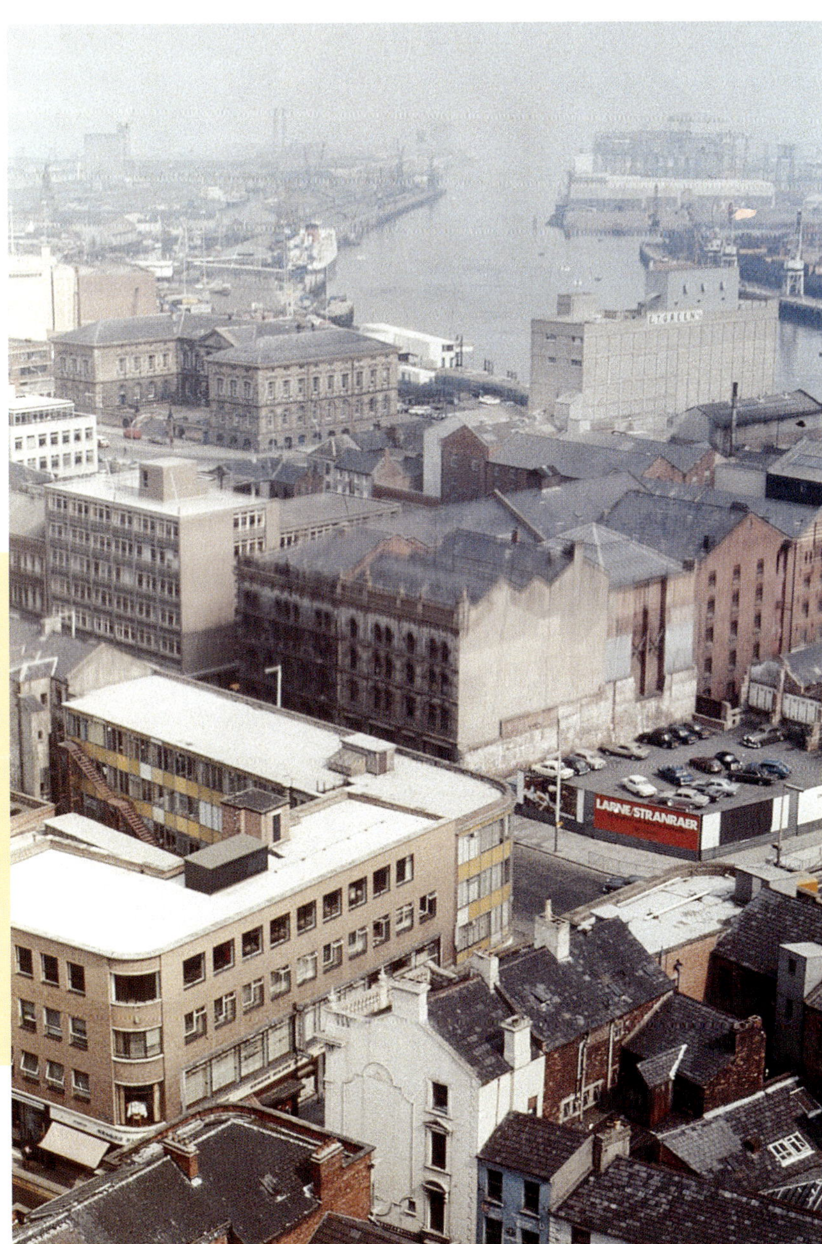

"*In the contemporary visual climate, I like the factories, the night lights, the world seen from an airplane. One of my life's greatest excitements was to fly over Washington at night.*"
Joan Miró,
Escritos y conversaciones
(Interview with Yvon Taillandier for
XX siècle), 1959.

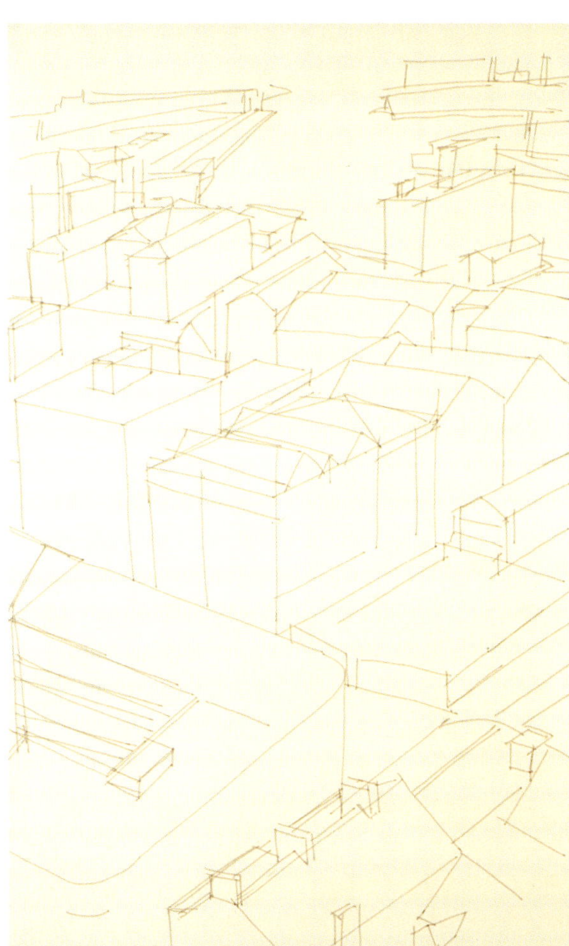

1 We center the scene within an elongated and vertical format to reinforce the bird's-eye view. The drawing is studied carefully, making sure that the vanishing points and the building arrangements are drawn correctly. This preliminary sketch is done freehand with a fine marker. You can also use a ruler if you do not feel confident making straight lines, although in this case some spontaneity will be lost.

2 The building in the foreground will have greater contrast and the ones in the background very little. This is why the shadow values are placed as follows: the dark sides of the first buildings with a very dark tone, and the intermediate sides with a medium tone, the same that will be used for the most distant buildings.

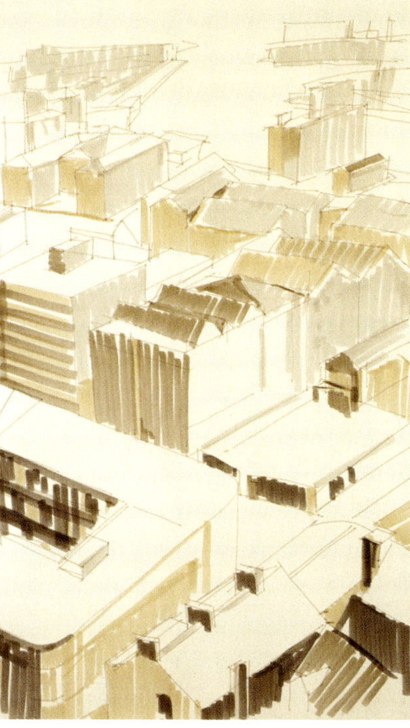

3 We continue working on the light and shadows. We apply a yellowish tone to the most illuminated areas to bathe the scene in a tinted light that will convey an atmospheric feeling, and a cool gray for the shadows to create thermal contrast. We also begin to define some architectural elements: cornices, roofs, and windows.

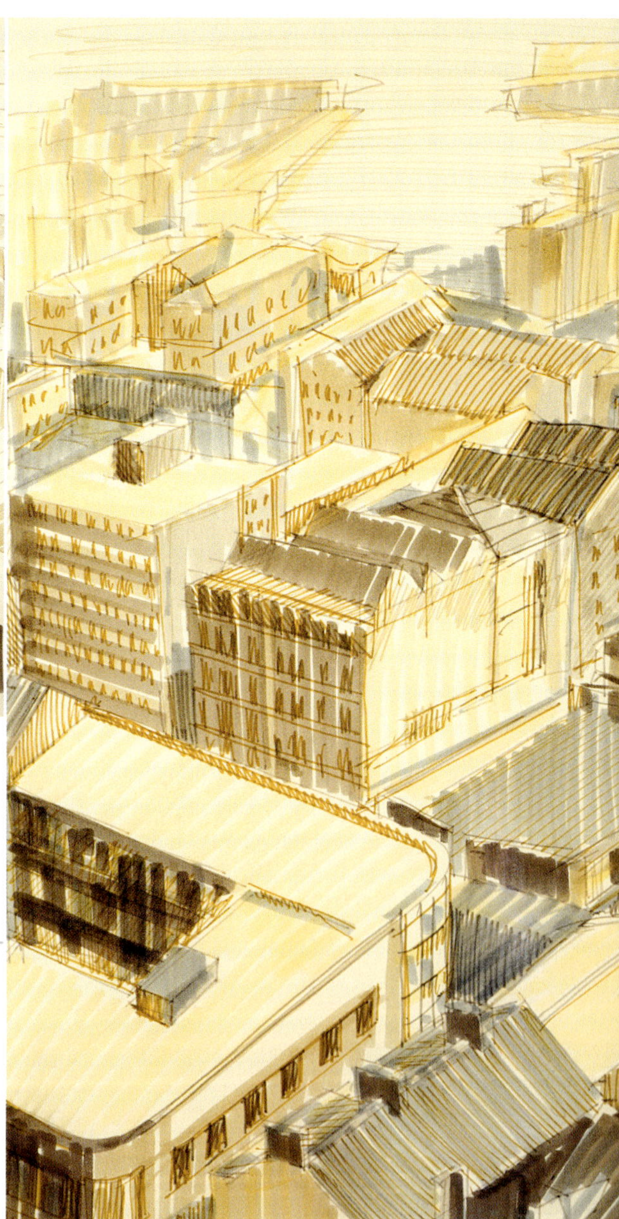

4 We continue defining the architecture and reinforcing the shadows with very dark grays, which are almost black in the closer areas and lighter in the more distant ones, avoiding too much contrast.

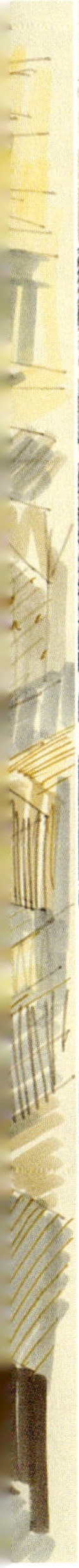

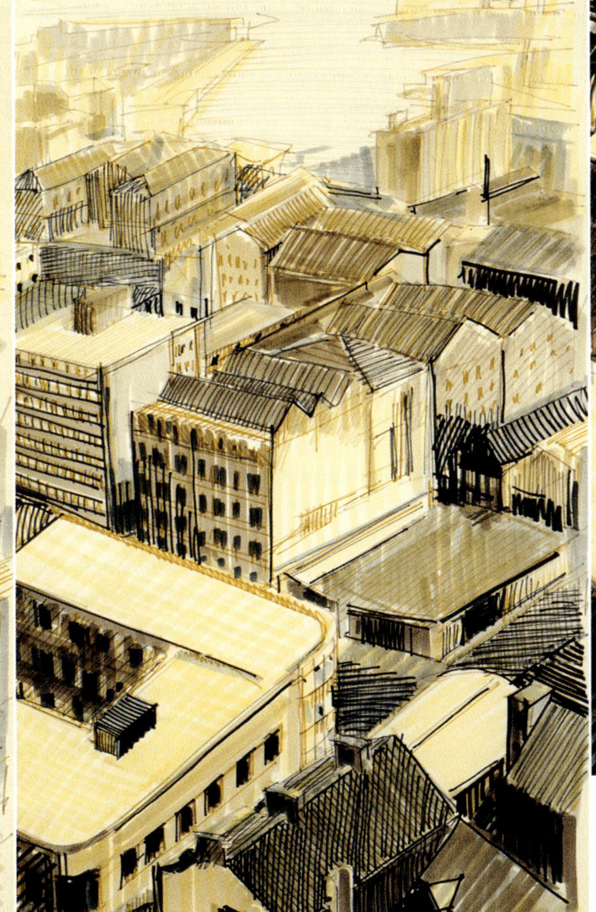

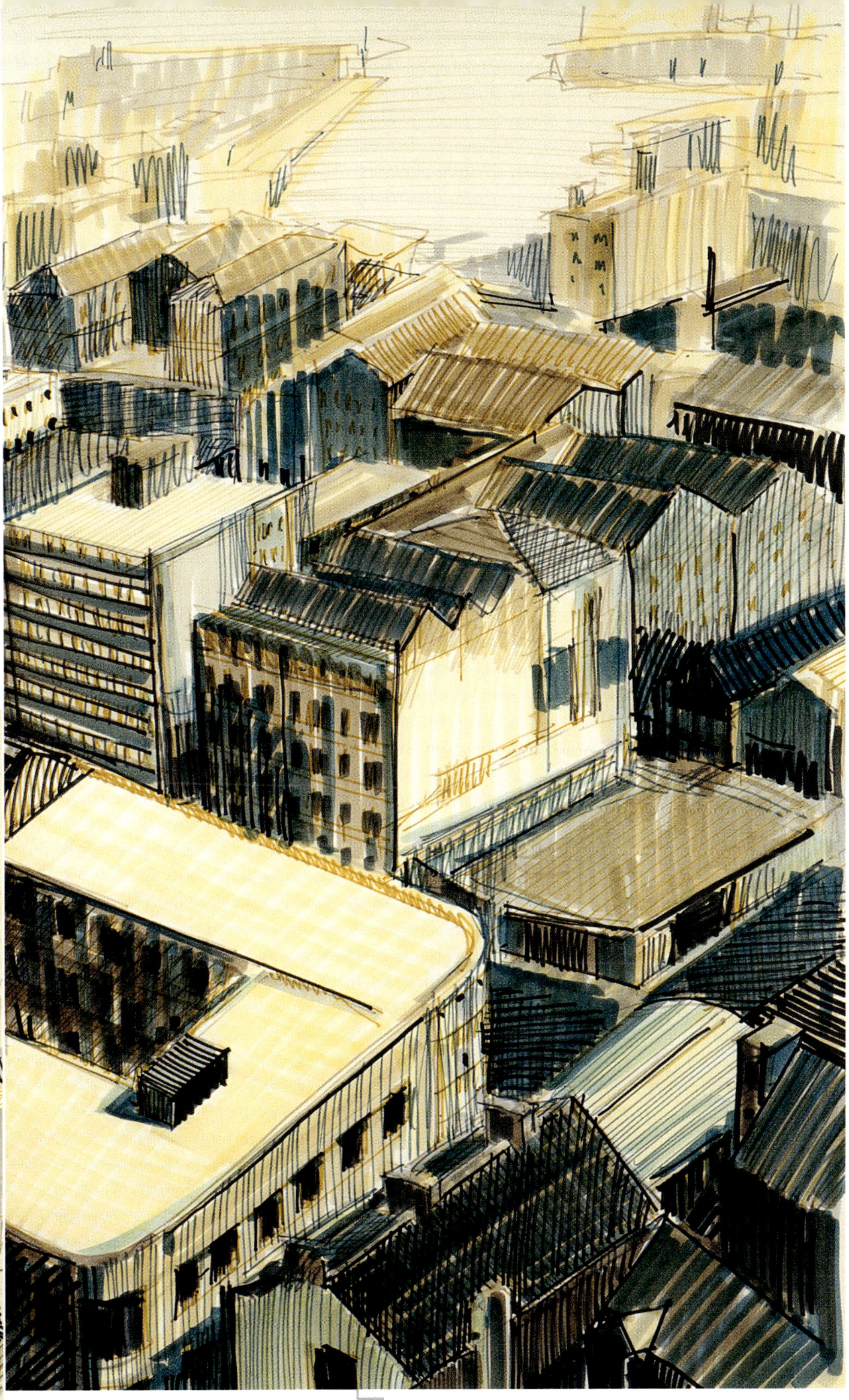

5 Finally, the lights and the details of the central and closer buildings are adjusted. Anything that is far away has little definition and little contrast; this is the key to making it appear distant. The blue lines of the shadows are a final touch that reinforces the thermal contrast originated earlier: warm light— cool shade.

From the same spatial structure, a grid made of diagonals, we can discover new landscapes if we vary the intensity, the definition, or the proximity (zoom effect). We can also produce creations with an abstract tendency with the use of lines and blocks of color.

In this image the artist's eye is directed toward the roofs and the chromatic variations between buildings. It is possible to exaggerate the colors a little bit by sacrificing the atmospheric feeling of the city to pause in that dynamic combination.

Here we pay attention to the atmosphere by inverting the light gradation. If in real life the distant grounds were light, in this work they are dark. It looks like nightfall or a distant storm is approaching. This inversion is a classical resource for creating depth by adding drama.

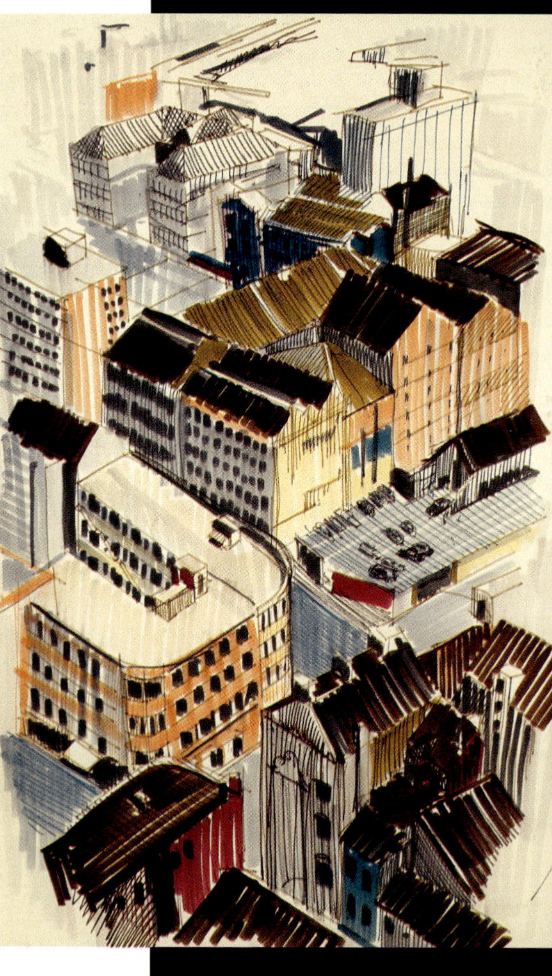

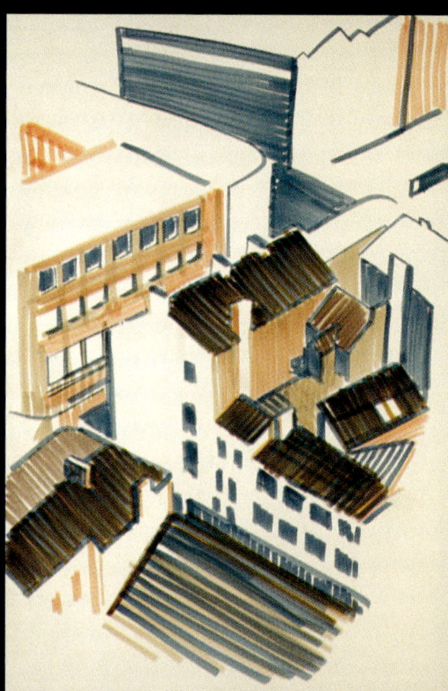

Emptiness and fullness are the two plastic effects in this work. By leaving the paper blank in many areas, a poetic effect has been achieved, creating a feeling of presence from absence, allowing the empty space to represent the volume itself rather than the surrounding one.

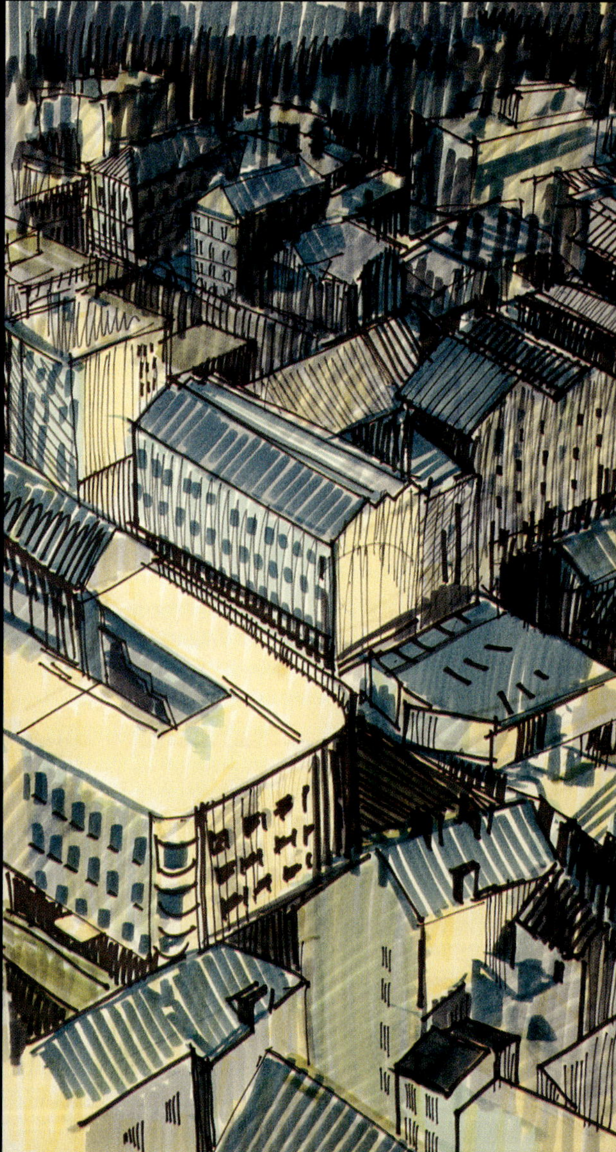

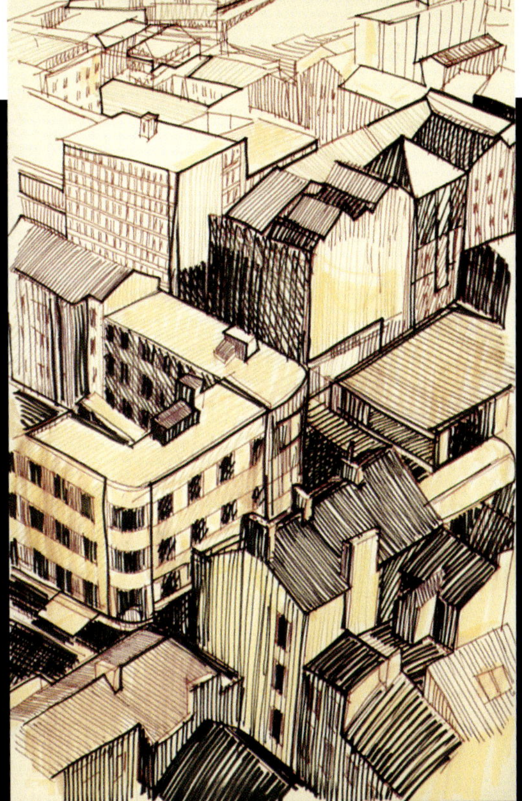

In this painting we have two areas divided by a diagonal. On one side, the close one, the shadows as well as the outlines of the buildings are reinforced with black, and on the other, the distant area—in the upper left triangle—there are hardly any shadows, as if an incredible light prevented us from seeing the buildings.

This is the result closest to abstraction. Through synthesis, the grid lines of the streets and the verticals of the buildings constitute a double panel, which at the same time acts as a conceptual and a formal structure.

We get visually closer to a specific area. Here, a single descending diagonal becomes the protagonist. It is perhaps the clearest work in this gallery, simple and beautiful.

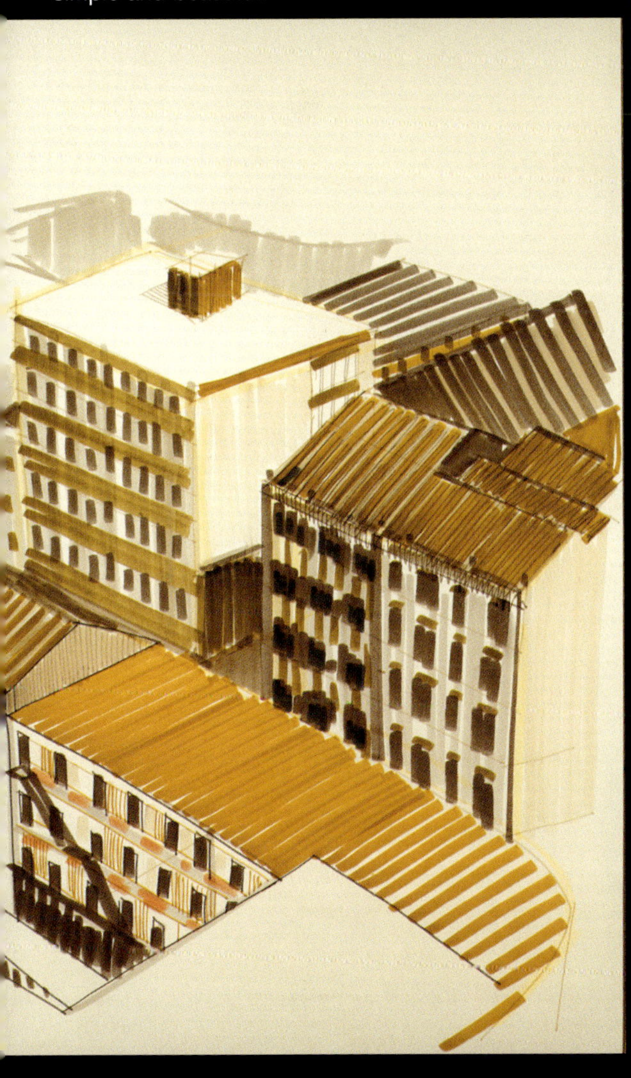

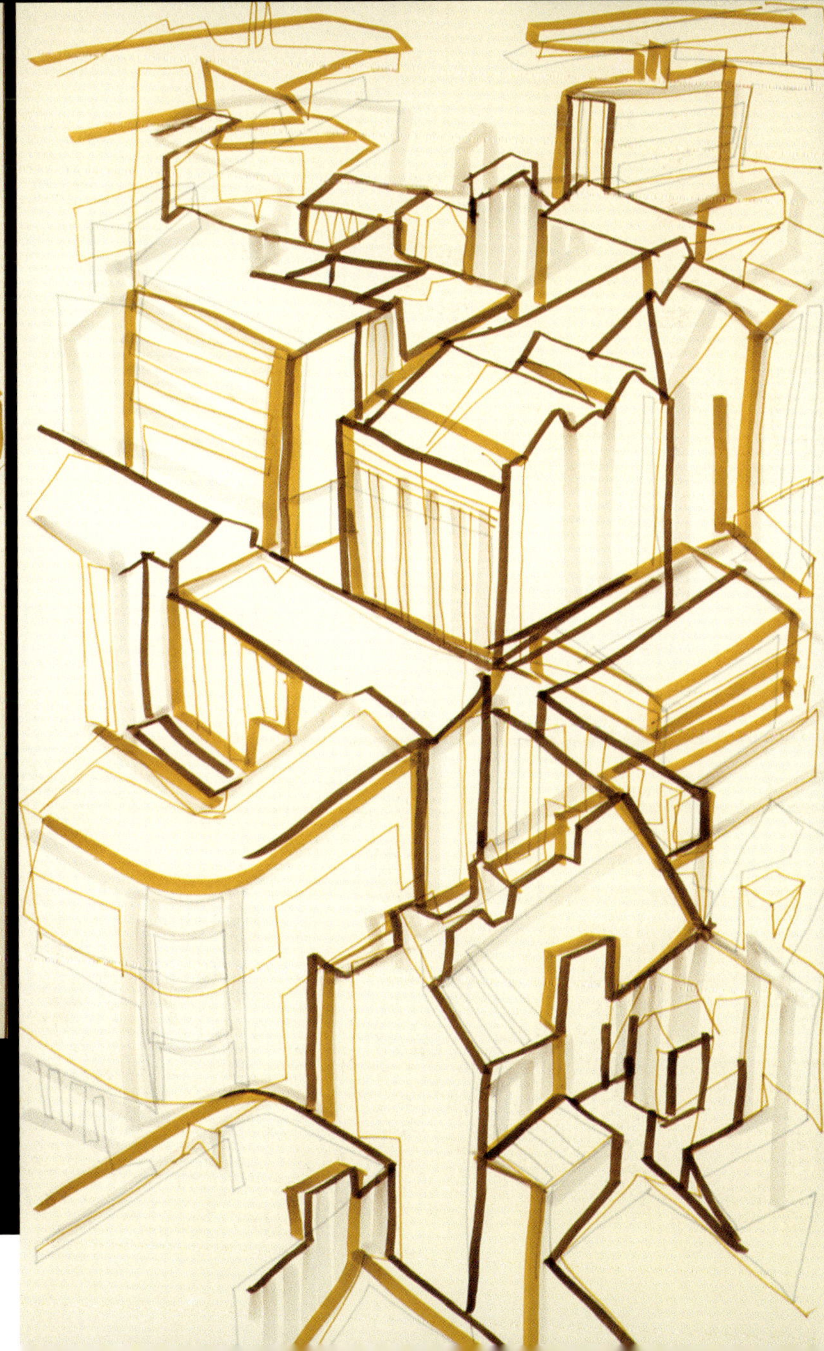

Other Models

A completely different space, but with many points in common, is discovered within an industrial environment. Josep Asunción has chosen it as a variation: the interior of a factory, with its architectural structures, machines, pipes, and so on—a true contemporary labyrinth full of suggestive and mysterious spaces.

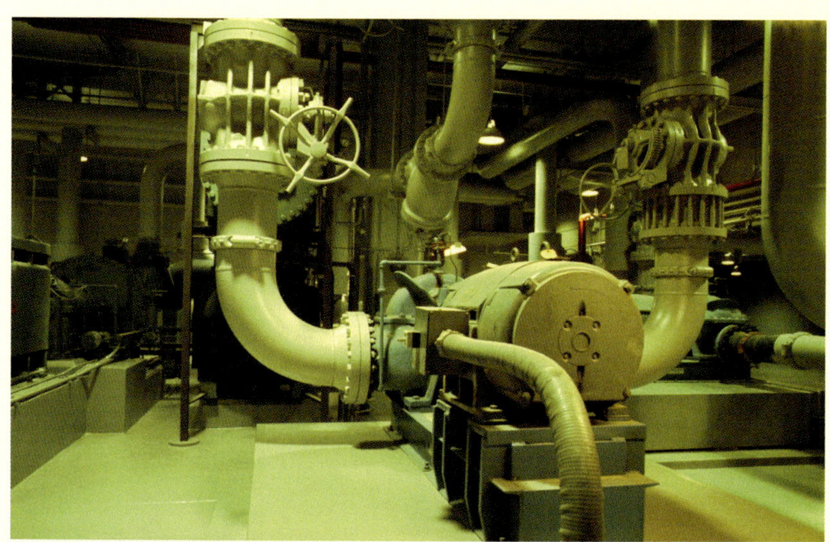

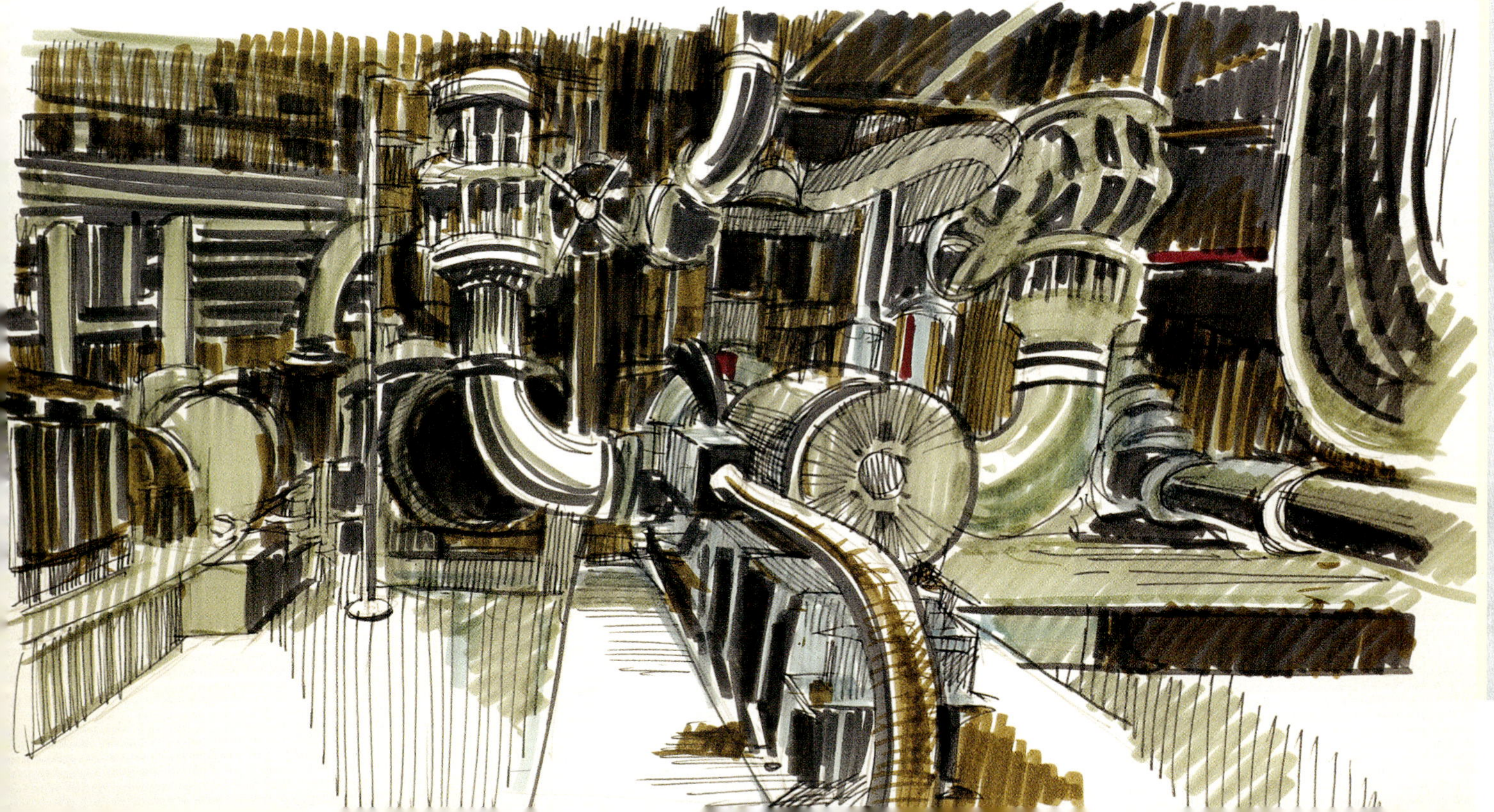

Other Media

Because markers are not viable for blending, we use a very common dry medium: the graphite pencil. With pencils of different hardness we create more or less intense cross-hatching and blend it with a blending stick until we create atmospheric cloudiness resembling city fog.

Other Views

Let's look at two views different from Hopper. First is a painting by Egon Schiele (1890–1918) with a distinctly expressionistic flavor. In it the artist focuses on the dramatic effect of the roofs' architectural structure, the narrow spaces that are created between balconies, and the little streets. In the other, Neus Martín Royo (born in 1968) develops a more lyrical realism, presenting a pleasant city bathed by a soft, clean light, characteristic of the Mediterranean. She uses soft colors, although she intensifies the chromatic value of certain areas to produce some idealization. In this work, like in Hopper's, the bird's-eye view prevails to eliminate the dominance of the buildings.

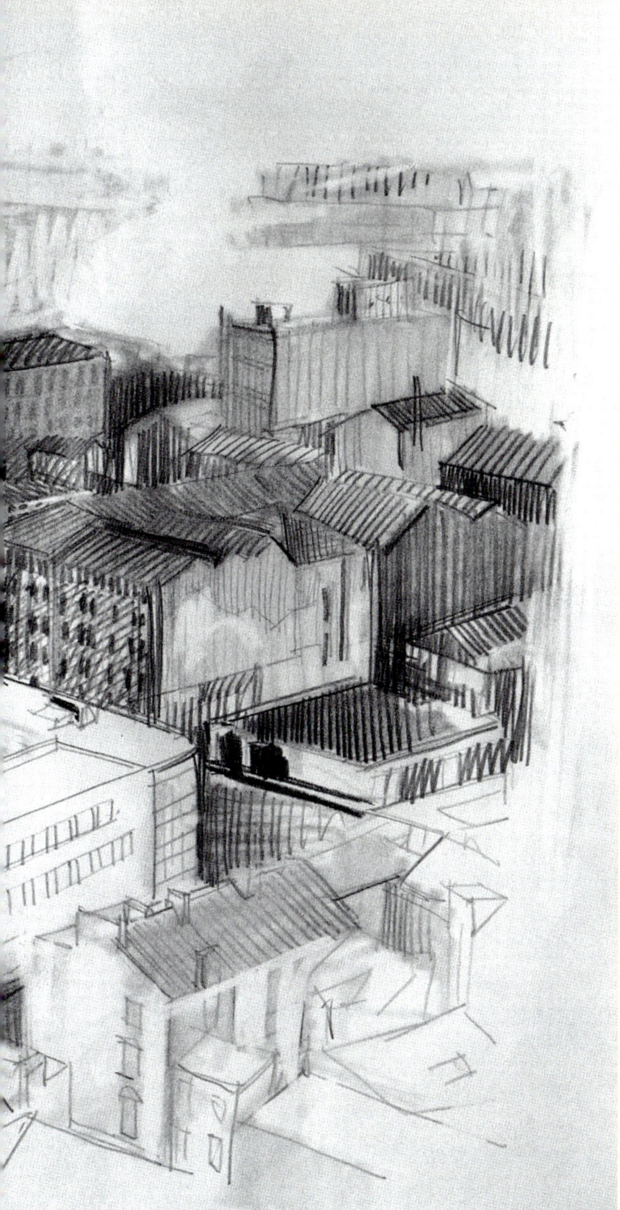

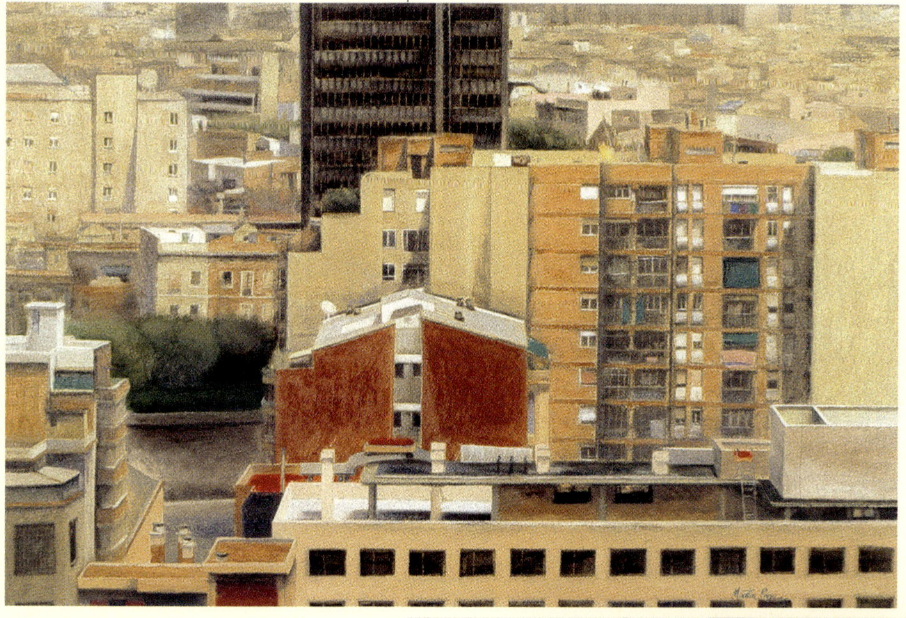

Neus Martín Royo,
2001: An Odyssey in Barcelona, 1996.
Private Collection.

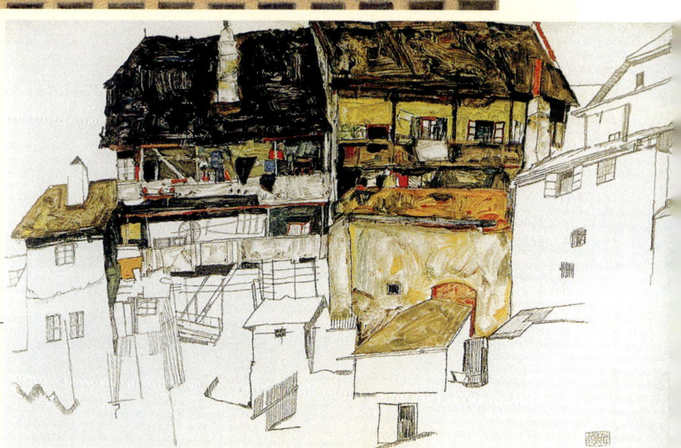

Egon Schiele,
Old Houses of Krumau, 1914.
Graphische Sammlung Albertina,
Vienna, Austria.

Natural, *Atmospheric,* and *Rural* Spaces

Aerial perspective is applied in the majority of landscapes. This technique was formulated by Leonardo da Vinci (1452–1519) in his *Treatise on Painting* written around 1500. Leonardo was an extremely restless painter, with the soul of a scientist. He dedicated many hours not only to the investigation of perceptive phenomena and to anatomy, realities that are closely connected to the problems of artistic representation, but also to the invention of various gadgets, turning him into a truly extraordinary person of his time. The aerial perspective by Leonardo is based on four principles: objects that are closer to the viewer are larger than objects in the distance, they are clearer, they have more contrast, and they have warmer colors. This implies that objects that are farther away are smaller, have less contrast, are blurrier, and are bluer. In the times of Leonardo, landscapes did not constitute a genre in their own right; they appeared as backgrounds in scenes with characters. Therefore we do not have any landscapes from the artist other than preparatory sketches.

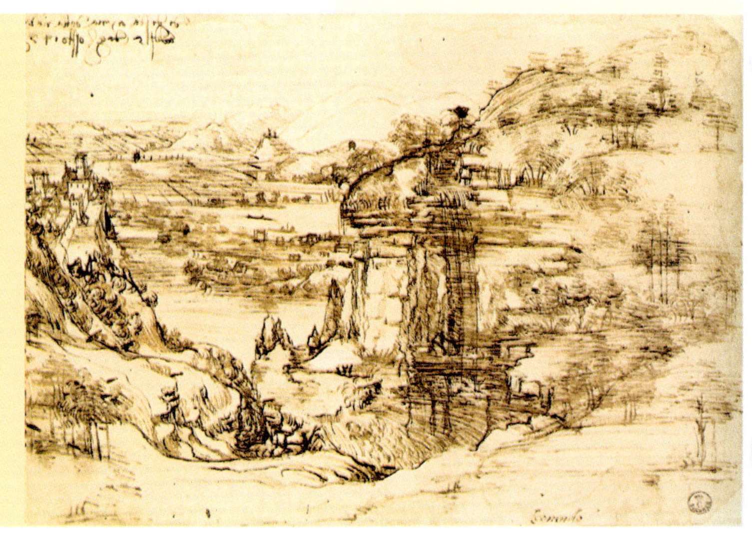

Leonardo da Vinci,
Study of a Landscape for Santa Maria della Neve, 1473. Uffizi Gallery, Florence, Italy.

Aerial Perspective: Representing Depth in a Rural Landscape

In this project, Pilar Valeriano approaches the aerial perspective formulated by Leonardo da Vinci, but she adds a factor that the Renaissance painter could not contemplate because of the times in which he lived: the focus. Based on a panoramic rural landscape, she applies the perspective step-by-step until depth has been achieved. The creative part of the project occurs when she acts as if she were capturing the landscape with a photographic lens, varying the focus. Therefore, she will be able to bring a specific area into focus, letting the others go out of focus, independently of its spatial placement and thus directing the eye of the viewer as she pleases. The medium chosen is oils on canvas.

"There is another perspective, which I call aerial perspective, because by the atmosphere we can distinguish the variations of distance between different buildings, which look like they are located on a single line."
Leonardo da Vinci,
Treatise on Painting, c. 1500.

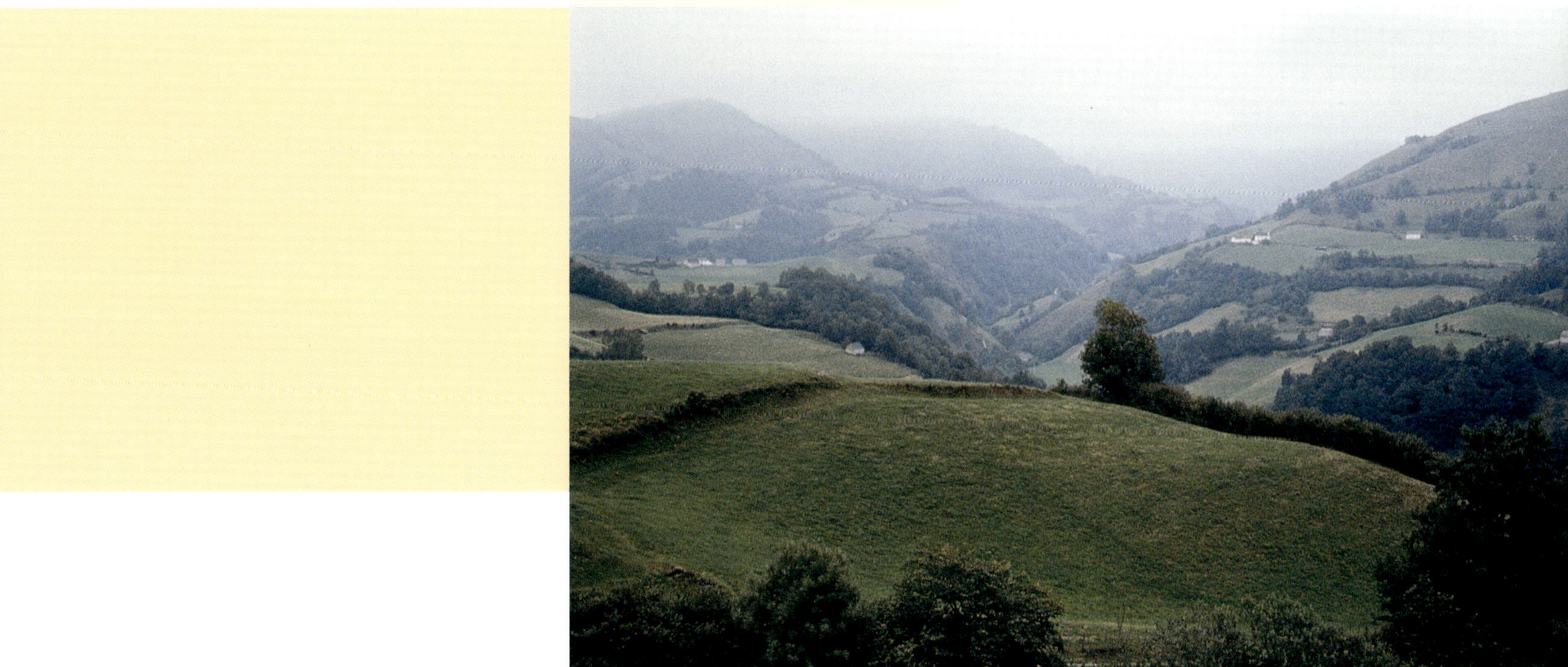

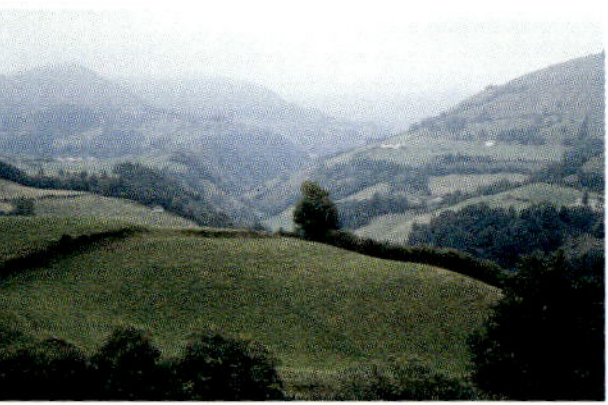

1 We lay out the initial sketch with a very soft (3B) pencil, drawing faint lines. These lines constitute the structure of the landscape by defining the areas of the space and sizing them proportionately.

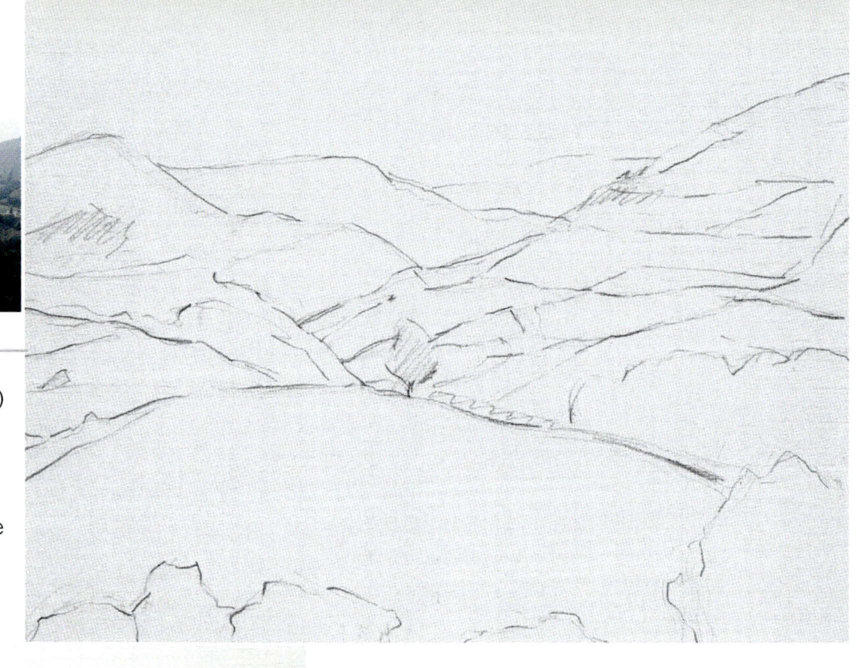

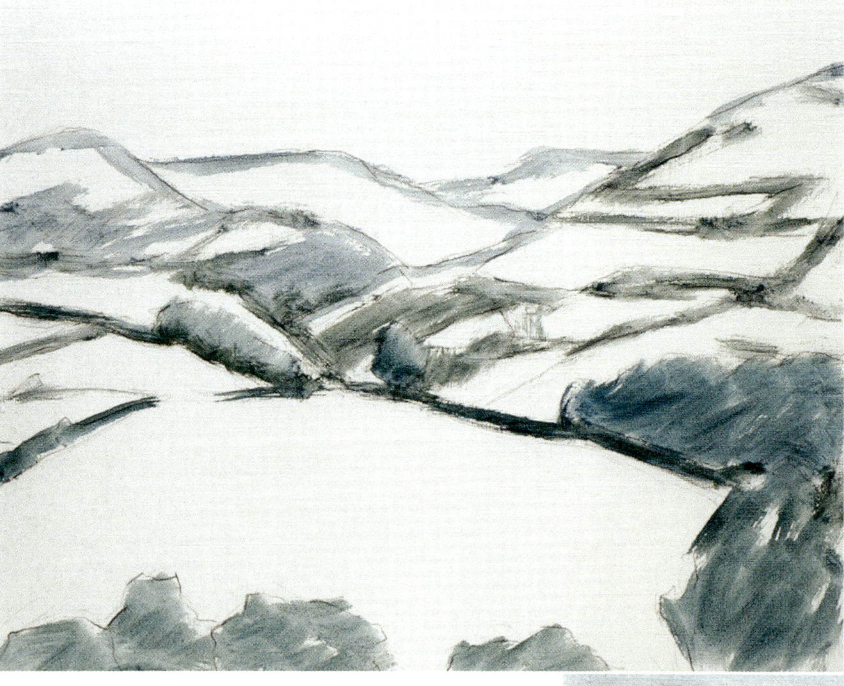

2 We draw the first color lines. They define the darker areas of the landscape, which coincide with the concentrations of trees. We apply a dark tone, but not too dark. It will be adjusted later.

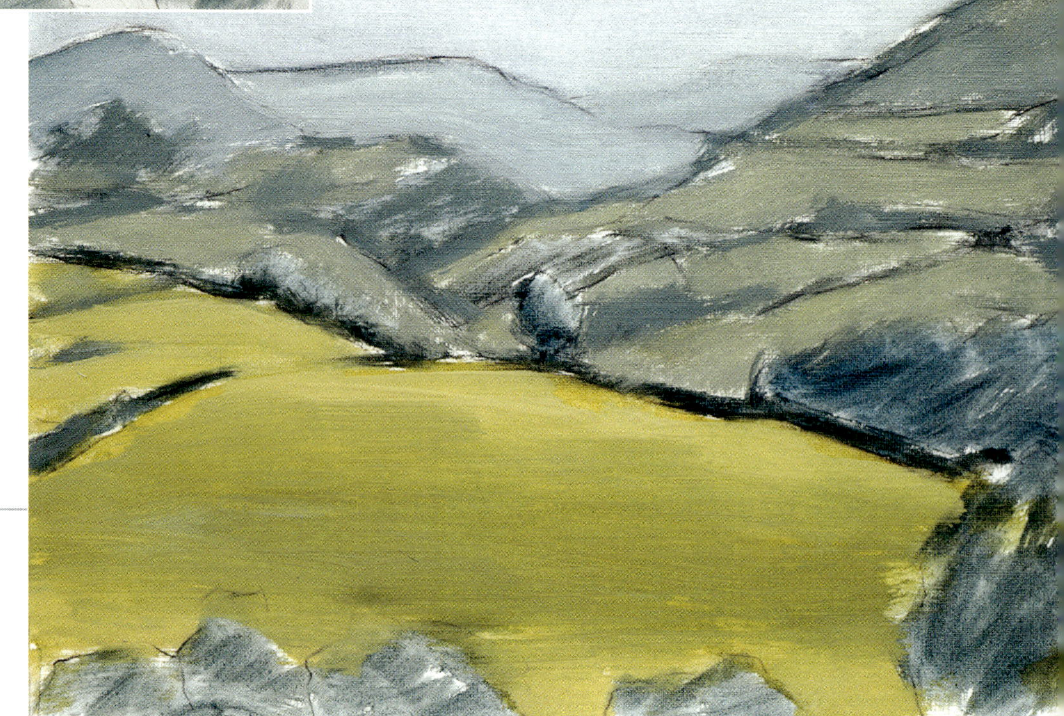

3 We complete the colors that constitute the general tones of the landscape, without overdoing the contrasts, and we define the color nuances, making them warmer in the foreground and bluer in the background.

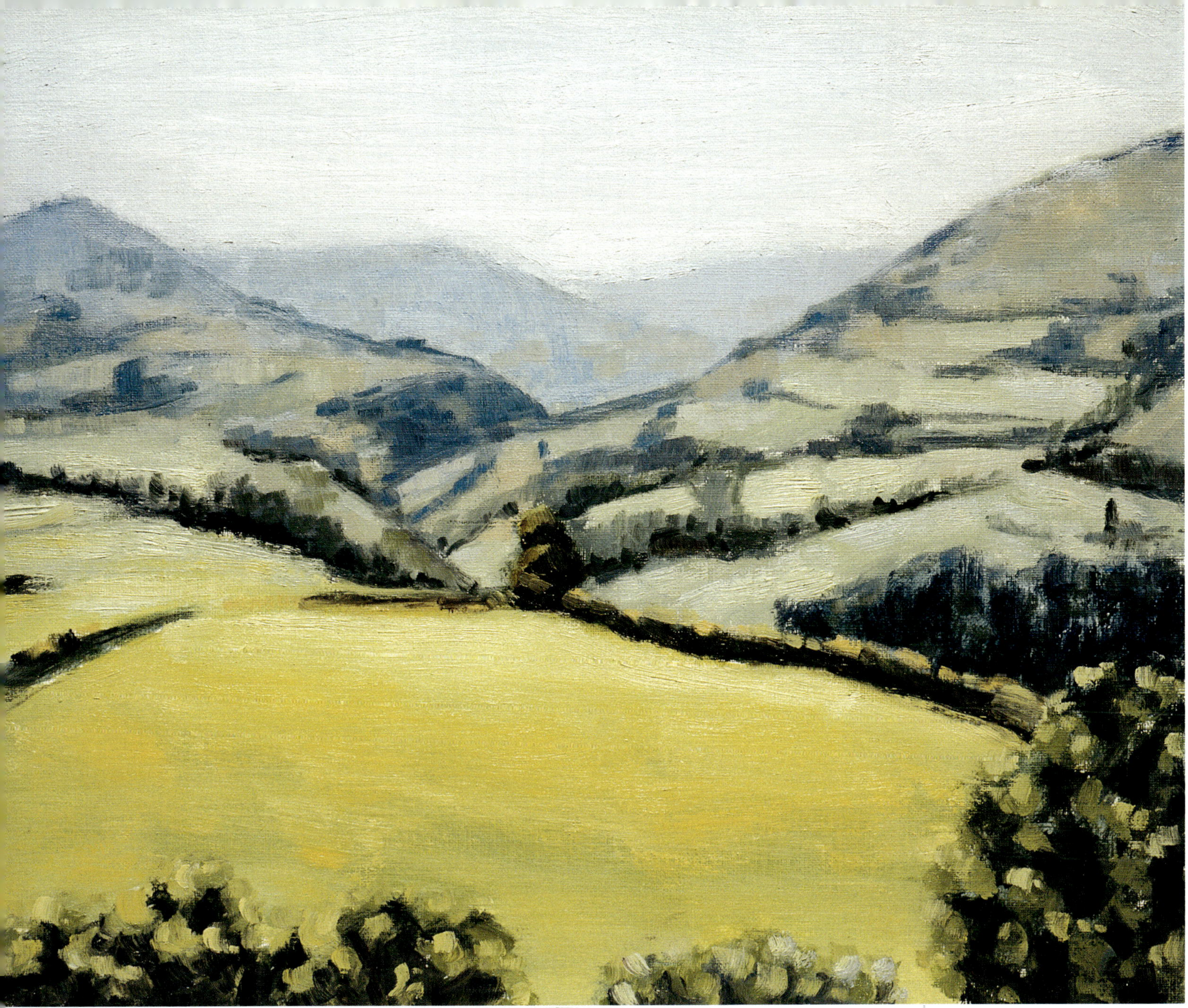

4 We continue defining the work by adding color and contrast. We model the volumes for each element—trees, mountains, fields— with larger blocks of color in the foreground and smaller ones in the distance.

5 To finish, we add blue for the most distant mountains and increase the contrast in the middle and distant grounds.

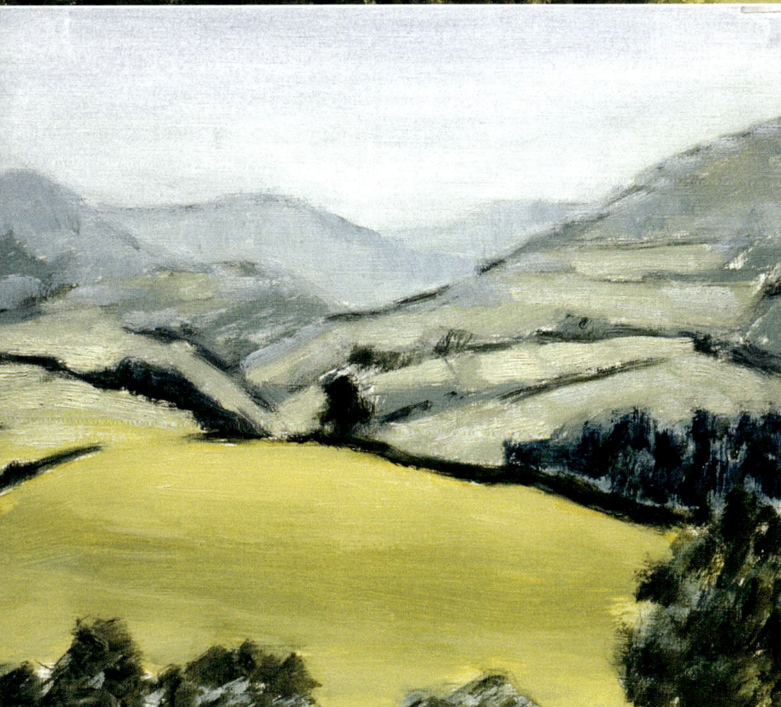

The variations in focus that Pilar Valeriano created in this gallery are based on the degree of clarity of the areas brought into focus and to their light and surroundings. This has created a new atmosphere, as if the time of day had changed.

In this painting the dense atmosphere, a fog that falls over the mountains, is the protagonist. This fog blocks the view because of the absence of contrast and the lack of focus that the blending has produced. Only the volume of the closest trees can be seen completely, although they are a little indistinct as a result of the diffused light.

This is the clearest landscape of the gallery. A clear day allows each element of the landscape to be seen with limpid clarity, even the most distant ones. This effect is experienced by any traveler who hikes up to high mountainous areas where the air is very pure and the light very clean.

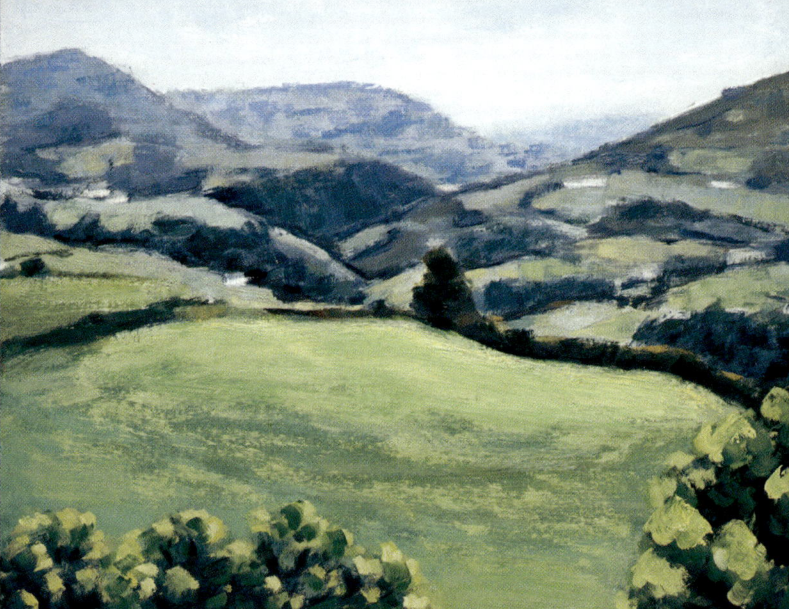

The focal point of this oil painting is the central meadow and its hedgerow. To highlight this ground, the artist has blended the background and the foreground by bringing them out of focus until they become unnoticeable—something Leonardo could not formulate five hundred years ago, because optics had not yet advanced to this point.

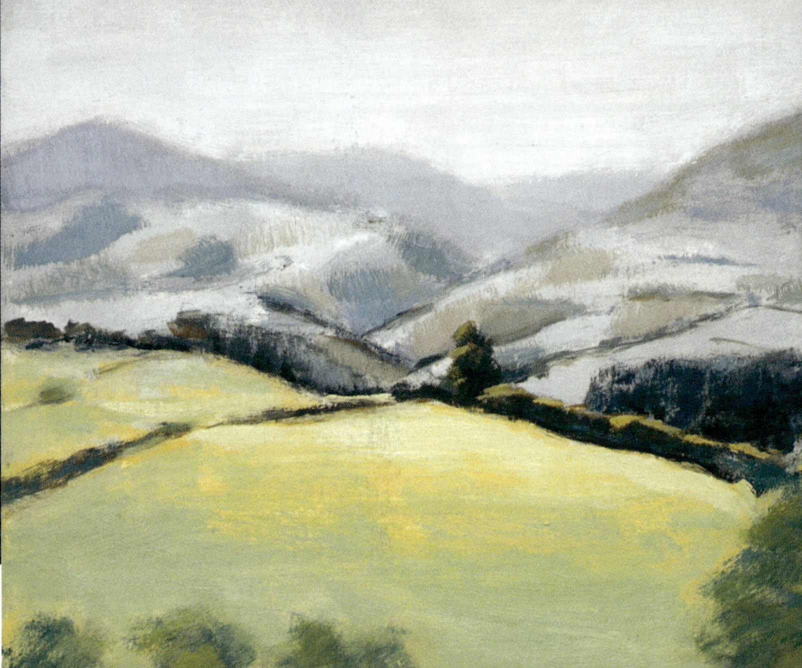

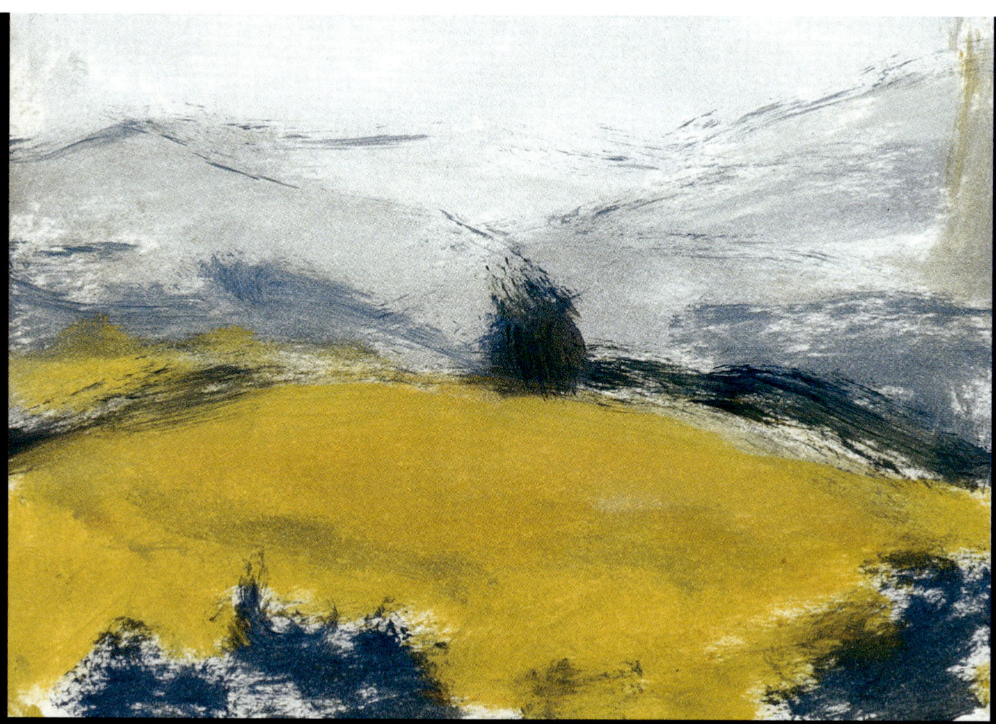

This is the most spontaneous landscape. In reality, it is a quick study done on a smaller support, but it has tremendous compositional and chromatic power. The main cause of this vigorous effect is the thermal contrast between the warm yellow meadow and the cold, distant blue background.

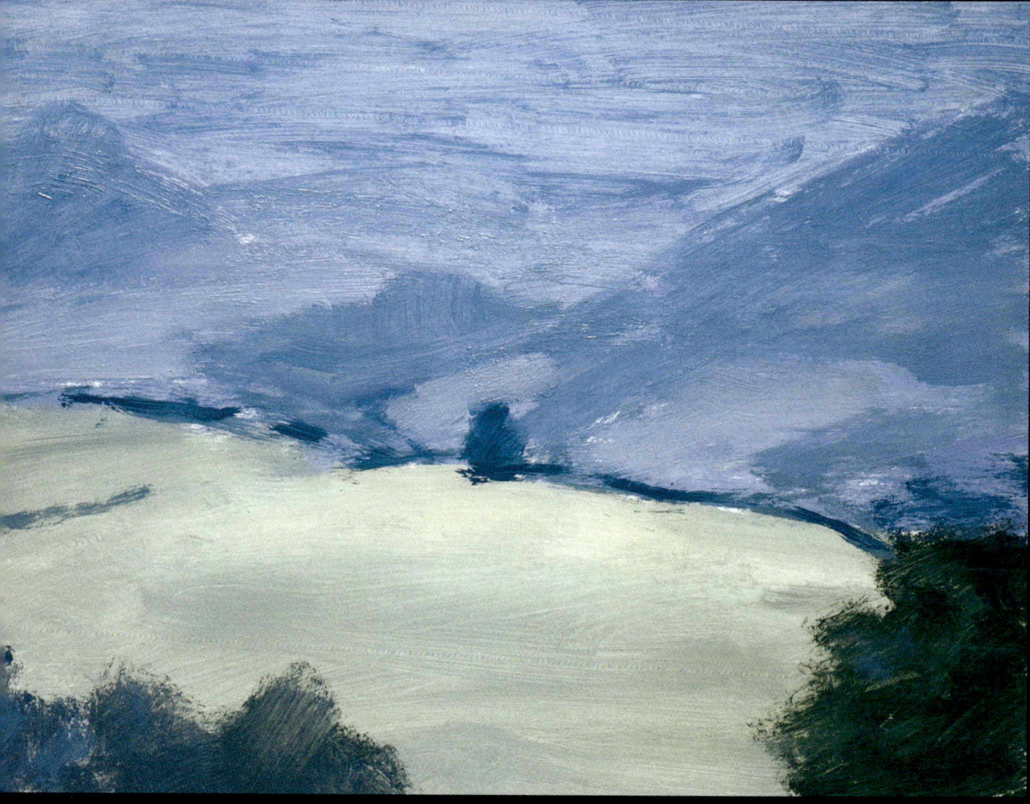

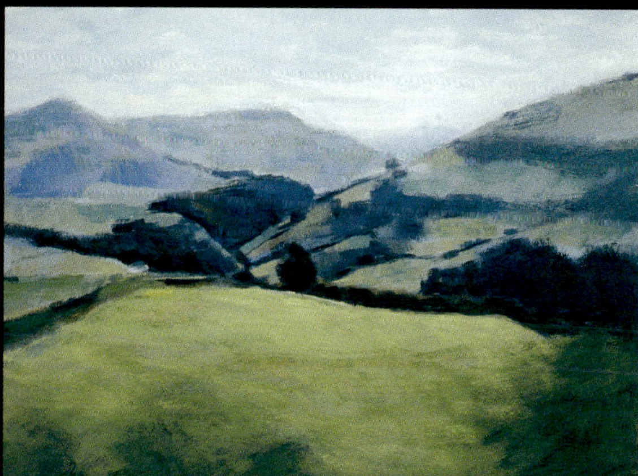

In this instance the artist has brought the central area of the landscape into focus. The valley that expands beyond the meadow is much lower than this. The rest is blended, thus losing its clarity and contrast. In terms of composition, the central diagonal line and the strong folds in the terrain are the powerful cloments.

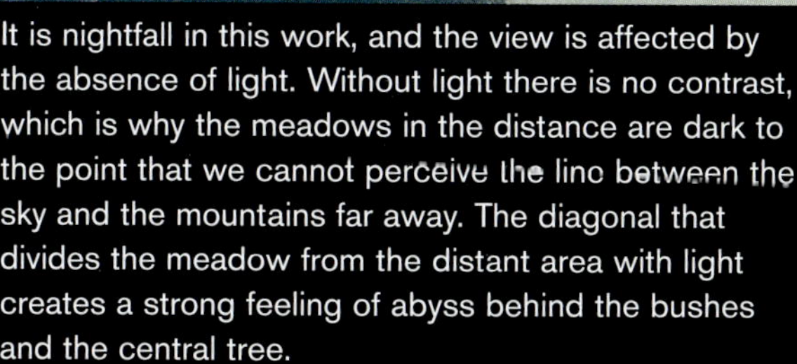

It is nightfall in this work, and the view is affected by the absence of light. Without light there is no contrast, which is why the meadows in the distance are dark to the point that we cannot perceive the line between the sky and the mountains far away. The diagonal that divides the meadow from the distant area with light creates a strong feeling of abyss behind the bushes and the central tree.

Other Models

In this case we have opted for a panoramic landscape that is somewhat different, more rugged, and without any flat areas, in which the vistas follow one another like a curtain, without any visible horizontal planes.

The use of aerial perspective is also possible because the variations in contrast, size, clarity, and temperature define the depth.

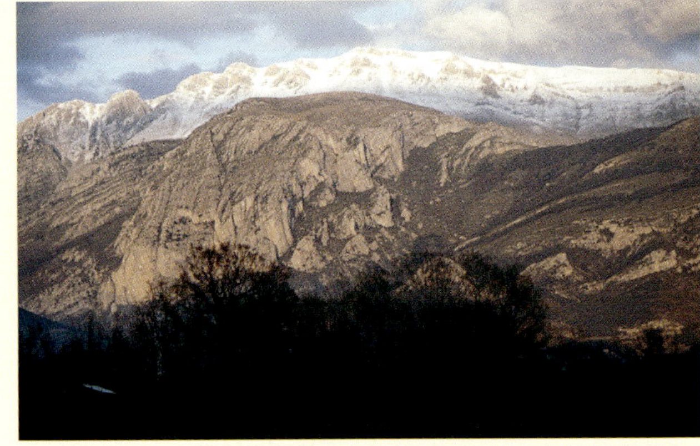

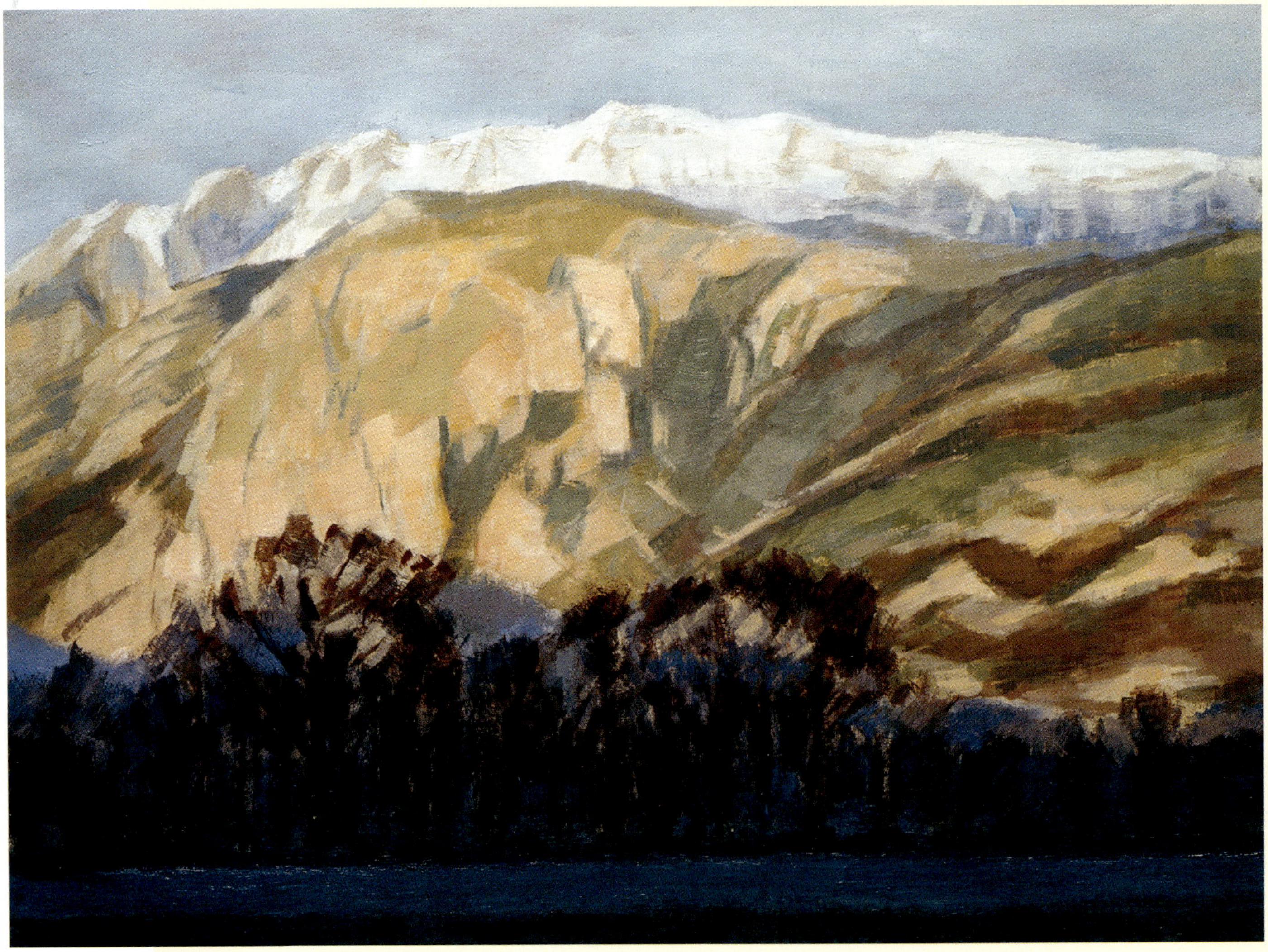

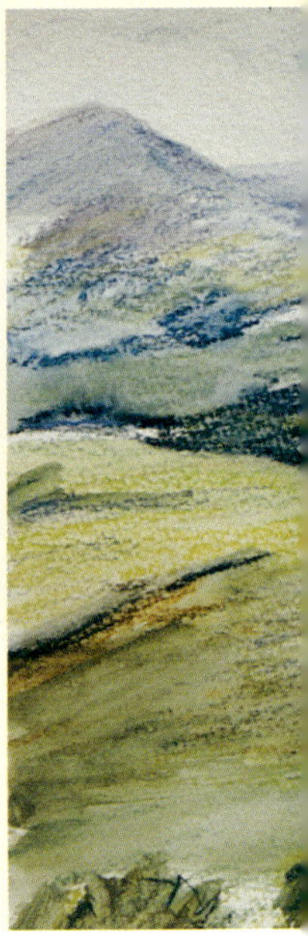

Other Media

In this instance, we have opted for the diversity of watercolor pencils. This medium makes it possible to draw lines and areas of color, if it is later wiped with a wet brush. The results are fresh and loose, as in a sketch.

Other Views

Paul Cézanne's (1839–1906) proximity to Pissarro and his trips outdoors to paint transformed his style, as well as those of many other impressionists, who are a mandatory subject in this chapter. Cézanne used to choose the point of view of his landscapes very carefully. In them the air and the light impregnated the canvas, illuminating the colors and the forms that were created with brushstrokes that constituted true impressionist touches. Cézanne applied a very personal language to the landscape: he created spatial depth when he broke down the grounds on the canvas, following an analytical yet intuitive process, which he constantly defined as *ma petite sensation*. He maintained the volumes, trying not to lose them in the distance to the atmospheric effect. He died of a sudden syncope during his daily encounter with Mount Saint Victoria, which he had painted many times during his life.

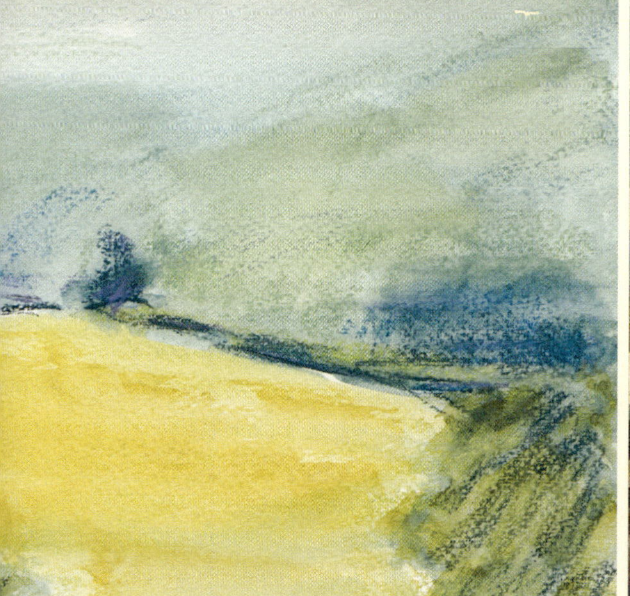

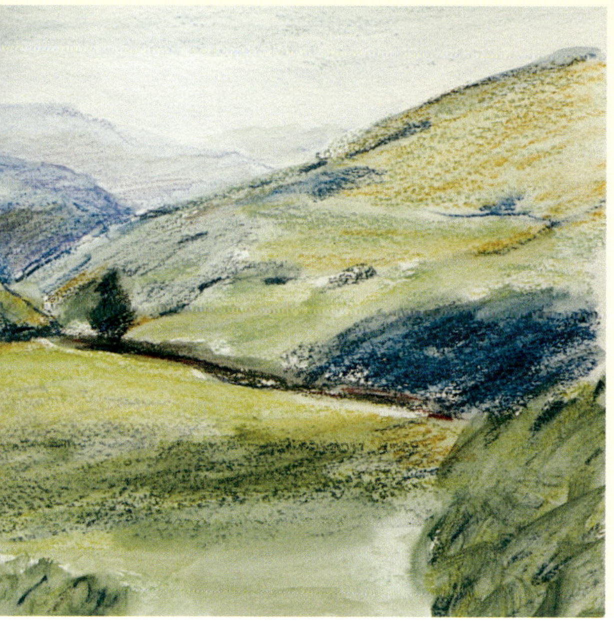

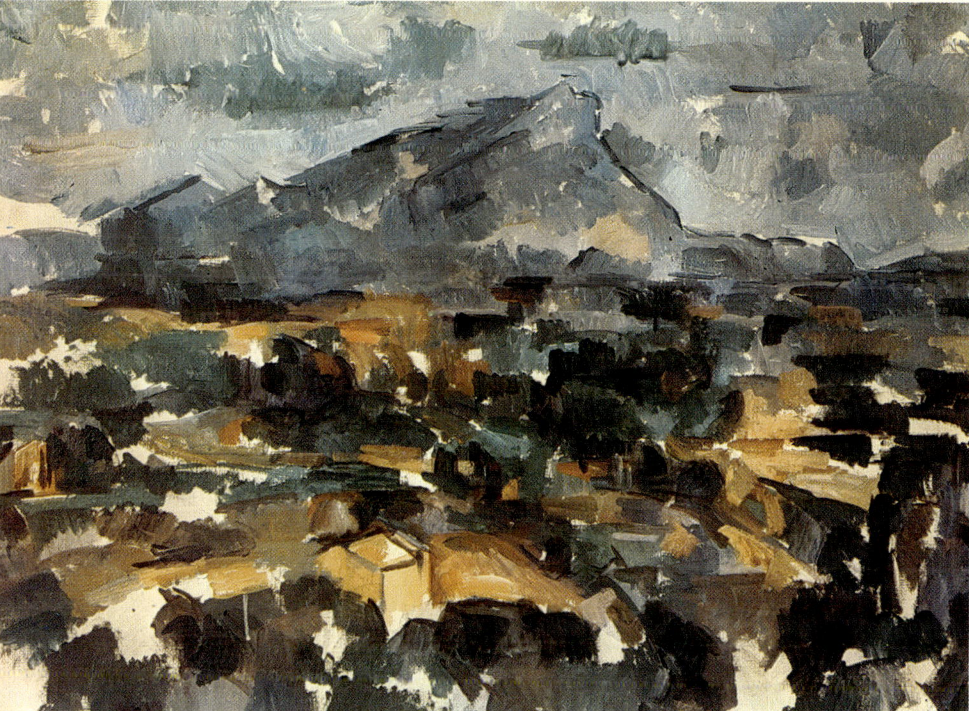

Paul Cézanne,
Mount Saint Victoria, 1904–1906.
Casa del Arte, Zurich, Switzerland.

Mobile, Connected, and Labyrinthine Spaces

Space can be approached in a symbolic or fantastic way. Stairways, bridges, tunnels, labyrinths, or caves are all allegorical and mythical representations that go beyond mere description. One of the greatest magicians of space was Cornelis Escher (1898–1972), who developed complex and impossible three-dimensional spaces in two dimensions. He was never interested in creating beautiful and interesting drawings, rather in visually reflecting his thoughts in each sketch. This is the reason why he devoted more time to reflecting than to creating. In *Concave and Convex* he invites us on an endless visual walk through the creation of a complex and ambiguous space. He produces an abrupt visual impression with an "inverted" drawing. The upper part becomes the lower part and the front becomes the back. Only people are left in an unambiguous relationship with their surroundings, which makes the viewer restless and dizzy.

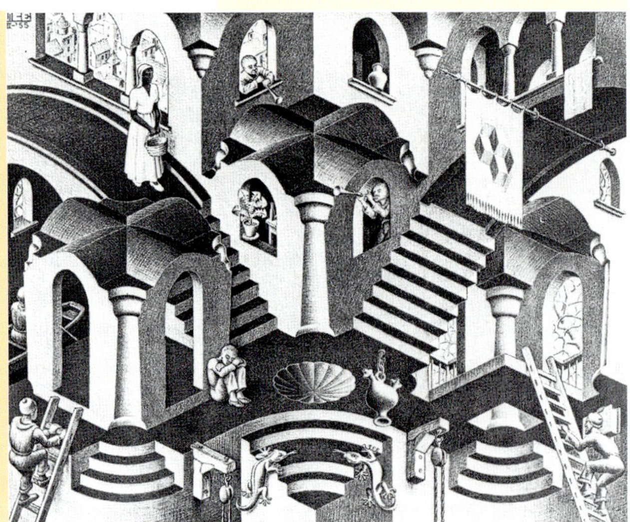

Cornelis Escher,
Concave and Convex,
1955. Lithograph.

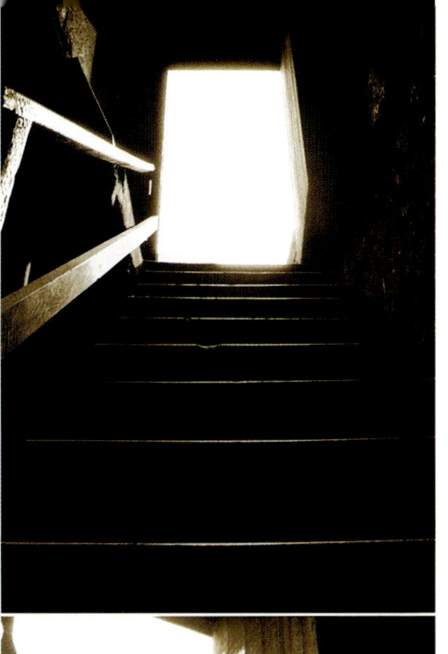

Ascent and Descent: The Stairway as a Symbolic Space

Transitional spaces permit transformation and change, providing multiple feelings: restlessness, hope, fear, suspense . . . In this perspective, Esther Pascual offers us a creative and risky work. The stairway is presented as the only possible space that connects two hidden realities: a luminous upper area, and a darker lower one. She chose oil paints as the medium, combined with collage, and applied on a wood panel, and different views of the same stairs are the model. All of this helps work the space in a creative way through symbolism and atmosphere.

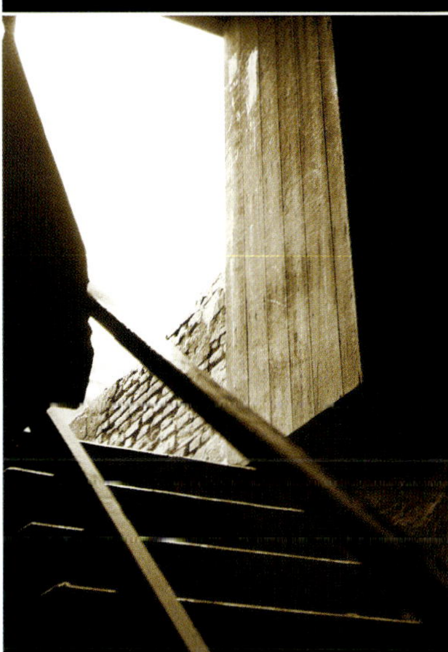

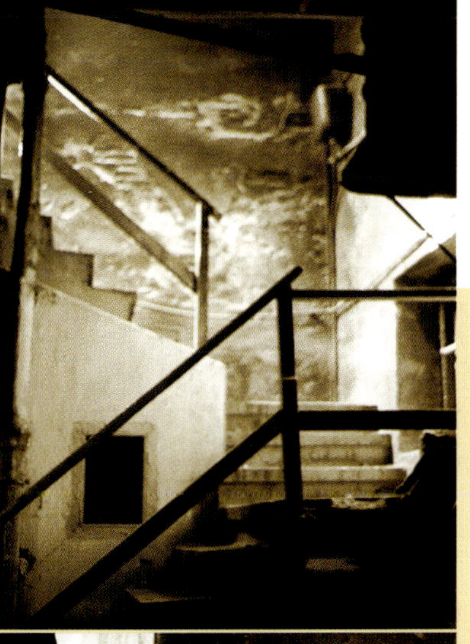

"The universe (which some call library) is made of an indefinite number, and perhaps infinite, of hexagonal galleries. (. . .) The lower and upper floors can be seen from any hexagon: endlessly. (. . .) One of the free walls leads to a narrow doorway, which opens to another gallery, identical to the first one and to all of them."
Jorge Luis Borges,
The Library of Babel.

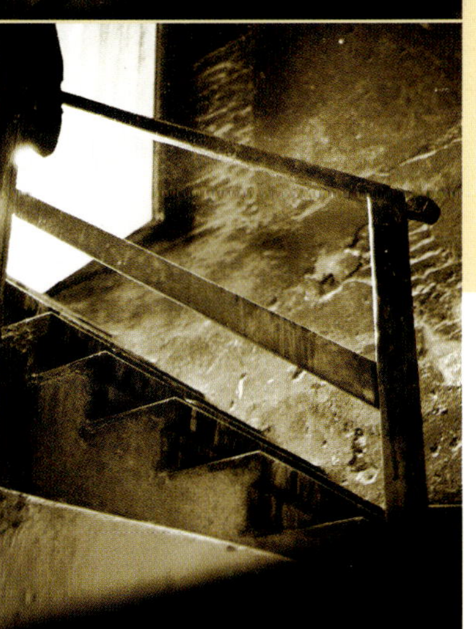

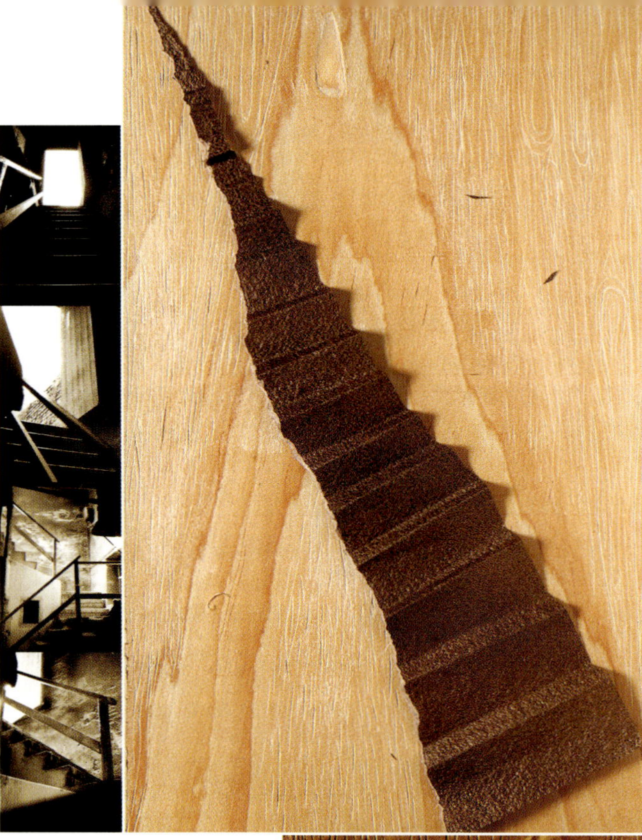

1 Before the painting begins, we scrape the wood grain with an awl to get the most out of the chosen material. Then we cut and fold different papers to create the shape of the stairs with collage. The stairs we created invite us to go up since they are wider in the lower part than at the top.

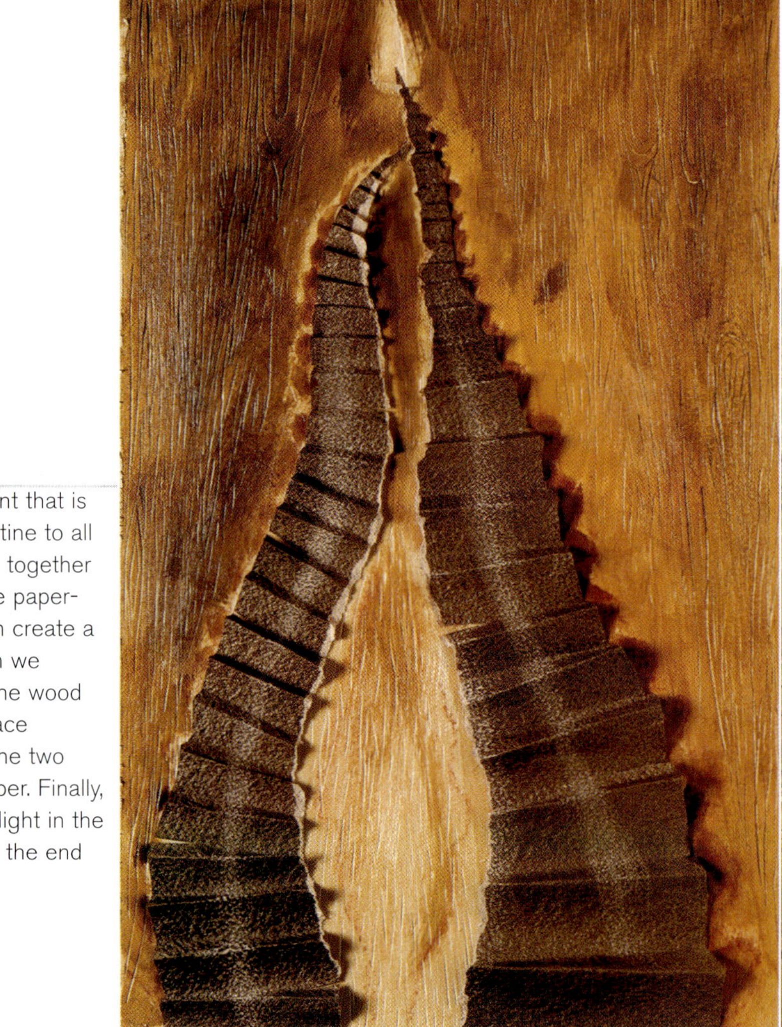

2 We apply oil paint that is diluted with turpentine to all the wood. We glue together two sections of the paper-folded stairs, which create a visual ascent. Then we continue to work the wood by sanding the space created between the two stairs with sandpaper. Finally, we create a small light in the shape of a door at the end of the stairway.

3 To intensify the atmosphere and to convey realism to the symbolic space, we resort to gloominess by exaggerating the contrasts. The background is darkened with shaded tones, and we highlight the light that surrounds the stairs with sienna tones.

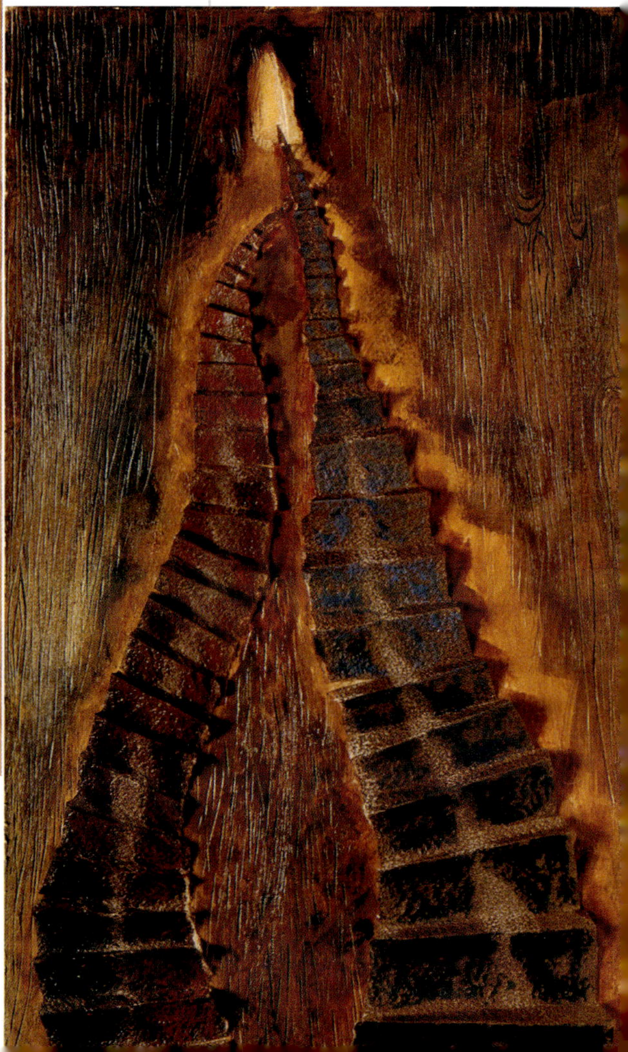

4 We work on lightening the dark areas. Highlights are applied in the upper part of the painting, and the stairs are emphasized by painting their projected shadows: dark for the staircase on the right and sienna for the one on the left. The collage representing the staircase on the left is painted with blue, and the staircase on the right with English red. This way we make two distinct possible paths, which reinforces their symbolic value.

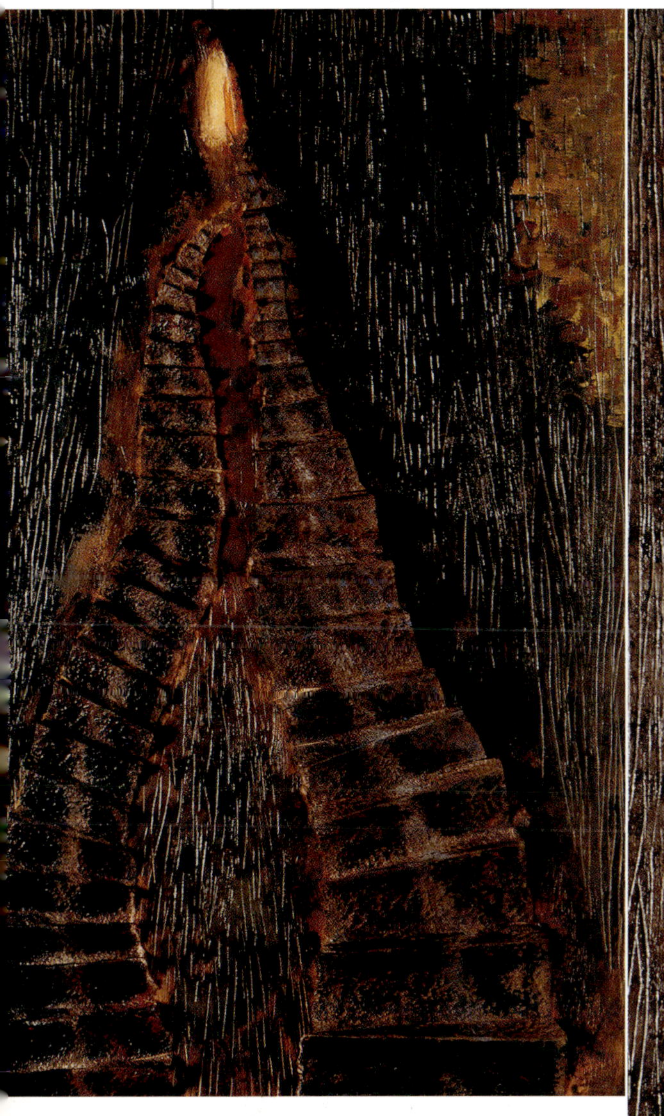

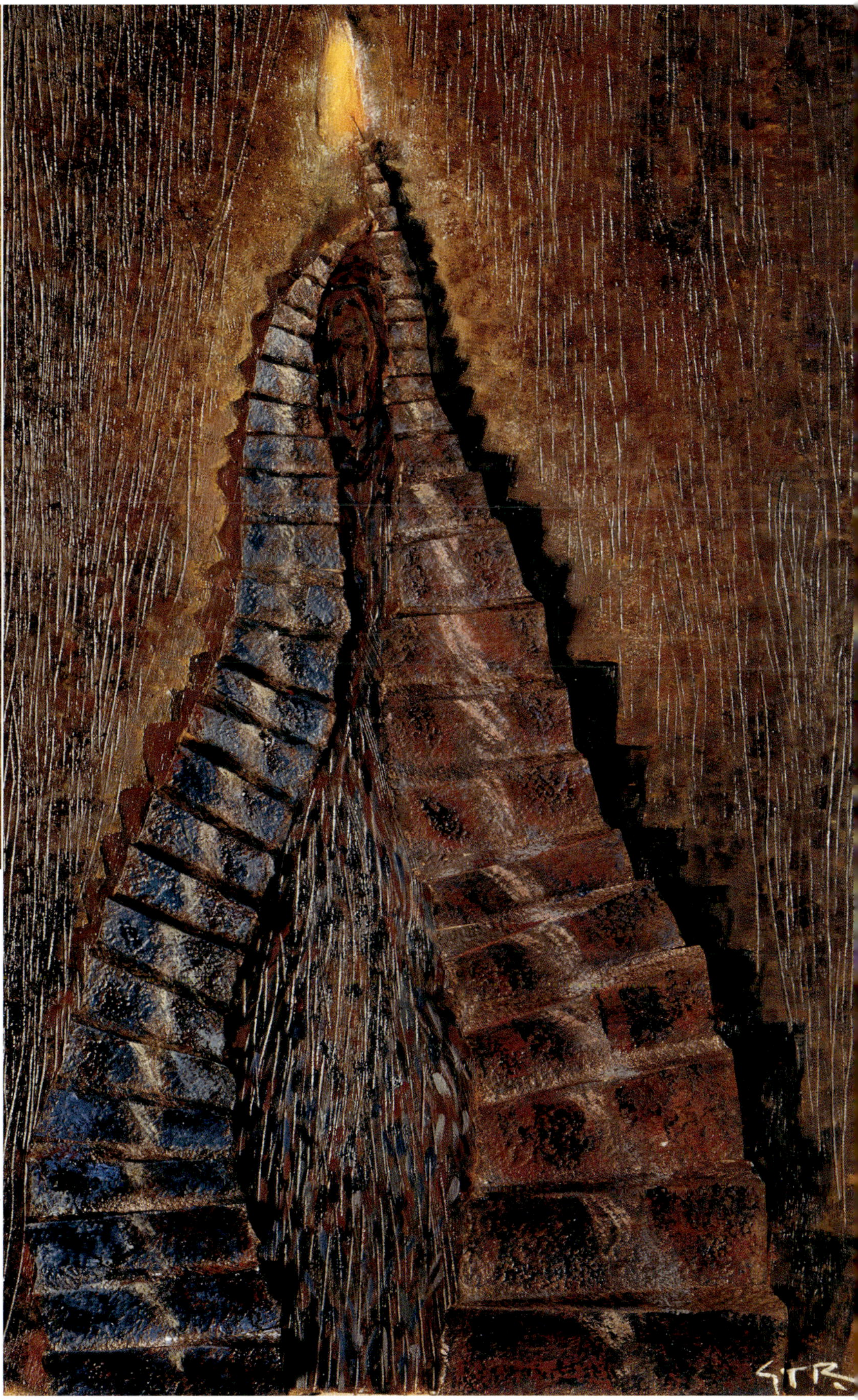

5 We blend the staircase with the background by applying a layer of very dark, almost black, paint. This emphasizes the only point of light: the opening to which the constructed stairs lead us. The hidden space becomes the protagonist and invites us into the unknown.

Other Versions

Wavy, narrow, doubled, and crooked stairs . . . transit spaces offer themselves as a metaphor of life itself. It is a theme with a strong existentialist content, of which we show rich and multiple variations that help us reflect and dream.

A dark staircase done in collage invades the support with a diagonal shape. The large, dark collage takes center stage in a directed and rigid composition. Grayish smoke at the upper part of the stairs reinforces the two-dimensionality of the painting.

This Z-shaped staircase presents the longest span. The distance places us in a space that is frightening, empty, and disturbing. Only ascending it offers us hope. This piece, with no use of collage, was done completely in oils.

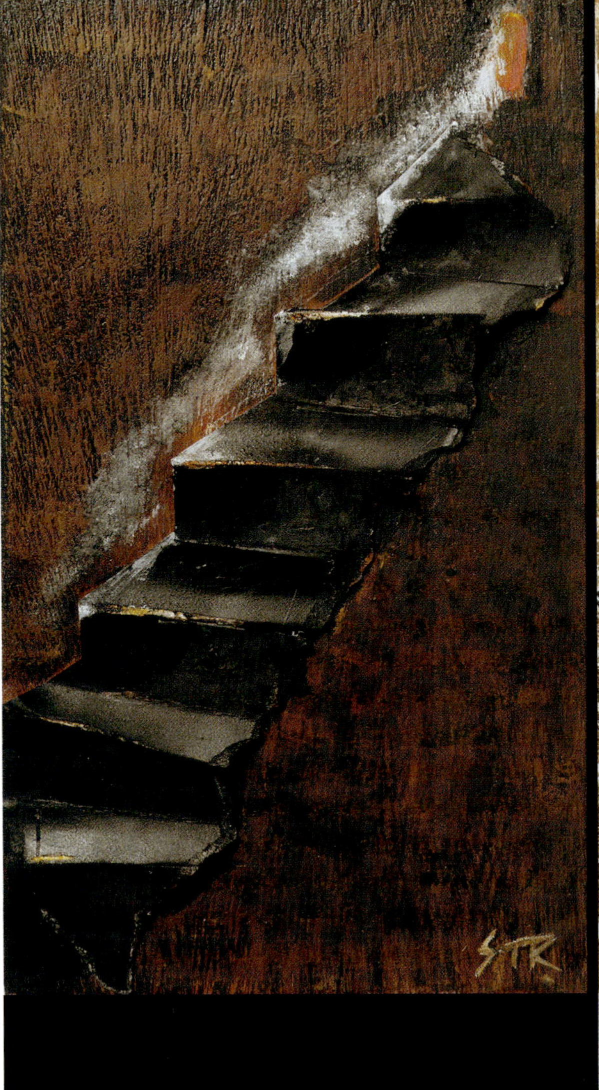

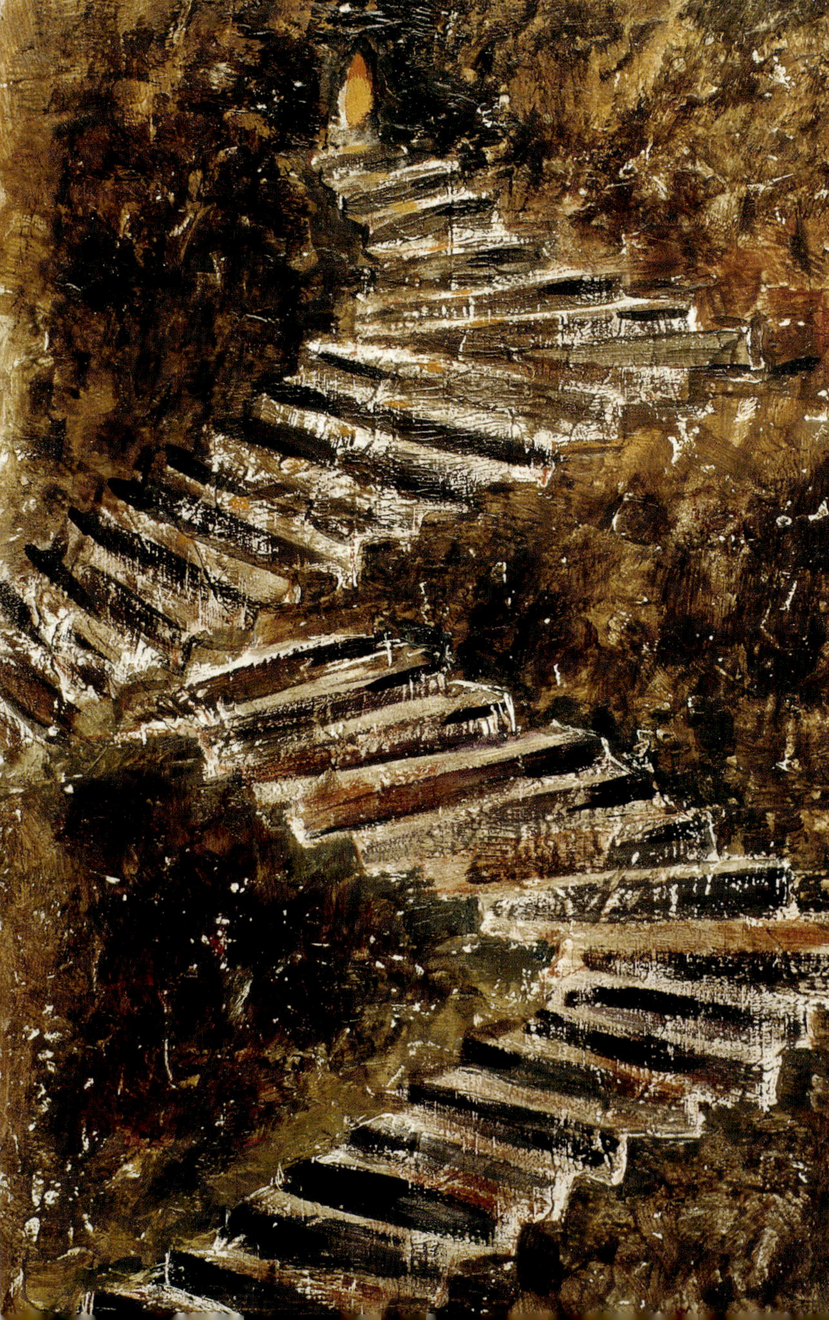

This painting constitutes the strangest and most abstract view of the gallery. The staircase looks crooked with a collage that is exaggeratedly curved toward the viewer. The lighter tones, ochres and whites, contribute the light in the collage. There is no exit in this work; the staircase is the light.

The blue collage placed in a whimsical manner, bending toward the left in the shape of a C, is an attractive composition. The projected shadows are worked with boldness and confidence. This is a near space that feels optimistic.

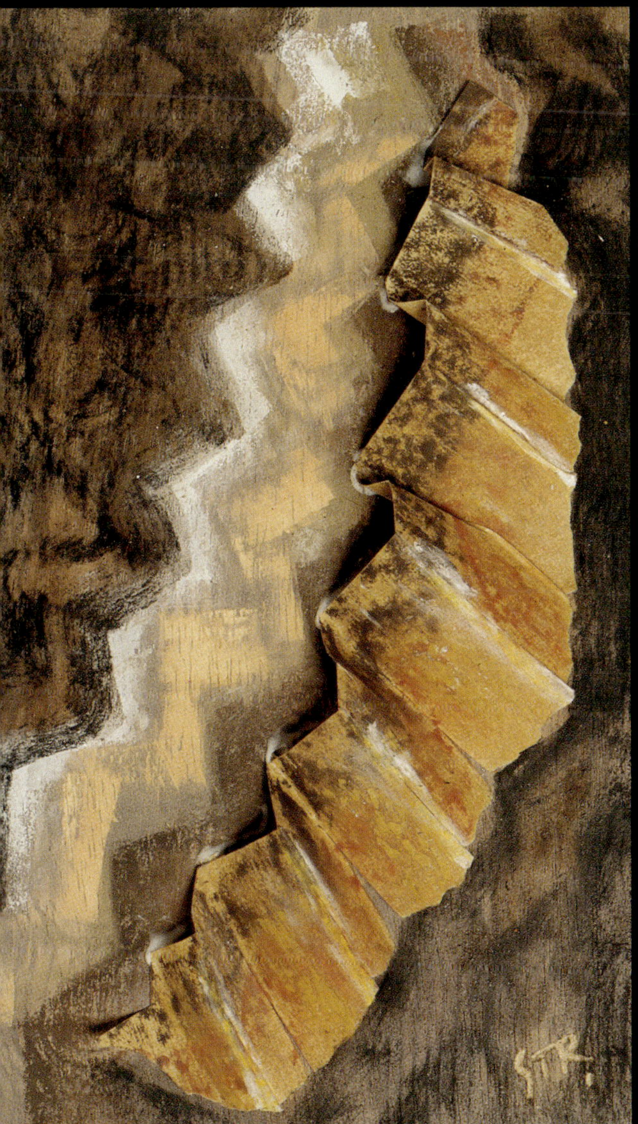

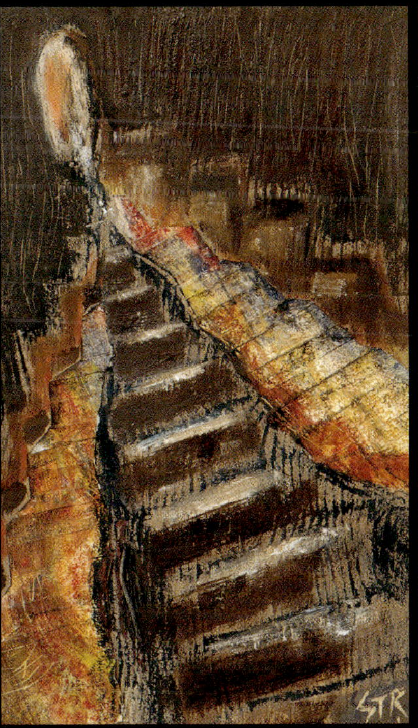

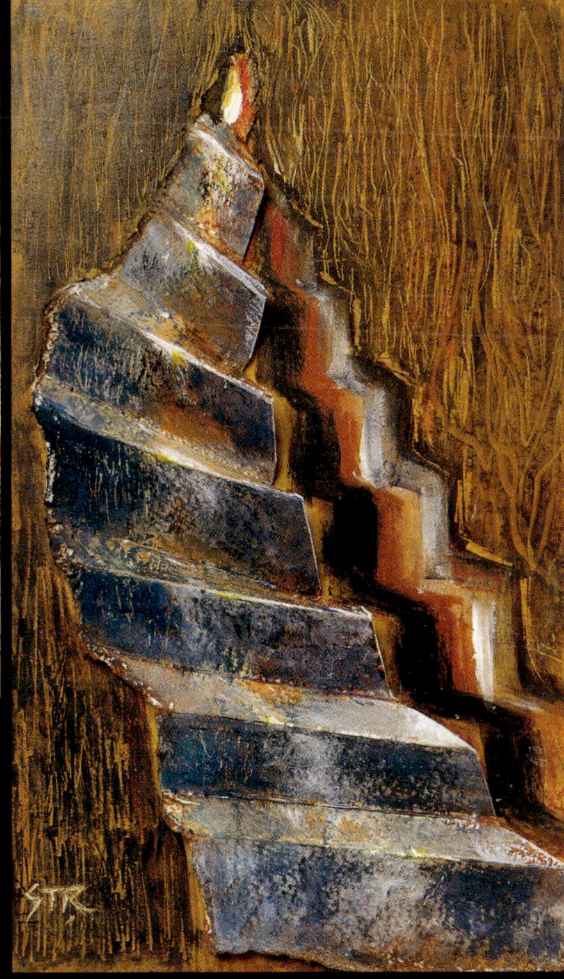

These three staircases leaning toward the left provide unstable and disturbing results. The side staircases, in various warm tones, contrast with the central staircase, painted with dark colors and drawn on with wax crayons. The creation of different ways up that lead to the same point invites us to reflect on life and death.

Other Models

Mobile spaces demand an effort and a difficulty that must be overcome. This is why they are ideal for symbolizing different issues that concern humankind. Esther Pascual has chosen a tunnel as her model. The tunnel symbolizes a road in the darkness to reach another landscape, another environment. In this case, the final tunnel on the ascent to the Valley of Núria, in the Pyrenees Mountains of Catalonia, offers us a charming and idyllic landscape on the other side.

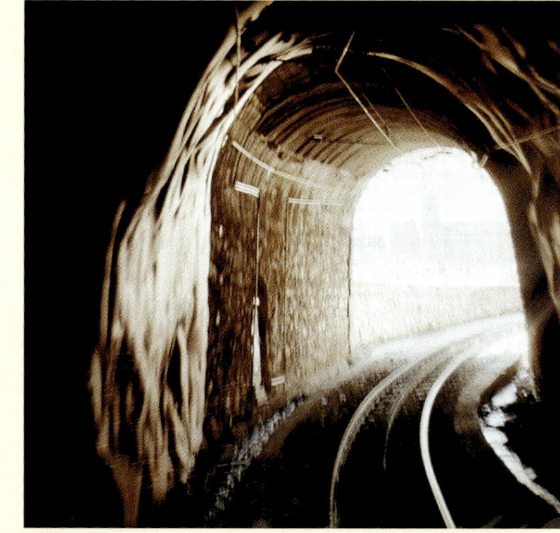

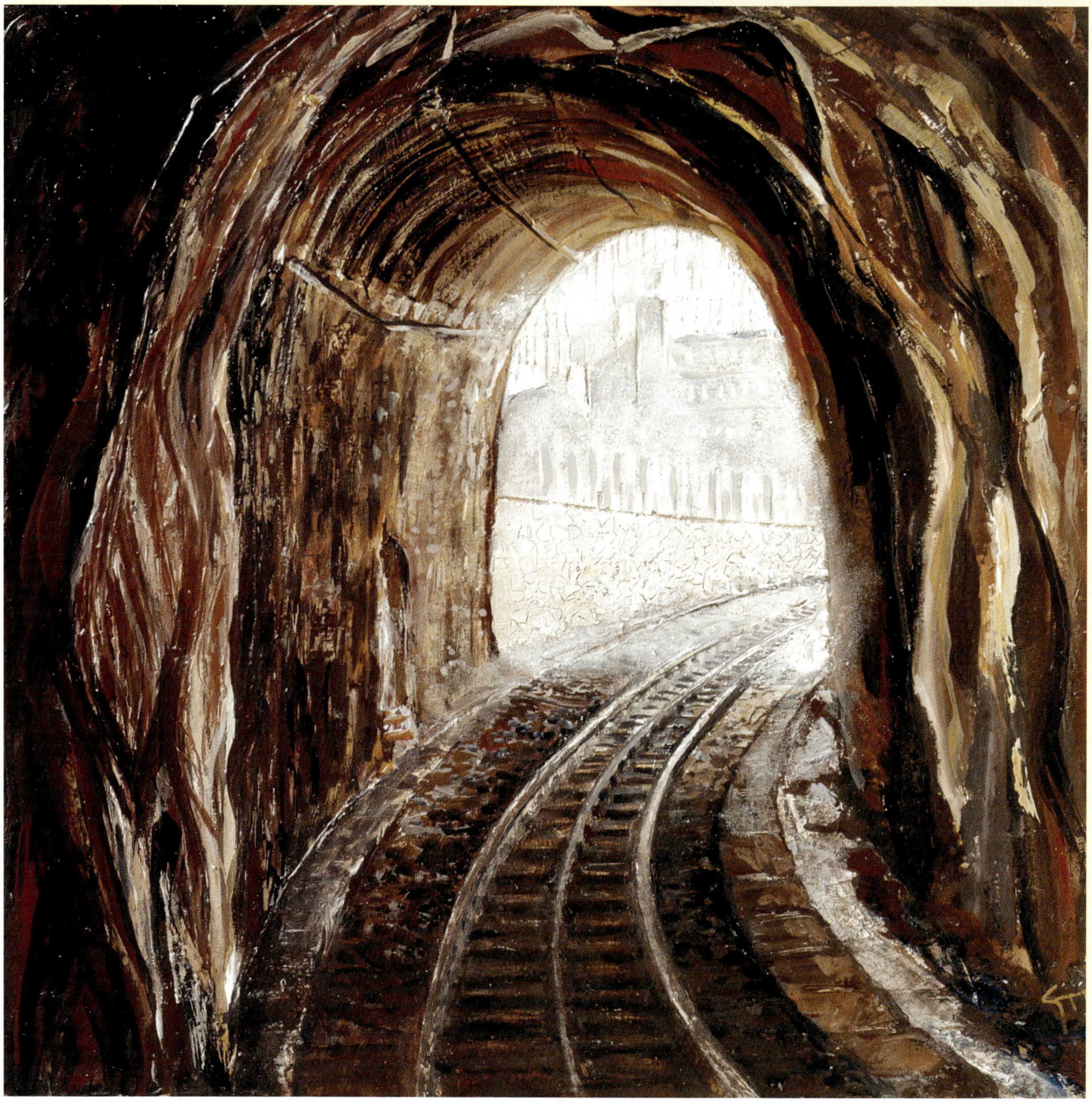

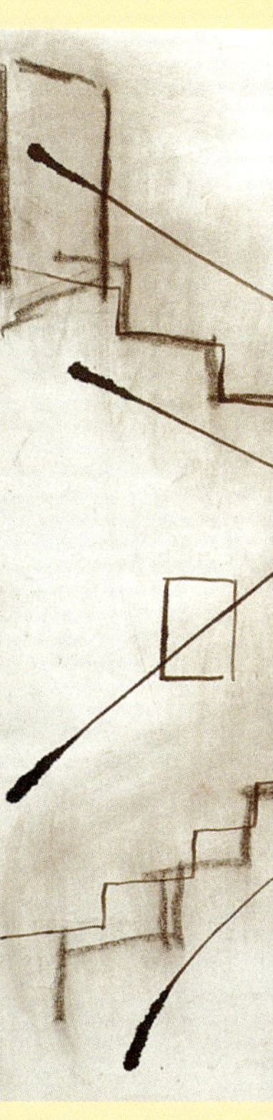

Other Media

To achieve very different results, the artist chose media more appropriate for drawing than for painting: ink, charcoal, markers, and crayons. The first work stands out for its austerity, placing us in a space with different levels, exit doors, and windows, and with the minimum number of lines possible. The second one takes us to a cavernous space; the ascent to the hole resembles more a mountainous terrain than an artificial staircase. The spatial contrast of emptiness and fullness that is visually perceived is conveyed by the contrasting media: markers are cold and direct, crayons inviting and atmospheric.

Other Views

A transgressor by nature, Alejandro Xul Solar (1888–1963) looks to us like a man who was able to live his freedom. Like William Blake, Xul Solar painted his visions, but proclaimed himself a visionary and a mystic without a defined religion. In *Walls and Stairs* he shows us different stairs laid out in parallel, which permit us to ascend through many paths to a single place. Another artist with an often visionary character was Giambattista Piranesi (1720–1778), an excellent etcher, and a lover of classical architecture and archaeology. In the series of etchings that he did on the subject of prisons, Piranesi attacked the rationality and perspective of logic, creating imaginary spaces that are intentionally complex.

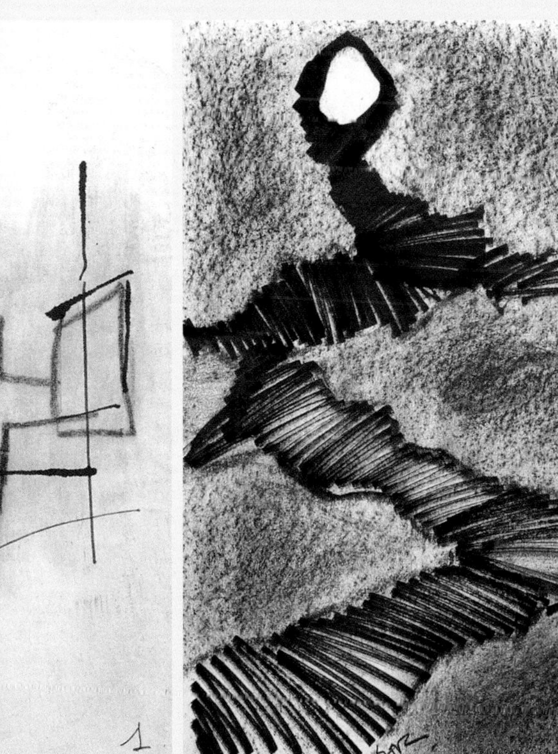

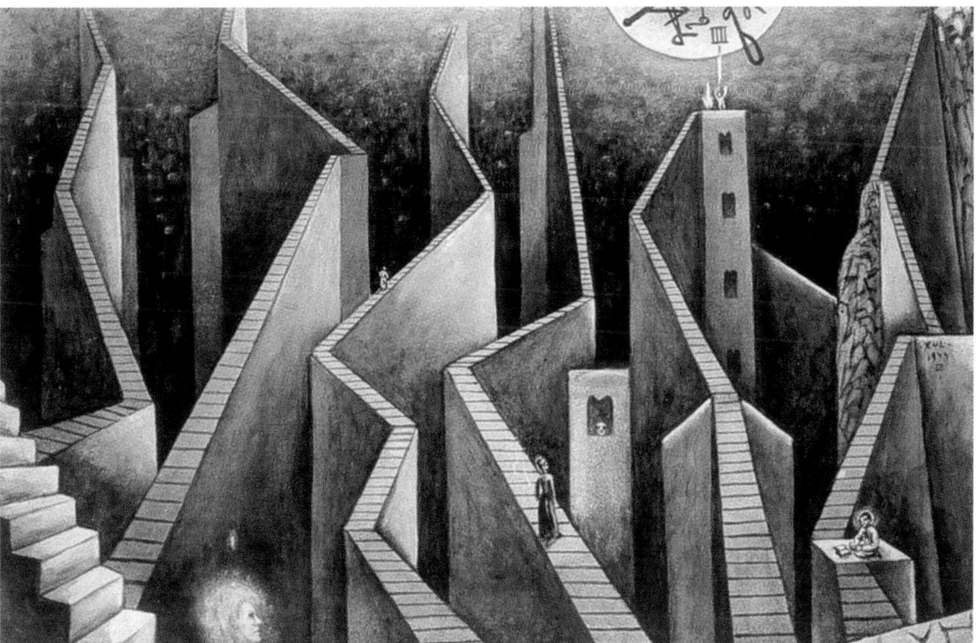

Alejandro Xul Solar,
Walls and Stairs, 1944.

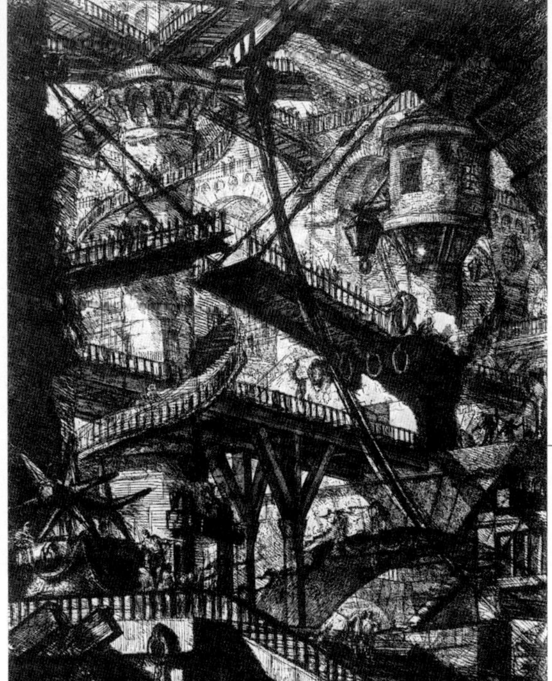

Giambattista Piranesi,
Prisons, Etching no. VII
of the Cárceri series, 1745–1761.

The relationship between the figure and space is a very
interesting research subject. We approach it in this
chapter from the standpoint of the internal spaces of the
figure and its surroundings. The first creative approach
looks for space in the human body, directing the eye of
the viewer in a selective and intimate manner. The other
two approaches examine the spatial relationships between
the figure and its surroundings. On one side is the interior
space, a private space occupied by a static body, and on
the other an exterior space crossed through by a dynamic
body, that of a figure executing an aerial pirouette.

Space in the

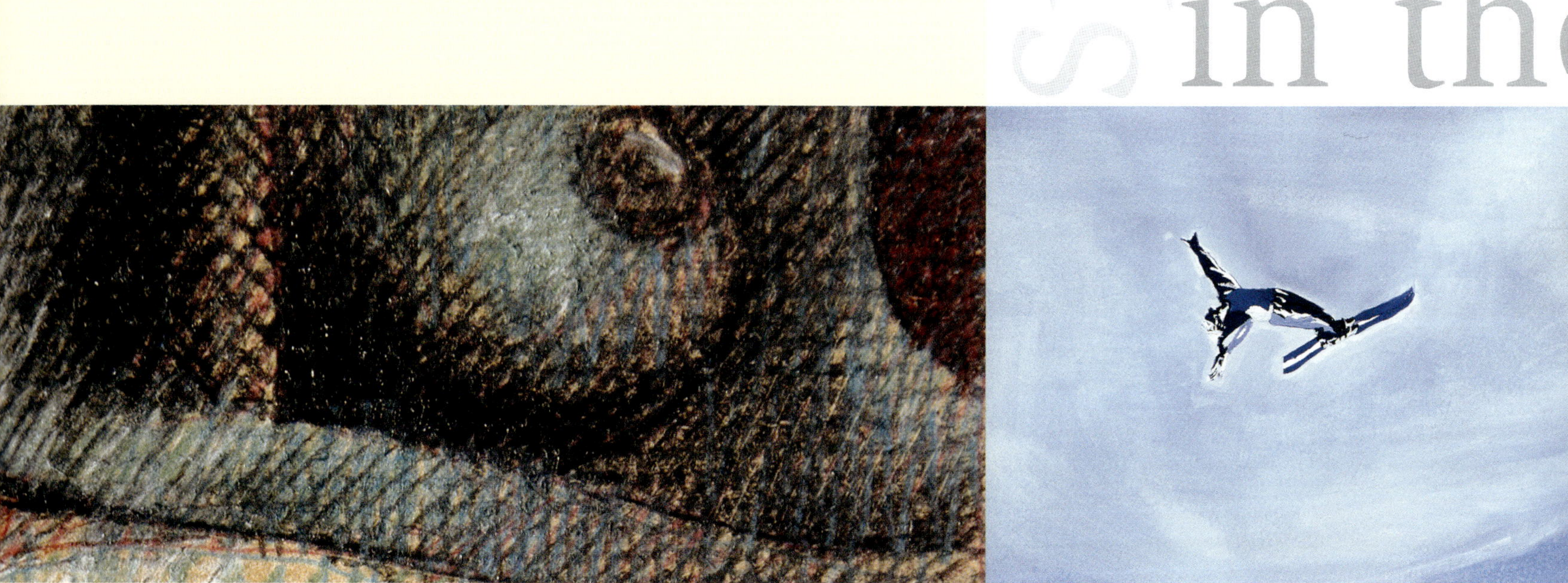

Human Figure

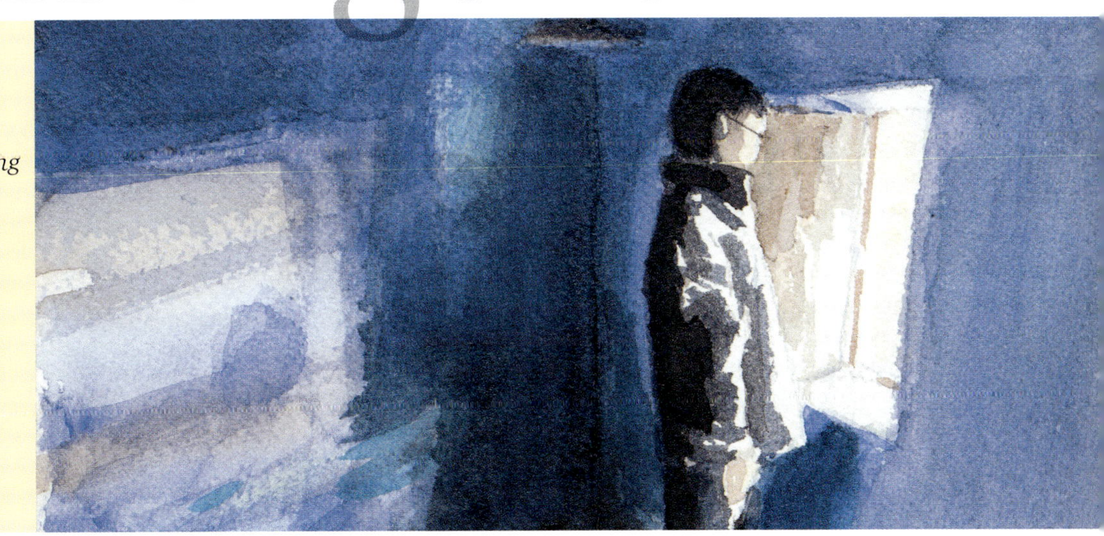

"*And now, where are we going? Aren't we stumbling forward, backwards, sideways, wandering in every direction? Are there still an up and a down? Aren't we wandering through an infinite nothingness? Doesn't emptiness follow us with its breath?*"
Nietzsche,
Gaya Science, Aphorism 125.

Forced, Near, *and Fragmented* Spaces

Finding spaces in the body without taking the surroundings into consideration is a very interesting challenge. To do this the artist works with moving closer (zoom effect) and with the framing. In his nudes, British artist Michael Leonard (born in 1933) creates an intimate visual contact with the model by bringing the body closer to the viewer, a proximity that conveys the humanity of the subject matter. This focus on the body is reminiscent of the photography of Mapplethorpe. In *Vanitas,* the artist creates an allegory of death caused by the AIDS epidemic. The work was obviously inspired by religious paintings of the Renaissance and baroque period: images of the dying Christ, the most well-known version being Mantegna's *Dead Christ.* Continuing with this iconographic tradition, Leonard presents the foreshortened nudes in *sotto in sù* (from bottom up), dramatizing the gesture adopted by the body.

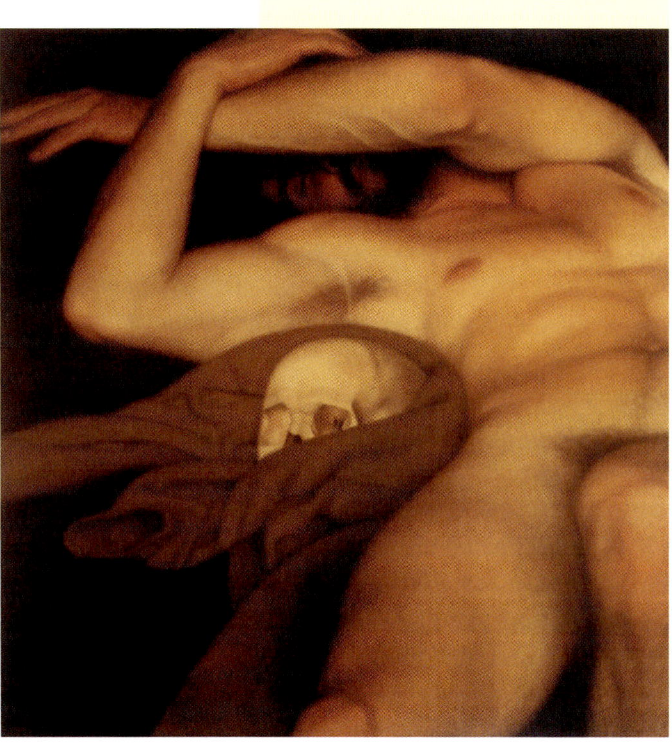

Michael Leonard,
Vanitas, 1991.
Private Collection.

Foreshortening: Varying the Framing and Zooming In on a Nude

Basing his works on a female nude in a foreshortened pose, Josep Asunción developed differently focused paintings without changing the point of view. To do this he framed several areas of the model's body and enlarged them to turn them into the subject matter of the painting. By focusing the eye on a fold, feature, gesture, or a volume of the body and arranging those details in a compositional form within a neutral space, he created unique works of art, of intimate and lyrical character. He created this work with graphite pencils of various hardness and color pencils on kraft or wrapping paper.

"If the body is rooted in the eye, the visual sensations encompass the entire organism."
Carolee Scheemann

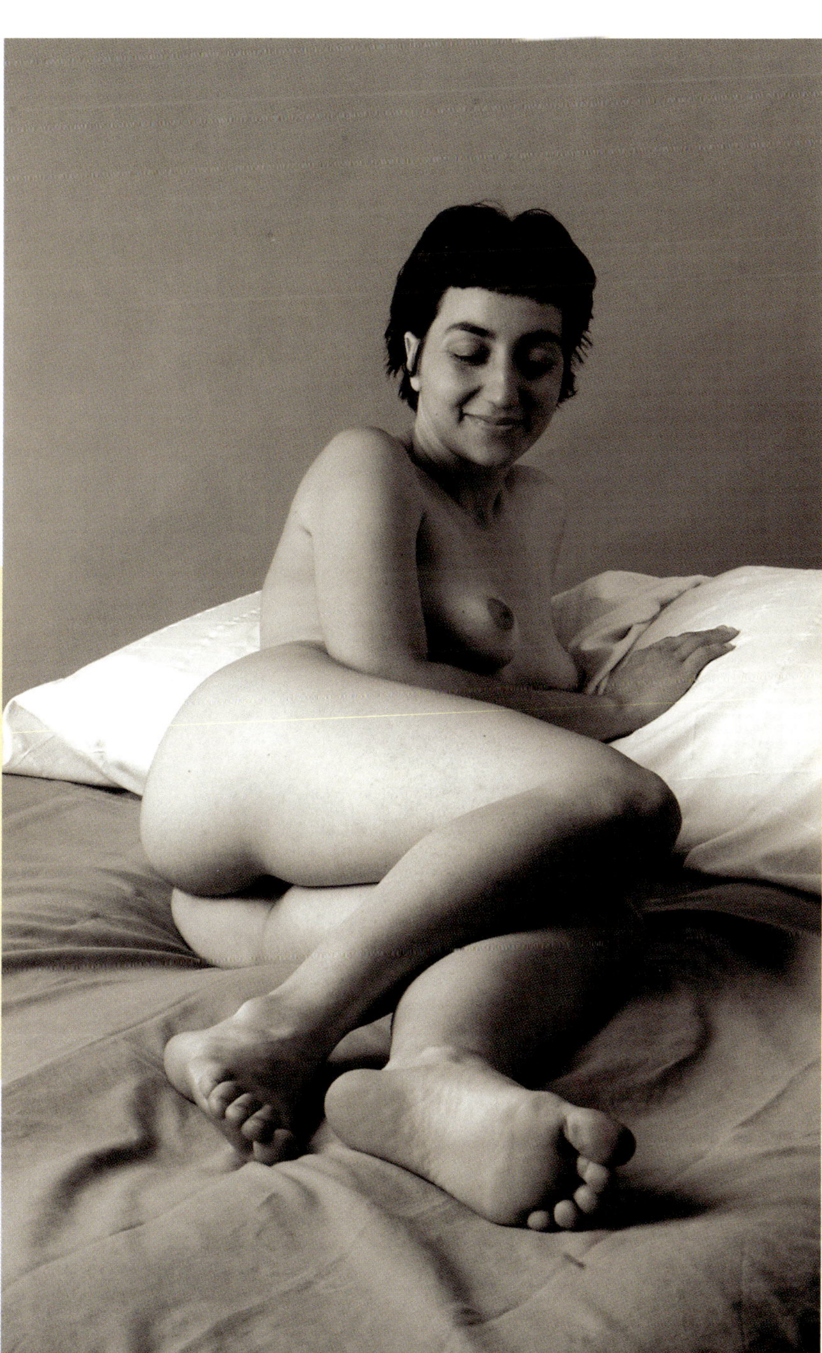

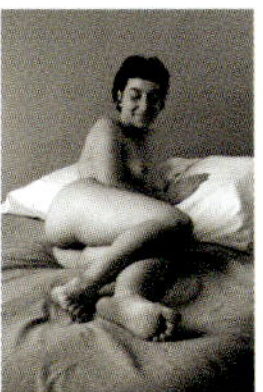

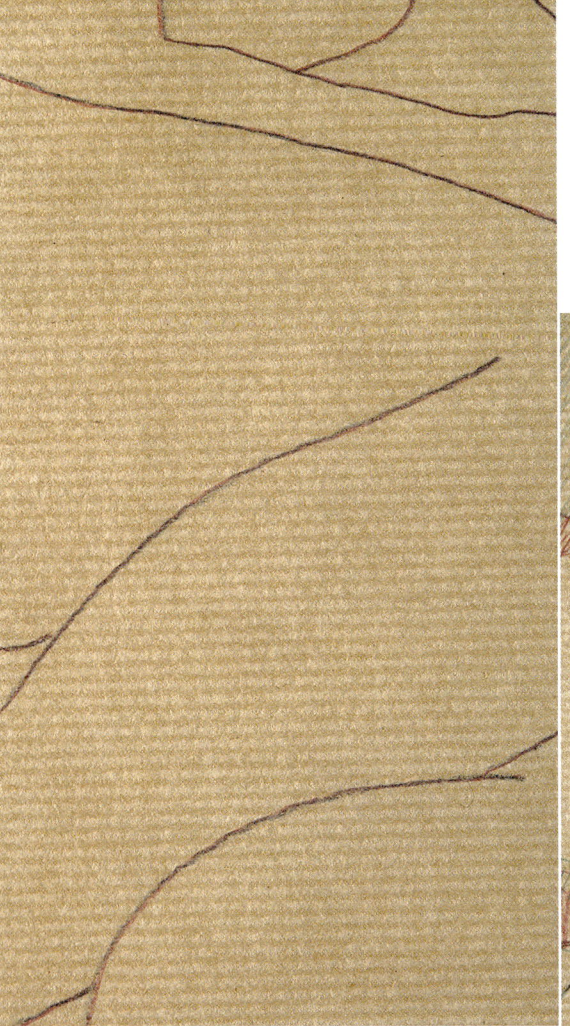

1 The layout that we create with a simple line drawing encompasses several parts of the body: legs, thighs, breasts, and an arm. These parts appear cut off without the silhouette of the body other than in small areas such as the armpit or an ankle. This effect forces the eye to concentrate on the interior volumes and spaces of the body.

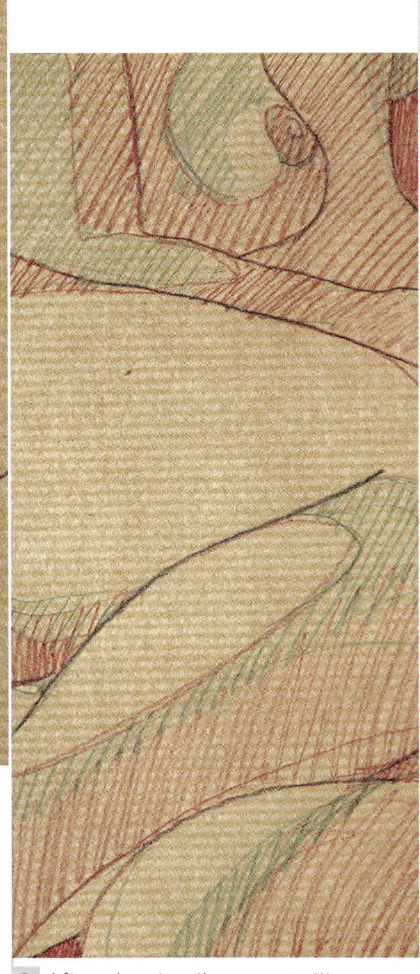

2 After planning the composition around the outlines, we introduce the main areas of light and shadow to begin creating the volume. We define the edges of both areas and apply two different colors with hatching. The green indicates the partially shaded areas and the red the darker ones.

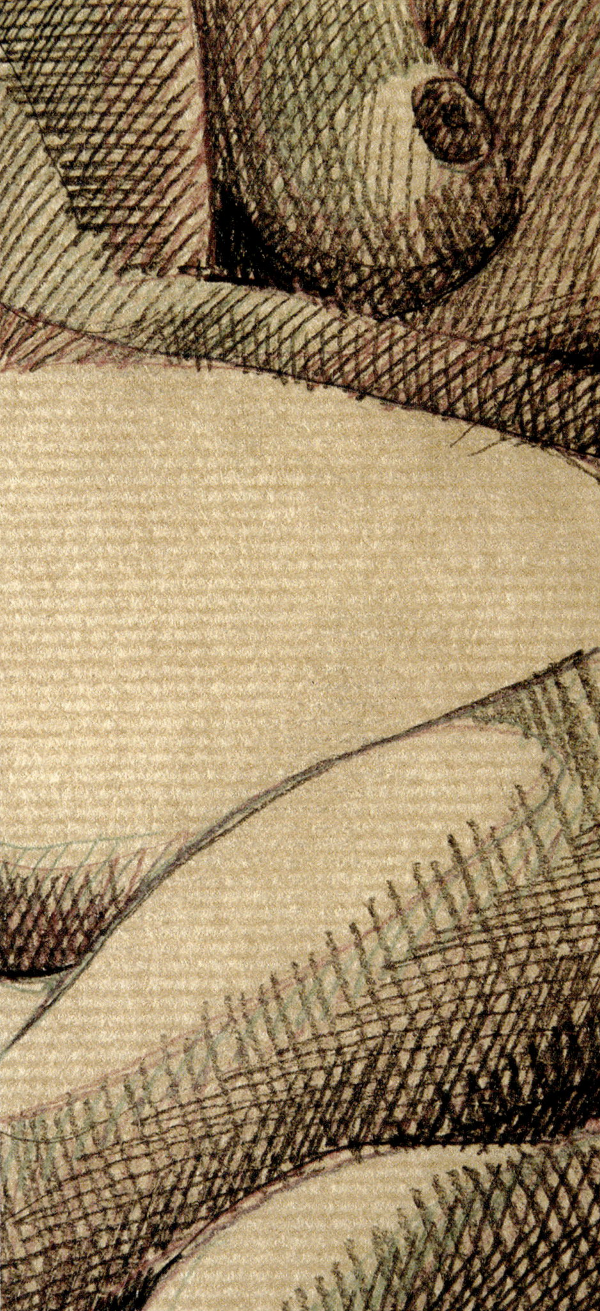

3 We continue drawing hatch lines in the areas of color to create different shadow intensities. This time we use HB graphite pencils for the general areas and 2B for the thicker and darker lines.

4 We intensify each area and incorporate 6B pencil lines to create very dark blacks. Observe how the lines lightly blend to create a natural modeling.

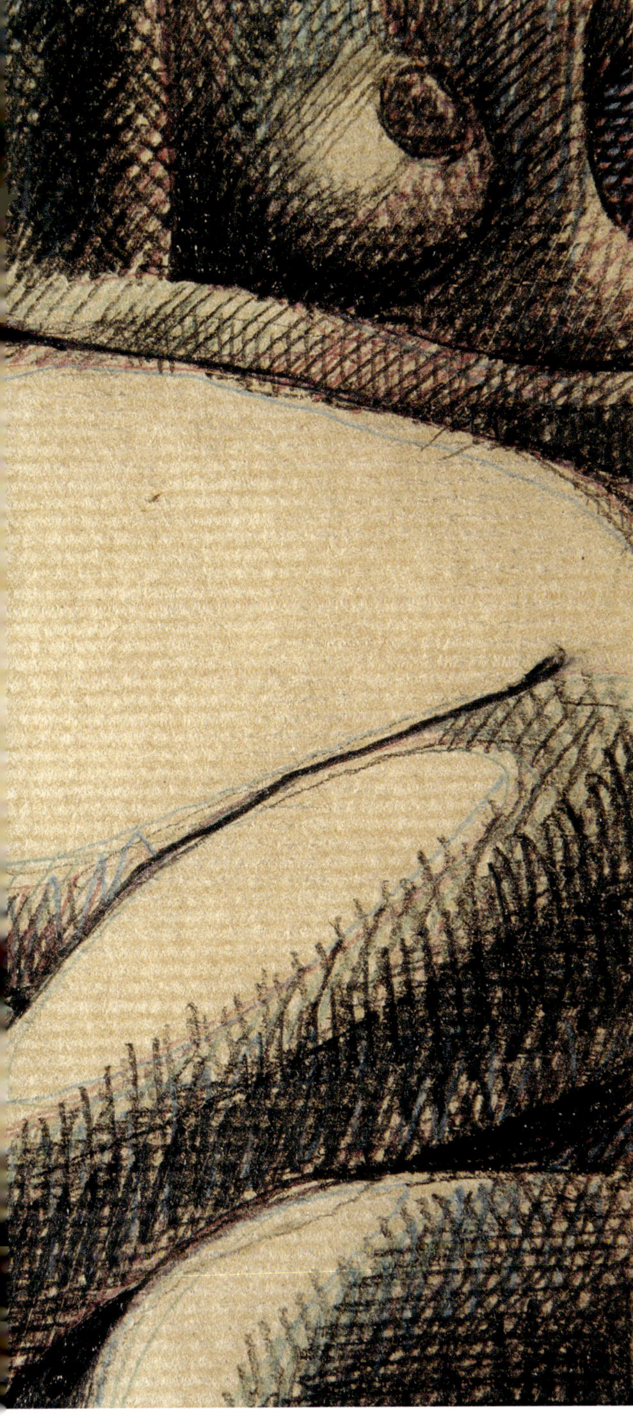

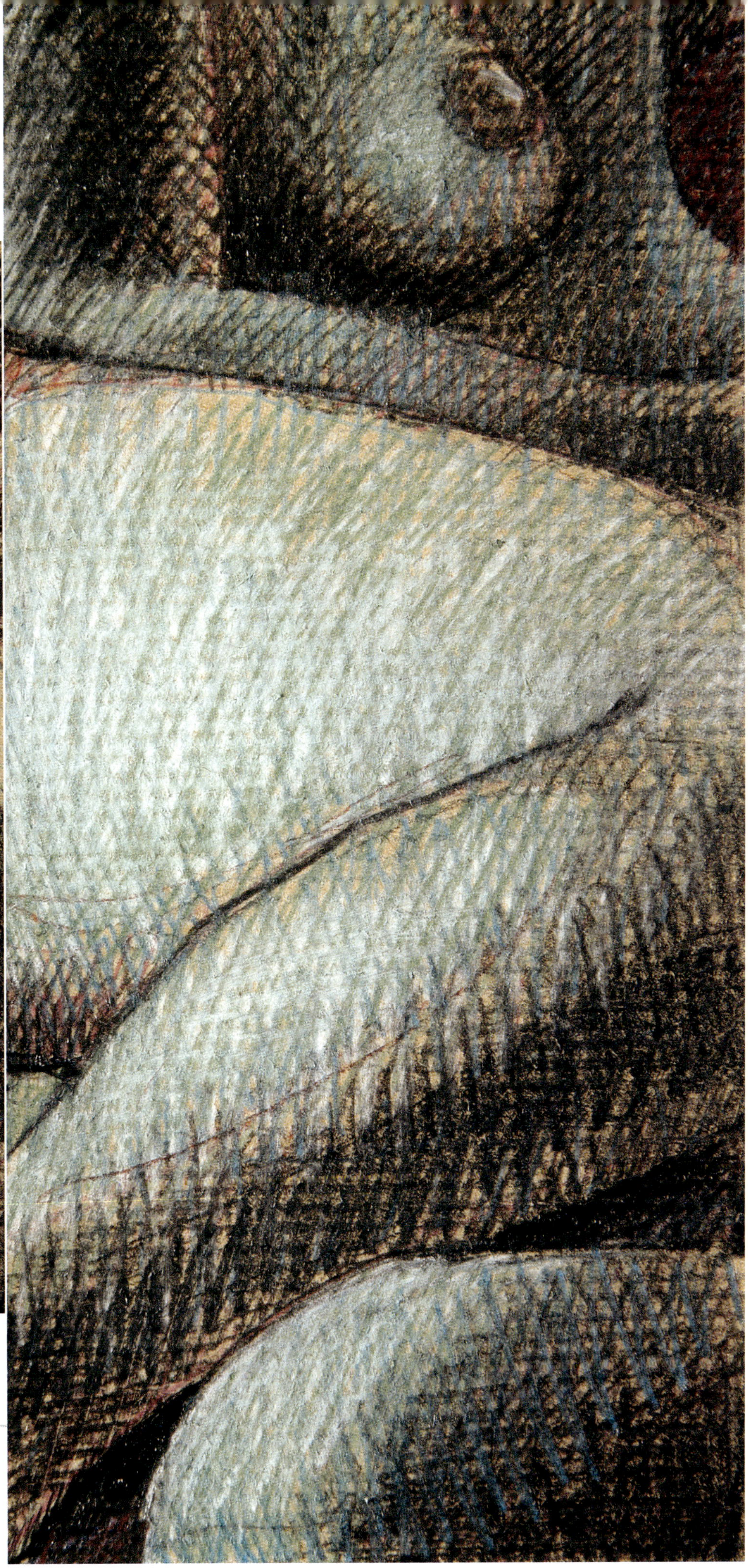

5 To finish, we shade the areas of light that had been left blank with hatched blue-green and white lines. Incorporating color into the light provides a greater feeling of volume to the model. Also, all the white space of the thigh is no longer perceived as an empty area and becomes a volume.

Other Versions

The forced perspective view of the model provides a rich combination of volumes and spaces. The foreshortening brings the figure closer to abstraction because it alters the normal view of the model and shows aspects that would be difficult to see unless viewed from unexpected angles, as can be seen in the different drawings of this gallery.

In the human figure, the directions of the extremities or of the gaze reveal new spaces. They act as signals that guide us to the areas we should look at. Here, the gesture of the hand describes the space of this pose. The hand makes an arc that connects perfectly with those made by the breasts. The body is open to the exterior.

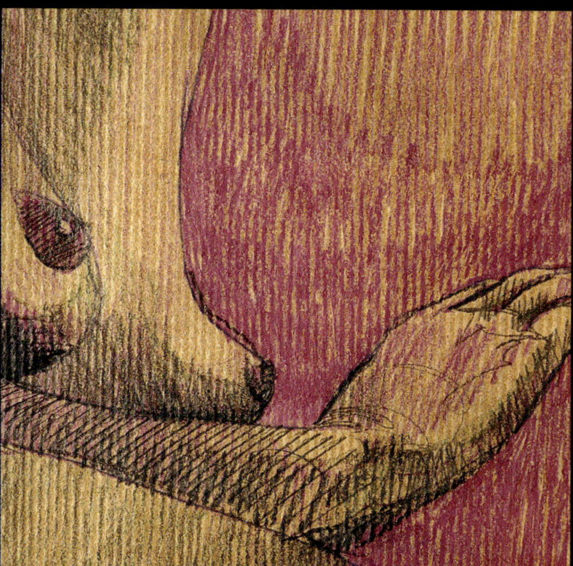

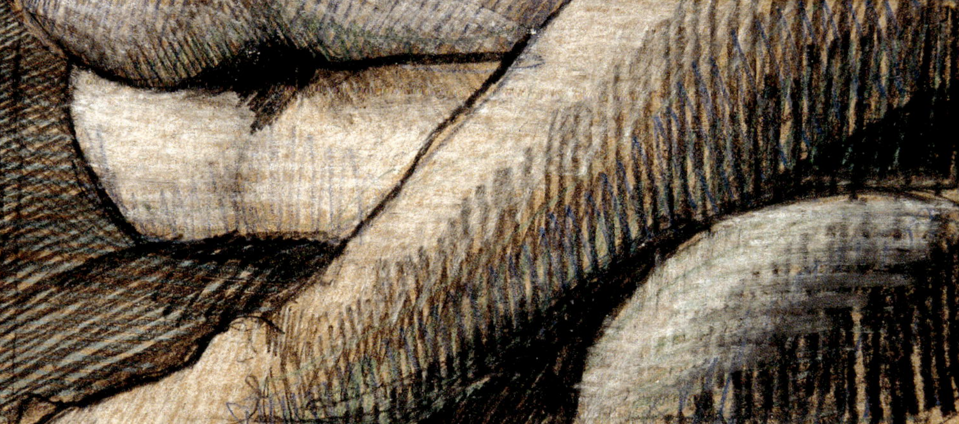

The horizontal composition of this work centers on the gestures of the thighs and legs seen from below. We see three grounds: a fragment of an enlarged leg in the foreground, the second leg with the suggestion of the ankle in the middle ground, and the two thighs in the back. The eye makes a round-trip journey.

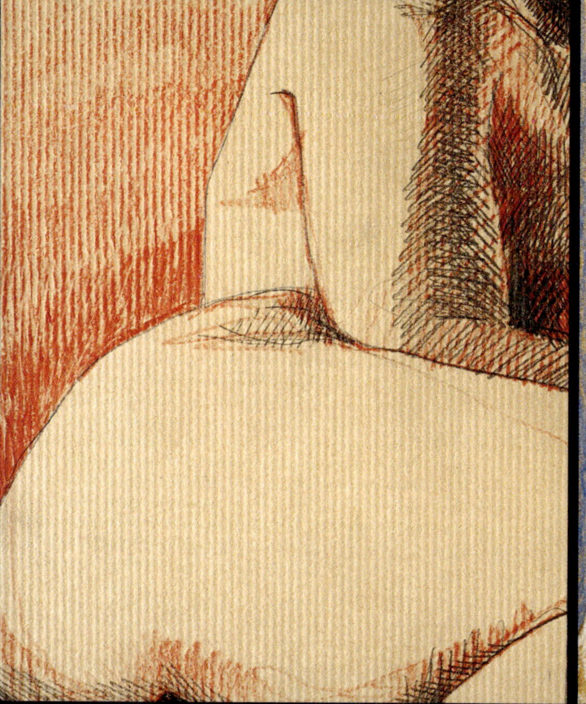

Here we see a balance between two large areas. In the foreground, the imposing volume of the large thigh captures the eye of the viewer because it is presented without any details, and is totally clean and well lighted. In the middle ground, farther away from the eye of the viewer, we see the beginning of the torso and the arm, in the shadow. It is a beautiful combination of volumes and spaces, light and shadow.

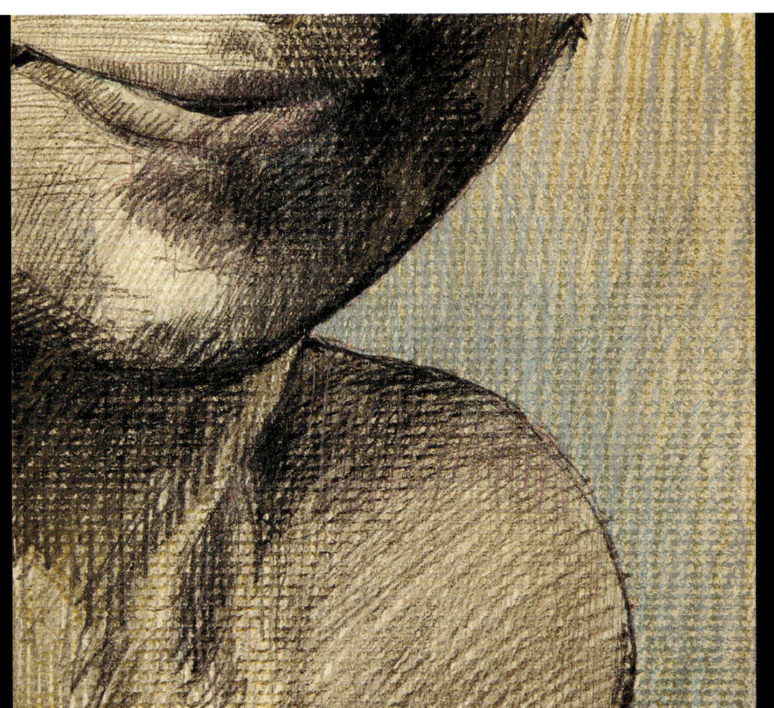

The enlarged view of the mouth, chin, and neck of the model brings us incredibly close to her as viewers, since close proximity is required to notice such small areas. We indicate the space that runs underneath the chin thanks to the chiaroscuro of the neck.

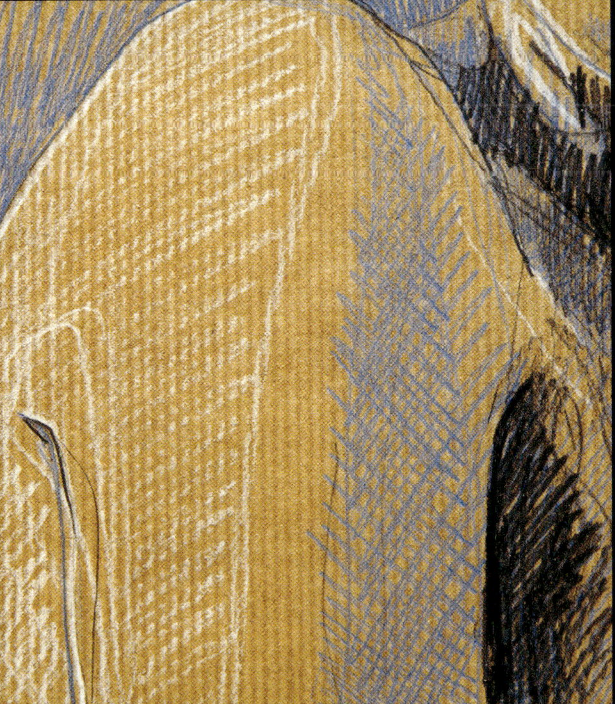

A shoulder is all that is needed to spark a suggestive visual journey up and down, like the ascent and descent of a mountain. The light and shadow contrast on both sides of the arm emphasize its roundness, providing volume and presence in such a way that the eye perceives a body, not a silhouette.

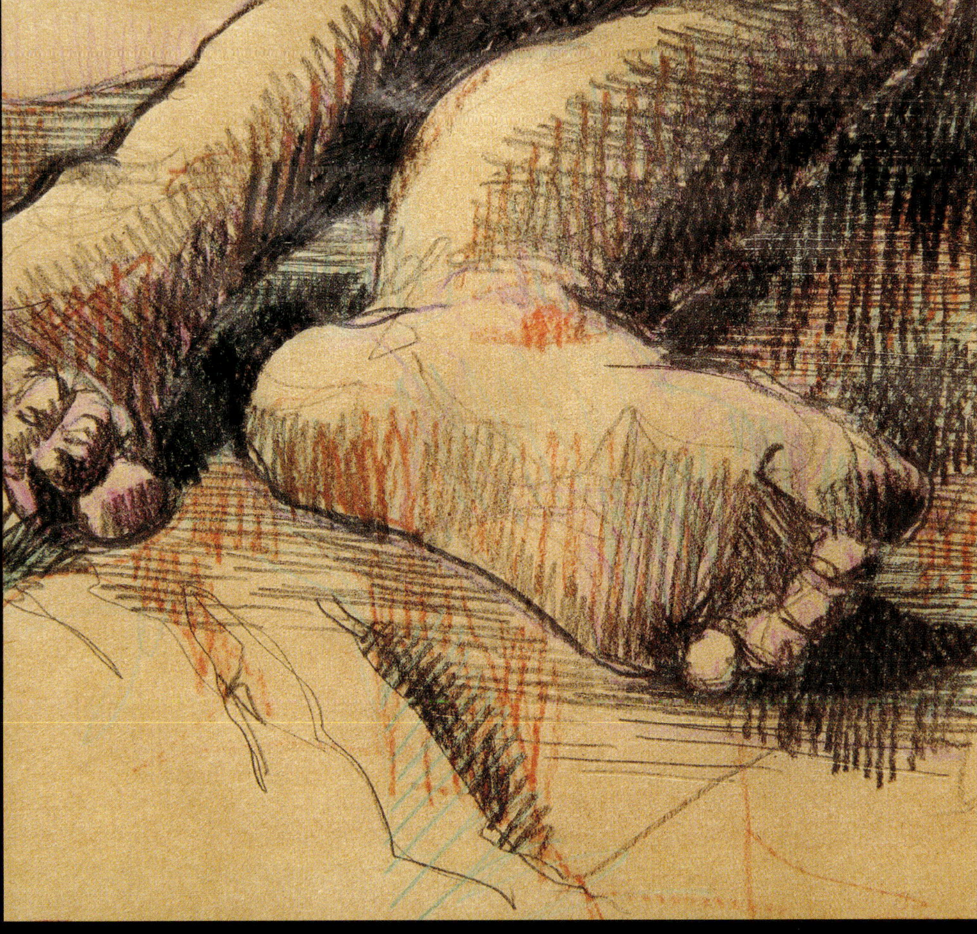

The feet create a composition formed by two triangles that spread apart like a fan on the horizontal ground. Like fingers, the toes signal a spatial projection away from the body while at the same time offering a visual entry to it.

116

Other Models

In this case, we have opted for a male model in a more static position where the musculature is emphasized and where we can see the disproportion created by the foreshortening on a body like this one. The position is similar to that of Andrea Mantegna's *Dead Christ,* but from a higher point of view. In the drawing, we can see clearly that the legs are extremely long compared with the torso, because of the *sotto in sù.*

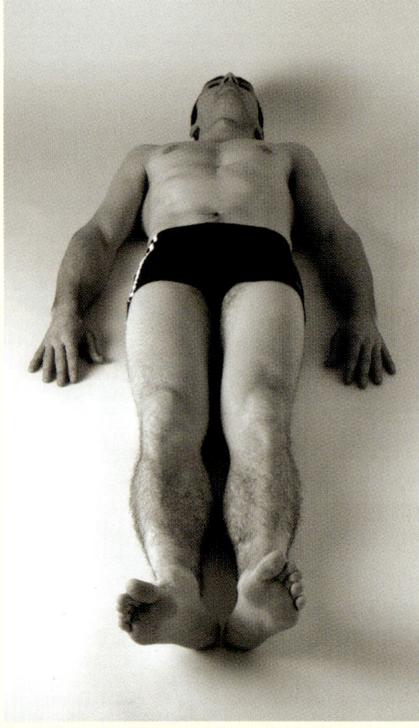

Other Media

As an alternative to texture created by the hatched pencil drawing, we propose areas of flat color gouache. With this new medium the features acquire a considerably different look. Flat colors make the image colder, more distant, looking like a poster or a pop-art image.

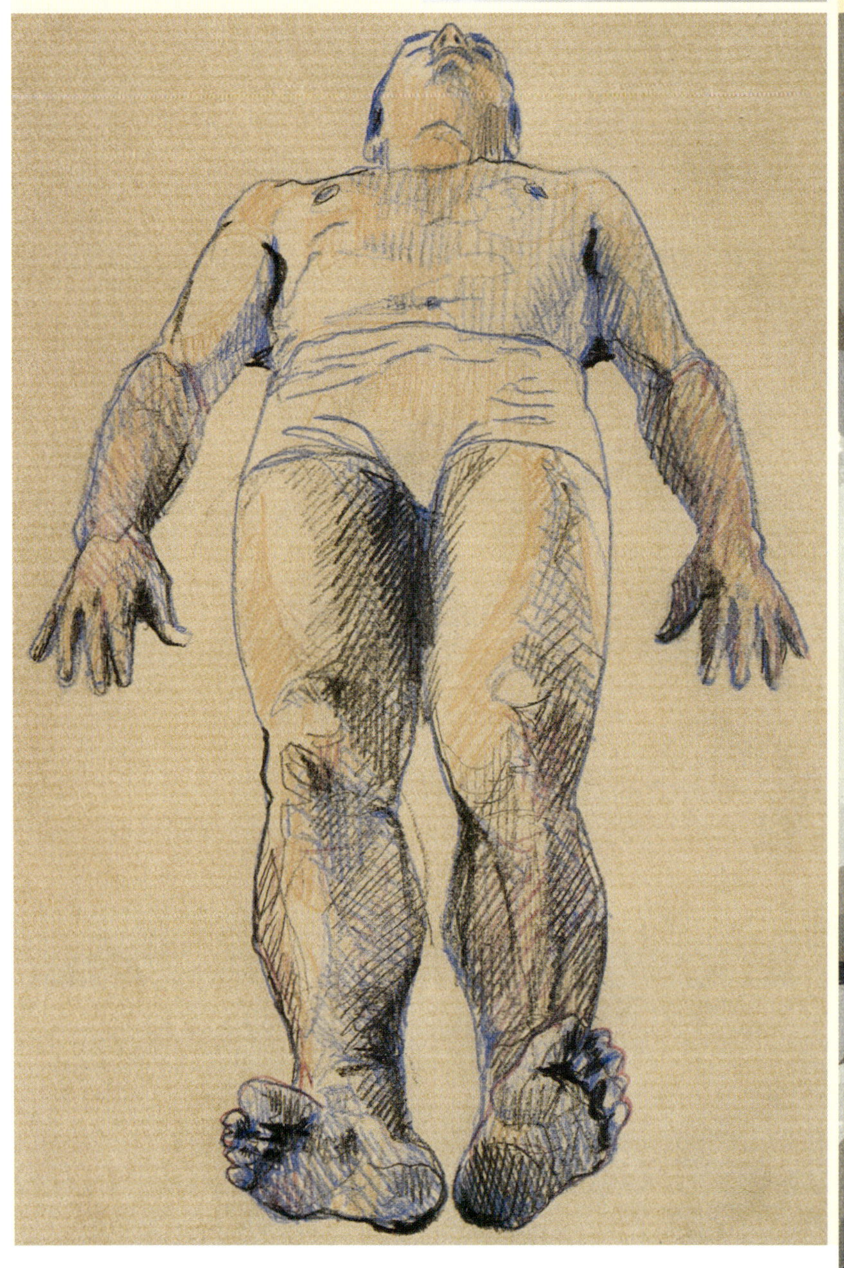

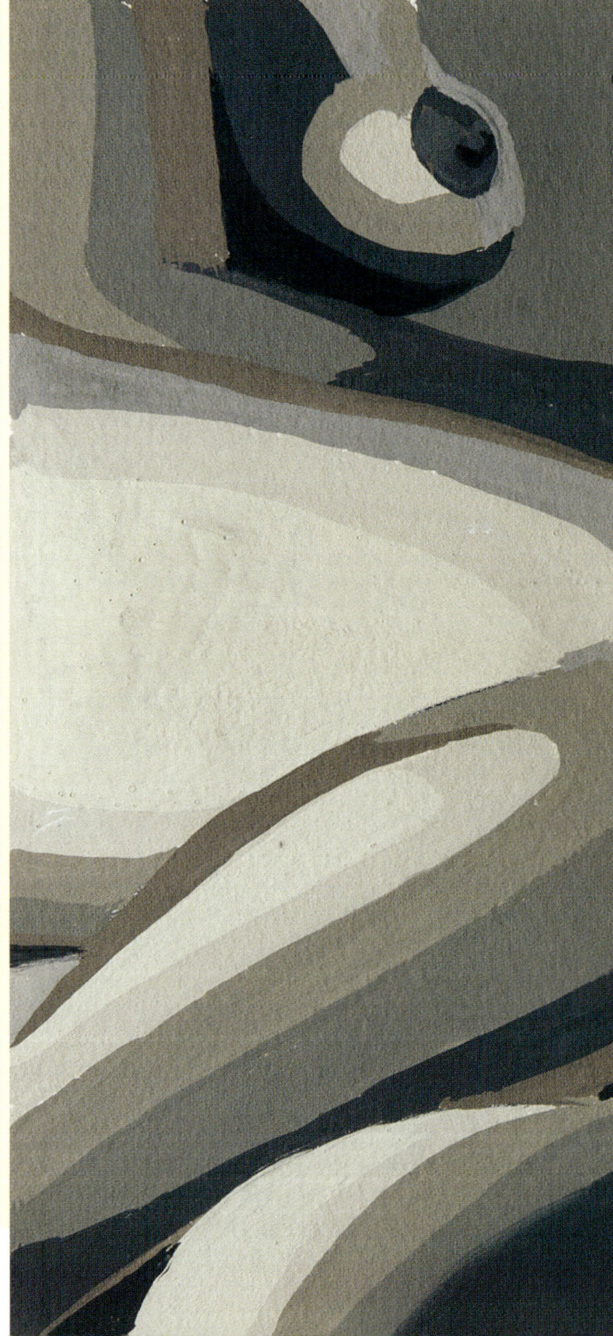

Other Views

Below we offer two different views of the same foreshortened figure, separated by a time span of five centuries. Andrea Mantegna (1431–1506) created provocative perspectives with a sculptural and voluminous look that were inspired by classical antiquity. After an illness he incorporated the theme of pain into his work. An example of it is the *Dead Christ,* achieving extremely expressive heights with foreshortening. Observe how he corrected the natural perspective, because the feet should be larger. This shows us the idealistic character of the painting.

Luis Caballero (1947–1995), a Colombian painter who focused on the male body, made nudes showing fragmented close grounds, whether in erotic poses, in combat, or dead. His focus shows the clear influence of Francis Bacon, Mapplethorpe, Goya's prints of the disasters of war, and Spanish religious paintings of the seventeenth and eighteenth centuries, as well as Colombian versions of those paintings.

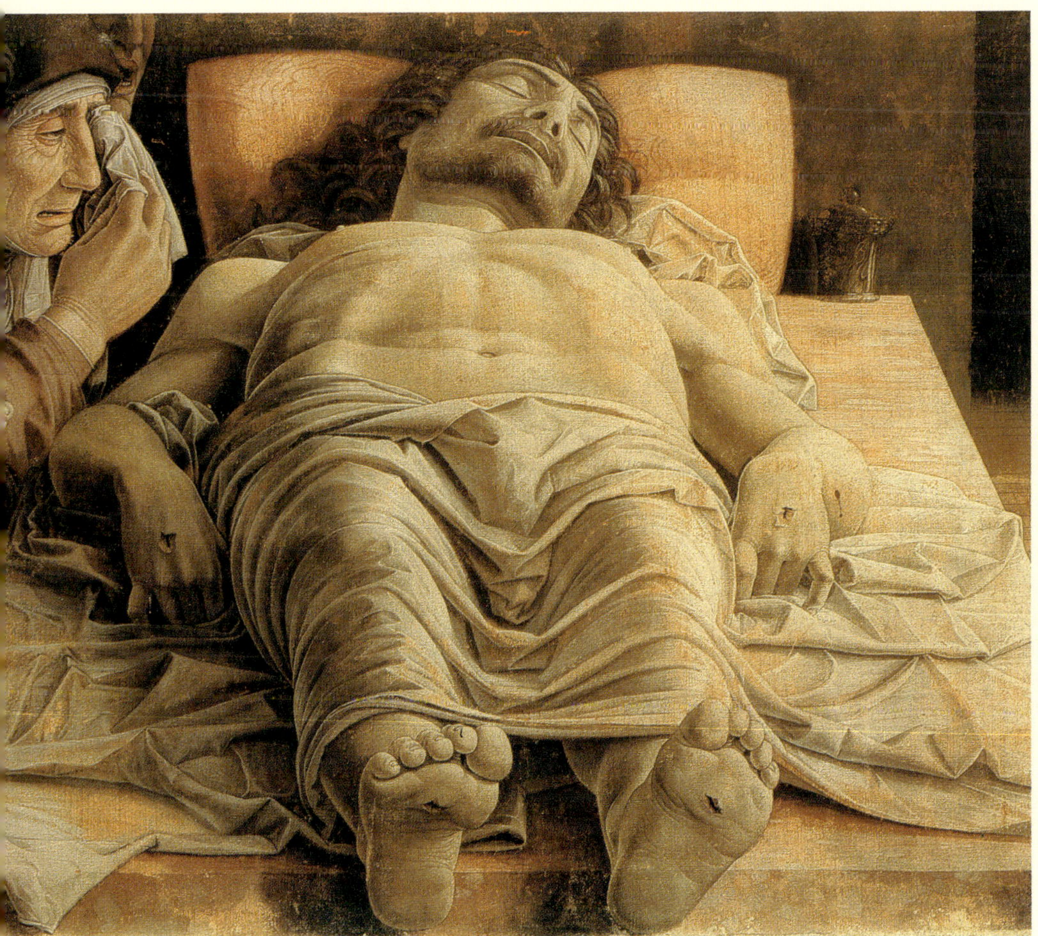

Andrea Mantegna,
Dead Christ, c. 1490.
Pinacoteca de Brera,
Milan, Italy.

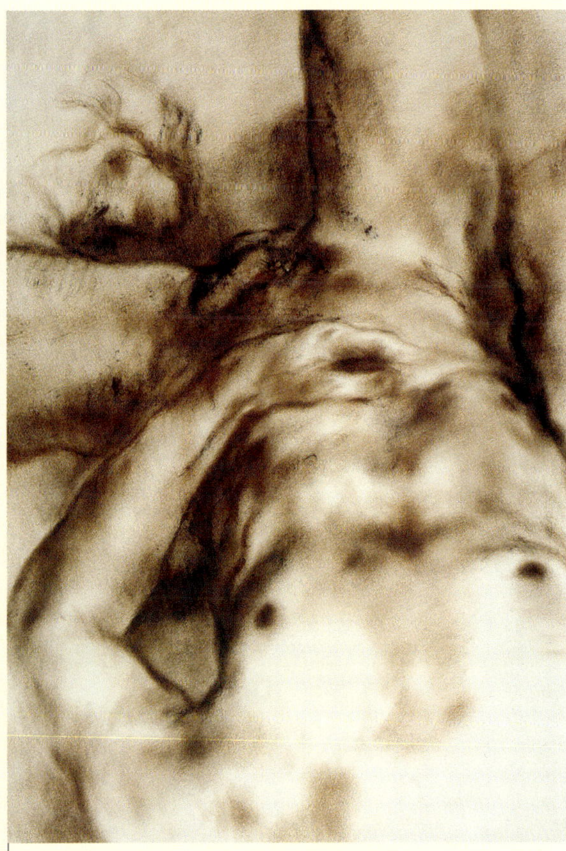

Luis Caballero,
Sin Título, 1990.
Private Collection.

Dynamic, *Spinning,* and *Weightless* Spaces

Space in the Human Figure

118

Edgar Degas (1834–1917), considered the painter of immediacy, had a restless and dynamic spirit; the most important goal of his work was to capture a fleeting movement. In 1866 he discovered the world of the theater, and he marveled at the movement that music generated in the bodies of ballerinas. His two great influences were Japanese art, from which he borrowed the off-center compositional style, and photography, a medium capable of capturing an instant. One of Degas's most beautiful paintings is *Mademoiselle Lala in Fernando's Circus,* a metaphor about human abandonment. In it he focused on the relationship between the artist suspended in the air and the architecture of the cupola. He carried out a thorough study of the space in numerous preliminary sketches, creating a very calculated composition, rich in diagonals and dynamism, without horizontal lines or a background.

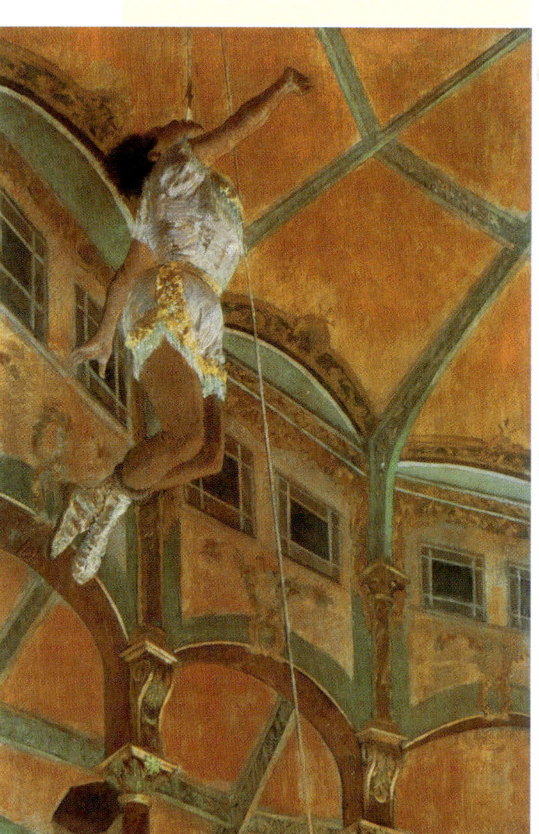

Edgar Degas,
Mademoiselle Lala in Fernando's Circus, 1879.
National Gallery,
London, United Kingdom.

Changes in Scale:
The Lyricism of Spinning
in Space

A skier's jump into the void inspired Gemma Guasch to capture the dynamism of the instant generated by the body suspended in empty and infinite space. Changing the size of skier and his position in the air allowed her to incorporate the immensity suggested by the empty space. The chosen medium is acrylic paints in blue tones, applied over heavy paper. In this case the versatility of acrylic paint helps create contrast between the density of the jumper and the vaporous sky.

"Dynamism is the simultaneous action of the characteristic and particular movement of the object (absolute movement) with the transformations that the object experiences in its trajectory in relation to the mobile and static environment (relative movement) (. . .) it is the lyrical conception of the forms interpreted in the infinite when manifested in its relativity between absolute movement and relative movement, between medium and object, until the appearance of a whole: medium + object."
Boccioni

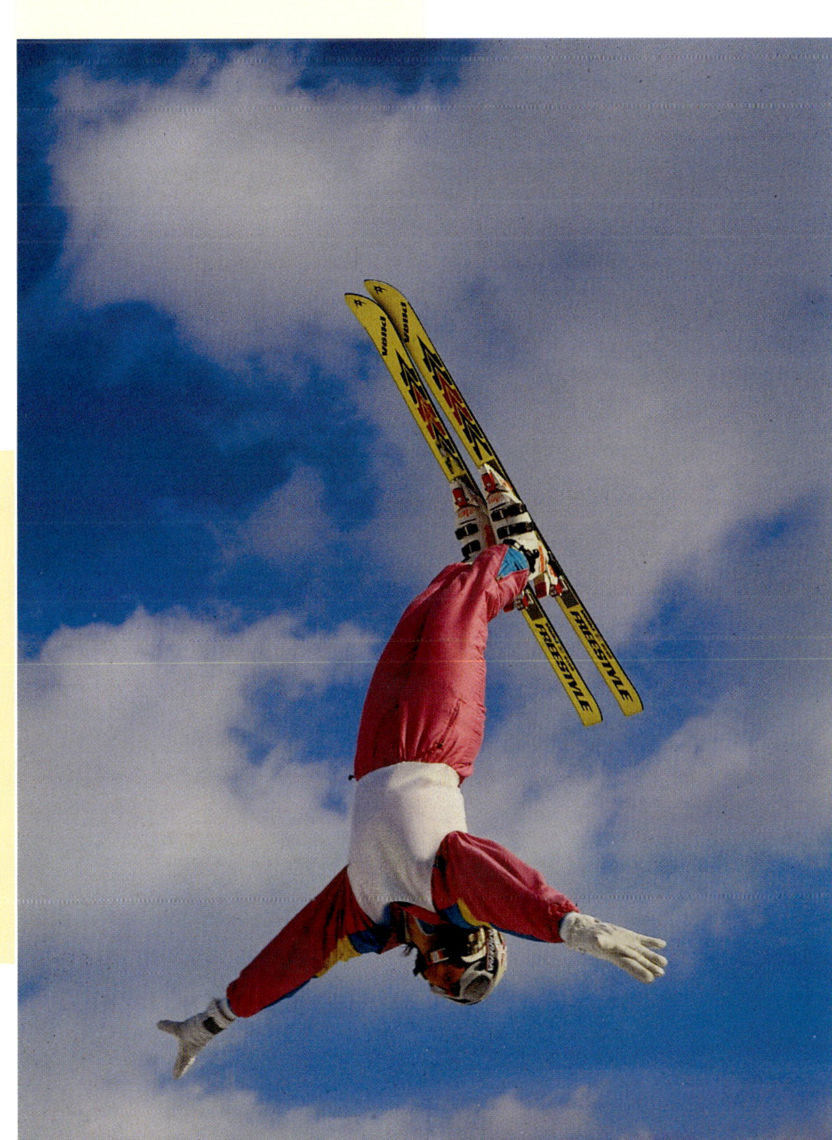

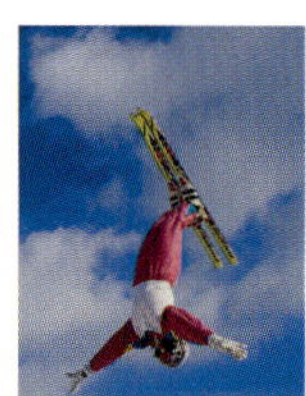

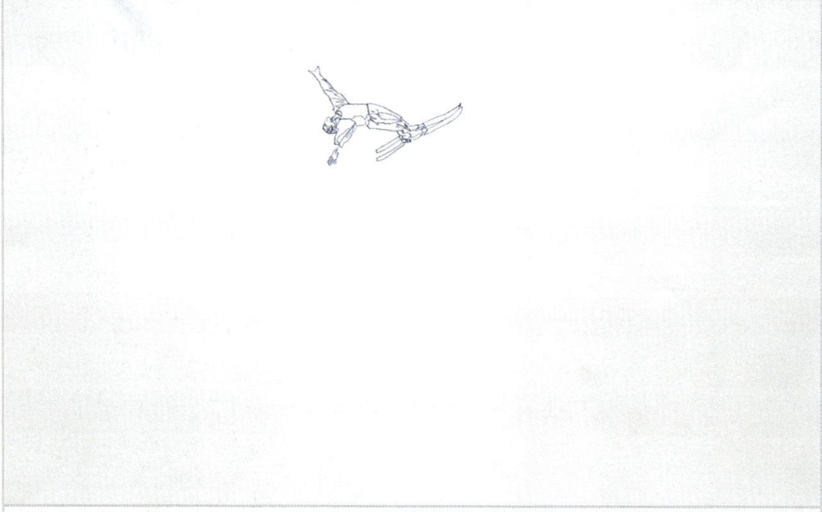

1 Before beginning we study the proportions of the figure so we can modify its scale. We reduce it and draw its outline while also altering its initial position. The chosen composition contrasts the empty and immense feeling of the space with the tension of the jump.

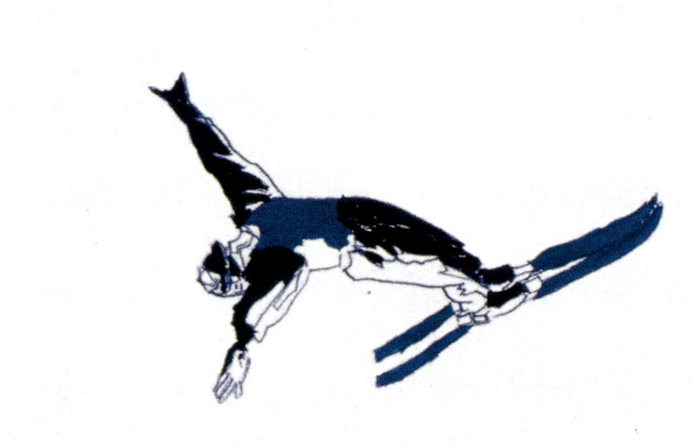

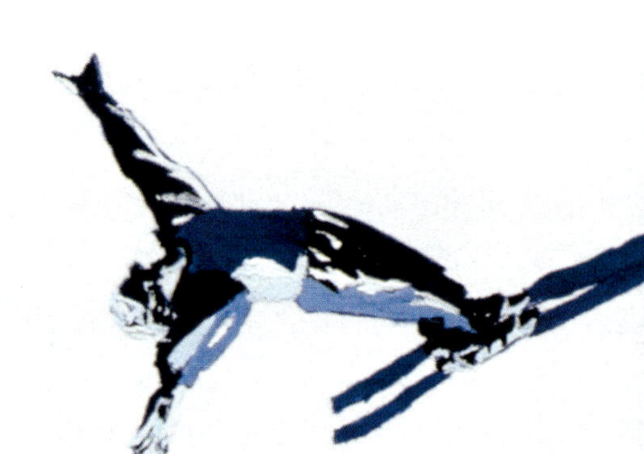

2 The darkest tones of the body are painted with dark blues. The arc formed by the immortalized instant of the jump becomes evident when different colors are applied to the body to give it volume.

3 The lighter tones of the body are painted with different blues. Now all its volume and density can be seen. The different tones of blue were previously chosen according to the lights and shadows that their presence generated in the middle of the sky.

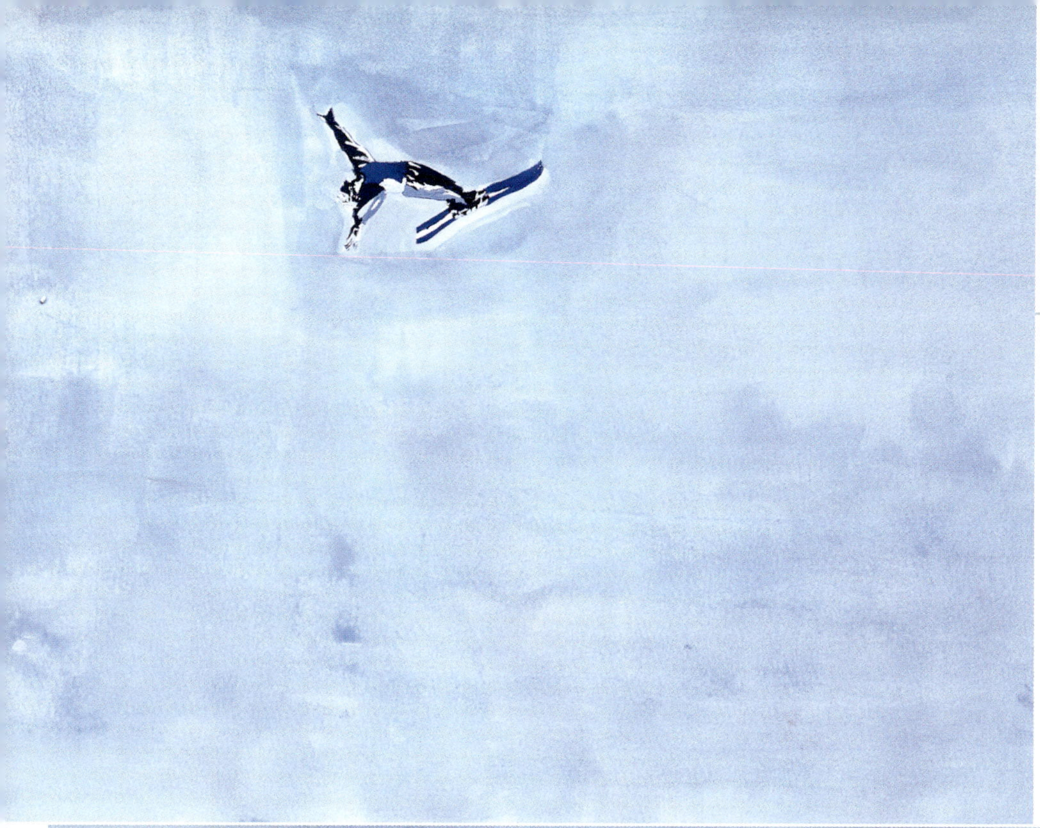

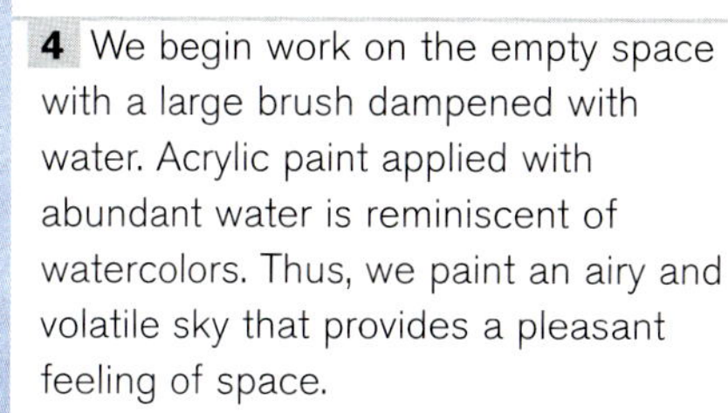

4 We begin work on the empty space with a large brush dampened with water. Acrylic paint applied with abundant water is reminiscent of watercolors. Thus, we paint an airy and volatile sky that provides a pleasant feeling of space.

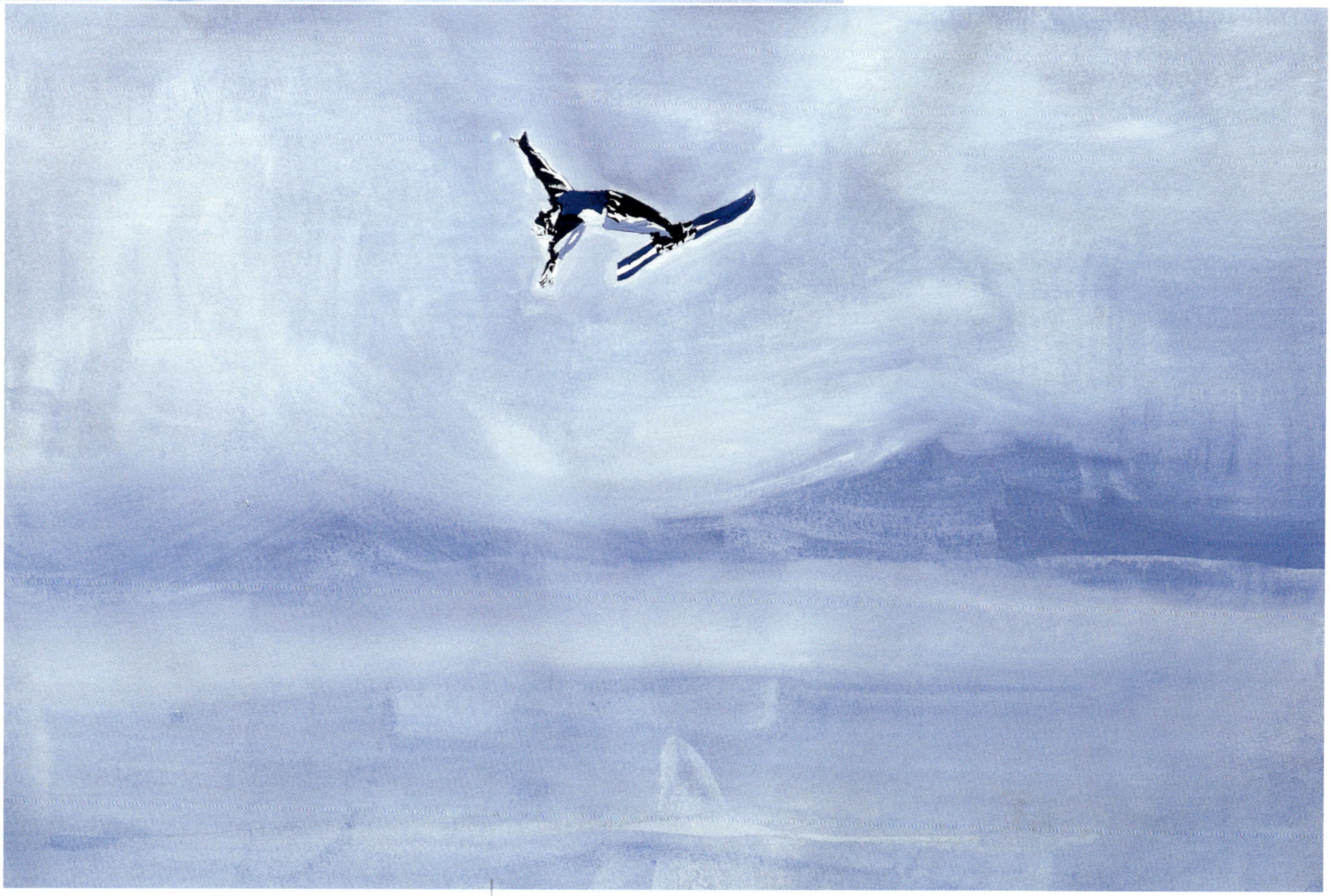

5 To finish, we have fun with the variety of tones that the sky displays. A few darker blue lines are reinforced, and white is added. With them the immensity and infinite feeling of the aerial spectacle becomes more vivid in the eye of the viewer. The result proves the poetry that empty spaces can convey by capturing an instant.

Gallery

Other Versions

We have created different compositions by changing the scale and the position of the skier. The perception of empty space interrupted by the presence of the jumping body generates very interesting and dynamic spatial sensations that encourage us to let loose and jump.

The skier is on the upper right corner of the paper, at full scale. The position captures the end of the pirouette that happens before the descent. The sense of space goes beyond the paper and suggests the experience of the jumper in the air before landing on the ground.

The immense and empty space overpowers this composition. The size of the skier has been greatly reduced to make it look as if the body is almost lost. Its position in the upper left corner of the image further reinforces the sense of spatial infinity and vastness.

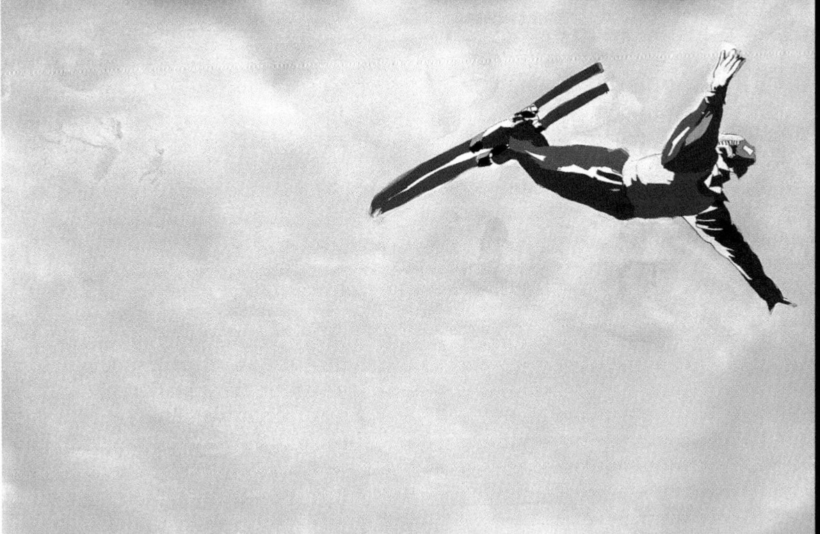

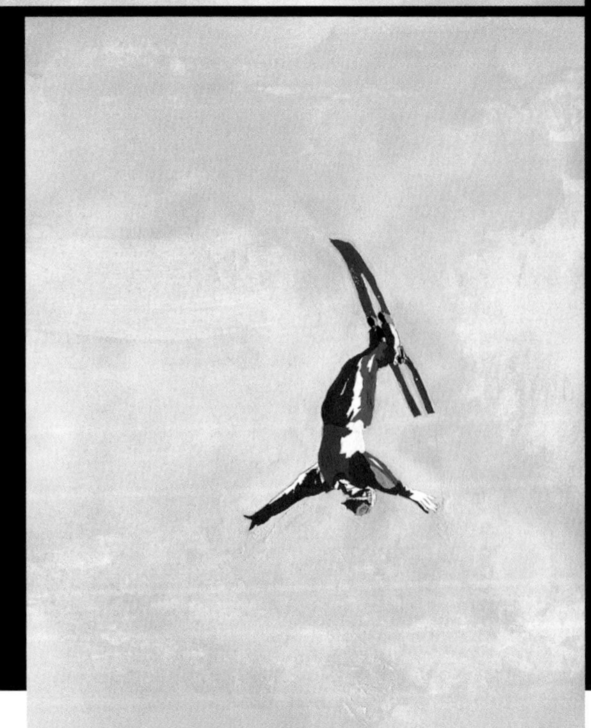

This end captures a fleeting moment in the jump, the moment when the jumper's body is totally inverted, defying all the laws of gravity. The scale of the body has been reduced a little. The verticality and central position create a composition that is perceived as unstable because of the jumper's inverted position.

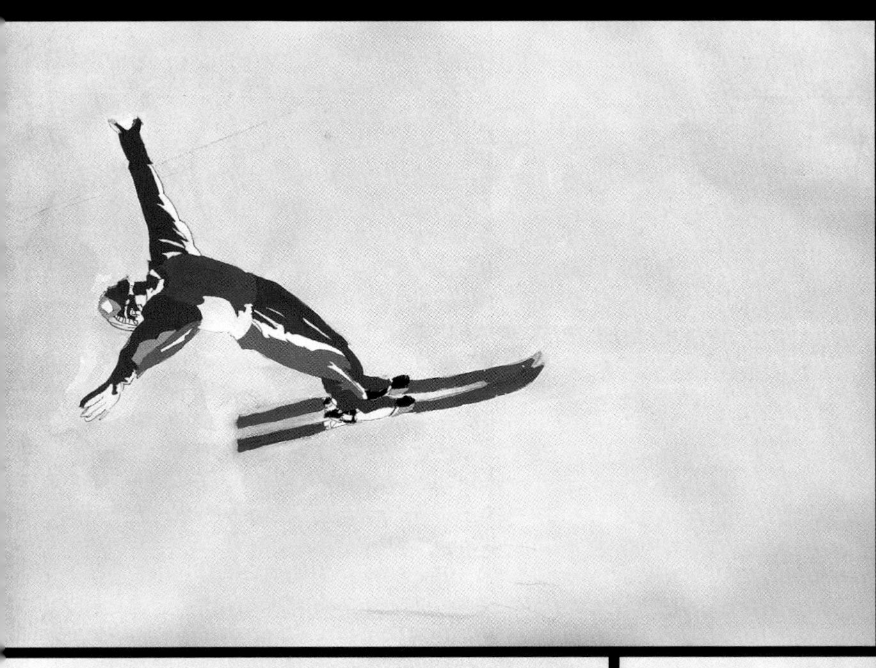

The moment captured here evokes the impulsive force of the body when it jumps into the air and the energy created to begin the turn in the air. The size of the skier at full scale places him close to the viewer. The composition is divided into two halves, the left one full and the right one empty, and this combination of fullness and emptiness balances the result.

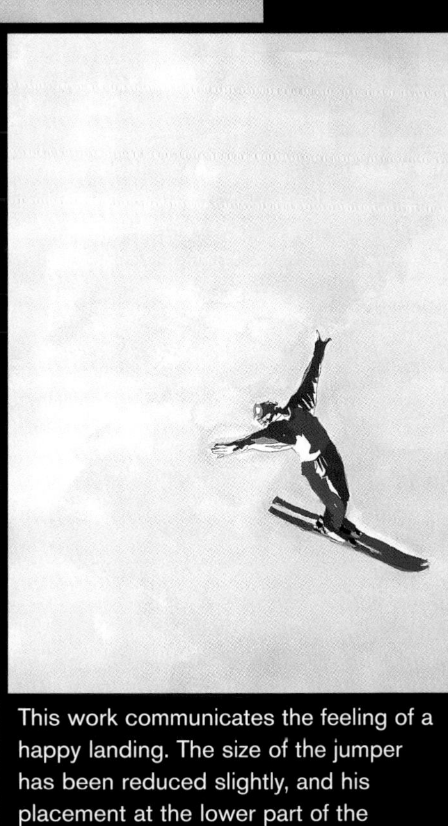

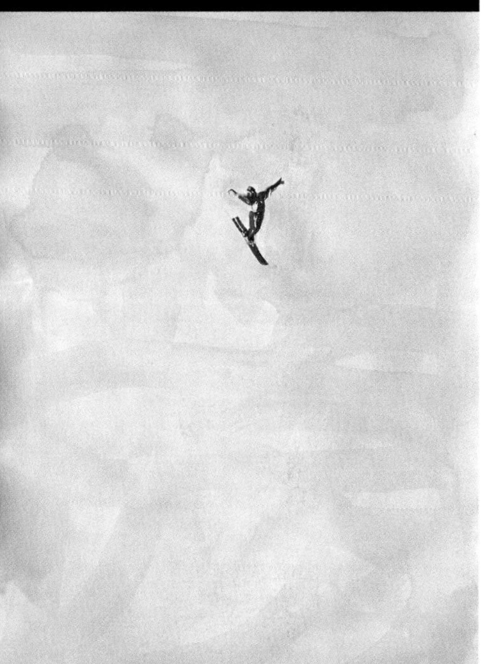

This work communicates the feeling of a happy landing. The size of the jumper has been reduced slightly, and his placement at the lower part of the painting shows the end of the jump. The experience that took place in the sky is almost finished, and there is a decreasing feeling of emptiness and weightlessness.

The small size chosen to represent the body of the skier in this painting places us in a space that is enormous and infinite. The composition reinforces the verticality thanks to the position of the paper and of the jumper. The spatial feeling is one of distance and loss, similar to that conveyed by birds flying in the air.

Other Models

Each time someone jumps, he or she defies the laws of gravity, if only for an instant. To vary the spatial feeling experienced in the jump, we propose a less risky jump. The idea is to immortalize the moment in which an athlete remains suspended in the air when high jumping. In this jump the body does not teeter in the vastness of the space but appears tense and rigid. The spatial feeling of weightlessness is not as intense, although it is more vigorous.

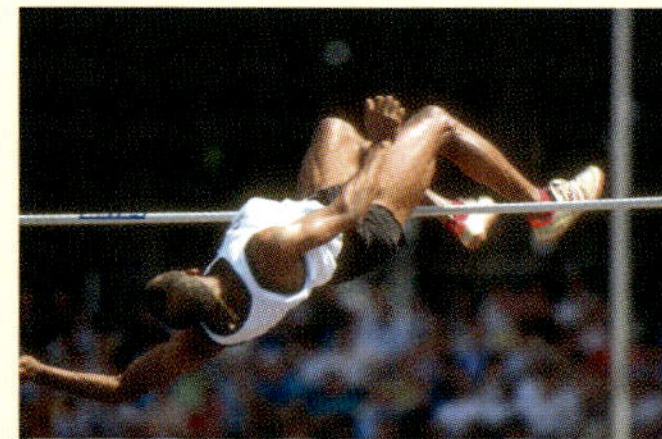

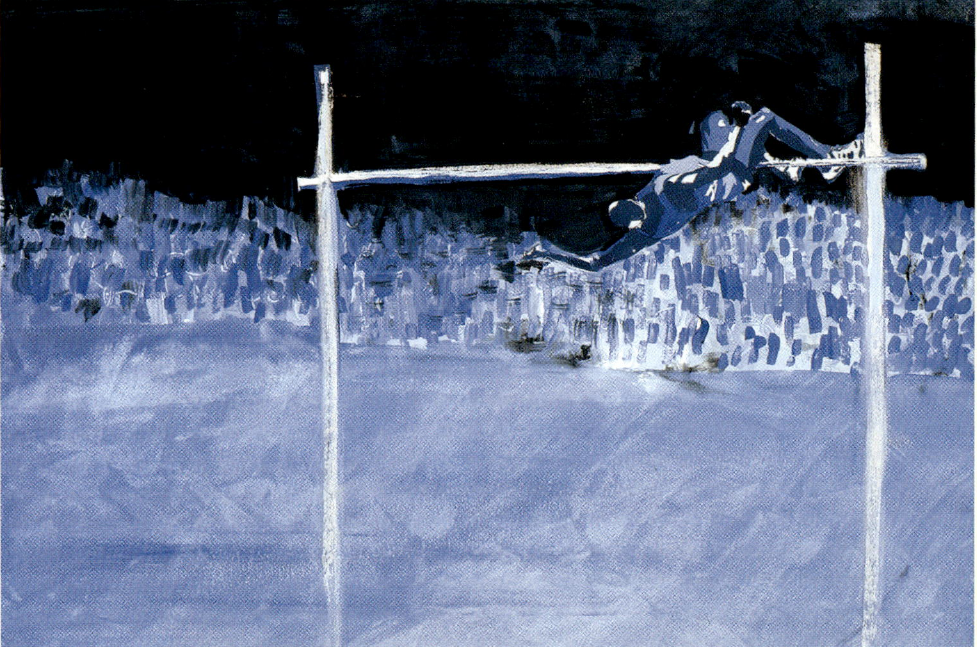

Other Media

The other medium chosen for this was pastels in tones of blue. This is the most artistic medium, which allows us to produce pleasant, atmospheric, and ethereal sensations with lines and blending. Combining hard and soft pastel sticks favors the difference of the treatment of the body with respect to the air. Hard pastels produce opaque blocks of color and direct lines, and they are ideal for providing the body with mass. Soft pastels, on the other hand, are blended with a hand or with a piece of cotton, and produce soft and airy tones, characteristic of the sky.

Other Views

Sandro Chia (born in 1946) belongs, with other artists, to what is called the Italian *Transvanguardia*, a phenomenon of the 1980s. These artists are not united by pictorial guidelines, but rather by a specific artistic attitude: the advancement of an individual and subjective revolution of "I, the artist." The works of art that emerged from this movement isolated themselves from beauty and spirituality, becoming uncomplicated and less desperate. In Chia we find reconciliation between tradition and the present. In his paintings, the poetry of Chagall comes together with the neoclassicism of Picasso, in an effort to give full freedom to his fantasy and imagination. In *Blue Grotto* a man in flames falling into a cavernous space is shown in a frivolous manner, with colors that are exaggeratedly bright and artificial.

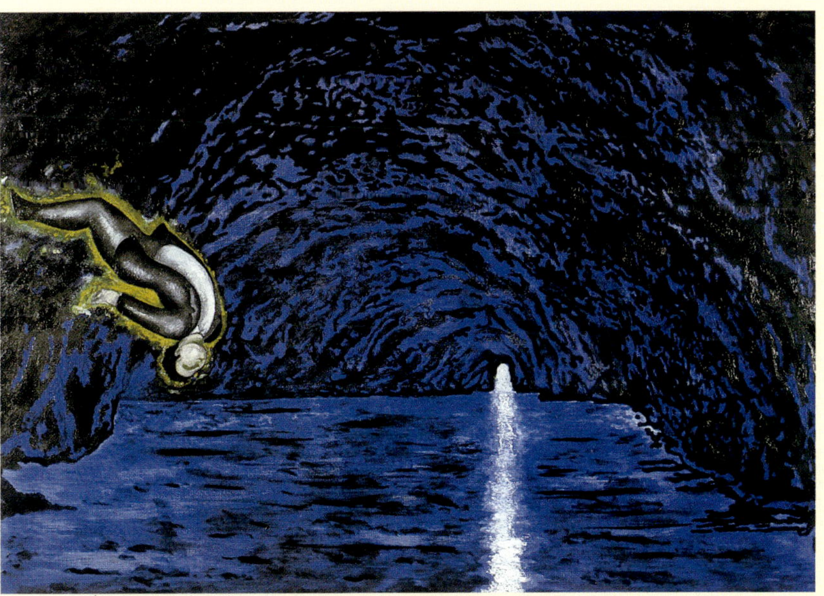

Sandro Chia,
Blue Grotto, 1980.
Bruno Bischofberger Küsnacht Collection.
Zurich, Switzerland.

Interior, Inhabited, *and Lived-in* Spaces

Wilhelm Hammershøi (1864–1916), a Danish painter who has influenced numerous contemporary artists, painters, photographers, and filmmakers, was one of the greatest exponents of the genre of human figures in interiors. Hammershøi's work achieved a mature style early on, and remained unchanged for thirty years. His most recurring theme was portraits of women indoors, usually maids, with their backs to the painter and in front of a wall or a door. In his work people saw erotic connotations linked to voyeurism, along the lines of Bonnard or Degas, his contemporaries. Architecture interested him enormously, but what he strived for above all in his work was light, a Nordic light that creates gray tones without many contrasts, what are now called "silent tones." This was quite an advanced concept for his time, a reason why he was not always well accepted.

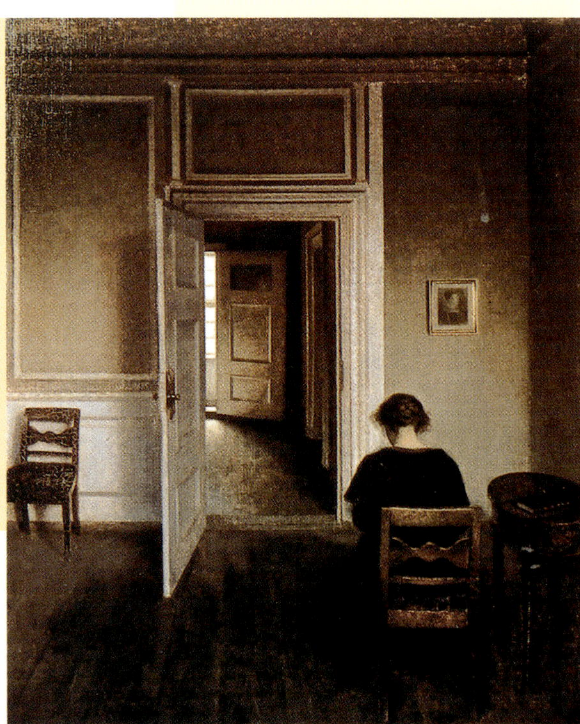

Wilhelm Hammershøi,
Interior with Seated Woman, 1908.
Musée d'Orsay, Paris, France.

Light in the Interior: Creating Intimate Atmospheres in Inhabited Spaces

In this creative approach we take on a classical theme whose origins are found in the Dutch baroque: the figure indoors in front of a window. Paintings of people in front of windows bring to mind that which was lost and produces the effect of visual inversion toward the interior, inviting the viewer to look inside himself. That introspective dimension is reinforced with the light and the atmosphere that bathe the room, creating enormous visual pleasure. Josep Asunción has approached this theme by photographing his son from various angles of an empty room, studying the relationship between his presence and the light that enters through a small window. He chose watercolors for their simple and delicate effects, as well as for the luminous effects that can be created with them.

"This bliss of passive contemplation is also, in the end, the one that spreads an enchantment over things past and distant and presents them to us, in the form of an illusion, covered in beautiful colors."
Schopenhauer,
The World as Will and Representation.

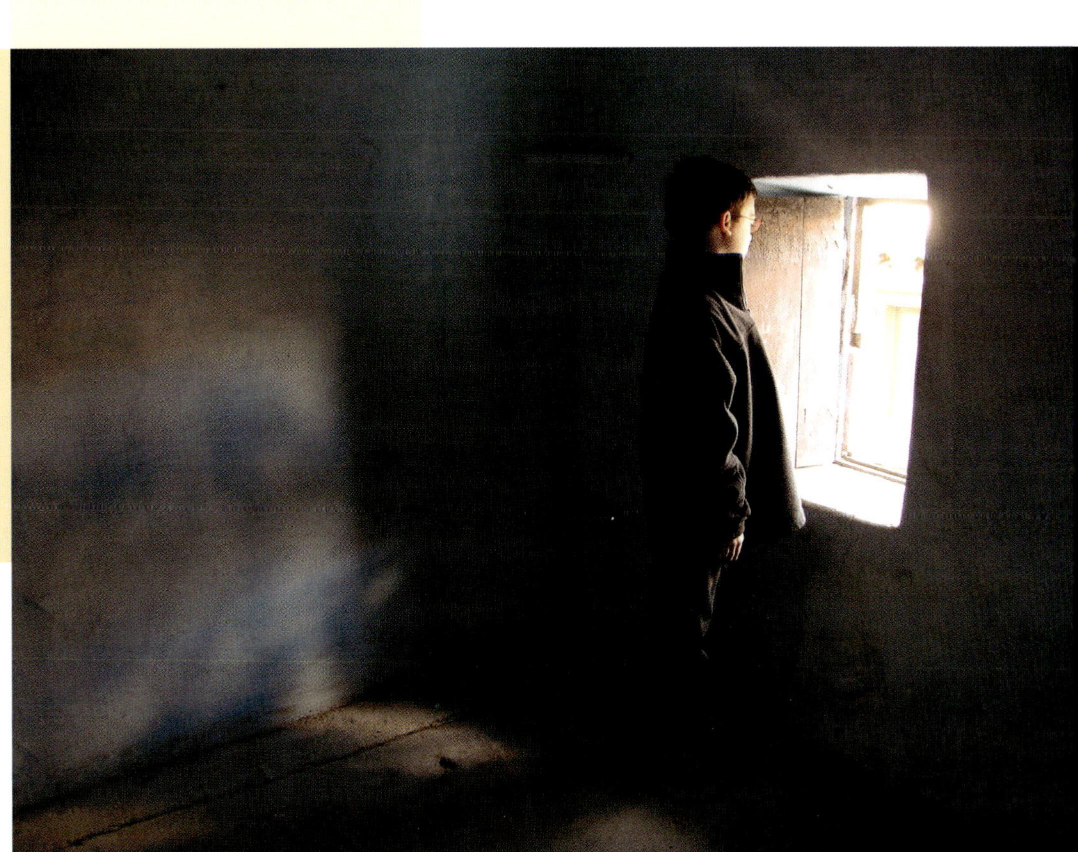

128

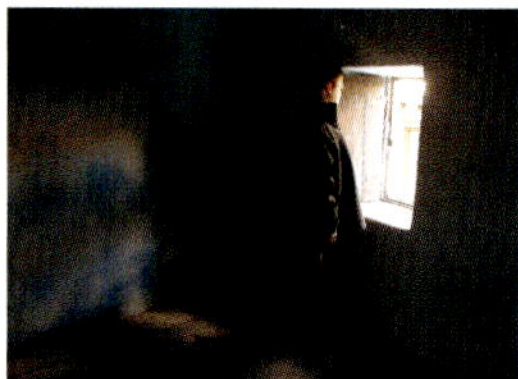

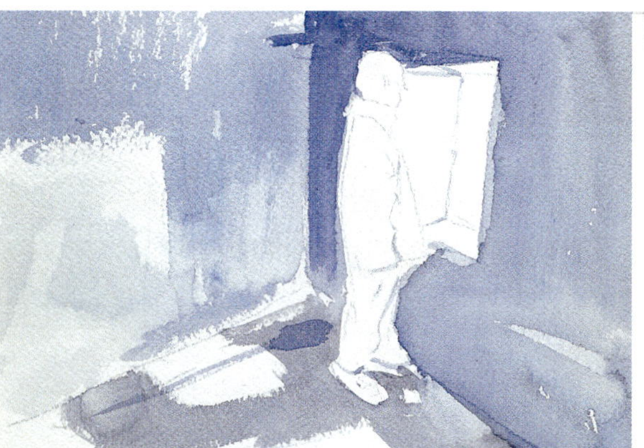

1 We lay out the drawing of the scene with brushstrokes of very diluted blue. Then the first blocks of color are applied—the ones that define the three planes of that corner, the floor and the two walls—with ultramarine blue and diluted indigo blue.

2 Next, we block in the shadows with a darker indigo blue, the ones in silhouette that can be seen on the figure of the boy and in the darker areas of the room. We leave the areas of maximum light blank. When using watercolors, white is represented by the white of the paper.

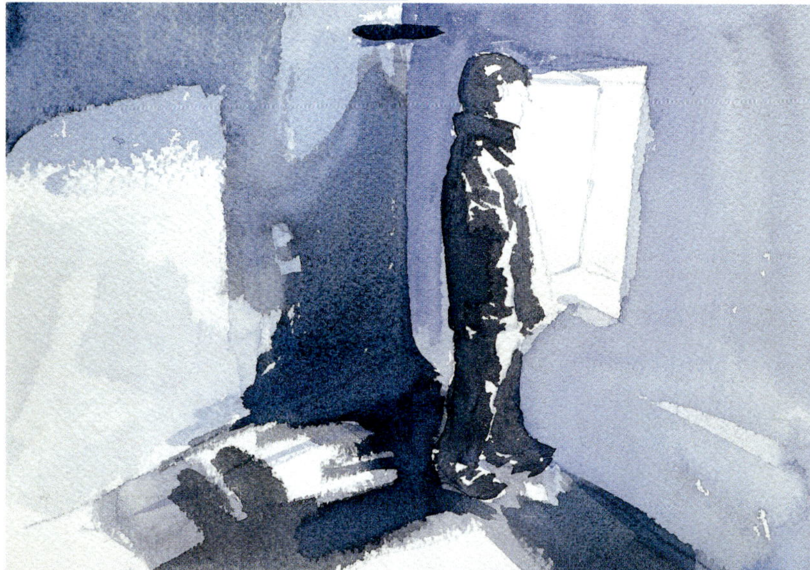

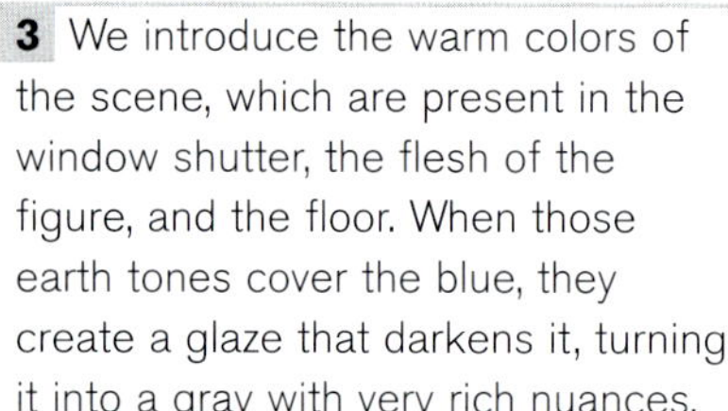

3 We introduce the warm colors of the scene, which are present in the window shutter, the flesh of the figure, and the floor. When those earth tones cover the blue, they create a glaze that darkens it, turning it into a gray with very rich nuances.

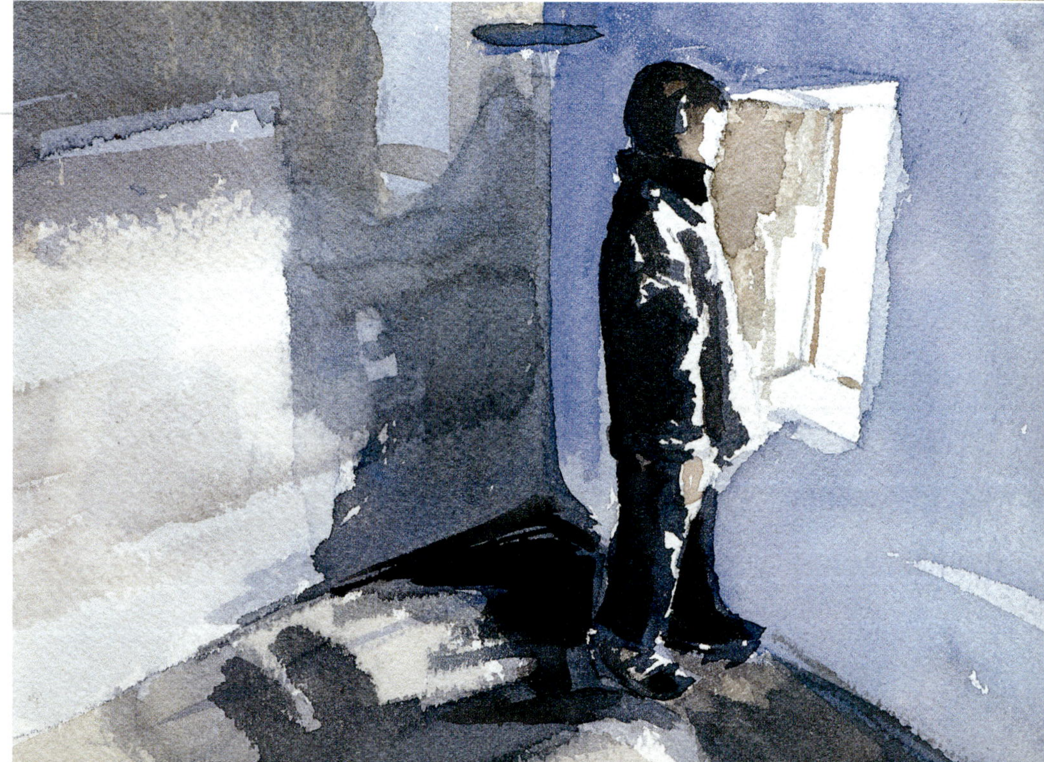

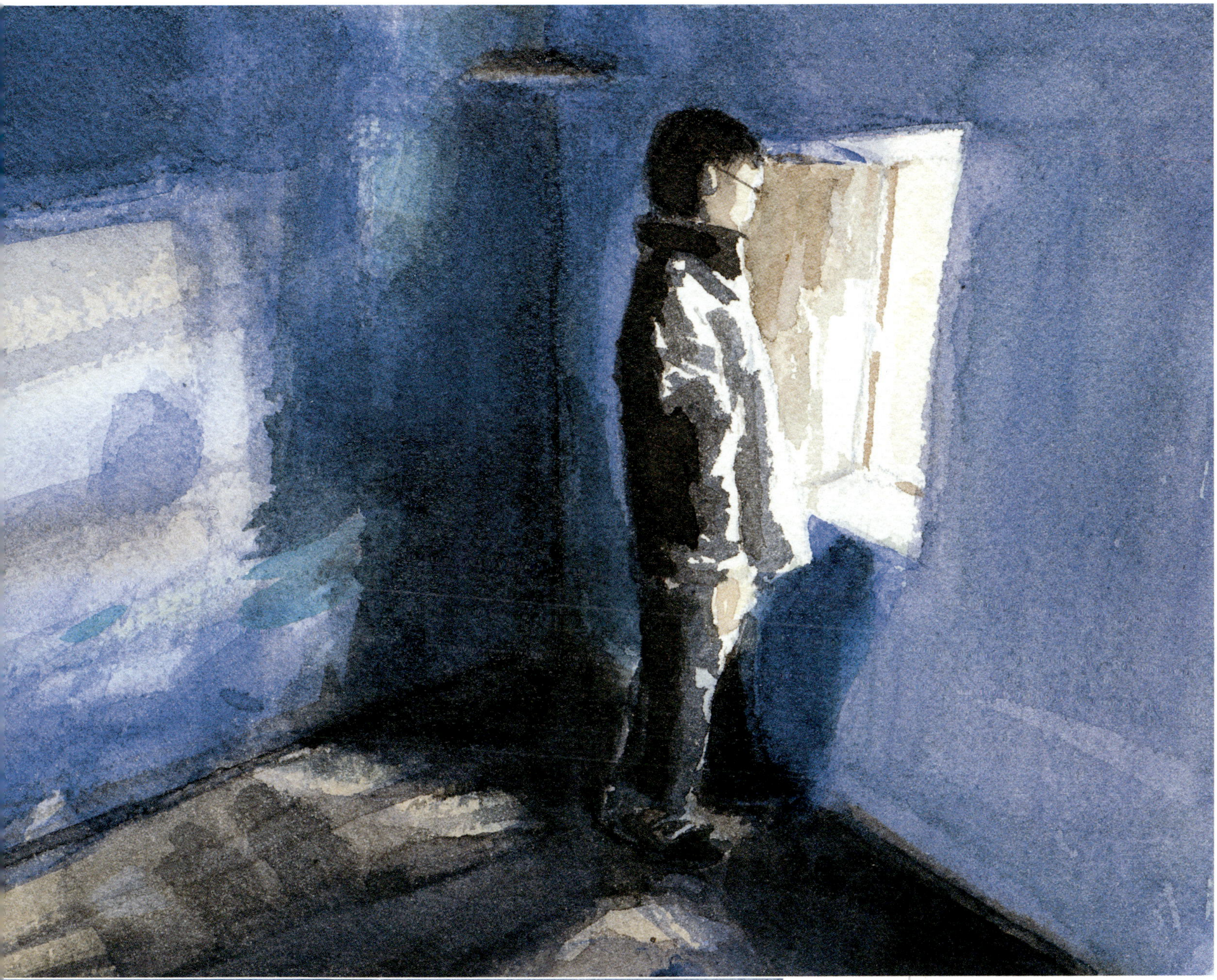

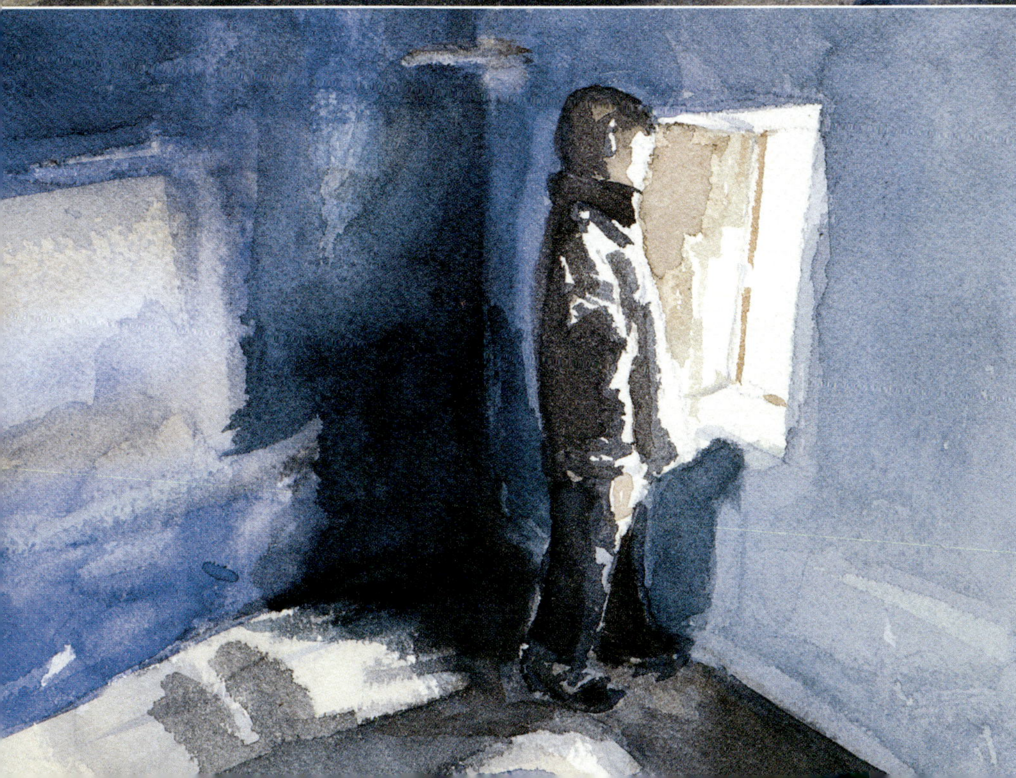

5 To finish the watercolor several more glazes are created with earth tones and blue colors. The shadows are now perfect. The space is dense, but it is bathed in light. With the final touch-ups we paint the boy's glasses and intensify the dark tones of the hair and clothing; this reinforces his presence.

4 We continue by adding transparent layers of Prussian blue and ultramarine blue to create a glazed effect. We wait until each layer is dry before we proceed with the next glaze to prevent them from blending together. Little by little the scene acquires atmosphere and density, without losing any light, because the reserved whites are still maintained.

Other Versions

The artist wanted to change the angle from which he was photographing his son to experiment with the relationship established between his figure and the space in which it is located. Depending on the location, the body is seen against the light or lighted from the side, which gives the work a dramatic or a lyrical feeling.

The composition of this work is centered and the room disappears amidst the total darkness. Only the effect of the outside light can be observed, in a tenebrous style; therefore the question here is, What is beyond the window? By painting the image from an elevated point of view, the model becomes somewhat deformed with a slight foreshortening and the window in a diamond shape, an approach that adds dynamism to the scene and creates enigma.

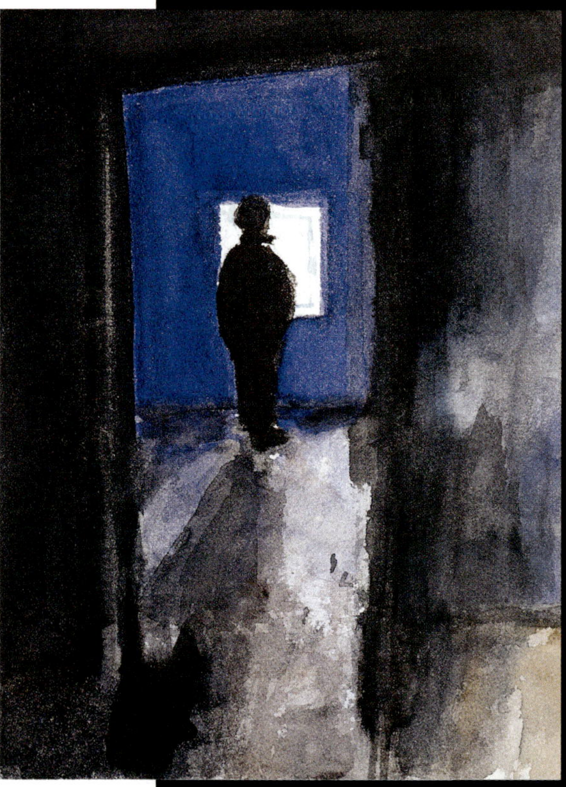

In this watercolor the painter is very far away, directly outside the room, behind a door, as if he were observing the person without being noticed. That distance indicates on the one hand respect, because it does not invade the scene physically, and on the other curiosity, because it reinforces the idea of voyeurism. This spatial approach was widely used by Pierre Bonnard in his paintings of *toilettes*, where he appears to be spying on a woman in the bath.

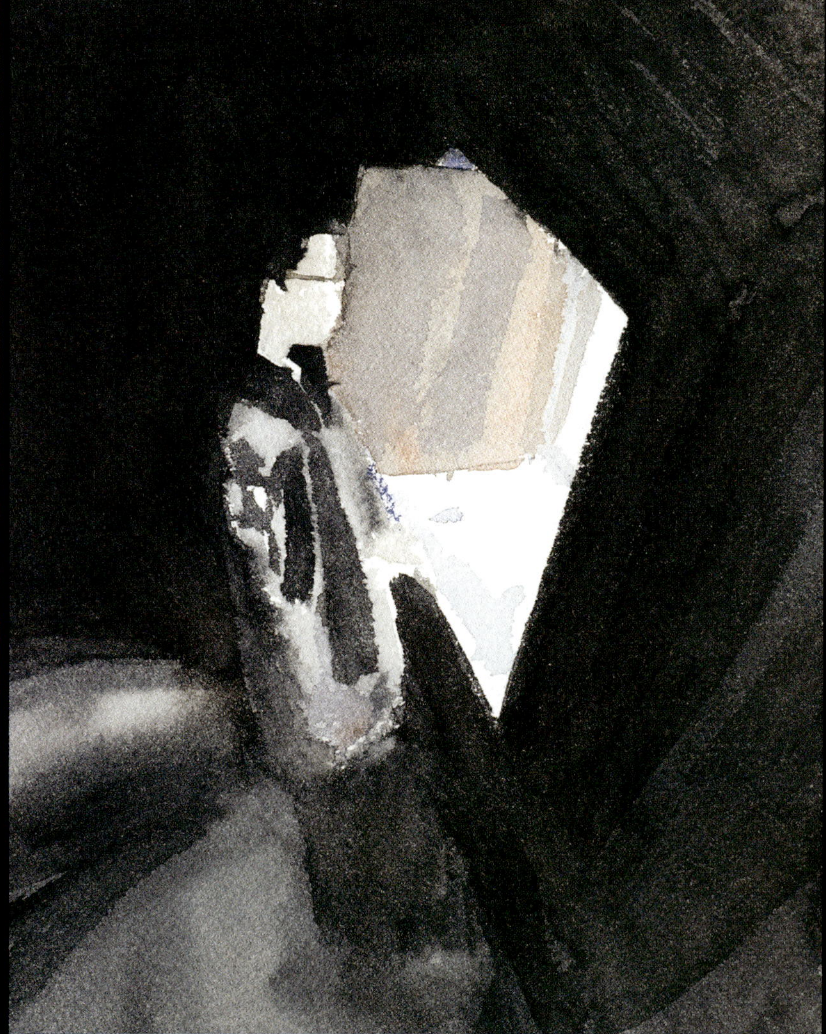

This work gives more information about the room's interior, the height of the ceiling, the dimensions of the window with respect to the room, the idea of emptiness . . . This effect is produced by the painter placing himself far away and by the low point of view, which indicates reverence toward the place.

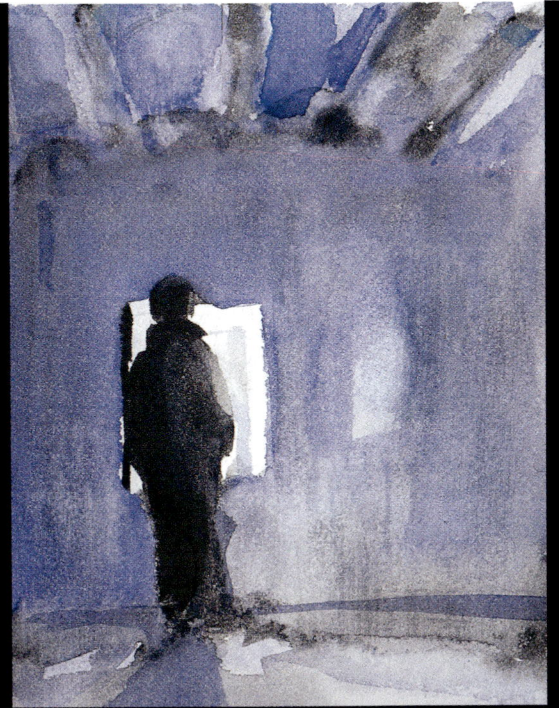

The boy stands with his back to the painter, like the maids painted by Hammershøi, but this time in front of a very bright light, in a radical chiaroscuro: a silhouette. The decision to place the light to one side of the composition indicates that the space continues on the right side, that the room is larger, and that it can be exited only from one point.

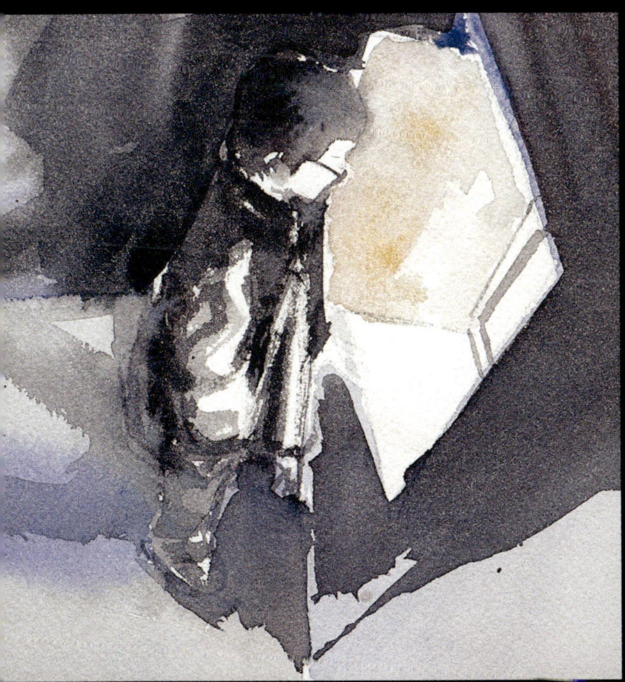

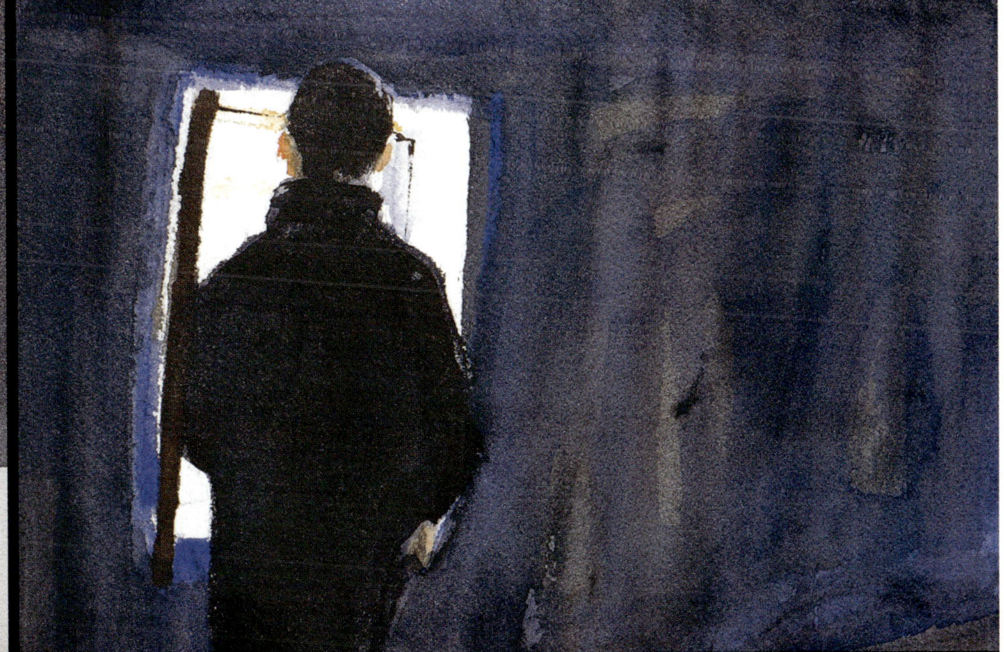

This angled view from above is the most forced of the gallery. To create the watercolor the artist had to climb up on a ladder. The window here is a perfect diamond, and the boy is in complete foreshortening. This angle is truly expressionistic and dramatic because it creates enormous distance between the painter and the model, as if he were being observed through a surveillance camera.

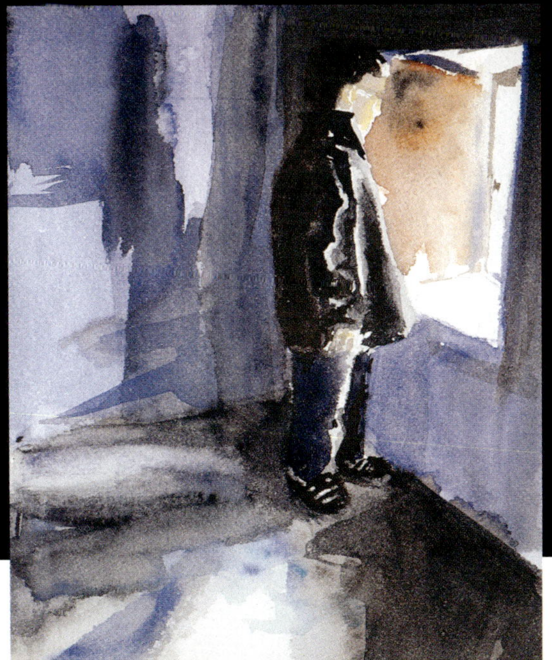

This painting is the closest to the one we saw in the step-by-step process, but in this case we changed the format, making it vertical, and we have lowered the point of view a little bit because the painter was sitting in front of the model. When the painter is lower than the model, the latter becomes more majestic and commands greater presence. The verticality also reinforces this effect.

Other Models

The figure indoors has been studied in intimate situations not only in private spaces but also in public spaces. In this case Josep Asunción wanted to work with human presence inside a subway station, an enclosed space, which is also conceptually open because of its public dimension. The behavior of a person in a place like this is automatic and functional, which produces an impersonal scene, although charged with expressive power.

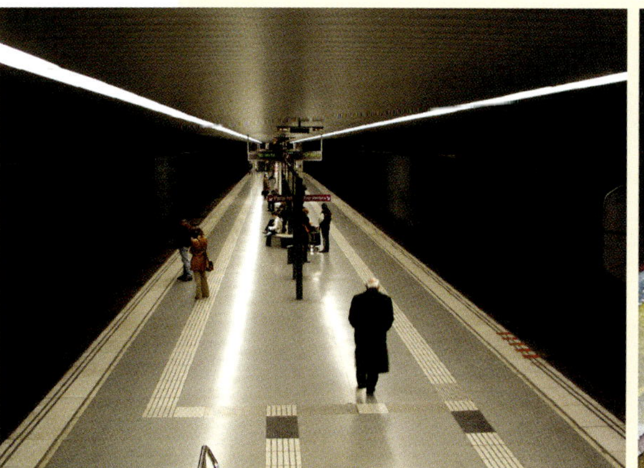

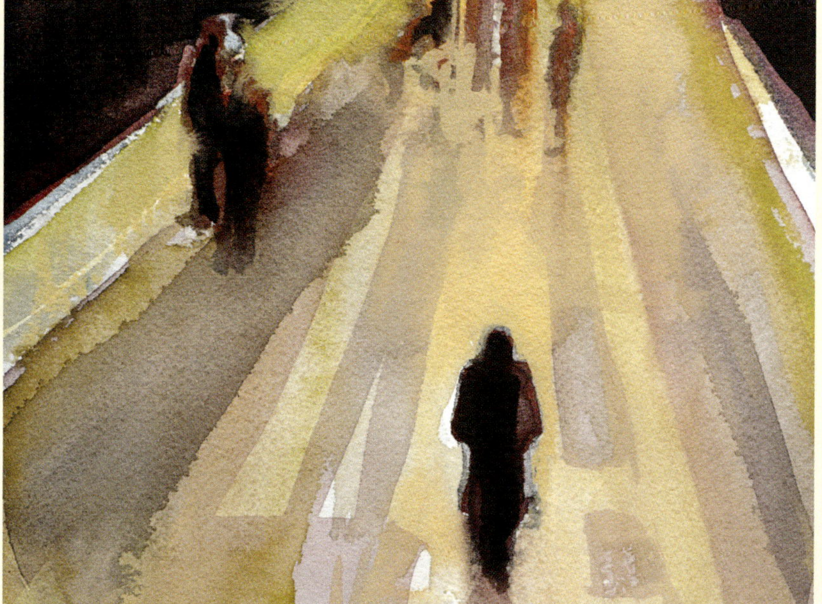

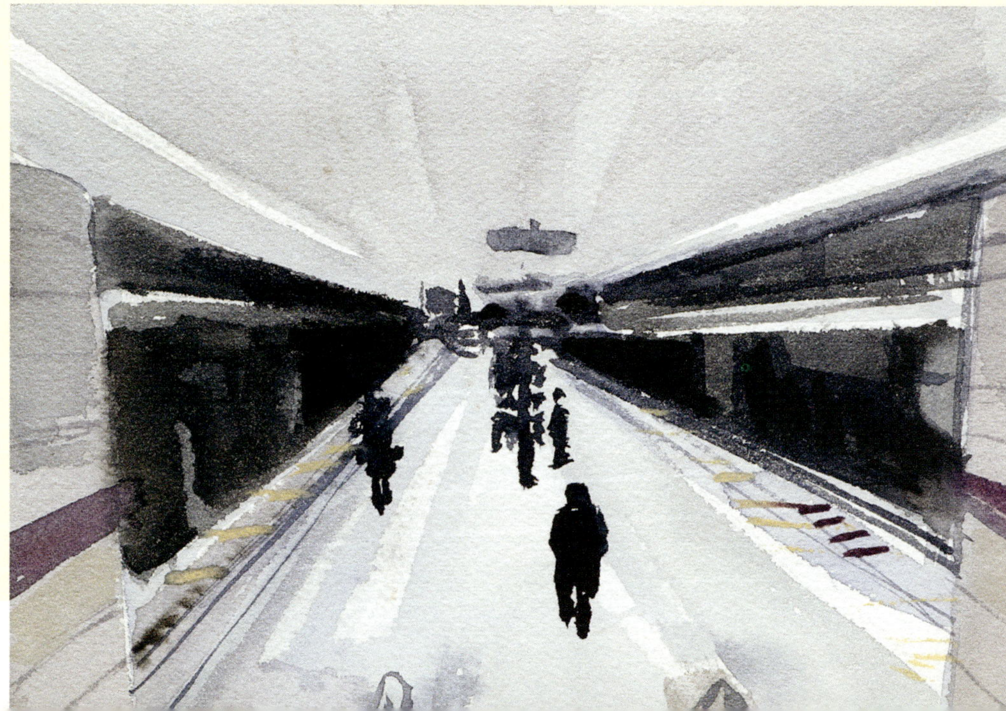

Other Media

The most appropriate medium for creating special atmospheres is oil paint. A dense and soft atmosphere, like velvet, was created with blending and *sfumato* techniques, caressing the model and the viewer.

Other Views

Here we see references to two great historic, scenic portrait painters. One of them is Jan Vermeer (1632–1675), the Dutch painter who was best able to express intimacy through the effect of the light that bathed his interiors. In his paintings he appears to stop time to allow the viewer to participate in the contemplative ecstasies of everyday life and simple things. The other is Henry Moore (1898–1986) and his portraits of the subway in London, which were produced under extraordinary circumstances, like he says: "People had become accustomed to rolling up their blankets around eight or nine in the evening, going down into the subway stations, and laying down on the platforms (. . .) it was like an immense city in the depths of the earth. When I saw this for the first time, almost by chance—I went in one of them during an aerial bombing—, I saw hundreds of Henry Moore figures laying down on the platforms. The visual effect fascinated me. I returned time and time again."

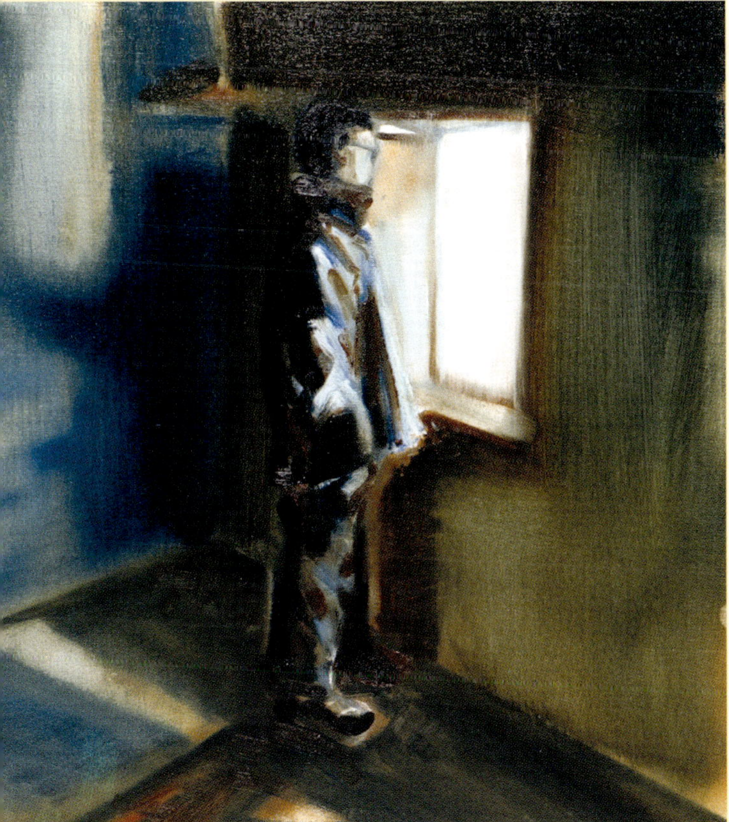

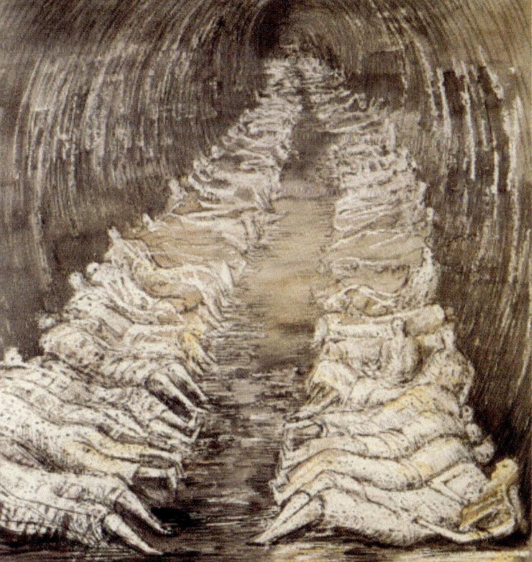

Henry Moore,
Perspective of the Subway Shelter
(Liverpool Street extension),
1941.
Tate Gallery,
London, United Kingdom.

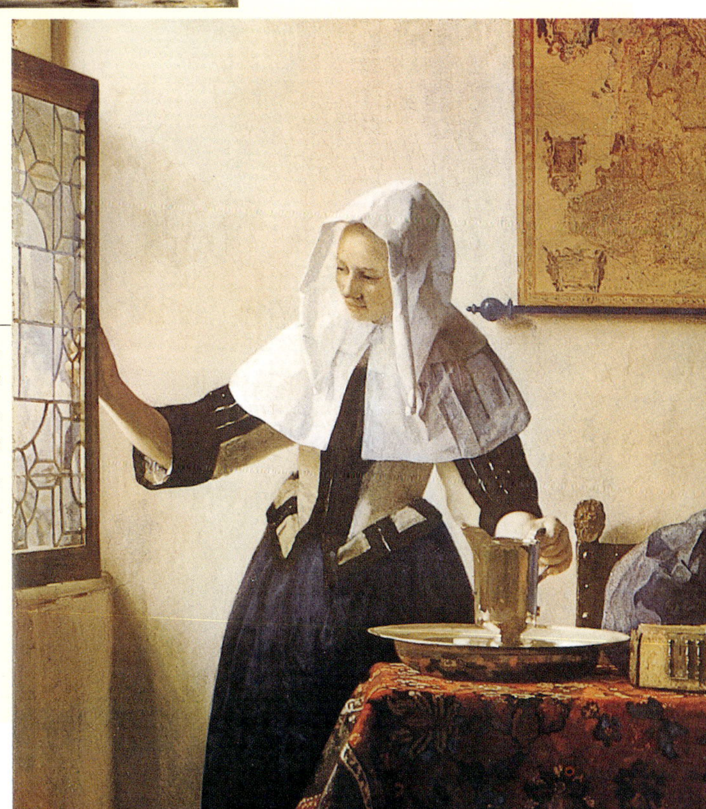

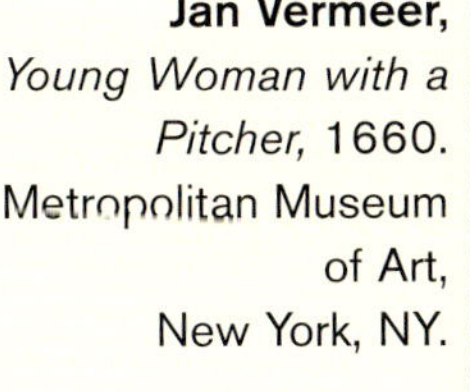

Jan Vermeer,
Young Woman with a Pitcher, 1660.
Metropolitan Museum of Art,
New York, NY.

Abstraction is characterized as being a genre devoid of
argument. There are no elements in it that can be
identified with the visual reality. Simple smears, lines,
areas of color, structures . . . in a specific space: the
painting. In this chapter we present two projects. In one
of them we produce a creative project based on
microscopic and organic spaces. In the other we begin
with structural and grid spaces.

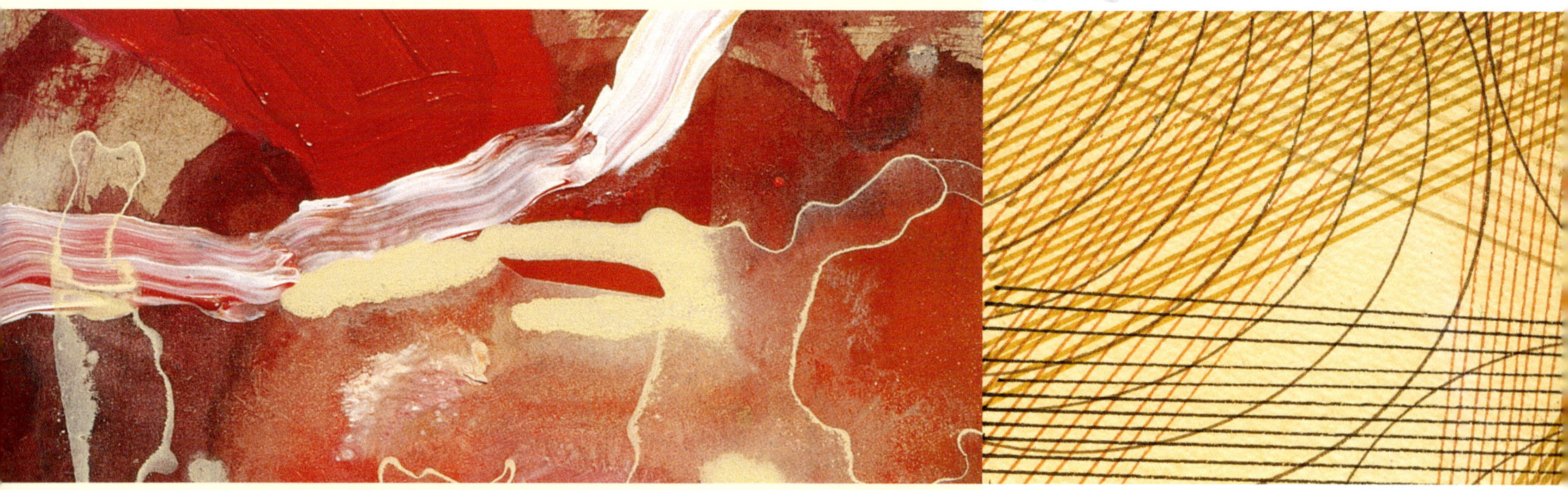

straction

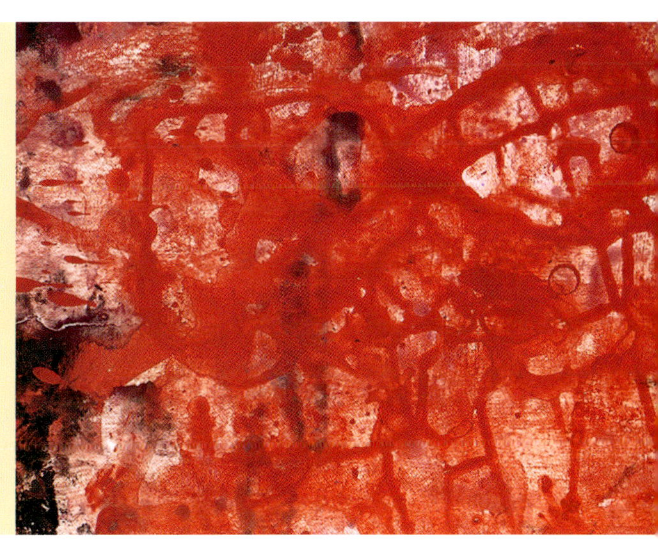

"Any map, smear, shadow, anything that breaks up the tyranny of the flat dimension of the paper, produces a suggestion, a possibility of space."
Henry Moore,
London, 1968.

Organic, Microscopic, and Fluid Spaces

Fascinated by what he saw through the microscope, the symbolist Odilon Redon created the first nearly abstract paintings. Barely one hundred years later, the Basque painter Darío Urzay (born in 1958) has developed this painted abstract vision in an exquisite manner, giving us paintings that suggest landscapes of the human interior. His paintings are in a fluid state along the lines of Pollock, Morris Louis, and Tápies. They flow by capillarity through the surface structure of the support and give us networks and conduits that suggest vascular systems of the human body, the skin as well as the interior of the organism. When he went to live in New York, he began pouring paint onto the supports and then tipping them to create glazes and other mixing effects. He finishes his paintings with resin to give the surface a terse and shiny feeling, canceling out any clue about the execution of the works. They are like mirrors that collect the image of the viewer and incorporate it into the work of art.

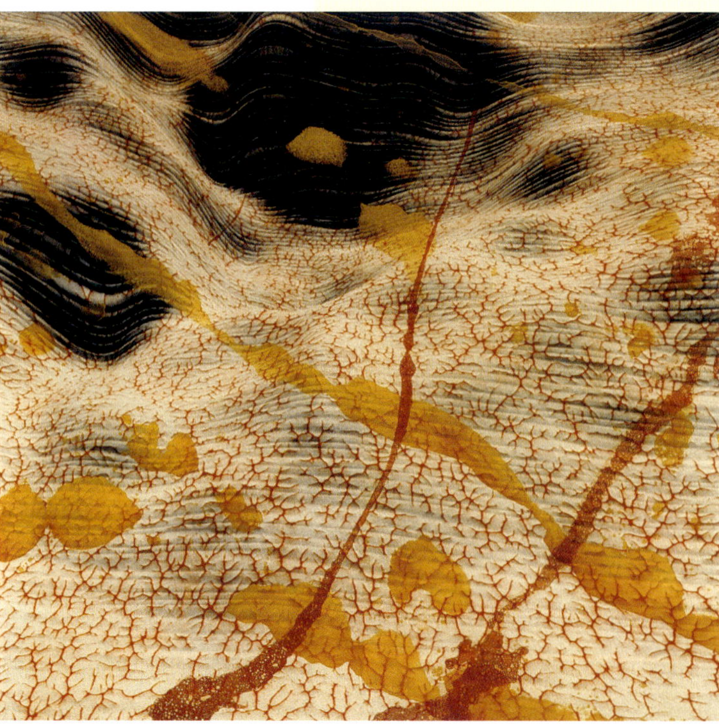

Darío Urzay,
Agnostic Site, 2000.

Bodies and Fluids: Abstract Spaces in Microscopic Images

Under the microscope we discover hidden spaces that evoke in us a fantastic
and suggestive world yet to be discovered. Gemma Guasch has chosen images
of cells seen in the microscope to use in the following approach. The images
of bodies and cellular membranes floating through a fluid space helped create
spatial abstractions. She chose to use acrylic paint on wood because its
versatility permitted her to use dense and fluid paint, combining impasto lines
with dripping and rinsing.

Space in Abstraction

*"The beauty of a composition mainly
depends on the variety, counterpoint,
contrast, and placement of all the
parts that enter into the work;
however, invention should rule all the
parts of the composition to regulate
the quantity of the more or less that
should exist in the painting and the
mood and properness of the person
making the composition."*
Mengs,
Works,
1780.

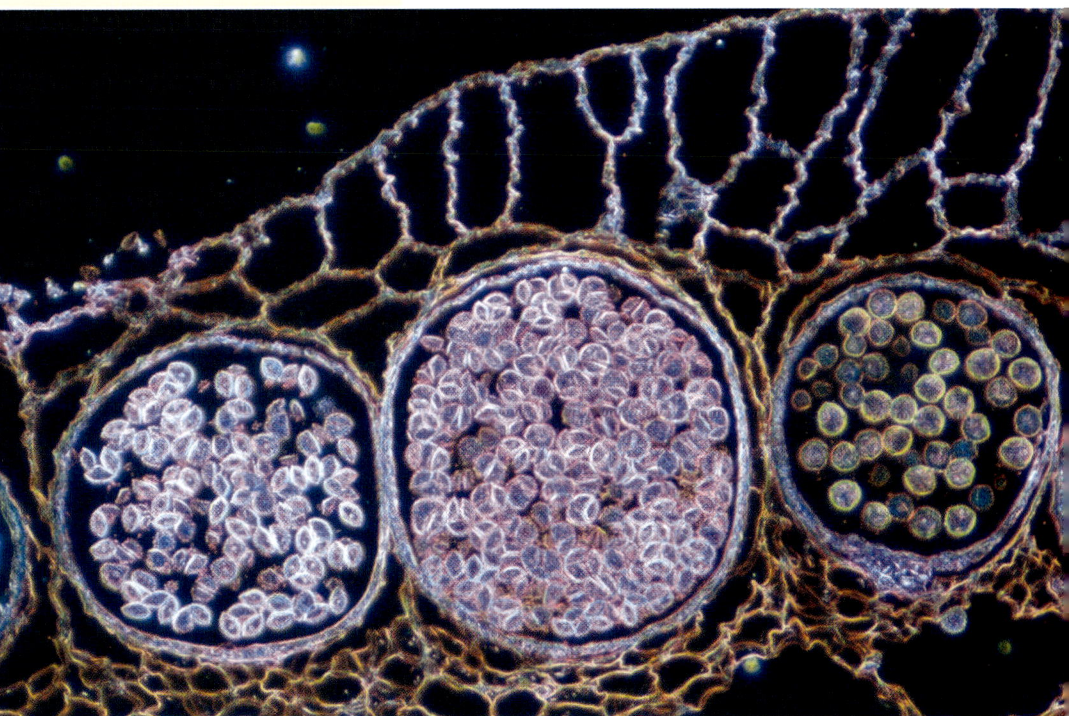

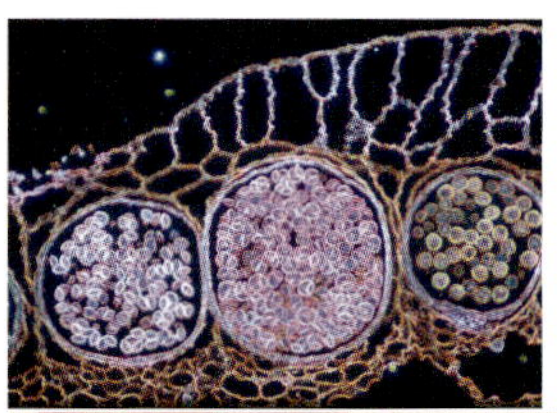

1 The support is painted loosely and irregularly to create a spatial effect that from the first moment highlights the different densities. We apply a reddish tone to create the body, and we allow the support to breathe.

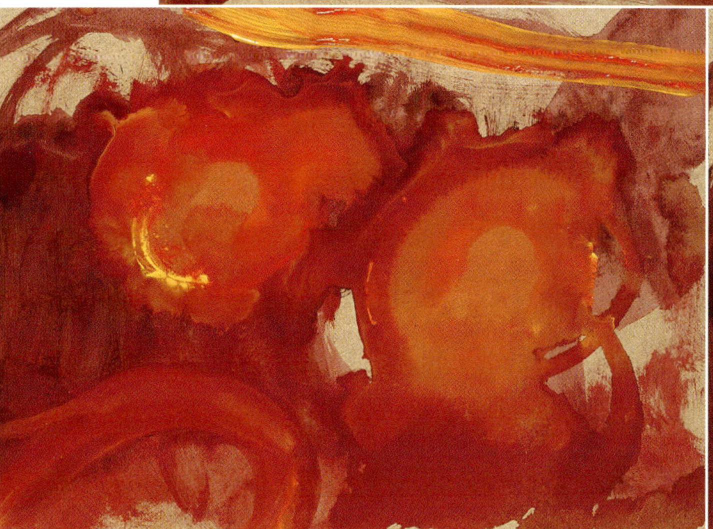

2 The spatial depth is reinforced by applying different airy lines in different tones of the same tonal range, more intense on the cellular bodies and loosely at the edges.

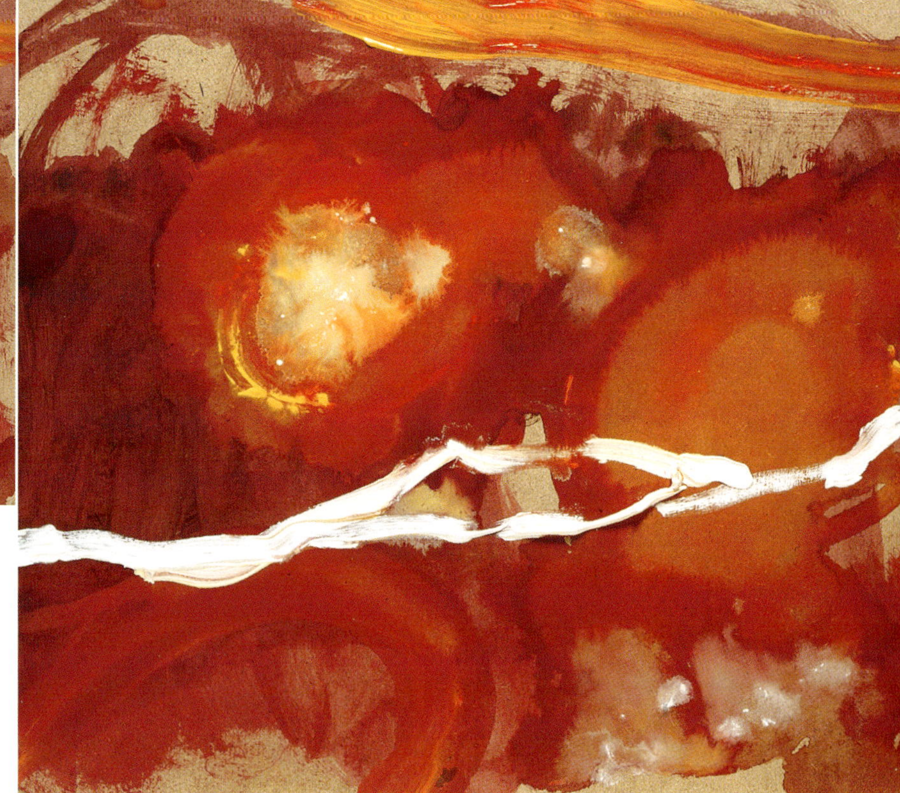

3 We intensify the spatial contrast with the application of various drips of white paint, which we distribute randomly across the support. Then we apply an important horizontal line in the center of the painting, thick, white, and organic, that divides the picture and situates us in the foreground.

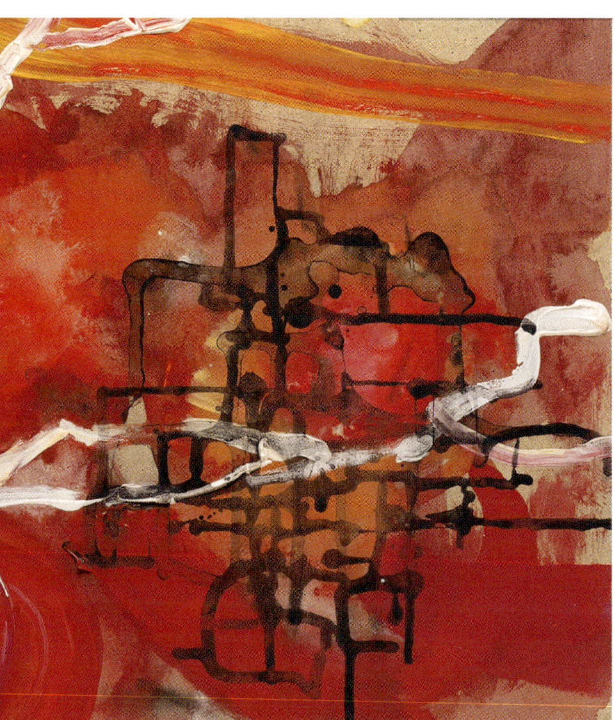

4 We reinforce some areas of the image with impasto to intensify the density of the different lines and add a more spatial feeling. Then we partially apply black paint in the right of the image, tipping the painting and letting the paint run to create a regular and ordered screen that is very different from the rest of the painting. We rinse it to moderate its intensity and provoke a contrast between blurry and defined effects that encourages spatial ambiguity by mixing and standing out at the same time.

5 Finally, the cream tones are applied by splashing and tipping the surface to make them flow, and light rinsing restores the light and spatial depth. The final piece is a cosmic and magic image suggestive of the cosmos.

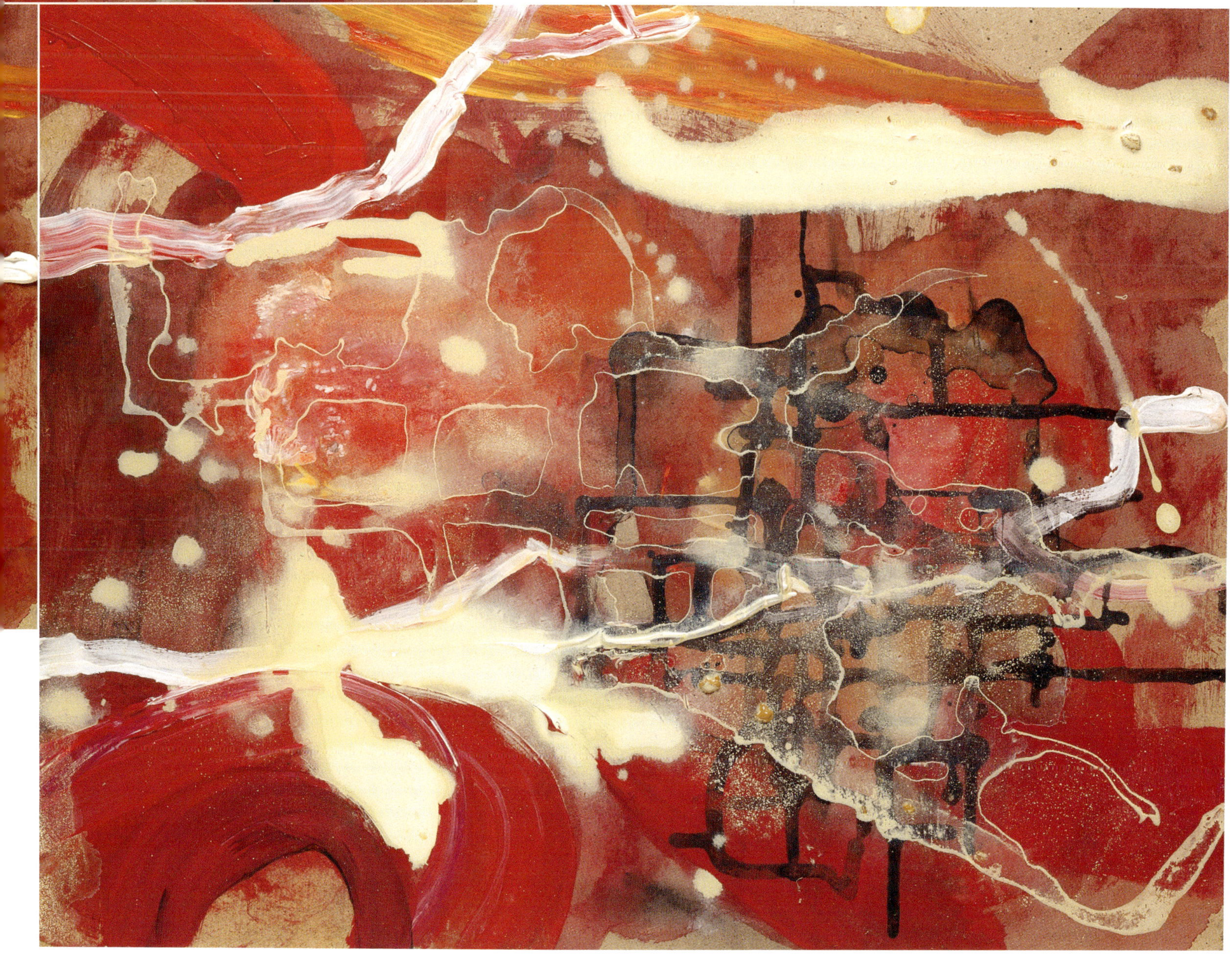

Other Versions

The vision of life contemplated through the lens of a microscope suggests an infinite number of spatial interpretations. They are lively images, changing, that flow unexpectedly. They organize themselves freely and change their scale, and silently multiply. Such are the different fluid spaces that Gemma Guasch created for this gallery.

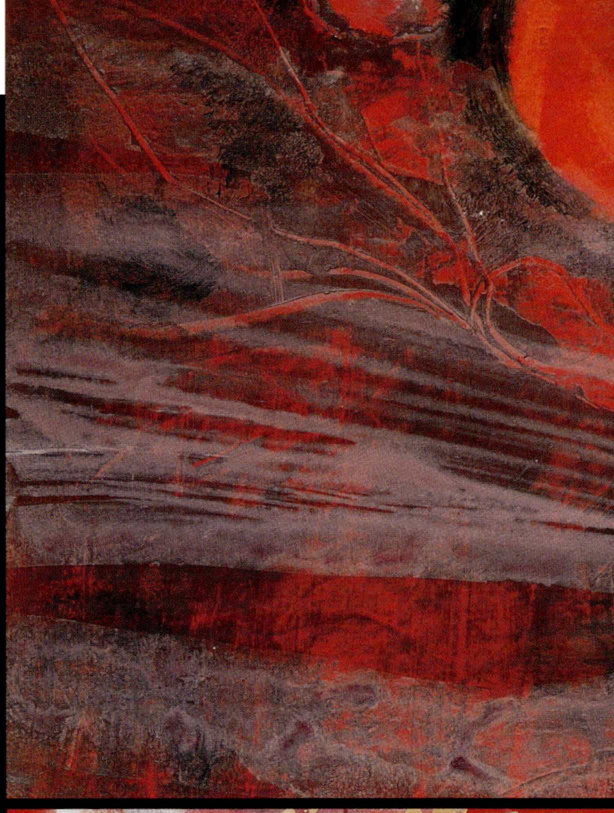

A decentralized version of the composition places the bodies in the upper edge and suggests a passing view of a space that overflows the edges of the paper. The bodies can be seen as holes created in an immense dark space that invades almost the entire image. Over this, a pink glaze covers the image to create a different spatial effect: a veiled space.

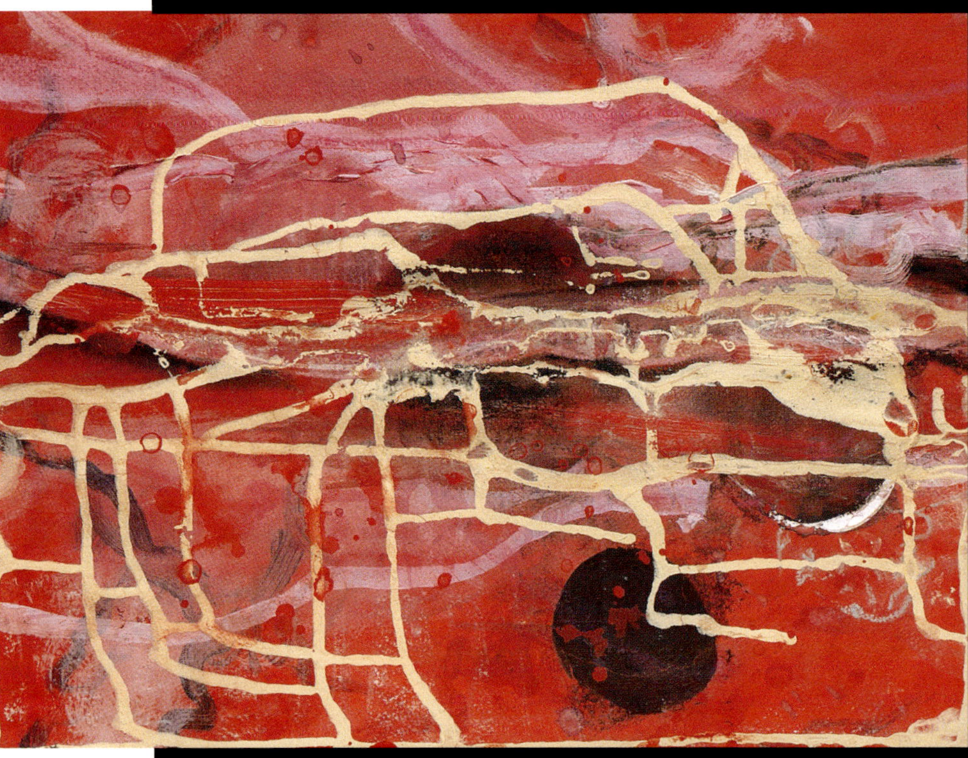

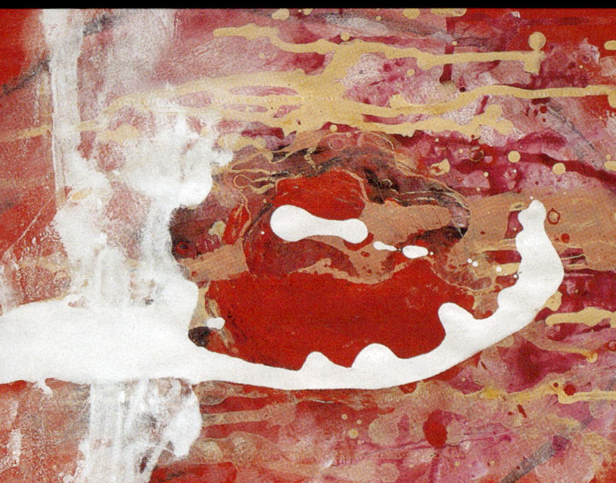

The proximity of the different circular elements places them in the foreground. Through a change in scale the deep space seems very near the viewer. The application of the defined whites in the foreground increases the spatial sensation and directs the viewer's eye to the center of the image.

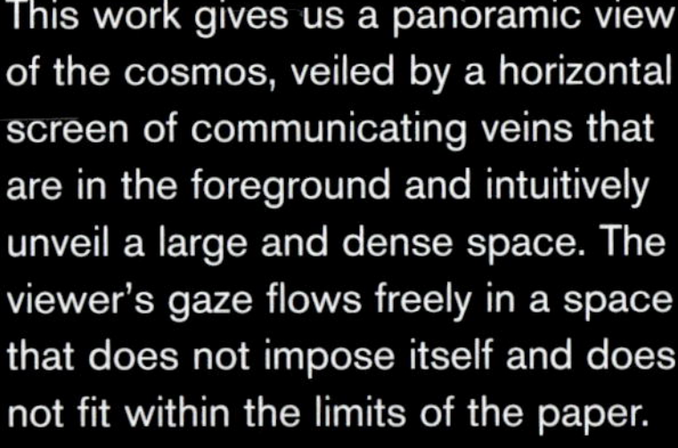

This work gives us a panoramic view of the cosmos, veiled by a horizontal screen of communicating veins that are in the foreground and intuitively unveil a large and dense space. The viewer's gaze flows freely in a space that does not impose itself and does not fit within the limits of the paper.

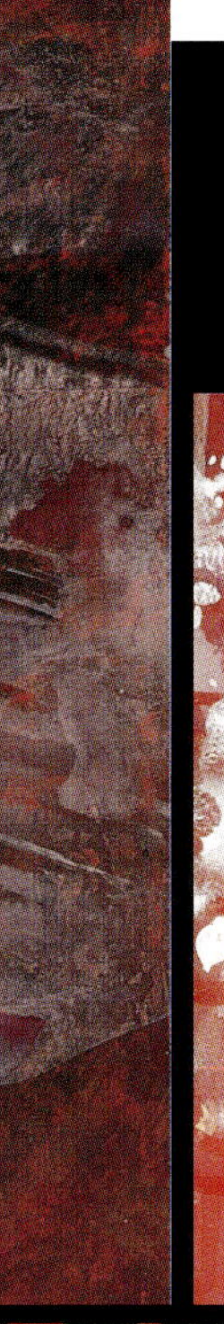

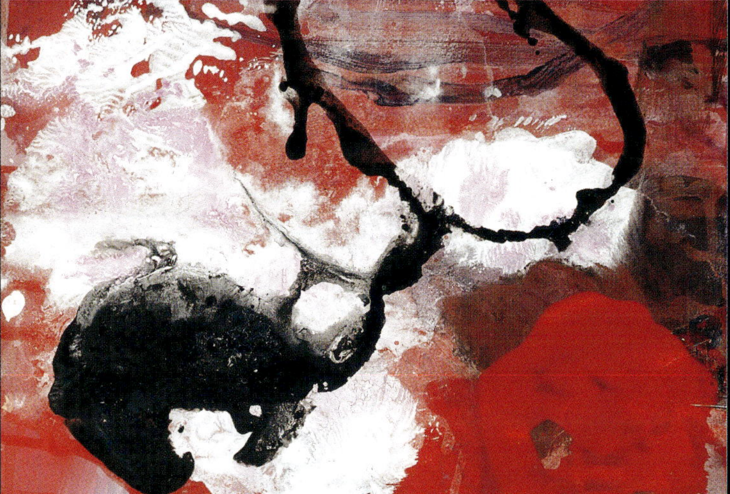

In this painting the bodies explode and fill the space with energy. The impasto of the whites and blacks is applied over the reds, as if they exploded from the center and spread out into space.

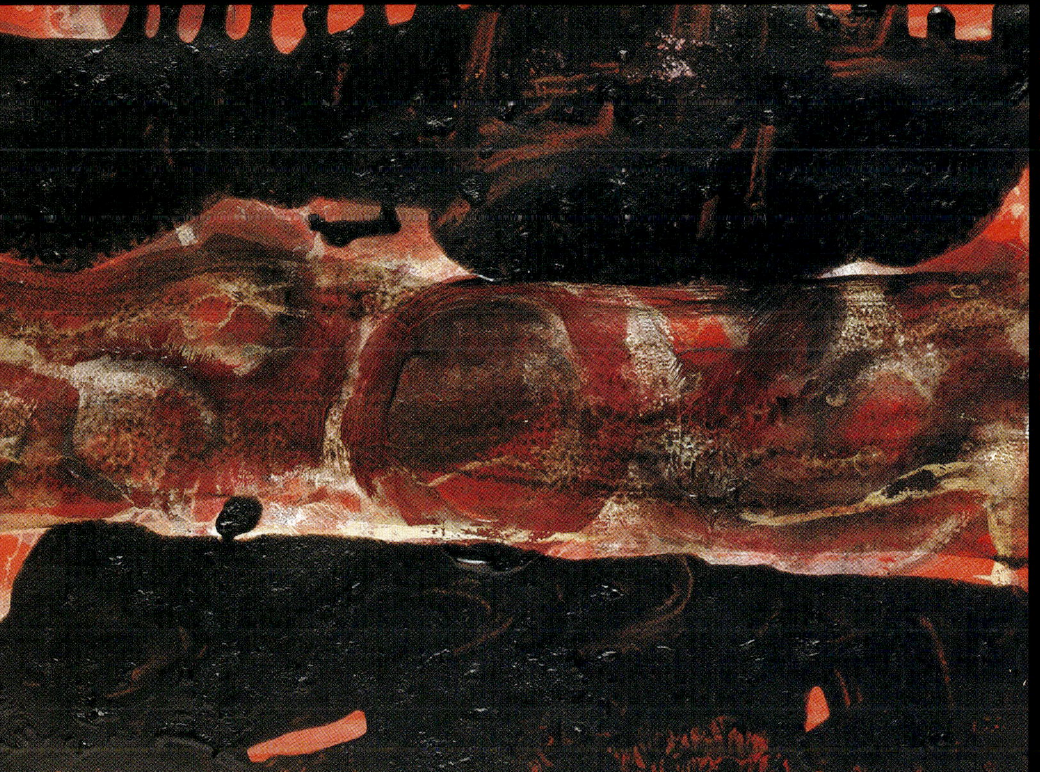

The spatial sense of grandiosity is achieved with a brutal close-up of a body, whose size and shape cannot be seen. This contrasts with a treatment of the interior space that is very discreet and monotonous without much variation but with an elegant reddish airiness.

The presence of two opaque, dark, and thick bands crowds the composition, creating an oppressed and directed spatial perception. Behind a veil of grime we can only just make out a sense of depth and life aligned in the center of the image.

Other Models

The mineral world also offers an endless number of spaces to be discovered; the different partitions of each stone show us new spaces that would fascinate any observer. Gemma Guasch has chosen, as an alternative model, the spaces created by the crystallography of the minerals. These spaces are harder and more geometric, but they offer diversity and contrast. They bring a new vision to abstraction: the creation of grids and flat spatial and geometric divisions.

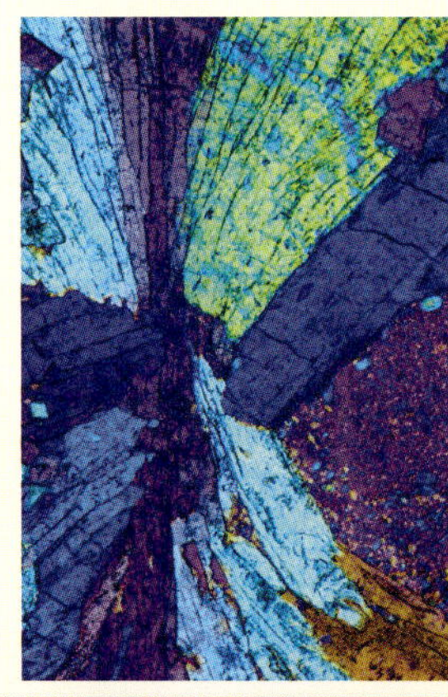

Other Media

The other media chosen by the artist is watercolor. This allows us to use the water to achieve different intensities without changing the light of the tones. The spatial effects are cleaner, because the different tones get stronger when they come into contact with each other. The fusion increases the sense of depth. The application of the black screen on the foreground was done after the rest of the composition was dry, so the effects on the other grounds would not be lost. Generally, this medium offers brighter and more luminous results.

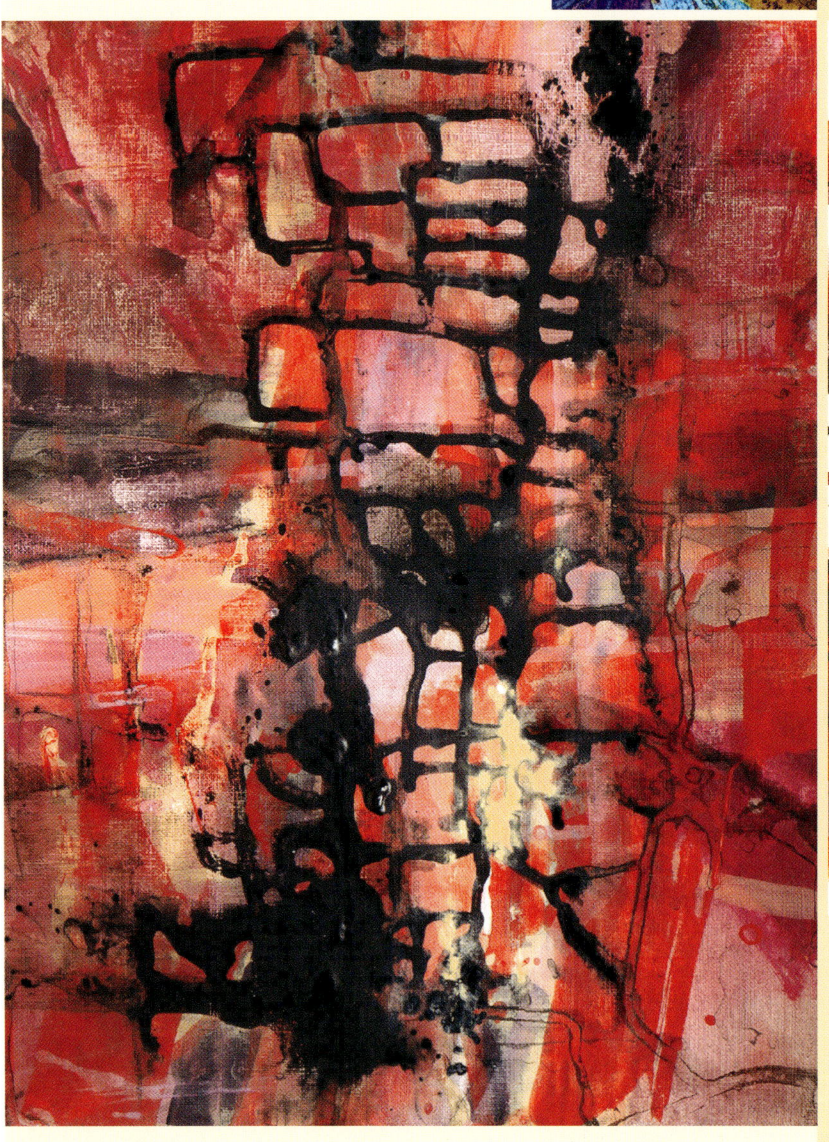

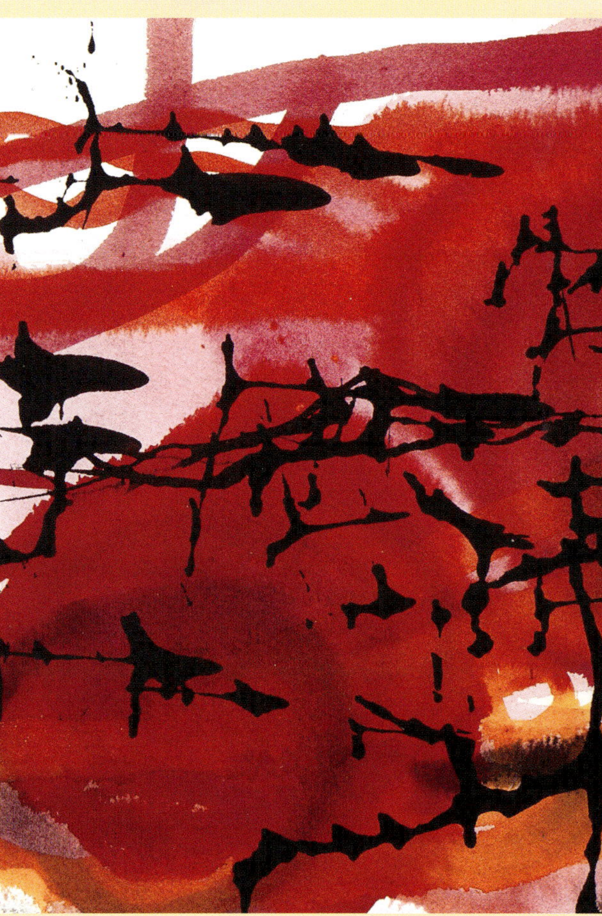

Other Views

If Darío Urzay approaches abstraction from the microcosm (interior flowing spaces), Baruj Salinas and Vicenç Viaplana go at it from the macrocosm (exterior flowing spaces). Through his work, Baruj Salinas (born in 1938) invites us to contemplate the universe. His motifs remind us of the spirals of star nebula, the tail of a comet, etc. He applies the paint in different ways; he uses acrylics, sometimes concentrated, sometimes diluted on the support itself, and encourages dripping. Vicenç Viaplana (born in 1955) creates in his canvases the suggestion of space with a subtle and elegant play of monochromatic chiaroscuro. In his paintings he creates the magic of that which is suggested, spatial visions of surroundings seen through translucent glass or veils that make them difficult to precisely define but that let us dream and imagine. Certainly, the microcosm and the macrocosm have the same plastic structure.

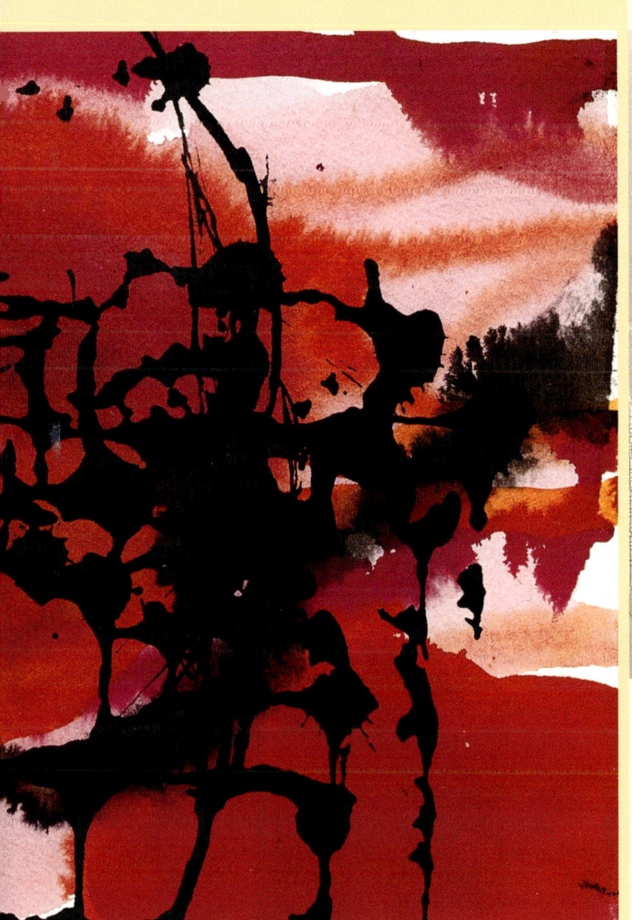

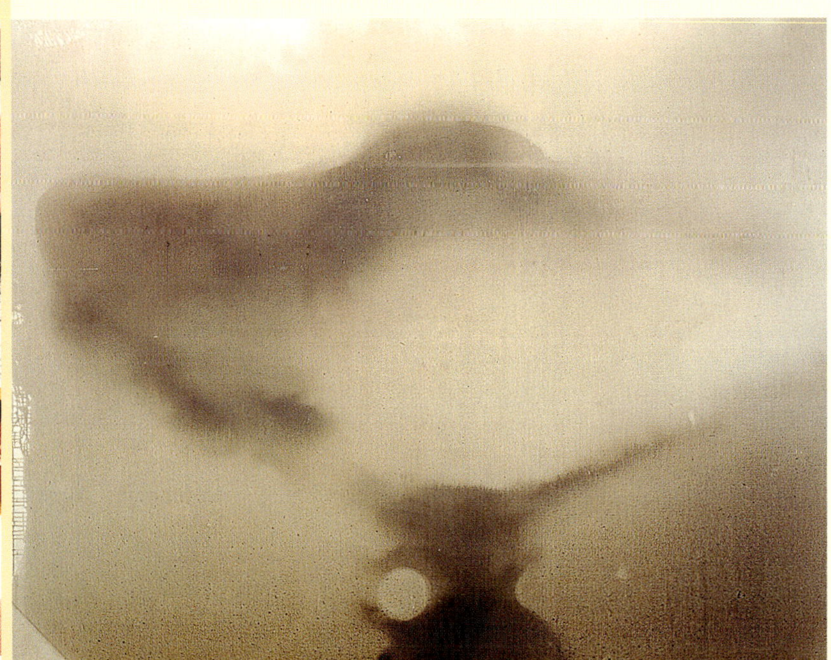

Vicenç Viaplana,
Sentimental Theory, 2000.
Private Collection.

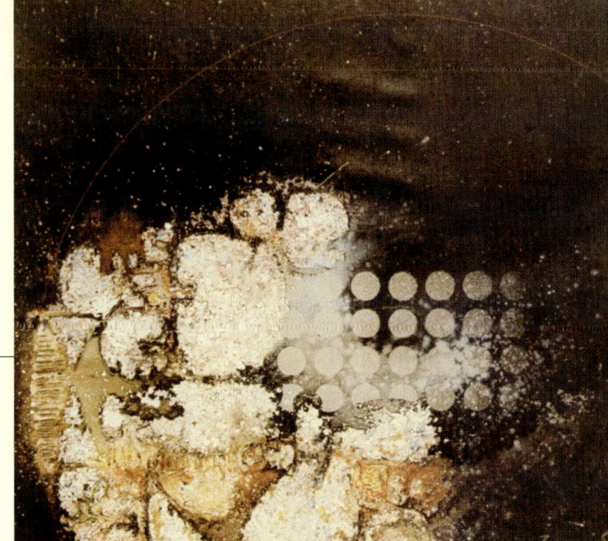

Baruj Salinas,
Panorama, 1973.
Private Collection.

Structural, Geometric, and Reticulated Spaces

With Sol Le Witt (born in 1928) we are surprised by the conviction that the artist has about his personal revelation, scorning frivolity and tenaciously working in a single direction. This attitude results in a solid and mature art, based on reflexive work, not at all systematic and greatly diverse. Sol Le Witt simplifies abstraction and codifies it in a basic language: straight lines in four directions, geometric figures, cubes, black and white . . . His conceptual abstractions are configured by repetition and series: "The idea becomes a machine that creates art." The creation of a visual syntax suggests that anyone can execute the work of art. When his work is applied to a wall, Sol Le Witt only has to indicate the formula for the combination of lines. The instructions are verbal, and a technician takes care of the execution. With this posture the artist's work is no longer a fetish. He makes it the same as a musical score that any musician can interpret.

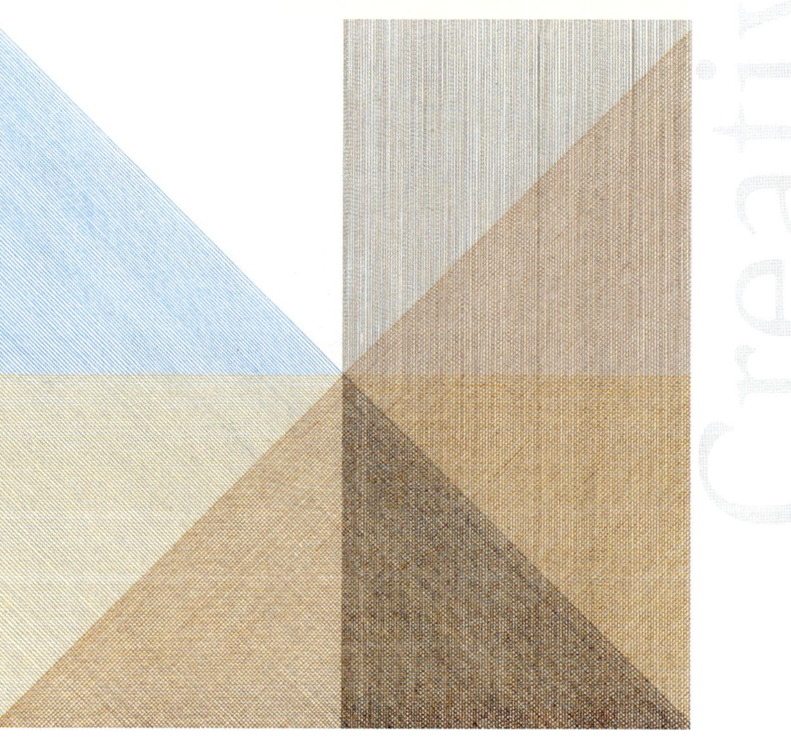

Sol Le Witt,
Four-Color Drawing in Half a Square, 1971. Private Collection.

145

Lines and Grids: Spatial Abstraction in Architectural Structures

Codified and simplified work is used as the basis for making the following geometric abstraction. The artist, Gemma Guasch, has taken the basic lines of the modernist architecture of the Temple of the Sagrada Familia (Holy Family) in Barcelona. By combining them she created new lines and grids that let us perceive new spaces inside the space. To make her work more like Sol Le Witt's she chose a simple and unpretentious medium in accord with the artist's philosophical principles: color markers and pencils on textured cardboard.

"The two opposite extremes that our planet is made from are: the line of horizontal force, that is, the trajectory of the earth around the sun, and the vertical and profoundly spatial movement of the rays that originate in the center of the sun."
H. L. C. Jaffé

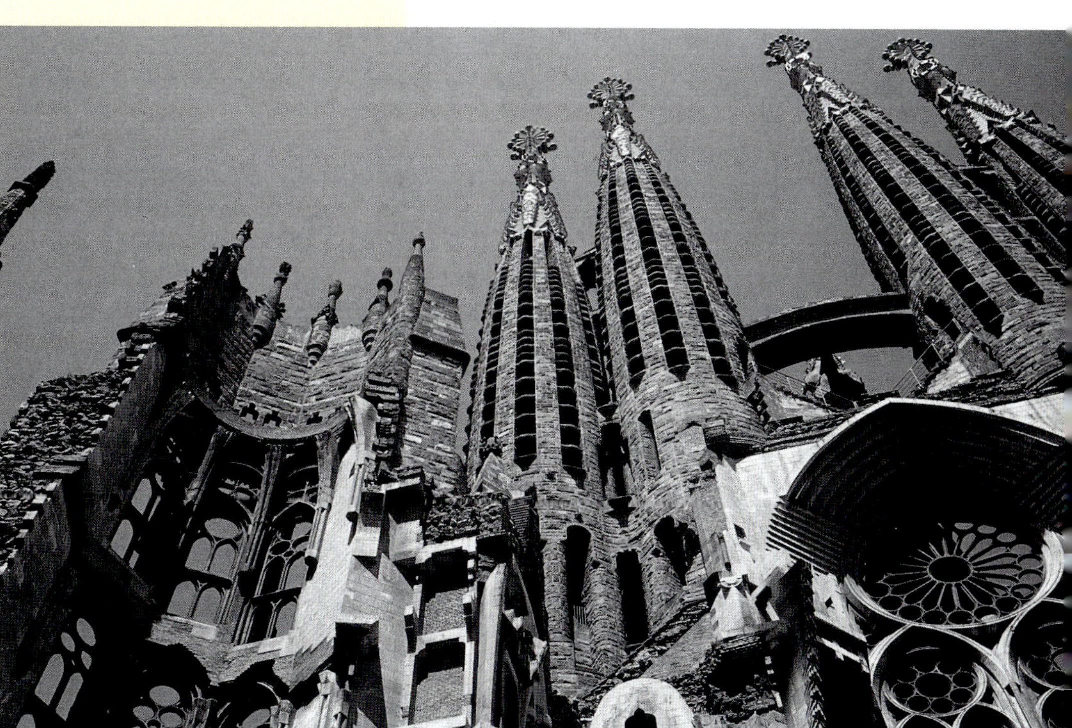

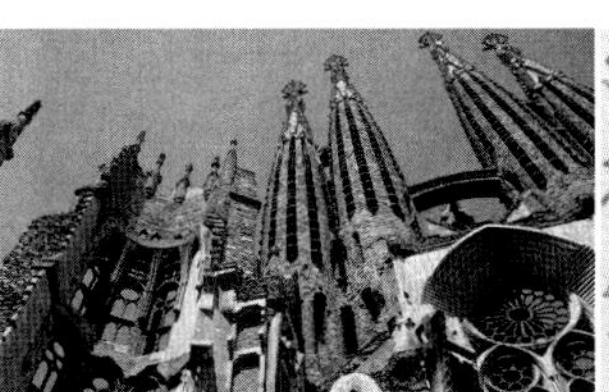

1 We draw angled parallel lines in opposite directions to highlight the idea of the pointed cone shape of the musical towers typical of the Sagrada Familia. The angle of the straight lines together with the tilted triangular space suggests an unstable and dynamic space.

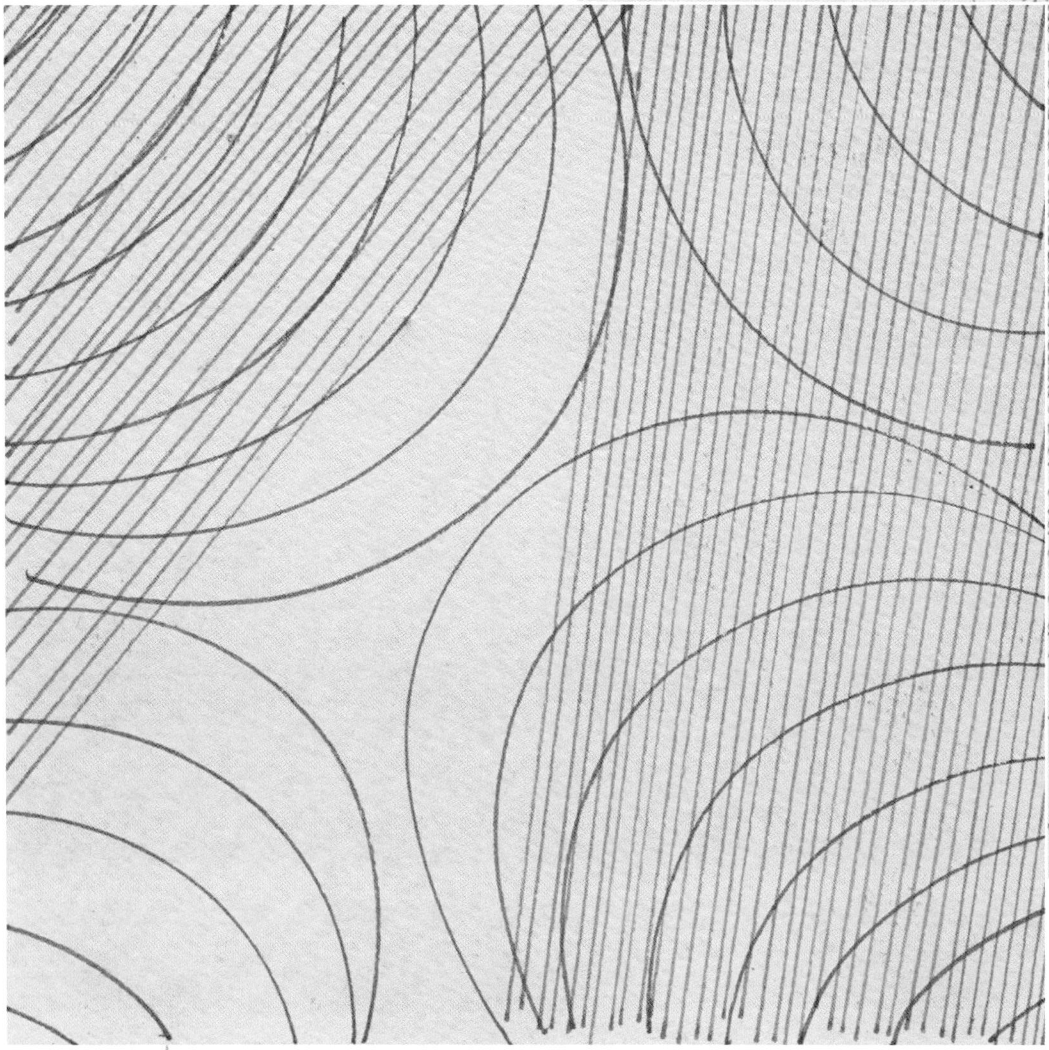

2 Because we are creating a geometric abstraction, we now take inspiration from the temple's rose windows. We fill each side of the paper with half circles. The overlaid straight and curved lines begin to describe a grid belonging to the paper and independent of the motif from which it was taken.

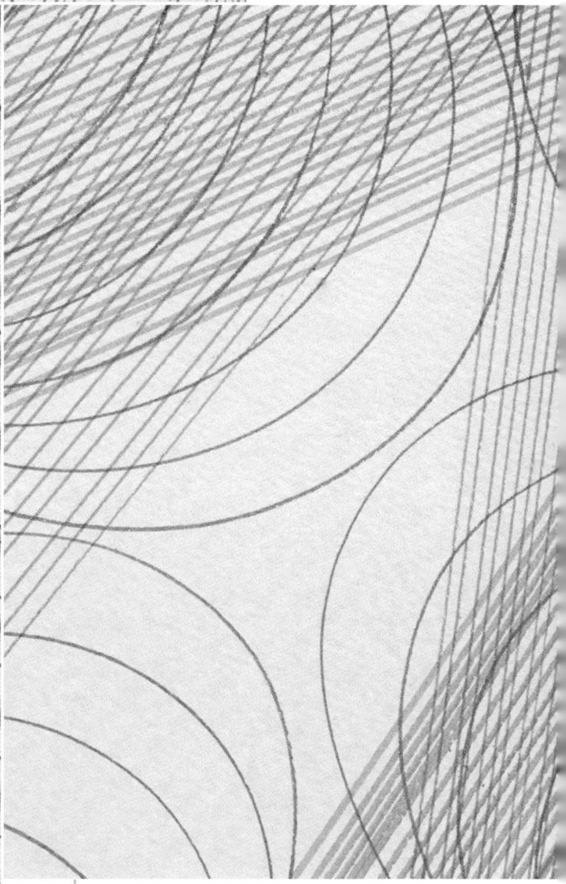

3 To intensify the effect of the angles we repeat the sloping lines, but change their position; by placing their starting point at the corner of the paper, we emphasize the sense of a triangle. The spatial feeling is more intense at the ends because the spaces created by superimposing the lines are minimal.

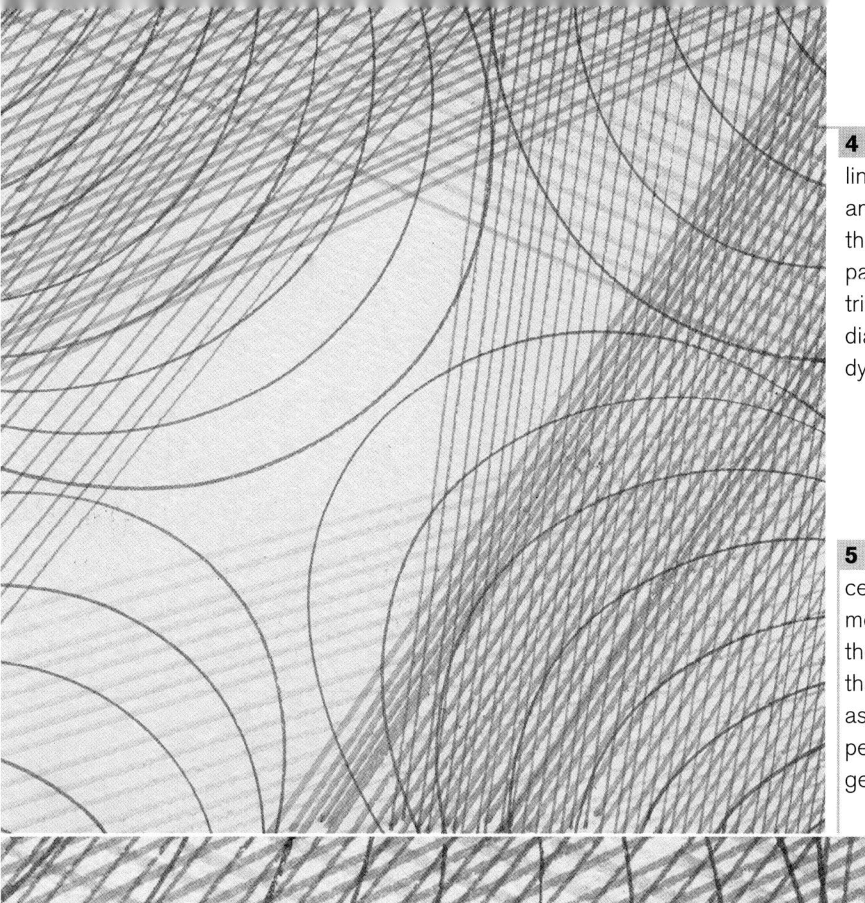

4 We go back to making the inclined lines, but we reverse their positions and draw them in a lighter tone, from the upper and lower edges of the paper. The formation of different triangles and superimposing the diagonals creates an active space, dynamic and tense.

5 We conclude the work with a central group of lines in a darker tone, moving slightly downward to continue the feeling of instability and movement that characterizes this work. The final aspect of the grid is unique, and it permits us to rediscover abstract geometry.

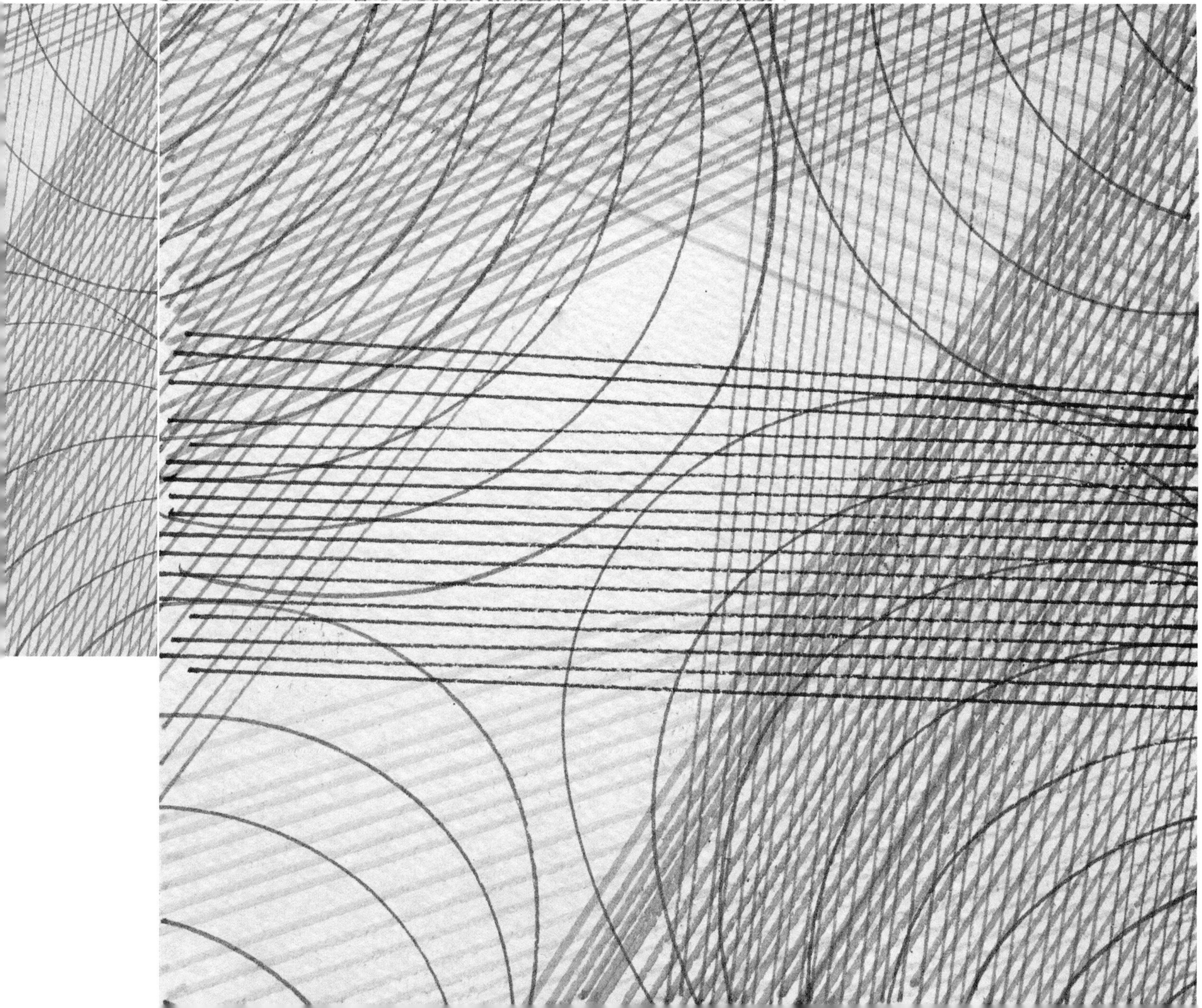

Gallery

Other Versions

Overlaying lines and curves in different directions creates special and unique spatial sensations. By just allowing ourselves to be guided by the imagination and varying the width and overlaying of the lines, we discover an infinity of spaces: minimal, full, dense, light, filled, empty, rigid, mobile, etc.

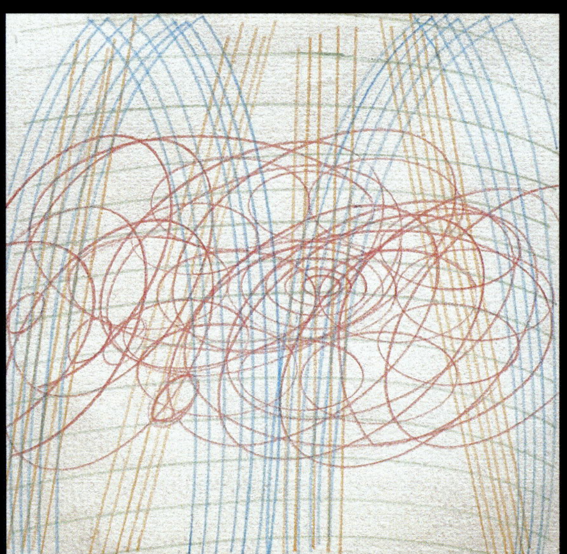

The combination of arcs and circles inspired by the vaults and rose window of the temple form a dynamic but ordered grid. The positioning of the horizontal and vertical curves is stable and solemn. This contrasts with the band of spontaneous circles that cross the center of the composition horizontally. An amusing balance between order and chaos characterizes the picture.

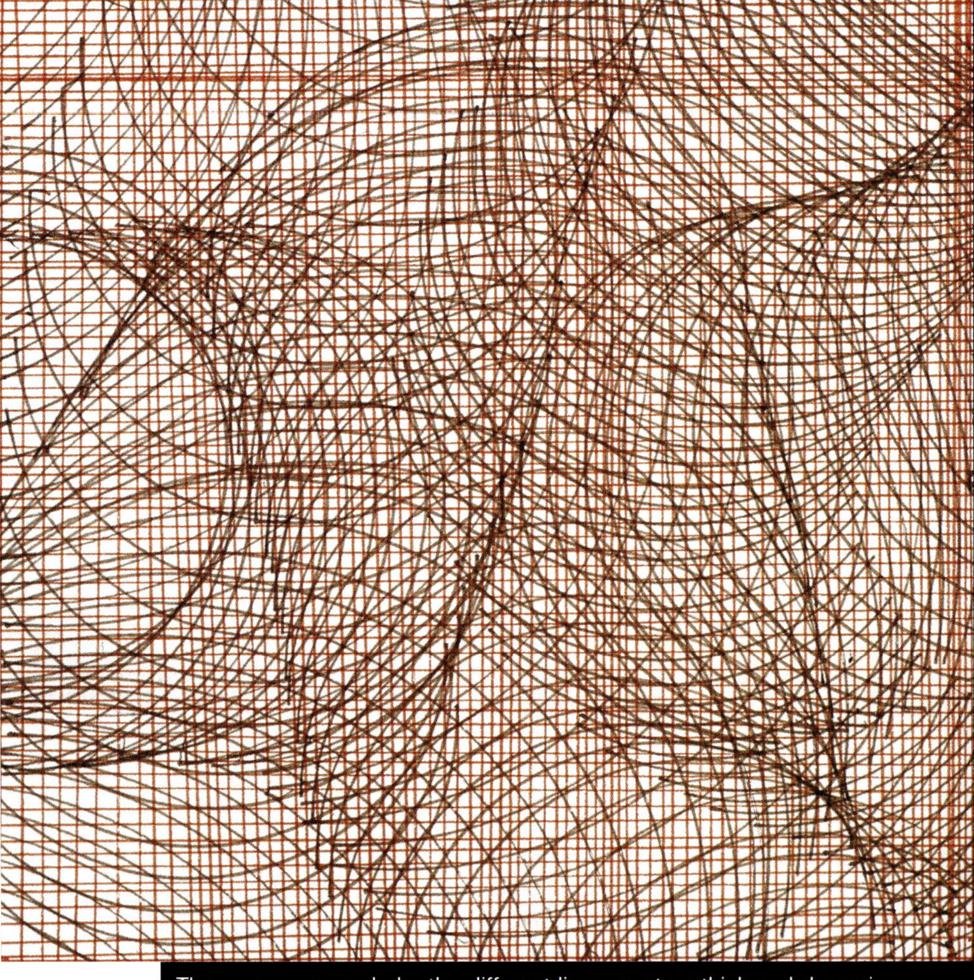

The many arcs made by the different lines create a thick and dynamic composition. The superimposed curves form spirals that go in opposite directions, reinforcing the movement produced by the grid. The final result seems to have a life of its own caused by the virtual movement.

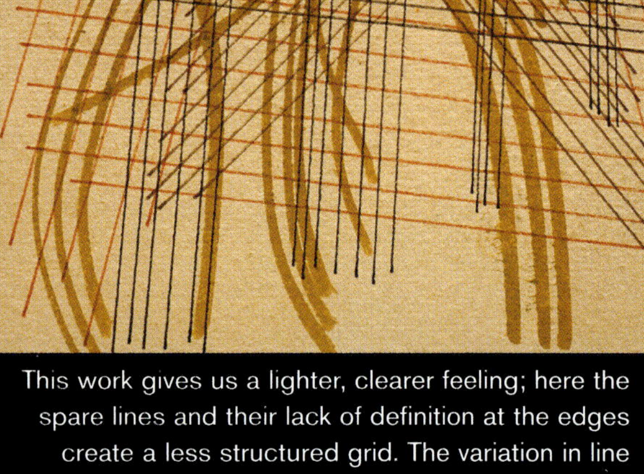

This work gives us a lighter, clearer feeling; here the spare lines and their lack of definition at the edges create a less structured grid. The variation in line weight and use of curves and angled lines give a feeling that the grid seems to be suspended in the air.

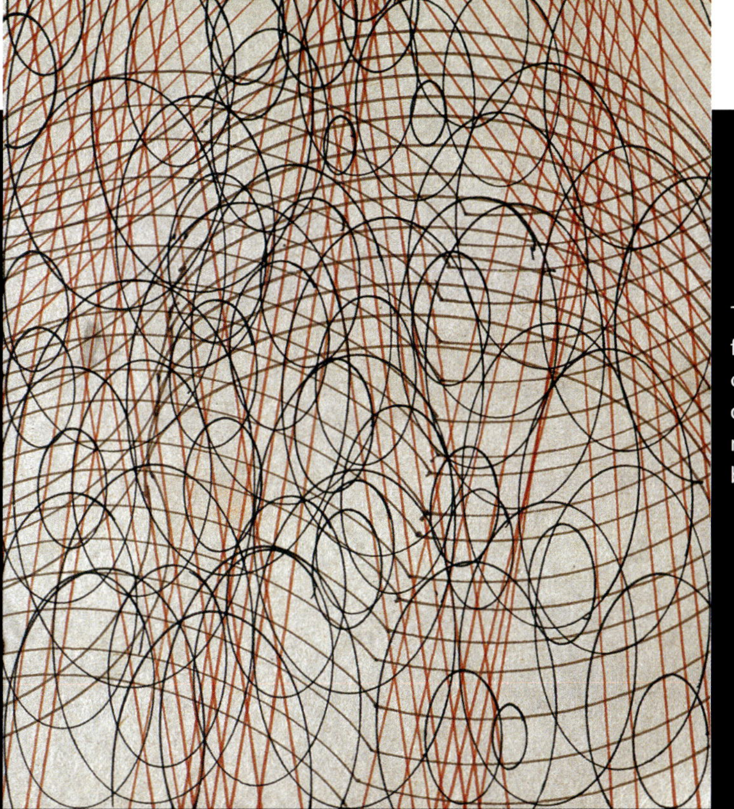

This image has a chaotic and vibrant feeling. The many lines, curves, and circles create a thick and full grid. The dynamic ascending feeling is reminiscent of a large number of soap bubbles floating in the air.

A surface full of different angled lines is given a sense of depth by a half circle that centers the group. Underneath, at the bottom, we can see the faint presence of a band of playful circles, which discretely support the image.

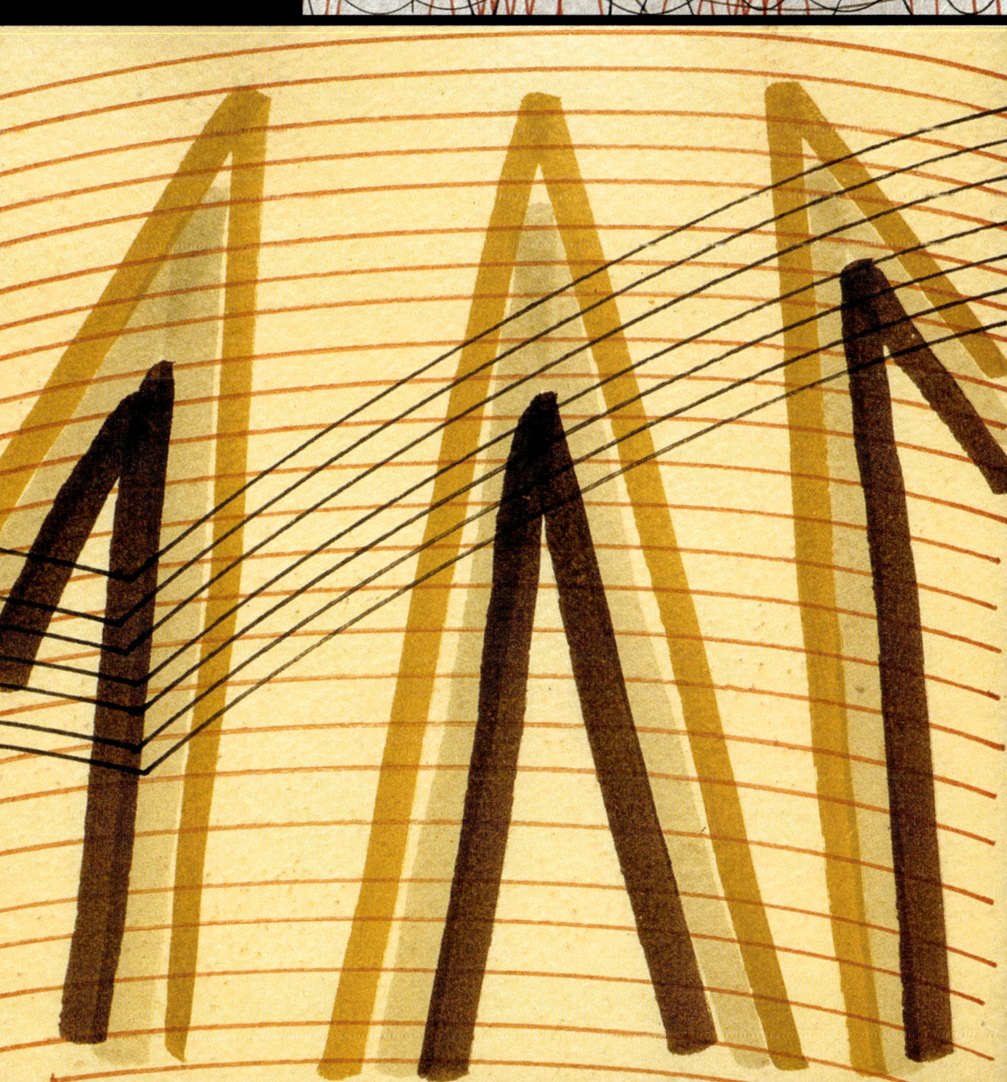

This piece is strikingly simple. The feeling of the grid is sharp and ordered because of the horizontal position of the curves and the three triangles that indicate the center. Just a few curves that remind us of a rainbow partially break up the whole.

New Approaches

Other Models

Any architecture or structure is valid when borrowing lines and curves for creating abstractions. It would also be valid to create them from nothing, without real references. In this case, the model is an old building in ruins showing structural references from construction of the past: Gothic and Romanesque arches that inspire the creation of an abstraction that makes a dense grid full of curved lines placed vertically and horizontally.

Other Media

Using drawing inks diluted with lots of water and applied with rollers and wide brushes, Gemma Guasch created a work that is totally different from the previous ones. The transparency and luminosity of the bands of ink create new and suggestive color spaces when superimposed. In the darkest areas light is regained by a final application of bleach with a nib pen. In the first drawing the curves make a fan shape across the image. In the second they are applied only on the angled bands drawn on the top and bottom edges of the paper.

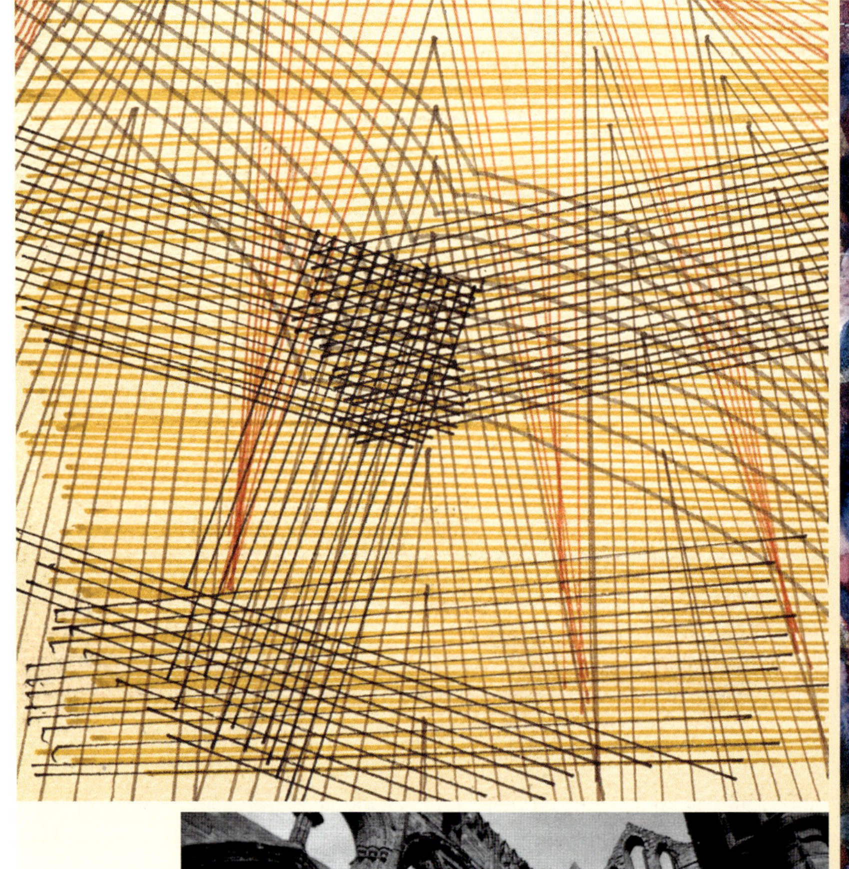

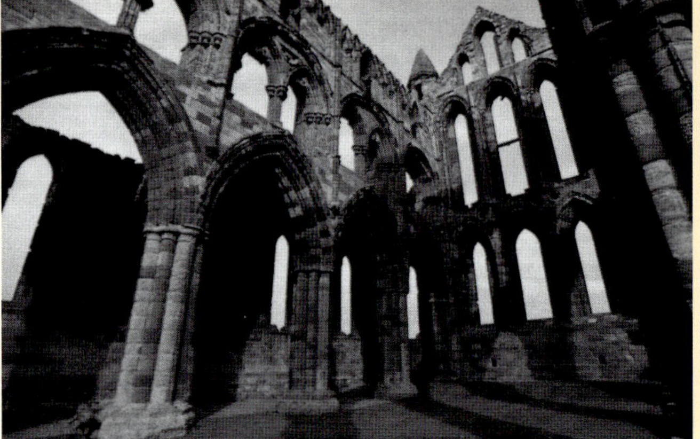

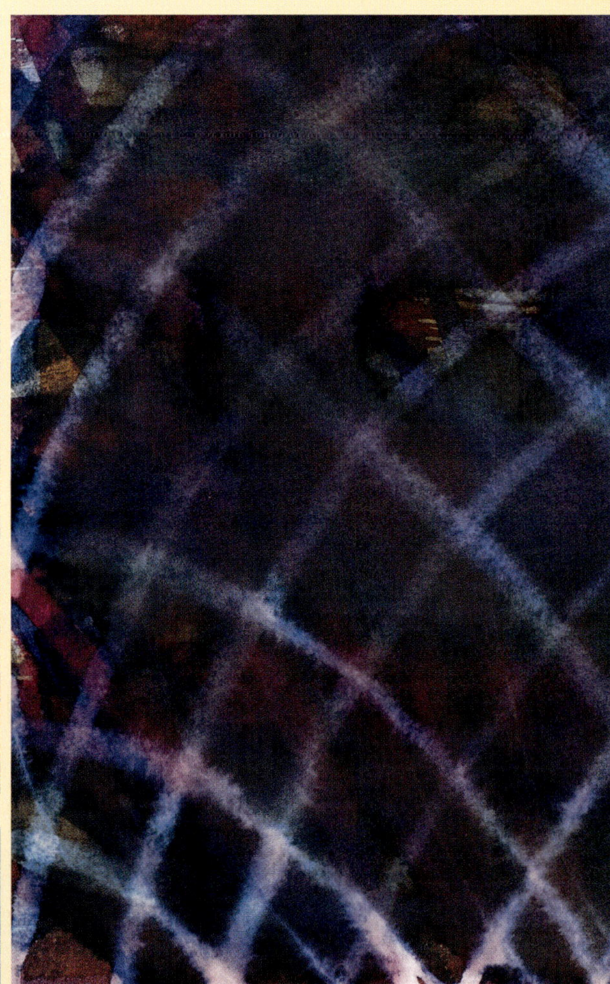

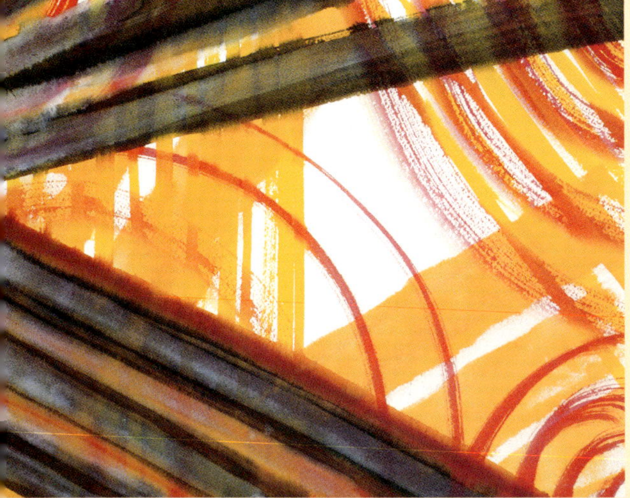

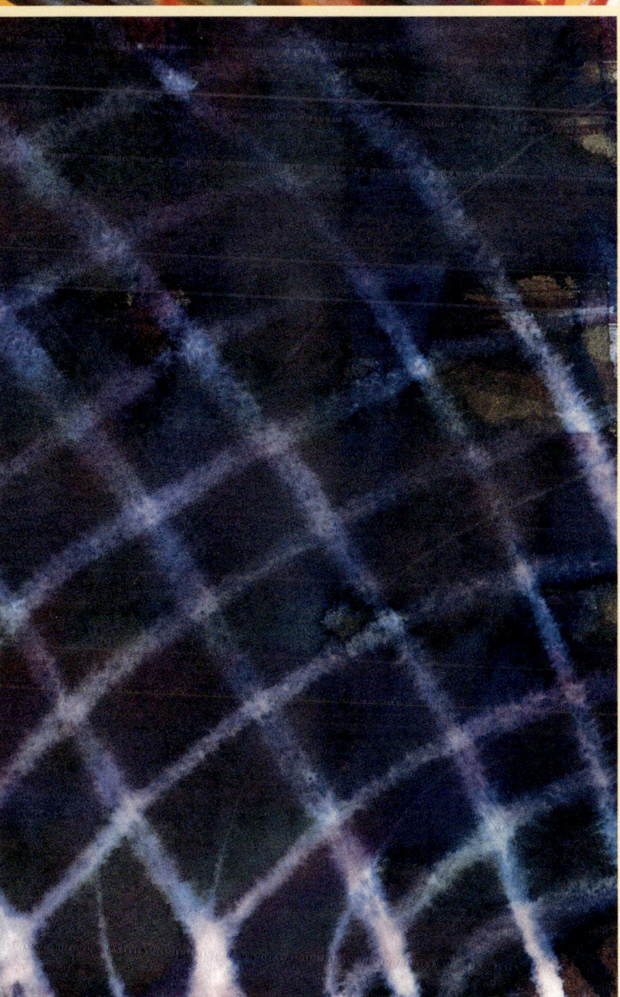

Other Views

Geometric abstraction gained worldwide popularity in the 1960s with the phenomenon known as op art (optical art). The artists in this movement worked with visual perception to create the sensation of movement. The virtual movement was born from this. In this line, the Argentine artist Eduard Mac Entyre (born in 1929), cofounder of the movement known as generative art of 1960, worked with geometric purity, space, and vibration. His search for optical effects, along the lines of Joseph Albers (1888–1976) or Victor Vasarely (1908–1997), was articulated in drawn circles based on generating points.

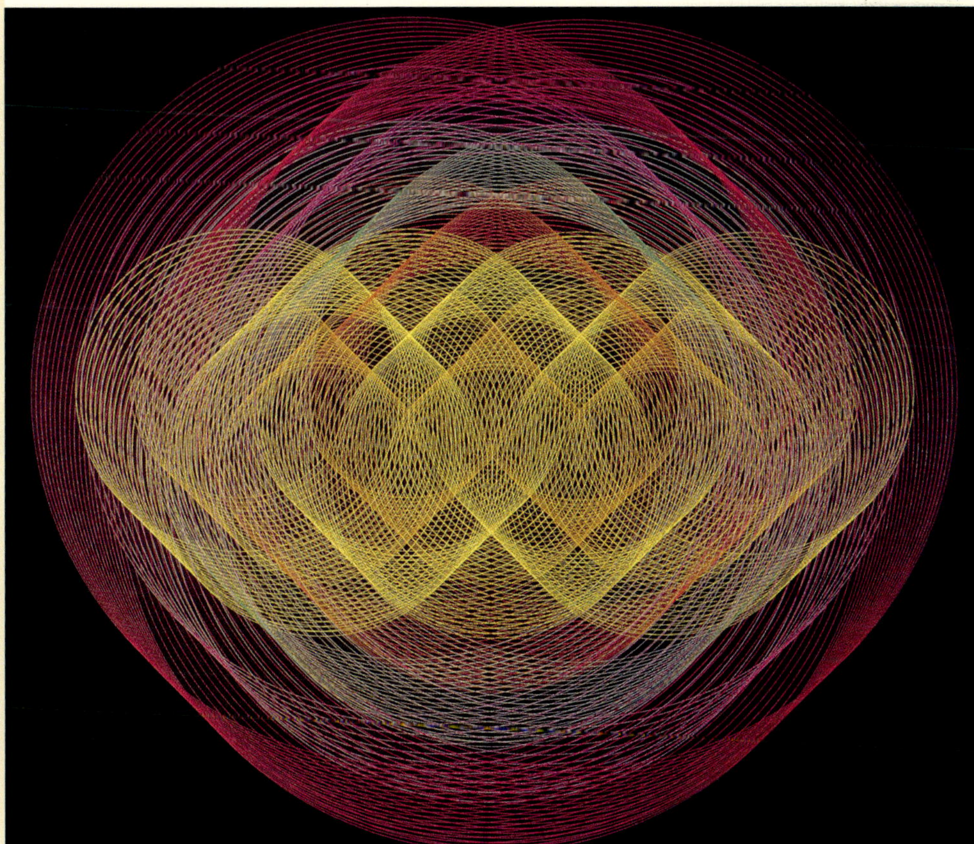

Eduard Mac Entyre,
Yellow Construction, 1969.
Banco de la República Collection,
Buenos Aires, Argentina.

Wet Media

Glossary

These media are composed of a mixture of pigment, agglutinant, and a solvent. They can be classified in two groups according to the solvent they contain: oil base and water base.

OIL-BASED MEDIA

The solvent used in oil-based media is an essence, which can be of either vegetable or mineral origin. The vegetable essences are essence of turpentine, which is more refined, and paint thinner, which is less. The mineral essence derived from petroleum is mineral spirits, a substitute for paint thinner.

Oils

Oils have been one of the most valued media in the history of painting. They have an oily and pasty consistency, made of tints or pigments mixed with an agglutinant: walnut, poppy, or linseed oil. It is preferably diluted with a vegetable essence, turpentine or paint thinner. It is available in tubes of different sizes from 1¼ oz. to 8 oz. (5 to 200 ml) or in 1-gallon (4-liter) cans. The prices can vary a lot according to the initial cost of the pigment. The earth tones are the least expensive, whereas the cadmiums can cost four times as much. Today, less expensive colors have been created, substituting synthetic pigments for natural ones.

Oil paints have a very slow drying process; this permits the forms to be blended and retouched, and allows more time for working on the painting. The colors are bright and intense, and lose little brilliance in the drying process.

Canvas, wood, or hard cardboard supports are recommended for use with this medium.

The most appropriate brushes are those with real or synthetic bristles; the spatula is recommended for use with impasto.

Wax Crayons

Crayons are made by mixing pure pigment with animal oils and waxes. Then they are formed into sticks of different colors that will make a thick and creamy mark. Their tones are intense and bright, and can be mixed on the support by rubbing with cotton, a paper towel, an eraser, or the fingers, which will create a smooth, bright, and oily texture. The colors can also be diluted with a brush or a paper towel impregnated with turpentine or thinner, to create a transparent effect. It is an ideal medium for the sgraffito technique, which consists of scratching areas of wax applied over a previously colored support with a sharp instrument (a blade or a craft knife) to create special forms and textures. It is also a very useful medium for making reserves: first, a drawing or an area of color is made on paper with wax colors, then ink or watercolor is painted over them.

Wax Crayons

Since the wax repels any water-base medium, the area covered with wax remains unpainted. Wax crayons are sold in boxes of assorted colors or individually at very reasonable prices.

Paper and cardboard are ideal supports. It is recommended to fix the artwork by spraying it with lacquer or a fixative when it is finished.

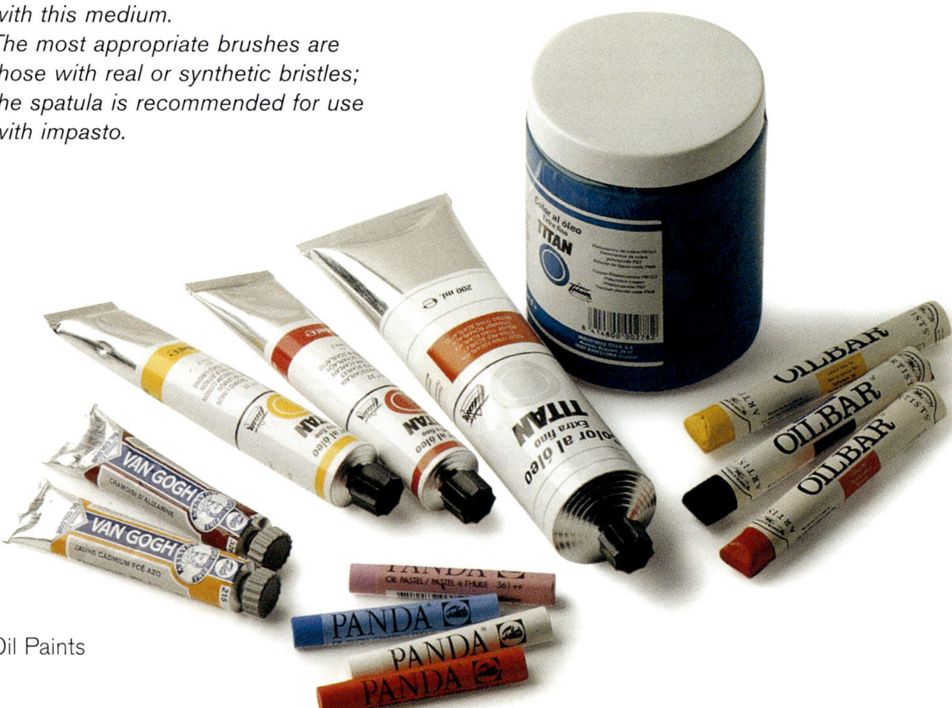

Oil Paints

WATER-BASED MEDIA
Regular tap water, or distilled water, which prevents granulation, is used as a solvent for this type of medium.

Acrylics
Acrylics are made with pigments bound with synthetic resins. They dry fast and do not yellow over time. Very versatile, they offer the advantages of watercolors when diluted with water, or the thickness of oils used without water. Acrylics are soft and creamy, like oils, so are ideal for impastos. They can be diluted with water or acrylic media. Glossy, matte, and gel media can be used to increase the shine and depth of color. Adding glycerin or a retardant medium delays drying time. Acrylics have a uniform, matte finish, but the gloss can be restored by applying a thin, transparent coat of acrylic varnish. Apply this only over completely dry paint, so it is wise to wait a day. The varnish can be matte or gloss or they can be mixed for a semigloss finish.

Acrylics come in tubes and cans at reasonable prices. A very durable medium, it will work with any applicator on almost any support.

Acrylic
Paints

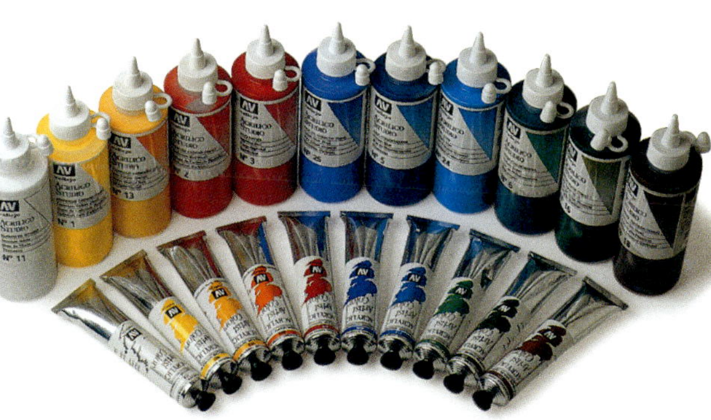

Watercolors
Watercolors are made of finely ground pigments mixed with gum Arabic as a binder with another substance for plasticity. Glycerin can be added to improve solubility and to prevent paint from cracking. Ox gall moistens paint, helping it flow over the paper.

Watercolor in
Cakes

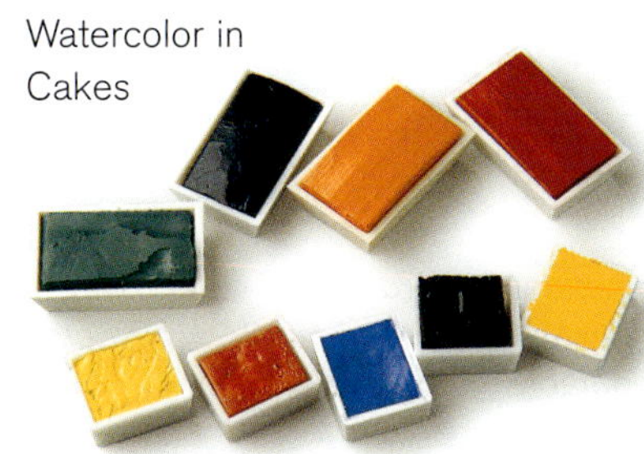

Watercolors are sold in either cakes or tubes and are available alone or in sets of assorted colors. Price is high; the smaller the cake the more expensive due to the quality of the pigment. Their chief characteristic is transparency. Mixing pigment with water reduces color intensity while increasing transparency and luminosity. There is no white in watercolor. When white is required, the paper can be left unpainted, or an opaque watercolor like white gouache is painted over the watercolors.
Sable brushes are ideal applicators but modern synthetic brushes cost less and create similar effects. Washes can be applied with a sponge, roller, or paper towel. The ideal support is watercolor paper, available in different weights and textures. It can be worked dry or wet. If wet, the paper must first be stretched on a board using adhesive paper tape.

Ink
Ink can be permanent or water-soluble. If not water-soluble, it contains lacquer, and is denser with a glossy finish when dry. Water-soluble ink has no lacquer and is used for making line and hatched drawings with a nib or reed pen, and for washes applied with a brush. It has a matte finish when dry as it penetrates deeper into the paper. Available in various colors, black is most commonly used.
Ink can be diluted with tap or distilled water.

Drawing
Inks

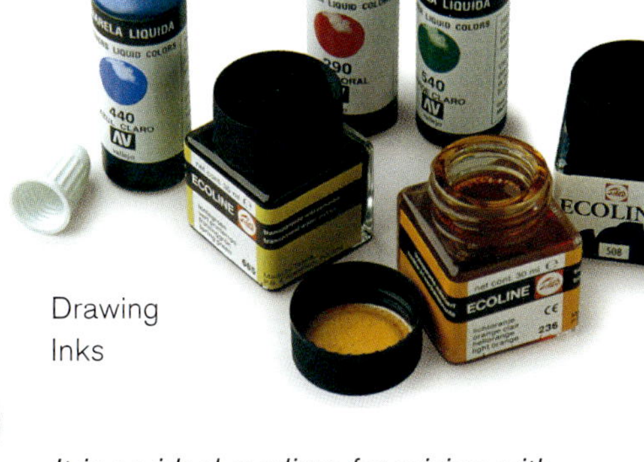

It is an ideal medium for mixing with other media to achieve special effects.
When using inks, fine lines can combine with washes. Quick, intuitive work is recommended as ink favors spontaneity and free expression. Ink is best applied with round brushes as they hold more water. Drawing effects can be achieved using nib or reed pens. Pens are available with different nibs to draw fine or wide lines. The more primitive handcrafted reed pen makes irregular, more expressive lines. Smooth or satin paper with some durability makes a good support.

Gouache

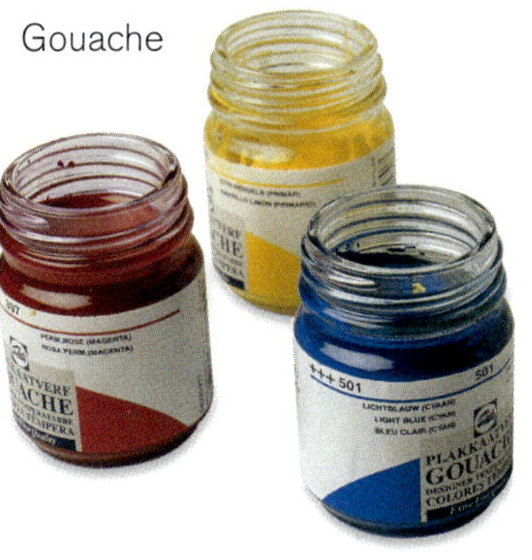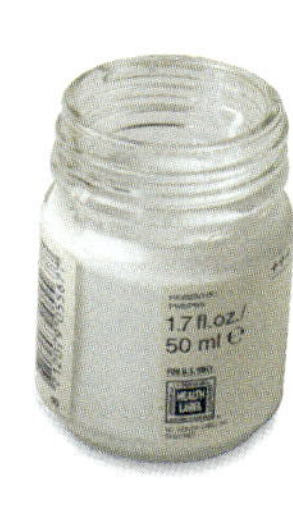

Gouache
Also called tempera, gum tempera, and opaque watercolor, gouache can be diluted in water, composed of pigment and gum Arabic. It is applied on paper, but is thicker and more opaque. The opacity allows it to be painted over dark paper. It can be applied with a brush or a roller in a creamy consistency, no impastos or glazes, so that after it dries, brushstrokes are smooth, uniform, and brightly colored. Sold in tubes and jars, this finish is perfect for posters, illustrations, and background for other media.

Glossary

Dry Media

These media are usually applied without a solvent.
They can be monochromatic or polychromatic.

MONOCHROMATIC MEDIA

These are media of a single color, which are gradated to achieve an extensive range of values.

Vine Charcoal

These are made of sticks of grapevine, beech, or willow, carbonized at high temperatures in an airtight oven. They are sold in boxes of several sticks approximately 6 inches (15 cm) in length and in different hardnesses and widths. The softest charcoal lends itself to rubbing and blending; the hardest is ideal for drawing lines and details. It is a very fragile medium, and drawing with shorter pieces broken off the stick is recommended. Various gray tones can be achieved by wiping with a rag or the hand. Charcoal should be used with a textured paper. When a drawing is finished, it should always be protected with a final coat of lacquer or fixative.

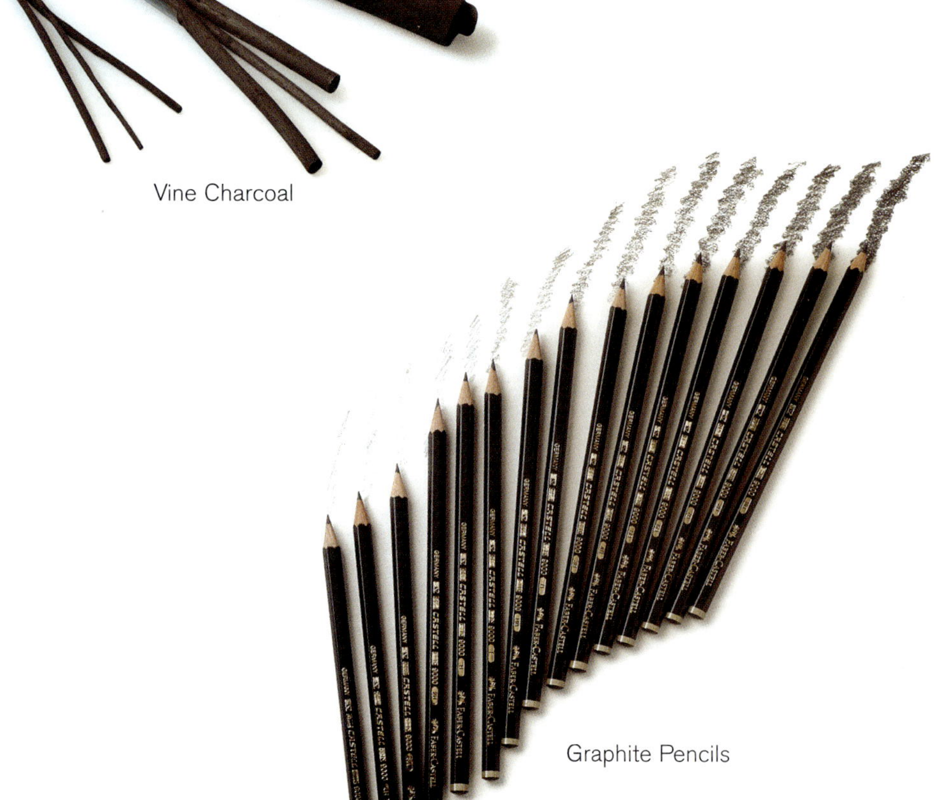

Vine Charcoal

Graphite Pencils

Graphite Pencils

These are very thin sticks known as leads, whose degree of hardness is determined by the amount of hardener (clay) mixed with them when they are manufactured. A universal system was adopted for identifying the different hardness of pencils. The letter B is used for soft pencils, and H for the hard ones, preceded by a number or coefficient. Hard pencils range from 9H (the hardest) to H, and the soft ones from 9B (the softest) to B. The HB and F grades fall between H and B. The soft pencils produce darker tones than the hard ones, making them ideal for shading and blending, and rendering expressive results. The hard pencils are more suitable for technical drawings, because they make precise lines and details and have a lighter tone. Generally, several grades of hardness are used in a drawing, to achieve a range of tones and expressiveness.

The universal support is paper; its weight, texture, and tone are chosen based on the desired effects. Normally, graphite can be used with any type of paper, except waxed or very glossy papers. It is a good idea to apply a fixative or lacquer when the work is completed, especially if very soft pencils have been used.

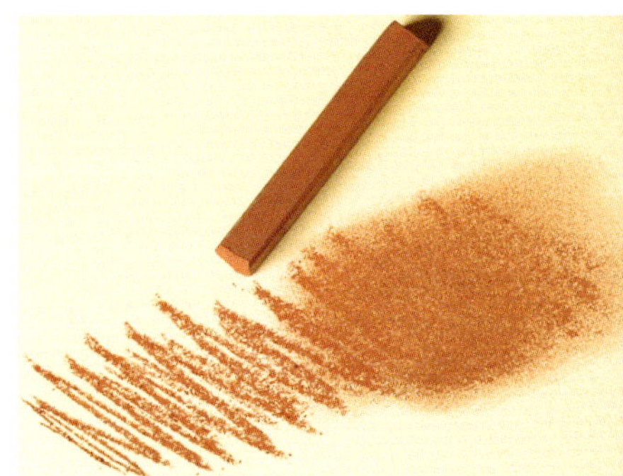

Sanguine Crayon

Sanguine Crayon

This is a terra-cotta–colored chalk made from hematite (an iron mineral) that has its own outstanding personality. A single color provides a full range of reddish tones. We can create excellent blended effects by rubbing with a rag or the fingers, achieving softer and more luminous effects than those obtained with vine charcoal. Vigorous erasing will produce watercolor effects. Sanguine crayon can also be combined with other drawing techniques (pastels, vine charcoal, graphite). The most appropriate support for this medium is one that has a little texture or that is velvety. A fixative or lacquer should be applied when the work is finished.

POLYCHROME MEDIA

These media are normally used in combination with other colors, although they can also be used monochromatically, thanks to the large range of tones available.

Pastels

Pastels are made from pure pigment mixed with a base of chalk and bound with glue. They are mixed to form a stiff paste, which is then cut and molded into sticks, and left to dry until they harden.

There are hard pastels and soft pastels. The soft pastels have more pigment and less binder, which causes them to break easily. They create magnificent bright, saturated, and velvety tones that are ideal for rubbing and blending.

The hard pastels have less pigment and more binder. We can use hard pastels for making a preliminary drawing and for details and finishing. They are the perfect complement to soft pastels.

They are sold in boxes of assorted colors or individually. Prices can vary considerably. The high cost comes from the quality of the pigment; the more expensive it is the less chalk in the mixture and the purer its tone.

This is a very painterly and versatile medium, and it allows working with line, glazing, impasto, rubbing, and blending. The artist can work with the side of the stick, with the point, or with the powder that comes from the stick, spreading it with a brush, the fingers, or a cotton ball.

It should be used with supports that are rough or that have a heavy texture to hold the pigment, and on resistant papers that can stand up to blending, corrections, and creating effects with an eraser. When the work is finished, it should be preserved with a fixative or lacquer.

Pastel Sticks

Color Pencils

These are made of pigments bound with kaolin and mixed with wax. Color pencils are easy to use and produce immediate results. They are used the same way as graphite pencils, but their finish is less greasy, softer, and glossy. They are ideal for making small-format works. The quality of the pencils depends on the quantity and quality of the pigment. Higher-quality pencils have better covering power. It is possible to achieve different intensities by varying the pressure applied with the pencil. Colors can also be mixed, by applying one tone over another using hatch lines. Some color pencils are water-soluble and their lines can be diluted with water. Paper is the ideal support.

Chalk

This is the name for pastels that are of a greater hardness. The composition is the same as that of pastels—pigment with glue—but they are usually hardened with resin. The most common chalks are white, black, sanguine, and sepia, but a wide assortment of colors is available. The finish of chalk is very graphic because it is applied as hatching and blended on the paper. It can also be applied to unsized lightweight fabrics, making use of their porosity, although this is not as common. When the painting is completed, it should be fixed with lacquer or fixative.

Color Pencils

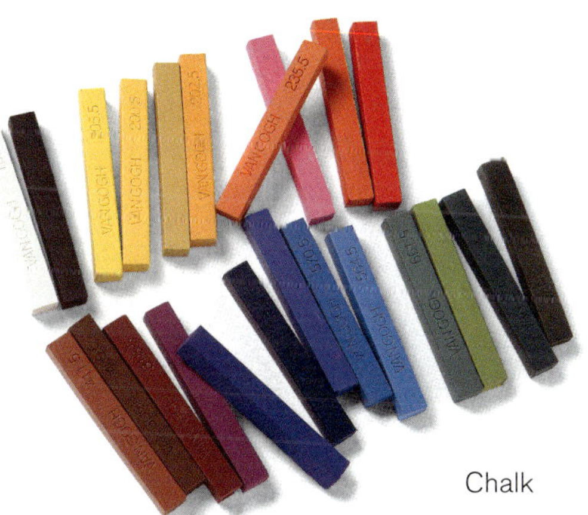

Chalk

Markers

Although the composition of the colored substances in markers is wet (usually an alcohol-soluble ink), they can be categorized as dry media, because they are applied directly to the support without using a solvent. The color in the marker passes to the support through a fiber point that must always be kept damp, which is why it is recommended that the caps not be left off markers for long periods of time. The most common support is paper, and the most commonly used technique is hatching.

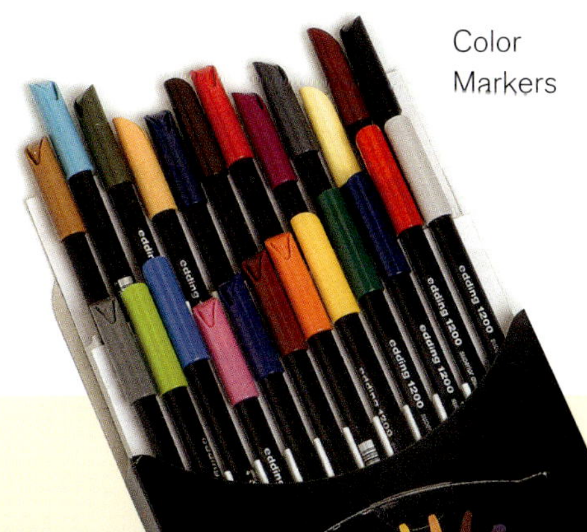

Color Markers

SUPPORTS

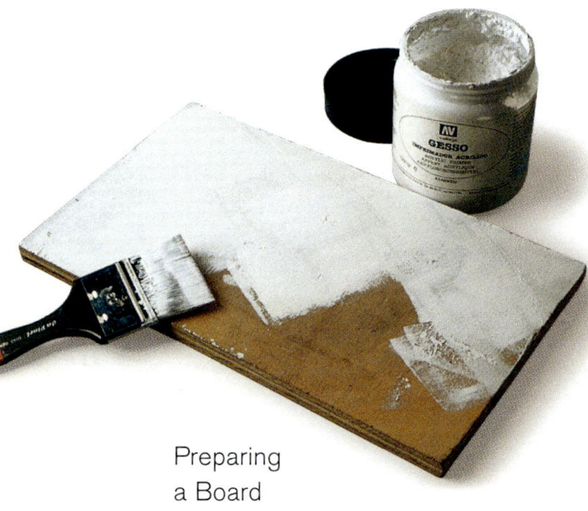

Wood

Wood is suitable for almost any medium. It must be prepared according to the medium that is to be used. First, the wood is selected, making sure it is dried and cured, with no resin, knots, or nails. It is best if it is not too well sanded. Then it is prepared, neither too much nor too little, as either extreme will make the adhesion of the paint to the support difficult, and the final result will be fragile and difficult to conserve. The porosity of the wood should be controlled with the appropriate product. Various materials such as gesso, casein, rabbit-skin glue, latex, or latex diluted with water can be used, depending on the painting technique we intend to use. Both sides must be prepared so that the board will not warp.

Preparing
a Board

Canvas
Panels

Boards and Canvas Panels

These are made with a cotton fabric primed with acrylic and mounted on a rigid support. They come in a range of standard sizes and in several textures. They are light and easy to transport.

Canvas

The canvases that are traditionally used for painting are made of vegetable fibers such as linen, hemp, jute, or cotton. They must be prepared to reduce their absorbency, but not so excessively that they lose flexibility, because a heavy preparation would cause the paint to crack. They are prepared with a primer. Primed canvas is available in rolls by the yard, or mounted on stretchers of various kinds, sizes, and formats. The sizes of the stretchers are international, each number corresponding to a specific length and width.

Paper

Paper is made of intertwined vegetable fibers, the most common nowadays being cellulose. The best is made with cotton, after which comes eucalyptus or pine (kraft paper), which have woody fibers that deteriorate more easily over time. Papers that are ideal for wet techniques and dry techniques are available, manufactured commercially under a wide variety of brand names.

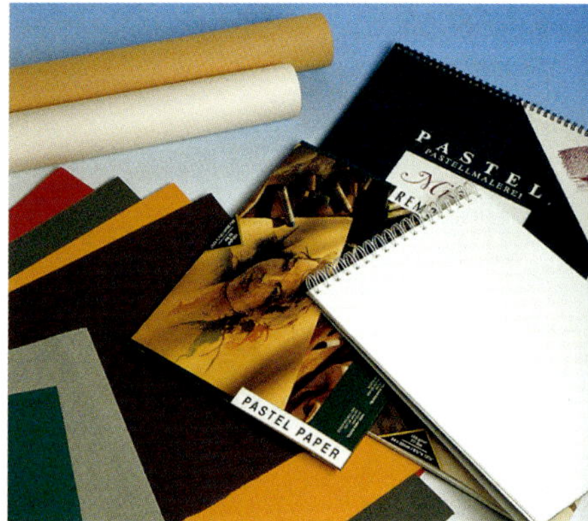

Papers

Canvas

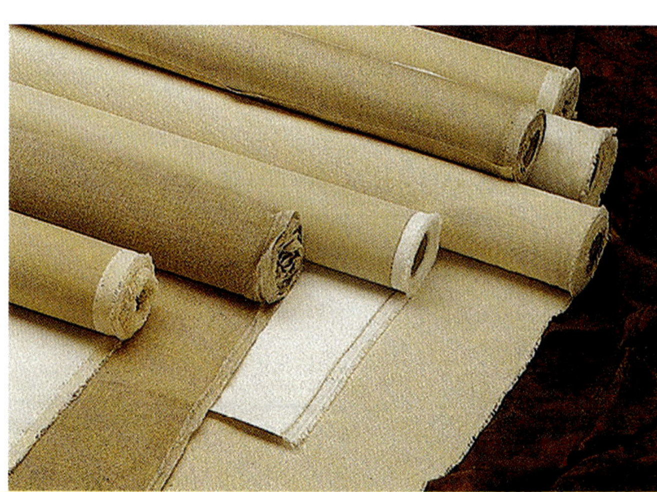

APPLICATORS

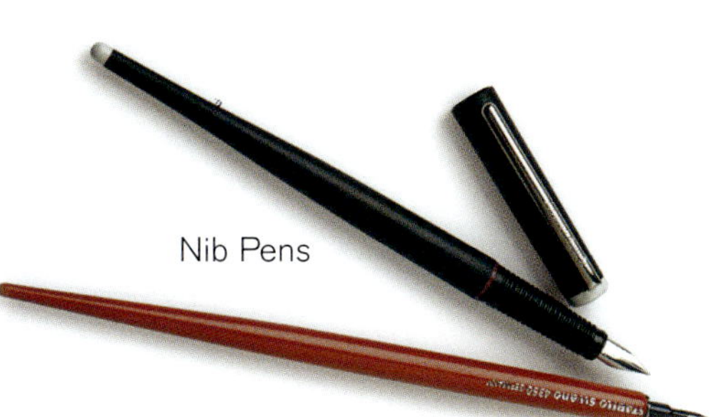

Nib Pens

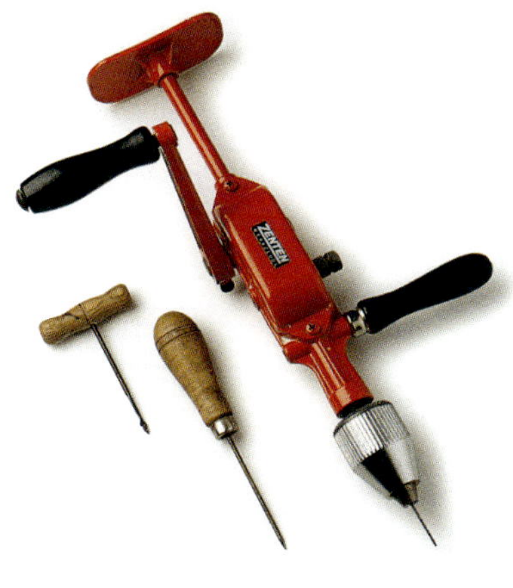

Awls

Brush

Brushes are composed of three parts: the hair, the ferrule, and the handle. They are available in several shapes and sizes. The choice of brush will be determined by the medium that is being used.
There are brushes with fine hair and stiff hair, and each group includes flat, round, and other shapes (filberts, brights, fan blenders, etc.). Each group has different sizes indicated by numbers. The types of hair used to make the fine brushes are sable, ox, otter, and squirrel, among others.
Stiff brushes are made with hog or boar bristles. Nowadays there are also brushes made with synthetic fibers.
Round brushes are usually made of fine hair and are most suitable for water-based media because they hold water better. The best-quality round brushes end in a point. Flat brushes usually have stiff hair and are most appropriate for oil-based media.

Nib Pen

This type of pen consists of a plastic handle and interchangeable steel nibs. It is an inexpensive drawing tool. Each steel nib makes a wider or narrower line according to its shape. The lines are even because the nib always dispenses the same quantity of ink. They are ideal for making details and hatching.

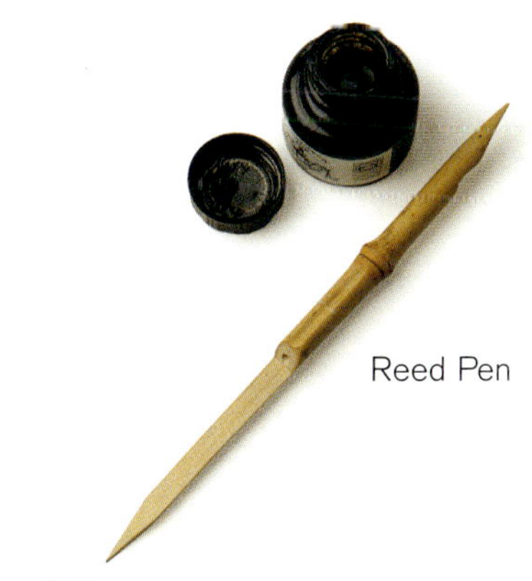

Reed Pen

Reed Pen

These pens are made of bamboo or reed and are very simple tools that can be made by the artist. Reed pens make irregular lines of varying width.

Sponge

Sponges are ideal for making washes and for glazing with water-based media. We can add or remove paint with a sponge, as well as wet the paper before using it.
We recommend having small pieces of sponge that can be held in the hand, to ensure more precision and control. Sponges can be hard or soft. The hard ones produce textured surfaces; the soft ones create smooth and even surfaces.

Awl

This metal rod with a wood handle has a more or less sharp point that is used to punch and create relief on rigid supports. It is useful for creating textures and expressive lines on wood.

Sandpaper

This is very rough paper that is used as an abrasive. Its composition is very simple: an abrasive powder, usually mineral, glued to a very durable paper. There are many different grades used according to the desired smoothness, and several compositions according to whether it will be used with wood, metal, or stone.

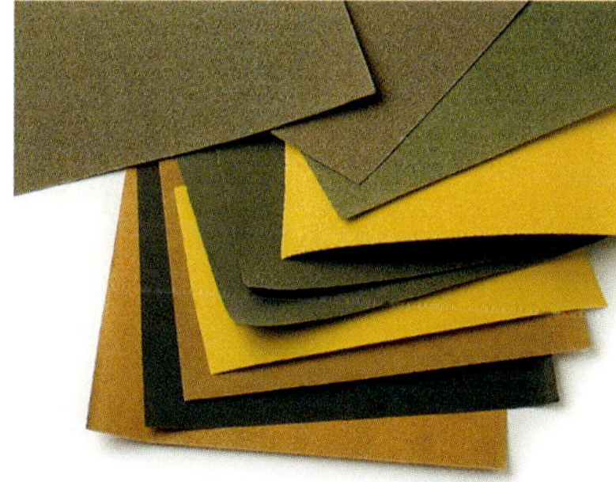

Sandpaper

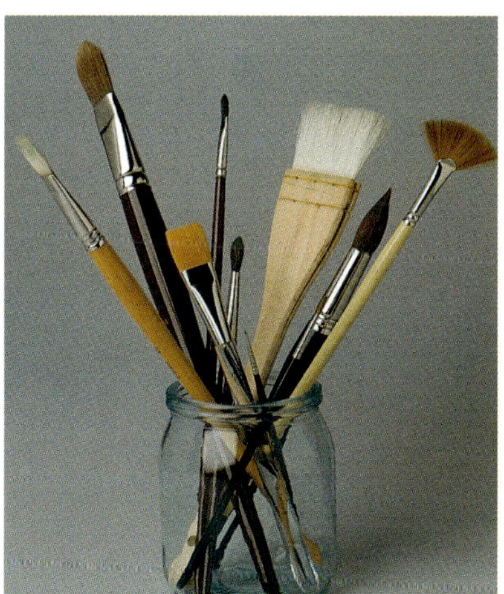

Brushes

Sponges

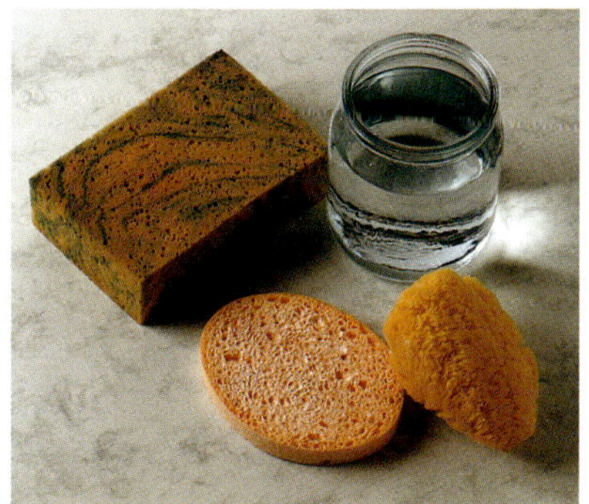

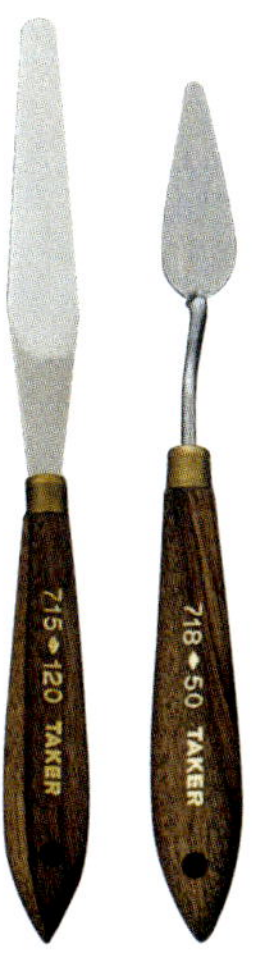

Spatulas

Spatula

This is an applicator in the shape of a knife or a palette knife. Spatulas are ideal for making impastos or for mixing colors.

Eraser

An eraser is not only used for removing pigment, but is also an excellent applicator. It cleans up colors, creates light and shadows, blends tones, and reinforces the lines made with wax crayons. We recommend soft rubber or plastic erasers for linear and heavy-duty work, and kneaded erasers, which are softer and easy to control, for light and atmospheric results.

Glossary

Techniques

A technique is the way a medium is used or a material is manipulated to achieve a specific plastic effect, although the term technique *has commonly been used as a synonym for* medium.

Rubbing
Rubbing is the action of smoothing a color until its edges blend with the background or with another adjoining color, making sure that no traces of the applicator are left visible.

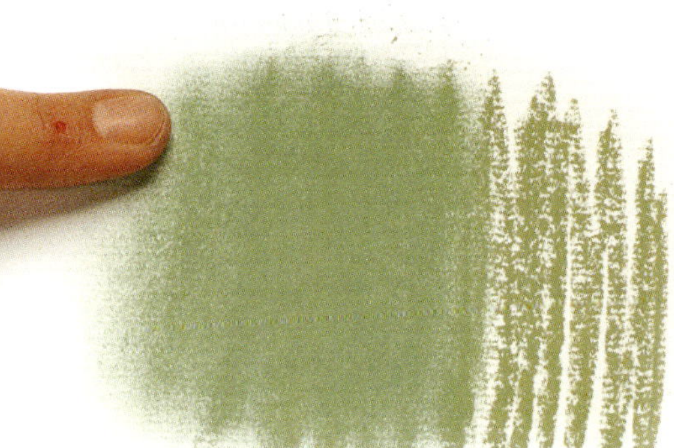

Rubbing

Blending
Blending is mixing paint directly on the support, taking advantage of the fact that the paint is still wet.

Blending

Impasto
This is the application of large amounts of thick paint with a spatula or a stiff brush, imparting a certain amount of relief to the surface of the paint.

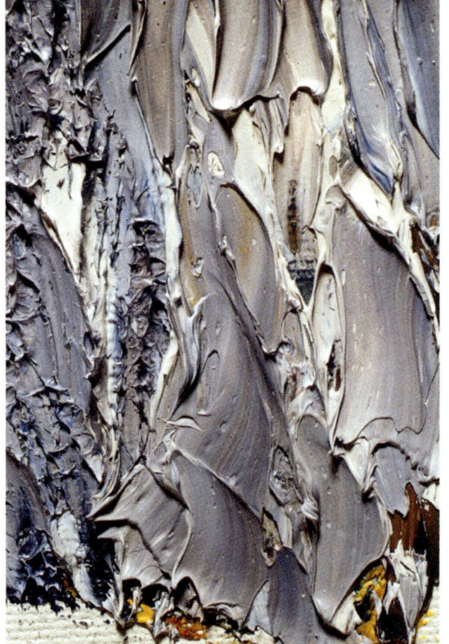

Impasto

Rinsing

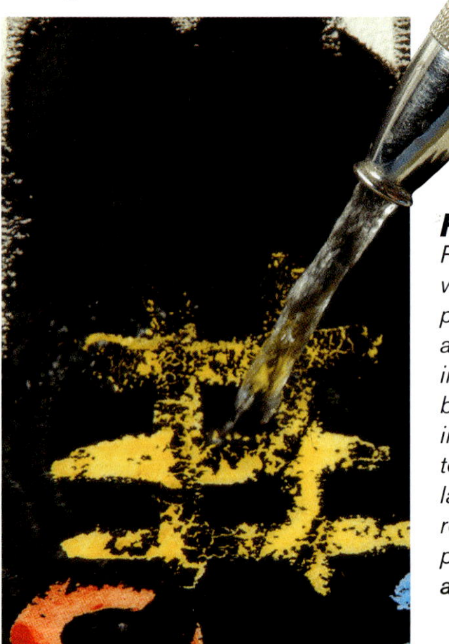

Hatching

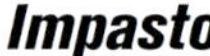

Hatching
This technique creates areas of color with parallel lines that can be overlaid to make fine grids. According to the distance between the lines and the amount of overlaid hatching, it is possible to make lighter or darker areas. If hatching of different colors is overlaid, they will optically combine and we will see the color of the mixture.

Rinsing
Rinsing is the technique of applying water to a painting to totally or partially eliminate a layer of paint and cause a worn effect on the image. It is useful only with water-based media (watercolor, gouache, ink, or acrylics). It is applied directly to the paint or with a sponge or large brush. The amount of paint it removes will depend on the pressure and the amount of water, **and whether the paint has dried.**

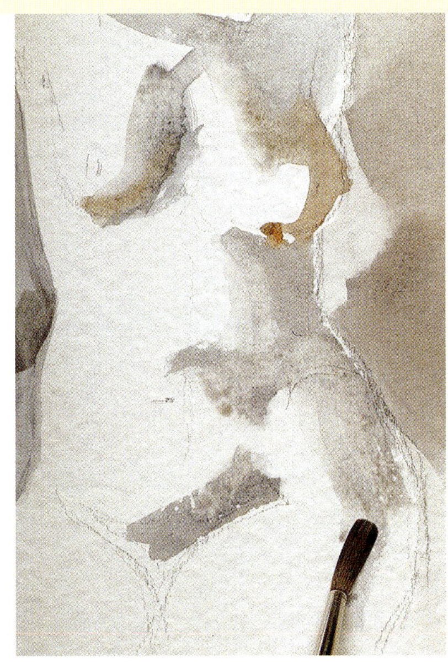
Wash

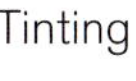
Tinting

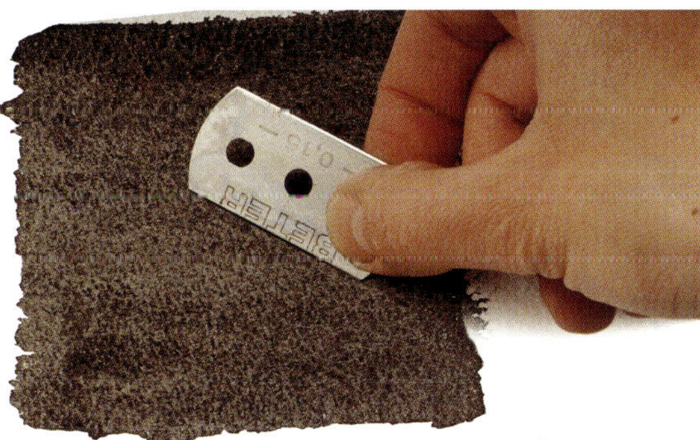

Tinting

This refers to modifying a color by mixing it with another color adjacent to it, that is, a neighbor in the color circle, such as yellow with orange, blue with violet, and so on.

Wash

This is a painting technique in which very diluted paint is applied to a support using wide applicators and without precise details.

Dripping

This is a painting effect produced by letting paint fall onto the support from a certain distance with more or less force and in small quantities, causing it to disperse in the form of drops.

Scraping

Scraping means partially eliminating a layer of paint using blades or needles to cause the background or a previous layer of color to emerge.

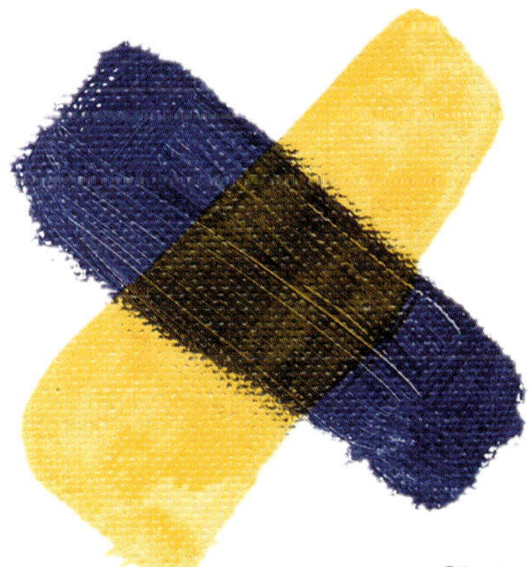
Glazing

Glazing

Glazing consists of totally or partially applying a transparent or semitransparent color over another color to vary its tone or value.

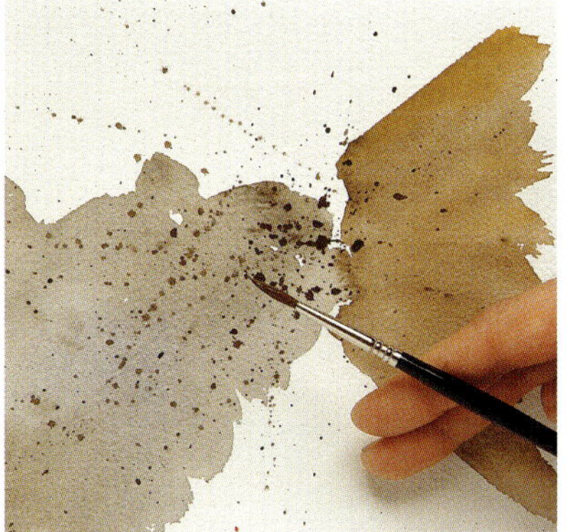
Dripping

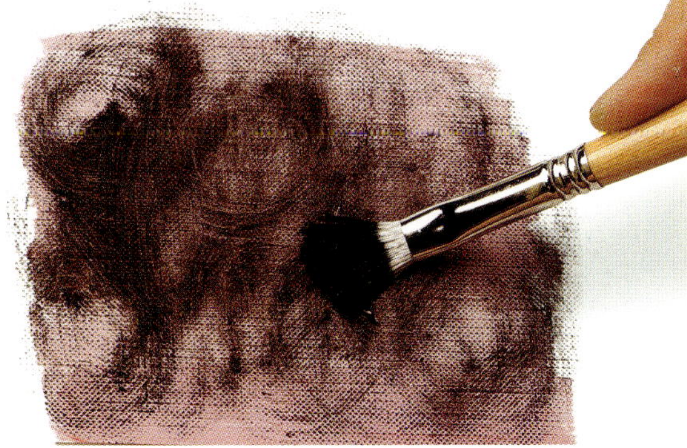
Scraping

Scumbling

This effect is achieved by scrubbing paint that is still wet with a brush, rag, or other applicator, dragging and partially eliminating the paint, leaving part of the background visible.

Scumbling

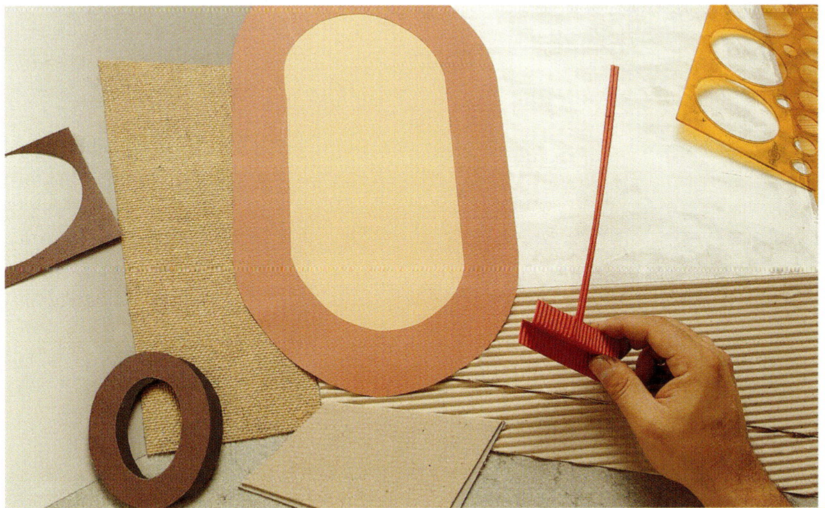
Collage

Collage

A collage is an image formed by gluing pieces of paper, fabric remnants, wood, sand, cardboard, or other materials to a support.

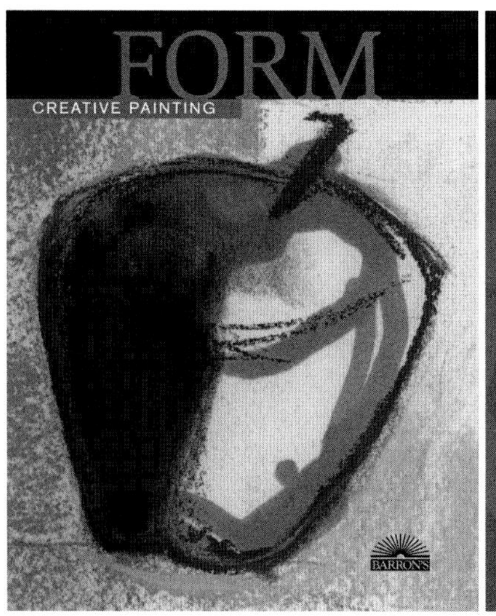
FORM
CREATIVE PAINTING
BARRON'S

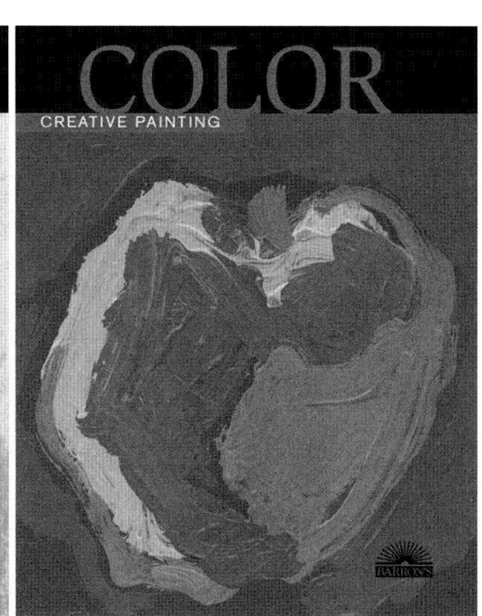
COLOR
CREATIVE PAINTING
BARRON'S

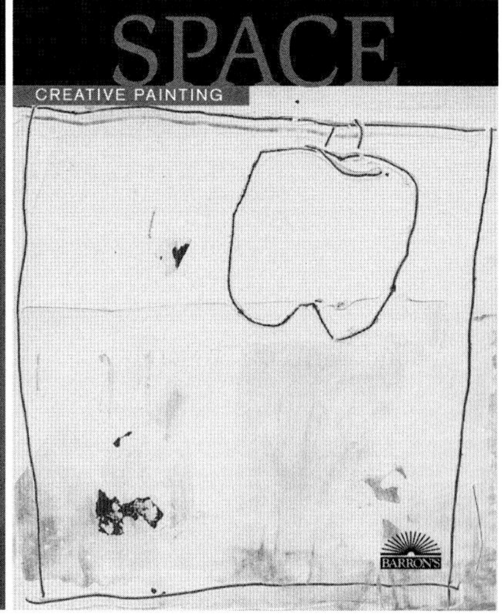
SPACE
CREATIVE PAINTING
BARRON'S

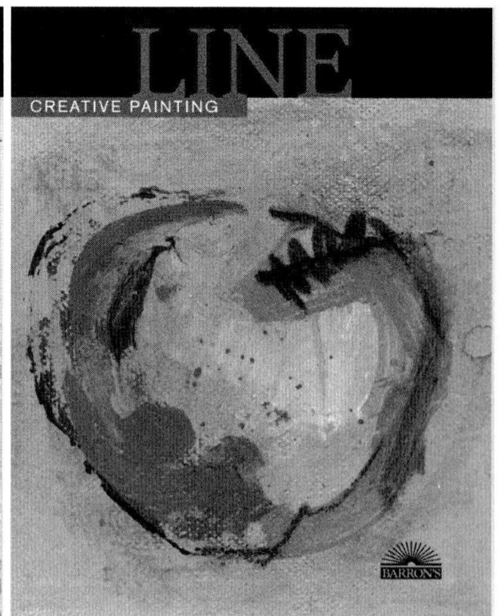
LINE
CREATIVE PAINTING
BARRON'S

SPA